William Maxwell

William Maxwell

A Literary Life

BARBARA BURKHARDT

UNIVERSITY OF ILLINOIS PRESS

Urbana and Chicago

First Illinois paperback, 2008
© 2005 by the Board of Trustees
of the University of Illinois
All rights reserved
Manufactured in the United States of America
1 2 3 4 5 C P 5 4 3 2 1
∞ This book is printed on acid-free paper.

The Library of Congress cataloged the cloth edition as follows:
Burkhardt, Barbara A.
William Maxwell: a literary life / Barbara Burkhardt.
p.   cm.
Includes bibliographical references and index.
ISBN: 0-252-03018-4 (cloth : alk. paper)
1. Maxwell, William, 1908– 2. Authors, American—
20th century—Biography. 3. Editors—United States—
Biography. I. Title
PS3525.A9464Z58   2005
813'.54B—dc22   2004018508

PAPERBACK ISBN 978-0-252-07583-4

For Craig

Contents

Acknowledgments   ix

Credits   xiii

Meeting Maxwell   1

Introduction   7

1. Childhood: A Lifetime of Material, 1908–33   19

2. First Fiction: *Bright Center of Heaven*, 1933–34   48

3. Breakout Novel: *They Came Like Swallows*, 1934–38   61

4. Mature Novelist I: *The Folded Leaf*, 1938–45   79

5. Mature Novelist II: *Time Will Darken It*, 1945–48   135

6. Turning Point: *The New Yorker* and *The Chateau*, 1948–61   171

7. The Novelist as Historian: *Ancestors*, 1961–71   205

8. Maxwell's New York, 1974–76   219

9. The Masterwork: *So Long, See You Tomorrow*, 1972–80   229

10. Summing Up: Late Short Works, 1980–92   257

Conclusion: Stand, Accepting   270

Notes   275

Index   297

Illustrations follow page 170

Acknowledgments

FOR A NUMBER OF YEARS, I have looked forward to acknowledging the people who helped me as I researched and wrote this book, who guided my scholarship and cheered me on, and it gives me great pleasure to cheer them in return. I am especially grateful to those who offered their time, knowledge, and support from the project's earliest stages, who read the manuscript as it evolved and offered both suggestions and encouragement. From the University of Illinois at Urbana-Champaign: Emily Watts, my doctoral advisor and model scholar, professor, and friend—a woman of great warmth, wisdom, and practicality; Jim Hurt, professor and friend, to whom I am indebted for his literary judgment, generosity, and goodwill; and George Hendrick, a devoted steward of American literature who first encouraged me to publish about Maxwell and introduced me to Richard Wentworth of the University of Illinois Press. From the University of Illinois at Springfield: Jacqueline Jackson, beloved writer and teacher; Larry Shiner, whose thoughtful consideration of the manuscript improved it greatly; and Ethan Lewis, who offered both editorial and moral support. Thank you professors, scholars, colleagues, and dear friends all.

The late William and Emily Maxwell welcomed me into their homes in Manhattan and Yorktown Heights, New York, over a period of nine years. Mr. Maxwell's generosity in conducting long interviews and sharing his time, letters, and memories was a gift that I now pass on to others through this volume.

Mr. Maxwell's cousins in Lincoln, Illinois, the late Dr. Robert Perry and the late Thomas Perry, offered special assistance with family stories, Lincoln history, letters, photographs, and grassroots research and became friends. Their joy for living and their pride in their literary cousin made it a privilege to know them. I am grateful also to Ted and Marlene Perry for friendship and support extended to me from Lincoln.

Mr. Maxwell's daughters, Kate Maxwell and Brookie Maxwell, along with his literary executor, Michael Steinman, twice read the manuscript carefully and offered suggestions and corrections that improved the book significantly. I am grateful for their time, consideration, and kind permission to quote from Maxwell's published and unpublished works and letters, as well as from the interviews.

Thanks to John Updike, Roger Angell, Blinn Maxwell, and Martha Landis, who agreed to be interviewed for this book. My appreciation also extends to the late Robert Henderson, Gene Yntema, and Bill Day, whom I was fortunate to speak with before their passing. I am particularly grateful to Mr. Updike for coming to Illinois for the celebration commemorating Mr. Maxwell's donation of papers.

Penelope Niven, biographer of Carl Sandburg and Edward Steichen, offered support and advice from the early stages of research through the publication process. Nicholas Day and Melanie England both assisted me at critical points in the development of the manuscript. Debbie Holmes lent her expertise in helping to prepare the manuscript, among many other kindnesses. I was fortunate to meet Michael Putzel, Mr. Maxwell's godson, in Washington D.C. and am grateful for his interest and editorial assistance.

I have benefited greatly from the assistance and goodwill of the staff from the Rare Books and Special Collections Library at the University of Illinois at Urbana-Champaign. Thanks especially to Barbara Jones, former special collections librarian; Gene Rinkel, archivist; Robert Wedgeworth, former university librarian; Paula Carns; Madeline Gibson; Nancy Romero; and Lyn Jones.

J. Michael Lennon introduced me to Maxwell's *So Long, See You Tomorrow,* for which I will be forever grateful, and offered advice and encouragement through the years. I was fortunate to have Richard Shereikis read my earliest writing on Maxwell and, as my advisor, help me begin developing ideas that led me to write this book.

I benefited from conversations with Rosina Neginsky, who also read several chapters, and with Ben Yagoda, Richard Powers, Betty Foster, Dennis Camp, Cullom Davis, Ned Watts, Ned Wass, Vibert White, Hammed Shahidian, Cornelia Spelman, Robert McGregor, Deborah McGregor, Cary Nelson, and Jana Van Fossan Dreyzehner. I am grateful for assistance offered by Ryan Roberts.

Special thanks to Richard Wentworth of the University of Illinois Press who supported this project for a number of years and to Rebecca Crist, managing editor, who cheerfully and professionally helped to bring the book to publication.

Thanks to those who gave me the opportunity to share and test my ideas along the way and whose recognition encouraged my work: the Society for the Study of Midwestern Literature, especially Roger Bresnahan, David Anderson, Phil Greasley, and Marilyn Atlas; the Sangamo Literary Circle of Springfield, Illinois; the trustees and benefactors of Lincoln College, especially the late president Jack Nutt; Friends of the University of Illinois Library; the Illinois State Library; the College English Association; the Illinois History Symposium, especially my respondent, Robert Bray; Bruce Morgan, Bill Aull, and Jim McGowan of *Tamaqua,* a literary journal, for welcoming my contribution to their special Maxwell edition; the Lincoln Library of Springfield; and the Vladimir Nabokov Society.

I also appreciate support and recognition received from the University of Illinois at Urbana-Champaign and the University of Illinois at Springfield.

I am grateful to all those who offered assistance with research, permissions, and photographs: Mary Kinzie for the Louise Bogan Estate; Nikki Smith for the Vladimir Nabokov Estate; Rosanna Bruno of Russell and Volkening for the Eudora Welty Estate; Kathy Kienholz and Betsey Feeley of the American Academy of Arts and Letters, New York; Pat Fox of the Harry Ransom Center for the Humanities at the University of Texas, Austin; Faith Goetz, sister of the late Robert Henderson; Elaine Maruhn of the University of Nebraska Press for the Estate of Wright Morris; Pamela McCarthy and Daniel Cappello of *The New Yorker;* Leigh Montville of Condé Nast for the Estate of William Shawn; Richard Ebersol of the Lincoln Public Library, Lincoln, Illinois; the Illinois State Historical Library; Richard Miller of the Wisconsin Historical Society; Jeanette Vogel and Hannah Przybylski of the Senn High School Library, Chicago, Illinois; Daria D'Arienzo of Archives and Special Collections at Amherst College; the Chicago Public Library; the Berg Collection and the *New Yorker* archives of the New York Public Library; Smith College; the Crane Society near Portage, Wisconsin; the Portage Public Library, Wisconsin; the MacDowell Colony, Peterborough, New Hampshire; Dorothy Alexander; Janice Delaney of PEN/Faulkner; Gayle Krughoff; and Kasi Burns of Chrome Photographic Services, Washington, D.C.

This book is dedicated to my husband, Craig. I extend my thanks to my father and stepmother, John and Jackie Stuemke, and to my parents-in-law,

Norma and Jack Burkhardt, and remember my mother, Gloria Stuemke, and grandparents, Warren and Alveda Smith, who were present through much of the research and writing of this book. Thanks to Sharon and Bob Lumsden, Lisa McCormick Mollison, Lawrence Stuemke, and Eric Copper. I am also grateful for the support of my friends Peggy Ryan, Julie Kellner, and Bill Kellner.

A William Maxwell Portrait: Memories and Appreciations, edited by Charles Baxter, Michael Collier, and Edward Hirsch was published as this book was in production, too late for it to be discussed in this volume. It offers loving tributes to Maxwell by a number of his literary colleagues and friends.

Credits

GRATEFUL ACKNOWLEDGMENT is made to The Estate of William Maxwell to print quotations from published works, unpublished letters, and manuscripts of William Maxwell; and to Alfred A. Knopf, Inc., a Division of Random House, Inc., for permission to quote from the copyrighted works of William Maxwell. Materials from the William Maxwell Collection courtesy of the Rare Book and Special Collections Library, University of Illinois at Urbana-Champaign, including the correspondence and manuscripts of William Maxwell, and the correspondence of John Updike, Eudora Welty, Vladimir Nabokov, and Wright Morris.

Grateful acknowledgment is also made to the following individuals and institutions:

Roger Angell: Personal interview and *New Yorker* office correspondence by permission of Roger Angell.

Louise Bogan: Published and unpublished correspondence, from speech quoted by William Maxwell, and from "Journey Around My Room" by permission of Mary Kinzie, executor of the literary estate of Louise Bogan. Letters of Louise Bogan courtesy of Amherst College Archives and Special Collections.

Shirley Hazzard: Memorial speech by permission of Shirley Hazzard.

Robert Henderson: Personal interview by permission of Faith Goetz.

Alfred A. Knopf: Materials in the Alfred A. Knopf Collection (correspondence and office communication of Alfred A. Knopf Sr., Alfred A. Knopf Jr., and employees of Alfred A. Knopf Publishers) by permission of the Harry Ransom Humanities Research Center, University of Texas, Austin.

Wright Morris: Correspondence of Wright Morris by permission of the University of Nebraska Press.

Vladimir Nabokov: Extracts from the correspondence of Vladimir Nabokov by arrangement with the Estate of Vladimir Nabokov. All rights reserved.

Frank O'Connor: Correspondence of Frank O'Connor by permission of the Estate of Frank O'Connor.

The Paris Review: Excerpts from "William Maxwell" by George Plimpton and John Seabrook, from *Writers at Work, Seventh Series,* edited by George A. Plimpton, copyright 1986 by permission of *The Paris Review.*

Thomas Perry: Correspondence of Thomas Perry by permission of Ted Perry.

Senn High School: Quotations from *The Forum* and yearbook photo by permission of Senn High School, Chicago, Illinois.

William Shawn: Quotations from *New Yorker* office memos courtesy of *The New Yorker*/The Condé Naste Publications, Inc.

Smith College: Quotations from *The Sophian* courtesy of Smith College Archives, Northampton, Massachusetts.

John Updike: Personal interview, correspondence, and speech by permission of John Updike.

Eudora Welty: Correspondence and speech of Eudora Welty reprinted by permission of Russell & Volkening, Inc., as agents for the author.

William Maxwell

Meeting Maxwell

SO LONG, SEE YOU TOMORROW was my introduction to William Maxwell. I read the novel outdoors on a warm September day in Springfield, Illinois. The narrator spoke with a striking simplicity, a combination of empathy and intellect that I found fresh and rare. And, perhaps most surprising to a Midwesterner, he did not recount a distant locale but spoke of life in Lincoln, Illinois—where he had grown up, a mere thirty miles away—and of universal truths emanating from a sensibility and landscape that I knew intimately.

A few years later, in 1991, I was presented an opportunity to interview Maxwell for a literary magazine. When my cab pulled up to Maxwell's building on East Eighty-Sixth in Manhattan, I stood for a moment looking up at the apartments and across the street to the park on the river's edge. Here was the home of the writer's adulthood, his second literary territory and the neighborhood that inspired "Over by the River," one of his finest stories. I remembered his words about the writer Colette in *The Outermost Dream:* how he had stood in Paris "day after day looking up at the windows of that row of houses on the north end of the garden of the Palais-Royal, wondering which window was hers, feeling a pull like that of the moon on the ocean"[1]—a pull precipitated by a love for her writing. Now Maxwell was the one inside, and when he opened the door I knew I was in the presence of someone very much like the narrator of *So Long, See You Tomorrow.* His gentle yet assured manner recalled the book's reserved wisdom; his voice echoed its natural cadence. Nattily dressed in a tweed jacket and tie, he was physically delicate, but a strength of spirit, a vitality shone from his eyes, from his open, welcoming face.

Inside, an expansive living room wall was lined with books he treasured. Some of the authors he knew personally—J.D. Salinger, John Updike, Maeve Brennan—others, such as Yeats and Tolstoy, had become his companions and inspiration through a lifetime of reading. A large-scale abstract painting hung on the wall, and a long, low bench with a needlepoint crocodile sat before the fireplace. He took me to a small back room filled with papers upon papers, odd furniture, a photo of his poet friend, Robert Fitzgerald (also a central Illinoisan whom he met at Harvard), and his daughter Brookie's drawing of the very park and river I had seen outside—the cover art for his first story collection. Maxwell had switched from a manual to an electric typewriter only in later years and preferred answering questions on his clattering Coronamatic. "I think better on the typewriter than I do just talking," he told me.[2] After carefully considering each of my queries, he rolled a sheet of paper into his typewriter and composed for up to five minutes at a time. He paused occasionally, his lips moving slightly as he reread the words through tortoiseshell glasses. Once satisfied, he turned the typewriter stand around on its squeaky wheels so I could read his response. The next summer, he arrived at the Croton-Harmon railway station wearing a broad-brimmed straw hat and drove me to his country home in Yorktown Heights. There, he suspended a long extension cord through the back window and brought his typewriter outdoors, where we sat for two afternoons at a picnic table on the patio overlooking a rolling lawn, flower beds, and an art studio that belonged to his wife, Emily, who served brie, bacon, and tomato sandwiches and berries with crème fraiche. Sitting by his side allowed me to read his words as he typed them. I could ask follow-up questions immediately, which made for a smooth interchange—a true conversation. Although this interview procedure may seem unusual, communicating through the typewriter was natural, even personal for Maxwell, a man who spent his career crafting stories at the keyboard. His nimble, sinewy hands, which John Blades of the *Chicago Tribune* aptly likened to "tree roots photographed in fast motion,"[3] embodied both the power and tenderness of his works.

Agilely swinging his legs over the suspended extension cord, Maxwell took me back inside to see a closet with letters stacked to the ceiling: his lifelong correspondence from friends, family, and the myriad writers whose work he edited at *The New Yorker*. He asked whether I would be willing to help him go through the papers, which he intended to donate to the University of Illinois. They were in fairly good order, but he wanted them organized differently. After that day, over a period of about five years, thick packages and cardboard boxes appeared on my doorstep—hundreds of letters, postcards, and notes he had received through seven decades. Among them, a 1945 letter from longtime friend Susan Deuel Shattuck tried to alleviate his concerns about the Illinois reception of his next novel, *The Folded Leaf,* based on his experiences at the university. Vladimir Nabokov's letters came with signature flourish: A butterfly drawn in exuberant colors punctuated the famous lepidopterist's "V." Eudora Welty's postcard from Mississippi's Mendenhall Restaurant pictured its famous revolving tables. She thought they "would have been good in the Beulah"—the fictional hotel in her 1955 novel *The Ponder Heart,* which she dedicated to Maxwell. And there was mail from the three Johns: Cheever, O'Hara, and Updike. The youngest of the trio, Updike wrote in 1992 thanking Maxwell for his years of editorial guidance:

> I've been pawing through my manuscripts at Houghton Library in Cambridge, trying to date my old poems for a collected edition and thought the old *New Yorker* letters might help, and couldn't help rereading some of the innumerable ones from you. What a torrent of encouragement and loving advice and undeserved flattery over the years! Where would I be without it? Somewhere else, I'm sure. And the sadness of thinking that you and I, you in your office with its view of Rockefeller Center and I in my Ipswich [Massachusetts] domicile surrounded by children and dinner parties, are figures of the past, characters in a drama whose scenery is all packed up and in the van. Anyway, if I've never said it before, thank you for all that caring and intelligence.[4]

Updike's tender tone is not unusual among the *New Yorker* contributors who worked with Maxwell. The correspondence reveals the close personal bonds the editor developed with his talented fold: As a well-regarded author himself, he felt an affinity for writers that they recognized and appreciated. Yet despite his genuine concern for their personal and artistic welfare, he maintained objectivity that guided them toward what he called their "essential quality." As Roger Angell, Maxwell's own *New Yorker* editor, recalled, "I think he was closer to the writers than anyone else [at the magazine]. He seemed to have intimate connections, intimate friendships, with almost all his writers." These relations constituted half of his dual life in letters and strengthened his resolve to write increasingly streamlined prose himself. By the time he published *So Long* in 1980, all he wanted was to say exactly what he meant "in the only exact way of saying it."[5] Indeed, caring so deeply about the language of other writers helped him to refine his own.

By the end of his life, Maxwell had corresponded for more than forty years with Updike, who accepted my invitation to participate in ceremonies honoring his editor's gift of papers and correspondence to the University of

Illinois in 1997. "Will we be anywhere near Lincoln?" Updike asked me. "On to Lincoln!" On a crisp April morning, Maxwell's cousin, Dr. Robert Perry, shepherded us through the ordinary streets and houses, the farms, fields, and cemeteries Maxwell molded into a literary place uniquely his own.[6]

* * *

When I saw Mr. Maxwell in his country house in 1994, he told me that it might be our last visit. He was getting older—he thought he had five years or so left—and must conserve his energy to finish the things he still wanted to do. That night I stayed up until three in the morning writing down every detail I could remember: helping Mrs. Maxwell carry in the groceries, the sausages she fixed us, his undiminished vitality. Yet it wasn't the last visit. To my great fortune, he continued to see me once or twice a year—the last time in December 1999, six months before his death.

In December 1995, Maxwell received the PEN/Malamud award for achievement in short fiction, and I flew to Washington, D.C., for the ceremony. He shared the honor that year with a much younger Chicagoan, Stuart Dybek, whose work had also appeared in *The New Yorker*. In the richly paneled, baroque auditorium of the Folger Shakespeare Library, the two sat on a bare stage prepared to read to the capacity crowd. Dybek was introduced first. The picture of an up-and-coming man of letters with a shock of brown hair and a tweed jacket, he delivered a graphic, gripping monologue from the perspective of a young man contemplating dating and sex in the 1990s. Ebullient and animated, he performed his story, controlling the stage as an actor behind the lectern, turning first to one side of the audience, then to the other. His voice rose and fell dramatically as he punched out explicit details of his narrator's love life, interjecting raw yet humorous language that would have been rejected by the *New Yorker*'s censors ten years earlier. Maxwell's face betrayed neither delight nor disgust. The audience roared with laughter repeatedly and gasped at the story's tragic turn. Dybek was a great success and received enthusiastic applause; he was indeed a fresh talent—a new *New Yorker* writer.

William Maxwell approached the podium slowly and adjusted his glasses. A literary patriarch nearing ninety, he had chosen "The French Scarecrow," a 1956 story about the comfortable yet not quite contented lives of upstate New York neighbors who garden in the country and lie on an analyst's couch in the city. He read modestly and softly, sometimes haltingly as shadows fell on his pages. The audience was hushed. The story's tension coursed beneath his words, beneath the gently muffled voice that one could imagine when reading *So Long, See You Tomorrow.* He offered no dramatic twists, no gesticulations—just words that evinced a commanding literary efficacy, a perfect emotional pitch tuned to the core of his characters' lives. The crowd acknowledged him warmly, as one would an erudite grandfather, and afterward he was greeted by a long line of readers bearing books for his signature.

It seemed that the past and future of *The New Yorker,* perhaps that of American short fiction generally, had met on stage that night. The evening was filled with appreciation for two superb writers whose work, though poles apart on many fronts, preserves part of our shared American experience. Yet although many were invigorated by Dybek's story, others may have winced a bit, longing for the days when Harold Ross, the magazine's first editor, published the essays of E. B. White. Clearly, Maxwell embodied the *New Yorker*'s legendary golden years. His forty-year tenure there began a mere decade after its founding, and he edited fiction by its principal luminaries. Even so, he was no relic: His work was conspicuously relevant to the many young people queued to meet him after the program that night. Standing among the Washingtonians and New Yorkers waiting their turn, I sensed their reverence for the novels they carried with them, for stories born in the heartland at the turn of the twentieth century that mattered even as the new millennium approached. They, too, were drawn to the quiet voice in the cavernous hall—to a voice that, through a long life of literary pursuit, echoed truths that were their own.

Introduction

THE FIRST PAGE William Maxwell pulled from his typewriter at the start of our many interviews explained what compelled him to write:

> I have a melancholy feeling that all human experience goes down the drain, or to put it more politely, ends in oblivion, except when somebody records some part of his own experience—which can of course be the life that goes on in his mind and imagination as well as what he had for breakfast. In a very small way I have fought this, by trying to recreate in a form that I hoped would have some degree of permanence the character and lives of people I have known and loved. Or people modeled on them. To succeed this would have to move the reader as I have been moved. This is the intricate, in and out, round and round, now direct and now indirect process that comes under the heading of literary art.[1]

For Maxwell, this process was guided by a historical imagination, a desire to make successive inquiries into the past. He often wrote of his native Lincoln, Illinois as it was before his mother's premature death during the 1918 influenza epidemic. Yet even as he sought to preserve memories, he continually refigured and reexamined them. They became a consistent source of material as he developed new fictional practices and challenged the bounds of the novel form.

Many American readers discovered Maxwell in the mid-1980s when Godine Press revived his work in elegant paperback editions graced by the cover art of his younger daughter, Brookie. More took notice in the 1990s when Random House reissued sixty years of his fiction and nonfiction in its Vintage International series. His death in Manhattan in July 2000, at age ninety-one, made the front pages of *The New York Times* and the *Chicago Tribune*, both of which made high claims for his place in twentieth-century literature, claims repeated in publications across the country and abroad. Readers curious about the universal praise for this quiet, underappreciated author found a collection of writing that vividly preserves the past and earns a permanent place in American letters with its powerful embrace of emotional experience and the beauty of its precise prose style.

Maxwell devoted his literary life to a dual exploration of his own history and the nature of fiction. He was first inspired by writers such as Virginia Woolf, E. M. Forster, and James Joyce, who were at the height of their powers when he came of age in the 1920s at the University of Illinois. His was a quiet yet dynamic literary path—a sustained effort to follow where his material led him. Through the decades, he experimented with narrative technique, bringing new form to his subjects as his view of them evolved over time. Early on, Woolf and company stirred him to create a distinctive form of the tradition-breaking Modernism they practiced: He brought tough subjectivity, in-depth psychological probing, and unremitting intensity to the substance of his life and Midwestern homeland. Then, in small stages over many decades, he pushed past his own practice to arrive at a distinctive form of American Postmodernism that questions and foregrounds how we come to understand the past, challenges how we can ever know what "really" happened, and candidly addresses the artist's struggle to capture the human condition. He explored and preserved his experience over decades yet found within it ever-changing possibilities. His work charts not only a journey through life but also the unfolding and deepening of artistic nature.

Maxwell remained loyal to his own terrain and sensibilities, maintaining a disciplined commitment that prevailed through literary trends and movements of the popular culture. Distinguished by its intimate, domestic focus, his work eschews the political, penetrates with raw emotion, regards people with prodigious empathy and respect, and yet assesses them astutely, with mature, distanced wisdom. Each of his works brings new form, new possibilities to his signature subjects—childhood and family life, the Midwest, the agony and acceptance of loss—while navigating the delicate balance between human will and fragility, between the concurrent tragedy and privilege of living. By the end of his career, he had spent more than fifty years exploring the interpenetration of life and art, melding the two most compellingly in his 1980 novel *So Long, See You Tomorrow*—the apex of his literary achievement, published when he was seventy-one.

Exploring the Past

Maxwell's life and works, like those of Joyce and Woolf, are closely entwined. Through seven decades of novels and stories, he never ceased to find new meaning in the places, people, and events that shaped him. Even after *So Long, See You Tomorrow,* a book that could stand as a summation of his autobiographical inquiries, he continued to uncover fresh layers, even startling revelations, in the late *Billie Dyer and Other Stories* (1992). Of course, authors have used personal experience as the basis for fiction throughout literary history—most obviously since Proust, as Maxwell pointed out to George Plimpton—but few have done so to such sustained effect. Roger Angell noted in 1996 that although other writers may have even stronger connections to the past, no other "shows it or uses it to such an advantage. It seems such a clear line from a writer, now in his 80s, back to the child Bill Maxwell, and the boy Bill Maxwell. And he's never tried to cover that up, or to be a contemporary person at the expense of what he has been or what his connections are, what he draws on for his fiction. It's quite remarkable. I can't think of any other writer in whom that seems to be as clear."[2]

Although we can understand Maxwell's novels without realizing that ten-year-old Bunny in *They Came Like Swallows* (1937), Lymie in *The Folded Leaf* (1945), Harold Rhodes in *The Chateau* (1961), and the elderly narrator in *So Long, See You Tomorrow* (1980) all derive from the writer's memories of his own experience at various stages, our reading of his work is enriched by recognizing this. At least one critic has noted that *They Came Like Swallows, The Folded Leaf,* and *The Chateau* serve as a Maxwell trilogy portraying a child, adolescent, and adult in sequence. The author did not intend for his novels to create this effect. In fact, he resisted writing sequels; most "aren't as good as the original book," he wrote to his father in 1944.[3] Yet a reader cannot help but notice that little Bunny who loses his mother in the first novel could have developed into Lymie Peters, the sensitive, motherless adolescent of the second, who, in maturity, could have resembled the introspective Harold Rhodes, the transplanted Midwesterner who travels with his wife to France after World War II in the third. In the narrator of *So Long, See You Tomorrow* we see their aged counterpart, the definitive Maxwell persona who, with wise and distanced retrospection, meditates on his childhood and his mother's death, the span of years that have brought him to advanced age, and what it has meant to him to be alive.

Perhaps no body of American writing so fully captures the development of one person from childhood through advanced years. The full stretch of Maxwell's works witnesses the psychological intricacies of a life that spanned most of the twentieth century—a deepening self-knowledge, a retrieving and reshaping of private experience, and breakthroughs in understanding personal history that can come only with age.

Some may consider heavy reliance on autobiographical material a weakness in fiction: Charles Shattuck, a lifelong friend and noted Shakespeare scholar, obliged Maxwell's occasional requests for literary advice and discouraged the return to autobiographical themes in his late career. The author himself told me that he admired fiction writers who do not seem dependent on their own lives for material, yet he thought that they were more dependent than they appeared. He came to believe, more and more strongly as he aged, that daily life produced patterns that could not be improved upon. Although secure in his artistic choices, he seemed resigned to the possibility that autobiographical fiction may be perceived as somehow limited in literary scope.[4]

With Maxwell's work, however, this is not the case: Ongoing self-exploration inspired some of his most powerful literature. The act of returning over and again to the stuff of an individual life over many decades, of maintaining a consistent set of personal concerns, allowed him to explore inner life and the nature of memory. His body of fiction reflects what we all do: repeatedly revisit our past, our childhood, our emotions, the things that matter to us. Perceptions and attitudes evolve while the material of the past, the emotional core, stays constant; our minds create myriad variations on personal themes in a lifetime's course.

The strength of Maxwell's work derives in large part from his decision to stay the course with his own material through an unusually long creative life. As a writer, he saw his childhood from myriad angles over his lifespan, as if going by it on a train, while we observe from a level once removed. Through his eyes, we view his past experience from various vantage points yet also witness how he responds to his memories differently over time. His autobiographically based characters represent every stage of the human cycle and reflect how the mind deals with daily life at every phase of development: from the boy who lives intensely in each moment and sees the world through the patterns and textures of his mother's home to the seventy-year-old man who experiences the opening of memory so that the past and present meet, stretched before him like the land and sky of his Midwestern landscape.

On a broader level, the series of Maxwell's autobiographically based characters offers a view of one American's trip through the twentieth century: A child of World War I, devastated by the Spanish influenza epidemic, faces social changes that displace the gentler, small-town world he knew. An adolescent struggles to find his way in a Midwestern college in the late 1920s. A native Midwesterner travels to France for the first time shortly after World War II. A New Yorker raises his two daughters on the Upper East Side at midcentury or relives his past on an analyst's couch. An elderly man finds clarity and comfort in memory as the next millennium approaches. Although Maxwell sustains his focus on inner experience and everyday nuances, his novels and stories render much of the texture of the twentieth century; we see how historical, cultural, and intellectual movements play out in the minds of his characters. Through each succeeding inquiry, he arrives at further insights that satisfy far more than a quest for self-knowledge. With intelligence and deceptive simplicity, he lays bare the tragedies, joys, and truths of a broad range of human experience.

Exploring the Art of Fiction

Maxwell's quest to preserve his childhood past, indeed to preserve all pasts from the ravages of time, led him to examine the nature of his life's work: the art of fiction. He began his career writing novels focused exclusively through his characters' perspectives without a narrator's commentary. *Bright Center of Heaven* (1934) shifts quickly between different characters' minds; *They Came Like Swallows* (1937) restricts each section to a single perspective. The purely introspective concentration illumines characters through both their understanding of the world and the limitations of that understanding. In both novels, action unfolds chronologically and in the second work is formally segmented, with no sign of the fluid movement of time found in his late fiction. Influenced by Modernists who were writing when he came of age, he composed this earliest work—particularly *Bright Center of Heaven*—in a more lyrical, less streamlined style.

The *Folded Leaf* (1945) introduces an intervening narrator, a sensitive yet objective voice Maxwell uses to universalize characters and situations through anthropological and classical allusions. In *Time Will Darken It* (1948), he expands these meditations by expounding on observations and ideas of importance to him, by using the narrator to state expressly the fundamental themes of his fiction. Time flows chronologically, yet these works are somewhat less structured: The narrator freely interjects his commentaries, and in the second novel conversations dictate progression, resulting in a freer, more relaxed pace.

In his work of the 1960s and 1970s, Maxwell makes the transition to first-person narration and drops the chronological timeline in favor of a new fluidity between past and present. Throughout most of *The Chateau* (1961), the only novel of this period, he continues with the style of narration found in his two previous works. Indeed, the narrator of *The Folded Leaf* or *Time Will Darken It* seems to have left the early-century Midwest to oversee a couple's postwar European adventure. However, the novel's brief epilogue makes the quick but essential switch that points his work in a new direction. Leaving behind the limitations of his characters' perceptions, he introduces a first-person narrator, an authorial figure who steps from behind the facade of fiction to reveal what *really* happened, what the French were *really* like. Although the Americans try to learn about their French hosts by examining the evidence, answers ultimately lie in the narrator's fictionalizing. For the first time, Maxwell lays bare the nature of his art, a method fully realized in *So Long, See You Tomorrow* and his late short fiction.

In 1963, two years after *The Chateau* appeared, Maxwell published "The Value of Money," his first work told completely from a first-person perspective and in a voice similar to that of the late Maxwell narrator. However, it is in the nonfiction *Ancestors,* a blend of family chronicle and autobiography, that he more fully develops the familiar narrator who shares both his history and his sensibility. After earlier aborted attempts at first-person storytelling, he was finally satisfied with a narrator who unifies generations of family stories while including his own, who explains his artistic focus on the minute details of human interaction and suggests a relationship between writing and history. The ancestral material also prompted Maxwell to free himself from chronology for the first time, to transition smoothly back and forth between past generations, between their times and his own.

So Long, See You Tomorrow represents the culmination of Maxwell's evolving literary technique and his final point of departure from Modernist methods. Here, he masters the first-person perspective and refines the voice of his wise narrator, one of his most vivid characters. The structure and content of his work combine inseparably. By weaving fact, fiction, and memory, integrating diverse elements and sources, and using a single metaphor to unify the whole, he achieves complete synthesis of subject and form. At this point, chronology proves inconsequential: The writer loosens strictures of time, suggesting that all moments can be lived on one plane.

In this final novel, Maxwell liberates the narrator from the natural limits of his knowledge: where memory and research fail him, the writer turns openly to fabrication. By presenting fiction explicitly, by making his art a subject within the work, he blurs boundaries between documentation and imagination, between experience lived and interpreted. His work challenges us, however gently, to see the continuum between experience and art, to live in a world of unpredictable tragedy while having hope enough to improvise possibilities and pursue higher truths. Yet just as he produces a complete union of form and subject, he takes the concept a bit further in "Billie Dyer" and "The Front and the Back Parts of the House," stories suggesting that literary art may actually have the power to affect life circumstances directly. After more than a half-century at the typewriter, he reveals fiction writing as a natural expression of experience—as a central approach to understanding and interpreting the world both around and inside him.

Exploring the Midwest

Maxwell once suggested, quite rightly, that what he did with characters was "more important than where they lead their lives." Even so, the emotional timbre and quiet culture of his central Illinois childhood provided the foundation for his distinguished fiction. Several works portray the New York and France of his adulthood, but most preserve what he called "the Natural History of home," the social atmosphere, idiom, and landscape of the early twentieth-century heartland. As he explained in 1991, "My imagination's home is the dead center of the state of Illinois, and when I have an idea for a story or a novel, much more often than not it is located in that part of the country. Or, perhaps I should say a facsimile of it. For I was removed from Lincoln at the age of fourteen, and so my childhood and early youth were encapsulated so to speak, in a changeless world."[5]

Maxwell's visceral connection to his native terrain accounts, in part, for his distinctive literary tone, for a power achieved through tremendous reserve rather than imposing drama. A memory from his early days on the East Coast makes plain the psychological hold of the Illinois topography on his imagination: While in residence one summer at the MacDowell Colony in Peterborough, New Hampshire, he took a day trip to Lake George with another colonist, violinist Sol Cohen. Cohen, who was behind the wheel, got lost on the return, and the two found themselves stranded in unfamiliar territory at dusk. "All around us were mountains, and I felt threatened by them," Maxwell remembered. "Only a flat landscape is reassuring to my unconscious mind. A landscape where you can see the horizon in all directions."[6] This affinity for illimitable vistas, for the sense of total exposure on the plain, plays an integral role in the aesthetic unity and effect of his work.

In essence, the prairie's physical presence forms the tenor of characters' lives. Maxwell's spare, graceful prose echoes the unadorned beauty of the prairiescape, the stark symmetry of uninterrupted soil and sky.

Among literary forebears who also claimed this territory—Sherwood Anderson, Edgar Lee Masters, Sinclair Lewis—Maxwell offers a distinct voice, a vision that is neither bitter nor sentimental. His realistic yet unfailingly respectful stance toward the Midwest results in a balanced portrait: While recognizing limitation, he finds beauty in the somewhat unremarkable aspects of the region's life and landscape. In particular, *They Came Like Swallows, So Long, See You Tomorrow*, and his late stories depart from the stifling stagnancy and isolation of *Winesburg, Ohio, Spoon River Anthology*, and *Main Street* by offsetting the region's provincialism with its refreshing simplicity and characters' closed-mindedness with their capacity for great love. Certainly a foreboding sadness permeates the air in Maxwell's Illinois, yet as his characters endure the desperation of the isolated prairie, they also experience moments of fulfillment and clarity, quiet epiphanies that emerge from the simple texture of their lives.

Unlike Anderson and Masters, Maxwell left his boyhood town as an adolescent, before he grew restless or felt the need to escape its boundaries. This early departure accounts in large part for his more affectionate view. His memories of Lincoln rest exclusively on observations from his youngest years, resulting in fiction that retains the fresh wonder of childhood even as it reaches the perspective of advancing age and wisdom. "I believe in Winesburg, Ohio, but I also believe in what I remember," he wrote in *Ancestors*. "Men and women alike appeared to accept with equanimity the circumstances of their lives in a way that no one seems able to do now anywhere." In retrospect, he recalled a teacher at Lincoln High School who reminded him of Anderson's Wing Biddlebaum, a *Winesburg* character ostracized for tenderly placing his hands on the shoulders of young male students. "There must have been other Anderson characters [in Lincoln] that I was not aware of," he reflected. "I never lived there again, and so I don't have an adult's perception of the place. For example, I don't know the part money played in the lives of people there. Or envy. Or desire. Men came home from work and watered the lawn or raked leaves into a pile and had supper and went to bed. Their calm behavior may have concealed all sort of horrors and lusts, but they weren't visible to me....I don't know whether I write about the 'real' Lincoln and I don't care; I write about a place that I possess in my imagination."[7]

Maxwell felt a closer kinship with Willa Cather, whose books he "admired" when he was young. Cather shared Maxwell's balanced approach toward Midwestern life in her portraits of the vast Nebraska landscape and the people who struggled to make it their home. Maxwell also recognized that his narrative style became more like Cather's as he got older. Although his earliest writings were more influenced by lyric poets, he "ended up in Willa Cather's corner," he said, "though she got there by way of Flaubert and I by a feeling that the way to write was the way I remember people speaking in my Illinois childhood."[8]

Among Midwestern writers he knew, Zona Gale was the most influential. Thirty years his senior, the Wisconsin author encouraged his writing career in its earliest stages and offered an example of how small-town Midwestern life could inspire serious fiction. Decades later, in his role as a *New Yorker* editor, Maxwell also worked with Wright Morris, a writer and photographer whose life and literary motives suggest strong parallels with his own. Morris's own mother had died within a week of his birth, and he had grown up in small Nebraska towns before moving to Chicago for high school. Like Maxwell's, his creative work sought to preserve the culture of his childhood in the heartland. In particular, Morris's photography was helpful to Maxwell, who consulted his prints of Midwestern farms as he wrote the novel *So Long, See You Tomorrow*. From an editorial standpoint, Morris also presented Maxwell the opportunity to work with an author whose background and sense of place mirrored his own—as well as one who faced similar literary challenges. For example, Maxwell noted that one piece Morris submitted to the magazine consisted of "writing that is mostly remembering," a pitfall that Maxwell sought to avoid in his own autobiographical fiction. Morris appreciated his editor's counsel on how to portray the "fading" culture of the early twentieth-century Midwest and responded:

> What you 'av done is persuade me that I may now have the appropriate distance and tone, to reconsider my early life and grand times. My very young and middle malehood is remarkably laden with events and sentiments that are now historic, and it is as history I would like to recall them.[9]

In his own work, Maxwell captured the years just before and through the aftermath of World War I—from about 1912 to 1923. The era's Midwestern domestic life serves as a touchstone, setting a fixed ideal for daily living. Home is his hallowed space, inextricably connected to his mother, who in her absence forms a vital presence. His love for this place of intimate, emotional connections fosters his focus on the small and unimportant within a scene—the interior over the exterior, the simple over the grand—similar to an approach in painting called "intimism" by Henri Bonnard, one of Maxwell's favorite artists. Within the family setting, we find the writer's vivid portraits of children: He casts their lives with instinctual understanding, depicting their pure, unfiltered view. From his earliest to latest work, he never seems more at home than when looking through a child's eyes. *They Came Like Swallows* offers his most concentrated focus on the psyche of youth, yet more than forty years later, he renders a boy's world with the same sense of recovery. At the end of his career, Maxwell layers his portraits of childhood with the hindsight of an aged man regaining his young self.

The voices of Maxwell's Midwesterners echo through his work. Partial to particular phrases, they speak in syntactical patterns that mark them as central Illinoisans of the early twentieth century. The author's ear for subtleties of the idiom was impeccable; his comments to *New Yorker* editor William Shawn during the editing of *So Long, See You Tomorrow* revealed his meticulous approach to recreating the language of his childhood home. Often the dialect is distinguished by fine points rather than patent distinctions—"I wonder why" instead of "I wonder," for example—a manner of speaking still familiar in the region.

Although Maxwell centered his creative life on the Lincoln, Illinois, milieu, his work ultimately benefits from a mingling of the regional and the cosmopolitan, as his native Midwest meets the New York and France of his adulthood. By the 1940s, a more detached intellect emerges. Although not as world-weary as the fiction of some of his *New Yorker* colleagues, his work offers increasingly complex, layered characterizations, remote objectivity, and free association resulting from his psychoanalysis. In his later work the heartland and East Coast coexist as Maxwell reflects on the full range of his experience. His prose becomes even purer, more streamlined, and increasingly reliant on facts.

* * *

My book is intended as an overdue introduction to a writer who seems destined for a special place in twentieth-century American literature. Tracing the development of Maxwell's art, it provides background on how he came to write his novels and short stories, and it examines his evolving approach to fiction writing and his contributions to the American literary canon. Perhaps most importantly, it attempts to convey the rich experience of reading and contemplating his work.

A study of Maxwell, it seems to me, might well begin with an understanding of what he called "three quarters of the material" he would need for his writing life: his childhood years in Illinois. As his readers know, the author has chronicled this time as no one else could; my aim is to set his work in context, to illustrate the circumstances through which his nascent sensibilities developed. After a discussion of his early years, my focus shifts to the novels, short stories, and nonfiction, to the unfolding of his literary life. The author once wrote me that he was "struck by the fact that literary projects that came into being one at a time and seemingly unrelated to anything else, in the end indicate a pattern that the writer—that this writer anyway—was not conscious of at the time."[10] I hope that this volume will help illuminate and interpret the patterns in Maxwell's writing and contribute to a better understanding of his literary world.

1

Childhood:
A Lifetime of Material
1908–33

Influenza

IN THE EARLY HOURS of January 3, 1919, ten-year-old William Maxwell lay feverish with influenza as the temperature outside dipped to ten degrees below zero. He had lost his usually enormous appetite on Christmas Day just as the dinner plate was placed before him by his Aunt Maybel, who put her hand on his forehead and took him to bed. Losing sense of time, he woke by turns to light, then to darkness. His whole family was sick: his brother Hap in a bed down the hall and his mother and father in a nearby town. This morning, nine days after Christmas, the telephone stirred his hazy sleep. From his room at the head of the stairs, he heard his aunt's strained voice speaking to his father on the other end of the line, then her heavy footsteps coming up the stairs.[1]

Almost a year earlier, the boy's father, William Sr., had read in the *Chicago Tribune* that a highly contagious and vigorous strain of influenza called the Spanish flu was spreading through American military camps and major cities. The Maxwells' hometown newspaper in Lincoln, Illinois followed the story as minor news. The big story was the Great War against the "Huns" in Europe and American boys being sent abroad to fight. In early March 1918, soldiers at Camp Funston, Kansas, were among the first reported U.S. victims of the disease, and thousands of American soldiers embarking for Europe in cramped troop ships came down with the flu. Most Americans associated the problem with soldiers going abroad, but before long, the troops returning on leave or as casualties carried the virus back to their bases and homes. By late August, soldiers in U.S. training camps suddenly began dying of a frighteningly severe form of the disease. The virus spread rapidly to the civilian population. Having mutated during its months in Europe, the new strain typically struck fast—"the passage from apparent health to near prostration [took] only one to two hours"—and often progressed to a deadly pneumonia that killed far more young adults in their twenties and thirties than it did any other group. In cities on the East Coast, hundreds, then thousands died, literally drowning in fluids that filled their lungs. From Boston, the flu moved swiftly west, following the railroad lines. Bodies were piled high in pine boxes and when there weren't enough caskets, in mass graves.[2]

As the alarming news reached central Illinois, families such as the Maxwells realized the epidemic was marching toward them. "There didn't seem to be any reason to think of the plague ever having to do with us," Maxwell recalled in a 1999 interview. "But in a gradual, remorseless way, it kept moving closer and closer. I know my parents were worried. I paid less attention to their words than to the sound of their voices. When they discussed it, I heard anxiety." On October 1, the *Lincoln Courier-Herald* reported that the county Red Cross had been asked to supply 5,000 influenza facemasks to highly affected areas. Maxwell's mother joined the seventy-five Lincoln women who answered the call to sew.[3] But masks did not stop the virus. On the main rail line between St. Louis and Chicago, the town of 12,000 lay in the path of masses of people traveling by train throughout the war, carrying influenza from major cities to small communities that dotted the prairie landscape. October 1918 was the deadliest month in the nation's history: Spanish influenza killed 195,000 Americans in thirty-one days, almost a third of the total U.S. death toll from the disease. Unlike its neighboring communities, Lincoln was slow to close schools and limit public functions. Thirty new cases were reported on October 16 alone. Schools and movie houses closed the next day, and all public gatherings were prohibited.[4]

On the evening of November 11, however, Lincoln and towns across the country and through much of the world celebrated the armistice ending the bloodiest war in history. Blossom Maxwell, William's mother, drove the family automobile through Lincoln in the victory parade with a gleeful William Sr. straddling the car's hood. The war was over, her husband had not been drafted, she was pregnant with their third child, and newspapers reported the flu pandemic seemed to be loosening its grip on the nation. Doctors believed those who had not yet contracted the disease had developed immunity, and by December the danger seemed to have passed in many parts of the country.

But after a brief reprieve, another wave swept the town. Advertisements for malted milk, thought to be the "right food" for before and after influenza, ran in the newspaper along with a public service announcement that admonished a young couple, "Don't kiss!" The *Courier*'s social column chronicled more Lincoln victims. Family friends Mr. and Mrs. Dean Hill, who appeared in Maxwell's late story, "My Father's Friends," fell ill with the flu. New cases were reported every day, and infected homes were quarantined. December proved a record month for deaths in Lincoln. By year's end, 2,000 cases had been reported since October, 602 homes had been placarded by the city board of health, and 97 residents had died.[5]

Blossom had reason to be afraid. Pregnant women were most at risk. Maxwell wrote on several occasions that she had premonitions of her death. But in the days before her baby was due, the epidemic in Lincoln seemed to be abating again. Dean Hill returned to work downtown on the eighteenth, and the second ban was lifted on the twentieth. Two days before Christmas only two new flu cases were reported, and the schools were preparing to reopen. The holidays were not the same, however. In nearby Springfield, Santa Claus made his annual appearance wearing a flu mask, but he was not allowed in Lincoln at all. Churches cancelled their usual programs and cantatas because there was no time to rehearse before Christmas, just a few days away.[6]

On Christmas Eve, Blossom and William Sr. boarded the train for Bloomington, Illinois, a larger community thirty miles north across the flat, frozen cornfields. Blossom's sister, Edith, lived there with her husband, an anesthetist at Brokaw Hospital, where the Maxwells believed it would be safer to give birth. They left Billie, as he was called, and his older brother, Hap, in Lincoln at the home of their father's sister, Maybel. As the writer recalled decades later, the morbid atmosphere of the house could be condensed to the prominent display in the living room of a framed sepia photograph of his grandfather lying in a coffin surrounded by floral tributes. A vase filled with peacock feathers completed the decor. The boys would have much preferred to be left with their beloved Aunt Annette, their mother's beautiful younger sister, but Annette had traveled to Chicago unexpectedly.

On Christmas, the day after his parents left for Bloomington, both boys came down with the flu at Maybel's. On New Year's Eve, a *Lincoln Courier* column mentioned that their parents had been stricken by the disease in Bloomington the day after Christmas and that their mother was particularly ill. Blossom gave birth to her third son, Robert Blinn, named for her family, on New Year's Day 1919. "Baby Born While Mother Ill With Pneumonia," announced a front-page story in the Lincoln paper. William Sr. was reportedly recovering, but his wife's condition deteriorated. She had developed double pneumonia.

When baby Blinn was two days old, Aunt Maybel received the dreaded telephone call from the boys' father. She climbed the stairs and gathered young Billie on her lap and Hap to her side. Tears streamed down her face. There was nothing more the doctors could do. Their mother was dead.

By the next evening, William Sr. was well enough to accompany his wife's remains home to Lincoln.[7] A story about Blossom's funeral appeared in the *Lincoln Courier-Herald* next to the news reports about the unexpected death of former President Theodore Roosevelt. Young Maxwell, still weak from the flu himself, found the rooms of his beloved Ninth Street home overflowing with friends and neighbors, out-of-town relatives, and floral bouquets "beyond description." The Presbyterian minister conducted the service in the living room, where his mother's coffin lay in the bay window, a somber scene replayed in novels Maxwell wrote decades later. Blossom was buried in Union Cemetery, a place he remembered for the comfort and peace it offered when his mother had taken him with her to tend his grandparents' graves. It appeared throughout his fiction as a site of silent communion between the living and the dead.[8]

His mother's death was the defining event of Maxwell's life and, later, of his literature. He often recalled that in that moment "the shine went out of everything." He learned that day that happiness is fragile, that no one is safe.

Lincoln, Illinois

Maxwell had been born into a gentler world. Before the Great War, middle-class families in Lincoln, Illinois lived in a neighborhood canopied by majestic elms; homes had wide porches and barns out back for horses and buggies. Without automobile noise, voices carried clearly down the street. Drama was supplied by town gossips rather than national tragedies. People walked to well-kept stores on the courthouse square, where Abraham Lincoln had argued legal cases in the only town that took his name before his presidency and assassination.

The town of Lincoln took pride in its legacy. The prairie lawyer had served as counsel and surveyor when the location was proposed as a county seat. In 1853, according to tradition, Mr. Lincoln bought two watermelons at a vendor's booth, called the landowners to the proposed courthouse square, cut the watermelons in two and christened his namesake town with the juice. A sculpture of a watermelon stands at the Lincoln train depot commemorating the event.[9]

The twentieth century brought progress and growth. The town built a Carnegie Library in 1902, where Maxwell borrowed his first books as a child, and a new county court house in 1905. Lincoln also boasted a small liberal arts college, a business college, twenty churches, three national banks, electric streetcars, two daily and four weekly newspapers, and a successful sand and gravel company owned by the McGrath brothers, who became Maxwell's new uncles after his father remarried. Thirty-six passenger and freight trains passed through every day. Most importantly, Lincoln was surrounded by the most fertile farmland in the world: from the town's edges, cornfields stretched to the horizon. Here and there a clump of trees or a farmhouse was the only marker between the eye and the setting sun. Farmers were prosperous and kept the town that way. Once established, they often built substantial homes and moved into Lincoln, leaving the crops to hired workers. The development divided the town and country people. Farmers who came to Lincoln in the evening after a day in the fields were snubbed by those whose fathers had done the same work but were now living within the town limits.[10]

The writer's father attended Eureka College, later known as the alma mater of President Ronald Reagan. William Sr. planned to become a doctor, but when his older brother died of typhoid fever, he came home to Lincoln to manage his brother's insurance agency. One day, on his way to the train station for a business trip, the young insurance agent caught the eye of Blossom Blinn as she rode by in a pony cart. Blossom, in her early twenties, was the middle daughter of Judge Edward Blinn, one of the most prominent country lawyers in Illinois. William began courting her when he returned from his trip, and they were married in June 1903. Their first son, Edward C. Maxwell, was born the next year. They called him Happy, which got shortened to Hap.

Their second son, William Keepers Maxwell Jr. arrived on August 16, 1908, a blistering hot Sunday at the height of the Lincoln Chautauqua season. That day, 5,000 people rode streetcars and horse-drawn carriages to the wooded Chautauqua grounds at the edge of town, where, for two weeks every summer, citizens of Lincoln, like those in communities all along the cross-country circuit, lodged in cabins or camped near the open-air auditorium that featured entertainment, lectures, and devotional programs from around the region and nation. The Chautauqua movement, founded on the shore of Lake Chautauqua, New York, in 1874, was a cultural phenomenon that swept rural

America before the mass media of radio and television reached beyond the cities. The *Daily Courier* reported that the 1908 Chautauqua season "merits the support of all lovers of high class and instructive entertaining." Just the day before, famed Chicago evangelist Billy Sunday preached to thousands about "Forces That Win," and the crowd viewed early moving pictures presented with a hand-operated machine. The morning of Maxwell's birth, a religious service featured a Des Moines pastor and the local choir, after which the Cadet Band played "inspiring and religious selections." The Honorable L. Y. Sherman, speaker of the Illinois House of Representatives, followed with an hour-and-a-half lecture on "The Anatomy of Humor." And, for the evening's finale, a man with a stereopticon projected reproductions of biblical master paintings on a screen while Father MacCorry told the story of Christ accompanied by a twenty-five member chorus.[11] Throughout his childhood, Maxwell vacationed with his family in a cabin every summer at Lincoln's Chautauqua, which appeared in his novels *Time Will Darken It* and *So Long, See You Tomorrow,* as well as in his short stories.

The same weekend, in the state capital of Springfield less than thirty miles away, racial tension that had been brewing all summer exploded into a riot. A white mining engineer had died of razor wounds inflicted by a black man and then, a few days before Maxwell's birth, the young wife of a white streetcar conductor claimed she had been dragged from her bed into her back yard and assaulted by a black man. In the days that followed, angry mobs lynched two black men, wrecked the small black business district, and burned forty homes in a black neighborhood. They destroyed businesses owned by white sympathizers and forced blacks to flee the city. The bloody weekend left two black and five white men dead and one hundred people of both races hospitalized. The accuser, Mabel Hallam, later confessed to a special grand jury that she actually had not been attacked by a black man but had been beaten by her white lover.[12]

"Husky newsboys" from the Springfield *Register* took the train to Lincoln carrying "enormous bundles of the...morning papers," breaking sales records at the depot with special editions about the Springfield race riot. Several days after the incident, the *Courier* reported that a black Lincoln man made remarks about Mabel Hallam that "in Springfield would have meant his death." Other blacks in Lincoln advised the man to go on vacation until the racial climate cooled. "It is well for the colored people of [Lincoln] that they refrain from utterances likely to inflame the people and their most valuable acts will be to suppress any signs of rowdyism that may appear on the part of the less valuable members of their race," the local paper advised. "[This] may go a long way in promoting the peaceful relations which now exist between the white and colored people [here] but which might be strained without much tension."[13]

No large-scale acts of violence were reported in Lincoln, yet racism was common, as it was in most small Midwestern towns. In neighborhoods such as the Maxwells', genteel bigotry marked most dealings between white families and their black servants. Maxwell recalled the prevailing notion among the white townspeople: "Negroes" were perfectly acceptable, "as long as they knew their place."

* * *

The community's atmosphere and history were reborn in the Lincoln of Maxwell's fiction, but it was domestic life that most thoroughly captured his imagination. When the author was two years old, his father bought a large house on Ninth Street diagonally across from the home of his grandmother and grandfather Blinn. In that house Maxwell found his hallowed ground, the place that became so much a part of him that its mere mention still moved him at the end of his ninety-one years. As a child, he absorbed every detail of the two-story late Victorian that later provided rich texture for his fiction: in front, the elevated curb offered an easy step from horse-drawn carriages (the hitching post is still there), and the lawn was bordered by a low black iron fence with one picket missing. The white lilac bush outside the dining room window and the violets in the yard emerged as symbols of hope and comfort in his novels.

Inside the house Maxwell's mother served tea parties with silver and china on a wicker cart, and his father's neighborhood orchestra rehearsed in the living room. Maxwell delighted in the window seats where he could curl up and read, the oriental rugs with intricate patterns for marble games, a notch in the tree that became his stepladder to the roof, the grandfather clock, smooth zinc kitchen counters, and a chair.[14] For him, all were part of the living home, so much so that as a writer he animated furniture and household objects as characters observing and commenting on a story's people and situations. The house on Ninth Street became the spiritual center of Maxwell's work. There were other dwellings—in Wisconsin, New York, and France—but Ninth Street inspired him to embrace domesticity as his artistic domain. His characters often live in this very home—or, as exiles, search for it in haunting dreams.

In Maxwell's mind, the world within the house was forever associated with his mother: "I didn't distinguish between the house and her," he wrote in

Ancestors in 1971. "When I was separated from it permanently, the sense of deprivation was of the kind that exiles know."[15] His special bond with her developed from infancy. He had been a fragile baby, weighing less at six weeks than at birth, and needed careful attention. In despair over his delicate health, his mother carried him gingerly on a pillow and was given no reassurance about his long-term survival until she took him to a pediatric specialist in nearby Peoria when he was three years old. He remembered taking off his clothes, standing on an examination table, and hearing the doctor tell his mother that, judging from the color of his lips and fingernails, he would live. "It was news to me," Maxwell said. "I never intended to die. I was pleased that I was going to live, but nevertheless, that hadn't been one of my worries. But a great weight must have fallen off her shoulders. I think the connection between us, this struggle that she had to keep me alive, produced in me an unbreakable attachment." Their bond formed the core of his childhood and the center of his own identity. As he wrote six decades later, he found in her physical presence "unfailing comfort and the immediate renewal of self-confidence." They had the same large brown eyes, and he so closely related to her that in his own mind their individuality blurred: "Which is his self and which is her?"[16]

The pattern of the family's life revolved around the father's schedule as a saleman for the Hanover Fire Insurance Company. Every Tuesday he caught the train to visit customers around Illinois, and on Friday he returned home where Blossom, Hap, Billie, and the family dog were waiting on the front porch. William Sr. helped found the Lincoln Country Club, and the couple took up golf. Music was his favorite avocation. The long-standing pianist for the Lincoln Rotary, he played popular showtunes of the day by ear—"from the 1900s through Rodgers and Hart, Gershwin, Cole Porter and Kern"—and was the regular host for rehearsals of the neighborhood orchestra. In his mind, however, boys should be boys. The younger William's penchant for art and reading, and his disinterest in the usual rough-and-tumble activities of boyhood, often put him at cross-purposes with his father. Through most of his career, the author portrayed his father as slightly gruff and distant, a parent who failed to understand his second son, "Their relationship is neither simple nor always the same. It includes both love and dislike. The man is not interested in hearing explanations for failure—not even legitimate ones. 'No alibis!' he says and turns away." The depiction softened in later years and writings as the author developed an appreciation and understanding of his father. With the perspective of age, he came to believe that his father gave him his "trust in life."[17]

One of the most compelling characters in Maxwell's work is his older brother, Hap, a rambunctious boy, a "holy terror" and remarkable symbol of a boy's ability to overcome adversity. When Hap was five, as his beloved Aunt Annette was ready to leave in her horse and wagon, Hap asked to go with her. She said he could not but did not notice that he already was climbing the spokes of a wheel to join her. When she flicked the rein, the horse pulled away, and Hap's leg caught in the spokes as the wheel turned. The boy's badly broken leg was amputated, but Hap nonetheless grew to be an avid athlete and outdoorsman: he won the singles tennis championship at summer camp and, with his pink cork prosthesis exposed, hopped to the end of the camp's high diving platform and performed a jackknife for all to see. Billie Maxwell was a baby at the time of the accident, so his brother's "affliction" (as his parents called it) was part of his childhood experience from the beginning. The brother of gallant physical courage inspired the future writer, while the pink leg propped against the bed reminded him what happens to young boys who fail to do as they are told.

In the back part of the house, young Maxwell was in daily contact with his mother's black household help. At the time, middle-class families in Lincoln often hired African Americans to cook, clean, and shovel coal for them. Hattie Dyer, whose own son, Billie, became the first black physician from Lincoln, served as the Maxwell's cook for many years. Billie Maxwell, who often took refuge with her in the kitchen, grew very fond of her.

Throughout childhood, Maxwell was surrounded by extended family in Lincoln, including many relatives who inspired characters in his future writing. Aunt Maybel, he told me, "sat for her portrait as Aunt Clara in *They Came Like Swallows*" as the woman who tells two young boys of their mother's death.[18] Grandmother Maxwell appeared most memorably in nonfiction as the staunch Christian woman who allowed her sensitive grandson to sit for hours cutting and pasting pictures from magazines. However, his maternal relatives, the Blinns, held a special place in his heart and imagination. His grandfather's term as president of the Court of Claims of the State led to his being known as "Judge Blinn" the rest of his life. Successful in both law and business, he was a kindly man prone to lending money and forgiving debts both large and small. Although he died of an infection from a ferret bite before Maxwell could remember him, he was held in such high esteem by Blossom and her two sisters, Edith and Annette, that his presence in the family was felt long after his death. Hap, who had been old enough to remember his grandfather, decided at an early age to become a lawyer like him. Originally from Vermont, Judge Blinn came west by way of Cincinnati, where he studied law and married Nettie Youtsey after settling in Lincoln in 1866, the year after President Lincoln's assassination.[19]

The Blinns had four children. Edith, the oldest, was actually an adopted cousin who served as an early example for Maxwell of an intelligent, academically inclined woman thwarted by nineteeth-century attitudes. As he describes in *Ancestors,* one of Edith's teachers left Lincoln for a job at Smith College and wanted to take his aunt with her, but Judge Blinn would not allow it. Edith, more reserved and serious than the other children, "might have lived a very different life and been rather a different person if my grandfather had believed in higher education for women," Maxwell reflected. Coincidentally, Maxwell married a graduate of Smith College decades later. Yet he did not forget the restrictions placed on his aunt, a memory that helped him write about women's lives in the 1948 novel *Time Will Darken It.*[20]

His mother's younger sister, Annette, provided a different example of womanhood. The beauty of the family, she was fun-loving, full of life, and beloved by her nephews. After Blossom died, Annette became the closest person to them. However, the family believed that she had made an "unfortunate marriage," the travails of which were not forgotten in the writings of Maxwell's adulthood.

Her younger brother, Maxwell's Uncle Ted, had a taste for finer things without a taste for earning them. Maxwell remembered that when he was three years old his father took him to a wheat field near Lincoln where Ted, hoping to change his precarious financial condition, had rented an airplane for $1,000 after the town agreed to pay him $2,000 if it took flight. The plane remained grounded, and after several hours William Sr. took his son home, while Judge Blinn paced his office, thinking about the $1,000 he would have to pay to relieve Ted of the obligation. Eventually, Ted became the elevator attendant in the courthouse where his father had once tried cases. Late in his career, in "The Man in the Moon," Maxwell offered an empathetic portrait of this uncle stung equally by misfortune and his own shortcomings.

Maxwell readers become intimately acquainted with these and other people from his childhood, all character models for his Lincoln fiction. Molding and remolding their joys and struggles over many decades, he firmly grounded their experience in the surrounding prairie, a place in time at once universal and very American. As an author, he depicted other places and other people, but these that he loved from an early age offered him a literary territory uniquely his own.

* * *

Maxwell's childhood changed forever when Aunt Maybel climbed the stairs to tell Hap and him of their mother's death. Suddenly, a series of housekeepers sat in Blossom's place at the table. William Sr., deep in mourning, paced the house with his sons, a memory that became one of the most compelling scenes in the late novel *So Long, See You Tomorrow*. To make matters worse, a former housekeeper wrote "poison pen letters" to Grandmother Maxwell falsely accusing the new widower of having affections for Annette, whose husband responded by limiting her visits to the boys. But the summer held a bright spot: Maxwell spent his entire school vacation with his Aunt Edith and Uncle Bill in Bloomington, where he saw circus parades, met new friends, and launched play boats in the fountain on their cul-de-sac.[21] For his father, the pall did not lift for a year, after which he began accepting party invitations and became more like himself again. Yet this was not the world he had known with Blossom. Overnight, it seemed, social life in Lincoln, as elsewhere, had been transformed. Prohibition hit, and suddenly respectable men and women were drinking and carousing, a development young Maxwell found unsettling. Even as an adult author, he always associated this period with distressing change: his mother's gentle world giving way to a fast and decadent one. Blossom's long, full skirts and upswept hair, her Gibson-girl womanhood, were replaced by flapper dresses and cropped pageboys. Late-night Charleston affairs supplanted her delightful afternoon tea parties. To the end of his life, Maxwell never developed a taste for jazz.

During this period, William Sr. began seeing Grace McGrath, a pretty young woman who, before Blossom's death, walked the children on Ninth Street to the kindergarten downtown and practiced with the neighborhood orchestra in the Maxwell living room. As a result, young Maxwell was not "faced with the prospect of living with a stranger" when his father announced his engagement. On October 5, 1921, in the presence of fifty guests, William Sr. and Grace were married at the home of the bride's sister, on a staircase landing amid a green bower of ferns. The *Lincoln Evening Star* reported the occasion as "one of the important and pretty events of the autumn season." Maxwell's father immediately sold the house on Ninth Street and "most of the furniture with it." For about a year the family lived in a rented home on an unpaved road while a new one was being built on Park Place, a fashionable new street with a boulevard and stone gate entrance. Having left the Ninth Street house one morning for school, Maxwell never returned; in his memory and in his fiction, it remained as it was that day.[22]

At Lincoln High School, Maxwell remained a studious boy who felt excluded from typical male activities. Books had always been his refuge, yet he considered *Treasure Island* his introduction to serious literature when it was assigned in his freshman year. "I reached the final sentence of the book and turned back to the beginning and went on reading," he remembered. "I read *Treasure Island* five times without stopping before I turned to anything else." That year he wrote his first story about "an aristocrat during the French Revolution who hid in a clock. If there were any French aristocrats in central Illinois in my boyhood I didn't know them," he said. "But at least we had a grandfather's clock in the front hall."[23] Although he would not travel to Europe until the summer he turned forty, his lifelong affinity with all things French was somehow sparked at an early age.

Leaving Lincoln

In 1923 the Hanover Insurance Company promoted Maxwell's father to vice president in the Chicago office, 170 miles north of Lincoln. William Sr. had turned down similar advancement in the company ten years earlier because Blossom had not wanted to raise the children in a big city. Now, tired of years of overnight business travel, "lugging that heavy grip from one small town to another," he accepted the offer. William Sr. and Grace moved in the spring, leaving Billie behind with Grace's older brothers and mother to finish his freshman year at Lincoln High.[24]

Blinn, Maxwell's little brother born at the time of their mother's death, had been staying with Grandmother Maxwell once a week. Those days "stretched to three or four," and as William Sr. prepared to leave Lincoln for the Windy City, his mother "threw herself on her knees before him and cried, 'Will, if you take that child I will die, it will kill me!'" The five-year-old stayed behind with his Aunt Maybel and Uncle Paul in a temporary arrangement that proved permanent.[25] Maxwell wrote that the decision was the only act of his father's life he ever heard him seriously regret. For Billie, it meant his little brother—ten years his junior—grew up in another town, and the two never knew each other well. Blinn rarely appears in his brother's fiction. After World War II Blinn joined his older brother, Hap, in the practice of law in Oxnard, California. The oldest and youngest Maxwell brothers worked together daily for most of their adult lives.

For young Maxwell the difficulty of being separated from his immediate family was eased by the McGrath brothers' light-hearted ways. The uncles were "very lively, generous men who treated me with great kindness, and were in the habit of stuffing ten dollar bills in my pockets, and enjoying my enjoyment," he told me. "I actually shared a bedroom with one of them that spring and when he went to bed at night the last thing he did was hang his toupee on a bedpost."[26]

When Maxwell finished his freshman year that spring, the McGrath uncles drove him north to return him to his father and Grace. They made a business trip out of it, stopping to see their company's gravel pits along the way. In Chicago they checked into the Hotel LaSalle, whose "mahogany and coffered ceiling far outdid any splendor" their nephew had ever seen, then took a cab up Michigan Avenue to Rogers Park to show him the cityscape on the way to his new North Side home.[27] Maxwell's departure from Lincoln at fourteen encapsulated his hometown in his mind and preserved it, suspended in time, as a century of dramatic change unfolded. Being forced to leave the small town of his boyhood before he outgrew it also meant he never felt the need to flee to more sophisticated pastures, as Sherwood Anderson and Edgar Lee Masters had before him. After college, he sailed to Martinique in search of something to write about, then he realized that "three-quarters of the material" he needed to sustain a literary career was already in his head.[28] He returned to Lincoln for his father's and Grace's funerals and sees to Annette in her old age, then never visited again. He much preferred the Lincoln in his mind.

Chicago

Rogers Park, the northernmost community in Chicago, was booming when his father and Grace arrived in 1923. Ten years earlier, the rural area had been home to 6,800 people, but by 1920 the population had soared to nearly 27,000 and, by 1930, to 57,000. As might be expected, the family found greater diversity among their urban neighbors than they had in central Illinois. Although at the time Rogers Park was almost exclusively white—out of more than 3,000 families, only five were "Negro" or "other colored"—the area was home to immigrants from Germany, England, Ireland, Sweden, and Russia. One of the city's fastest-growing neighborhoods, it became known as a "cosmopolitan community" with "handsome buildings, fine beaches, parks, and good schools."[29]

Maxwell's first look at Nicholas Senn High School must have been a shock. The imposing limestone structure was bigger than any building in Lincoln and, with an enrollment of 3,400, housed twenty times more students than Lincoln High. At first other boys ignored him, but Hap mixed easily and smoothed the transition by getting his younger brother into a high school fraternity—a group of boys he could speak to, who knew his name. After his first lonely weeks, he gradually "became more at home and ultimately very happy" in the new school with "every conceivable opportunity." Indeed, the move to Chicago became one of the most positive developments in Maxwell's young life—"a stroke of fortune," he later recalled. Senn High School offered him a wholly new environment, a better fit for his interests and aptitudes. Relieved that athletics was not the only acceptable activity for male students there, he wrote for the *Forum*, a student literary magazine, and took art classes in hopes of becoming an illustrator of children's books. Academic standards were so high that he later found his first year at the University of Illinois a "come-down."[30]

Maxwell had never felt accepted by another boy his age until the move to Chicago; among other indignities, he had not learned to throw a baseball and so considered himself an outcast. At Senn he met Jack Scully, an athletic and ruggedly handsome young man whom he considered his first real friend. "He liked me…because I *was* different. He loved mavericks," Maxwell told me. They were indeed a pair of opposites: William, the mild-mannered student at the head of the honor role, weighed 108 pounds, and Jack, at 155, became a top school athlete and could take on any boy in sight. Their close and increasingly complicated friendship continued through their college years and beyond, as Maxwell later modeled the character Spud Latham after him in the 1945 novel *The Folded Leaf*. At Senn, Maxwell also met Susan Deuel, a bright student who shared his enthusiasm for literature and art. She later joined William and Jack at the University of Illinois in Urbana, where she lived most of her adult life as the wife of English professor and Shakespeare scholar Charles Shattuck, who also became a lifelong friend of Maxwell's. Yet even as he was developing these lasting friendships at Senn, Maxwell still did not feel understood by his father, a circumstance exacerbated when he did odd jobs in the senior Maxwell's office in the Chicago loop during school vacations. On the forty-minute ride south on the El, his father, concerned for his son's social life, insisted that he put away his Russian novel and read the bridge column in the *Chicago Tribune*. But the younger Maxwell could not be dissuaded: When his father was not looking, he "stopped thinking about bridge…in order to go on with *The Brothers Karamazov*."[31]

Bonnie Oaks

Young Maxwell was not long for his father's corporate world: After his junior year at Senn, he took a job on a farm ten miles outside Portage, Wisconsin, where he could read Dostoevsky without looking over his shoulder. "Bonnie Oaks," as it was called, was no ordinary farm; in later years he likened it to the farm in Anton Chekov's *The Cherry Orchard*. Mildred Ormsby Green and her husband, Harrison Green, a Milwaukee attorney, had inherited the property from her family. Buoyed by Mildred's ebullient personality and love for the creative temperament, it became a retreat for authors and musicians—an informal artists' colony—in the twenties and thirties. As the Greens' daughter writes, "The summer months became legend. Mildred was a warm and hospitable woman whose genuine interest in people drew them to her....From the bootblack to the artist, the very young to the very old." The estate was idyllic and extensive; wooded land rolled through wild flower meadows to a calm creek perfect for rowing. In all, fifteen buildings dotted the property, most of which had been built in the mid- to late nineteenth century: the Main House, where the Greens lived, several guest houses, a boat house, woodshed, carpenter's shop, and chicken coop.[32]

Several noted artists became regular guests at Bonnie Oaks. Beginning in 1922, renowned pianist and Juilliard professor Josef Lhevinne spent twenty-two summers there where his grand piano, sent annually from New York in a crate, occupied the first floor studio of the "tower" across from the main house. Lhevinne, who often encouraged students and other New York musicians to stay at the farm, slept on the second floor, while the third floor, originally a huge water tank, became another studio after renovations—and the retreat where Maxwell eventually wrote his first novel. In 1931, Jean Toomer, author of *Cane* and one of the most prominent figures of the Harlem Renaissance, came to guide students of the Gurdjieff philosophy in a communal living experiment at Portage, bringing the group to Bonnie Oaks many times to study in its seclusion.[33]

Bonnie Oaks was a halcyon world to the artistic high school student. Here he not only soaked up the intellectual and creative atmosphere but also met Zona Gale, one of the primary literary mentors of his life. She had won the Pulitzer Prize for her play *Miss Lulu Bett* just four years earlier and was a good friend of Mildred Green. Although Gale's work became neglected later in the century, she had a national reputation at the time and was the first acclaimed writer Maxwell knew. "If you picked up a magazine there was a very good chance you'd find a story of hers in it," he wrote in a tribute to Gale for the *Yale Review*. In an interview, he exclaimed, "Oh God, what a lovely creature she was! And so kind to me." Gale was probably the first feminist in Maxwell's life. Fluent in the artistic, cultural, social, and political movements of her time, she was an active national voice on women's suffrage, pacifism, prohibition, civil liberties, and racial equality—not to mention the future of the novel. She exemplified a highly successful, independent woman who had made her way in a male-dominated profession early in the twentieth century. Unlike his Aunt Edith, Gale attended college, graduating from the University of Wisconsin, and ventured to New York in her twenties, as Maxwell would. There she wrote for the *New York World* to support her "real" work: fiction that most often captured life in her small Midwestern hometown. Although Gale and her young protégé shared this literary calling, ultimately her path differed from the future *New Yorker* editor's. In 1911, after ten years in Manhattan, she published her first novel, *Romance Island,* and later that year received first place out of 15,000 entries in a short story contest conducted by the *Delineator*. She returned home with the $2,000 prize money to live the rest of her life as a writer in Portage.[34]

There, twelve years after Gale's return, Maxwell met her the day he arrived on the train from Chicago. One of Mrs. Green's daughters greeted him at the station and, on their way to Bonnie Oaks, stopped to deliver a box of strawberries for Miss Gale's father at the writer's Greek revival home on the Fox River. While Miss Green spoke with Mr. Gale, Zona spoke with Maxwell: "I remember her showing me a Hiroshige print of some men walking in the rain, and a parchment lampshade with cutouts and explaining that they were of mystical significance. She also—and it is the one thing that always makes an adolescent's head swim—treated me as an intellectual equal. There was thirty-four years difference in our ages, and I was by no means her intellectual equal."[35]

The next day, while Maxwell was pulling weeds in the Greens' vegetable garden, he heard the telephone ring. Gale was calling to invite Mildred and "the little Maxwell" to dinner. He remembered it as one of the best days of his life: "When I was talking to her I felt I was conversing with a celestial being, in a world of light." Indeed, Gale introduced him to an alluring world of letters and intellectual pursuits. She was engaged in correspondence with the most famous American women writers of the day—Edith Wharton, Willa Cather, Charlotte Perkins Gilman, and Anzia Yezierska—and showed him their letters. He recalled "a note from Elinor Wylie, a letter from A.E. and others. These were talismans." At the time he met her, Gale had grown increasingly interested in mystic and psychic phenomena partially as a result of her mother's death two years earlier. Her credo—that life is more than we believe it to be—left a permanent impression on him, influencing his own way of observing and thinking about the human condition. As he remembered, "It was understood that I would make something of my life, but meanwhile it was life—the secret nature of all things that were something more than they appeared to be—that's what she talked to me about."

After the first dinner, their visits "fell into a pattern"—a member of the Green family delivered him at the Gale's and then went about the family shopping. "I came to talk and we talked," he recalled. "Her voice was both sad and humorous at the same time. Suddenly the car would be waiting at the curb, and it would be time for me to go. I had been immeasurably enriched, in ways that I didn't even try to understand." At first, he wrote down everything she said, but later found that he couldn't: "I said good-bye on the front steps and at that moment a curtain came down over my mind and I could not to save my life have told anybody what had happened inside that house or even what we talked about."[36]

Gale's impassioned *Portage Wisconsin and Other Essays,* published by Alfred A. Knopf in 1928, offers a glimpse of the concerns consuming her when they met. These writings seem to lay out the very essence of her conversations with the young man in the light-filled office at the back of her stately home and suggest she was an ideal mentor who sparked his interest in the years before he decided to become a writer. Through hindsight and knowledge of his own novels and stories to come, we can say that these meetings with Gale were a revelation for the seventeen-year-old and influenced his approach to the art he would later claim as his own. Her ideas about literature, for instance, and the novel in particular, spoke directly to the way he himself would write as a mature author. For Gale, the "naturalistic" or "realistic" novel of the time captured sordid, dramatic, and bleak aspects of common existence while ignoring its "brighter" implications; she called for a future fiction that would lie somewhere between the photographic "records" of naturalistic novels and the "human imaginings" of romanticism. Neither turning its back on base realities nor resorting to sentimentality, her "novel of tomorrow" would find significance in the simple patterns of daily living, in "the mysterious beauty of the commonplace." Artists, she believed, should find "excitement in the presence of life," not just for "acute situations"—the "tragedy, the zeniths, the nadirs"—but for "life's sheer deadly death-dealing routine." She longed for regional color, for American authors who would concentrate on their "native sources": "the growth of the individual: marriage, the great American home, relatives, traditions, and the accepted virtues in the route of [their] civilization."[37]

All this, of course, became Maxwell's own field of labor in years to come, and Gale lived to see his first fruits. On a visit to the Zona Gale home, I could imagine them sitting together at her mahogany desk or looking across the sloping lawn to the river below: an impressionable, book-loving, and somewhat romantic young man enchanted by her pontifications on literature and serious concerns for the state of the nation's fiction. Most likely, her conversations first planted in him the notion that art could emanate from everyday town life—even from Lincoln, Illinois—and that his "native sources" could be developed as subjects for fiction. Her "novel of tomorrow," with its reconciliation of the realistic and romantic, foretold the dark realism Maxwell later coupled with his reverence for homeland, a quality that fostered a distinct clear-sightedness, a dual and balanced view that set his work apart, particularly from other Midwestern literature. By example, Gale also taught him that fiction could be a viable career: She and her parents lived comfortably in a house that her writing had built them.

Gale's essays indicate that she may have spoken in high-flown, philosophical terms with a dramatic flair; her intellect clearly impressed Maxwell, whose more linear manner of thinking may explain why he remembered her discussions only in generalities. Even so, he connected with her. She shared his interest in stories of human nature and sought a higher meaning in everyday life, particularly in her small Midwestern hometown. She probably encouraged her young friend to heighten his sense of wonder and perception through what she called a "special grace of seeing"—to find and interpret the unexpressed, to record what lay beneath the familiar externalities of human life. For Maxwell the writer, this quality—an emphasis on the unsaid, on the power of silent epiphanies—became an intrinsic part of his artistic sensibility and work. Gale may also have introduced him to the "new psychology," which she held great stock in, particularly as it applied to the novelist: "The secret of understanding of human beings is now something in which all the world may share."[38] After Gale's death in 1938, Maxwell had his own experience with this "new psychology," using what he learned in Freudian analysis to deepen characterization in his novels of the 1940s.

Maxwell returned to the farm, off and on, for the next twelve years and continued to see Gale during his stays. In both Mildred and Zona he found women who encouraged and nurtured his literary interests—indeed introduced him to what a literary life could be—and helped put him on the path to becoming a writer.

Senior Year

After his first summer at Bonnie Oaks, he returned to Chicago for his senior year at Senn, where his English teacher had a friend at the Chicago Public

Library: "Once a week a crate of books would arrive and we would dive into it," he remembered. "I sometimes read six or seven plays and novels over the weekend. Shaw, Barrie, George Moore, Galsworthy, de Morgan, H. G. Wells, Conrad—whoever was admired among contemporary writers in the year 1925." He also tried his hand at writing and illustrating as associate art editor for the *Forum*. On the "Vacation Travels" page of the October 1925 issue, he wrote a piece comparing his time at Bonnie Oaks to spending the summer on the *H.M.S. Pinafore*. The opening paragraph reveals his views of his father's corporate world versus the life he found with the Greens. "One of the pleasant things about life is that one never knows what is just around the corner," he writes:

> Having resigned myself to the sad fate of spending the summer in an office in the loop, and of being a small and quite unnecessary cog in the "wheel of industry," I was suddenly whisked from my job in a most miraculous manner to one of the loveliest places on earth, a little Wisconsin town whose name had five "o's" [Oconomowoc] and heaven only knows how many other letters. Instead of by a magic carpet or a flying horse, I was carried there via the North Shore Line, but that did not make it one bit less exciting.[39]

More impressive, however, is a five-part series Maxwell wrote on American artists, based on paintings he viewed at the Chicago Art Institute through his high school years. Working with the editor of the institute's bulletin—a Miss Fishkin, whom he thanks profusely at the end of each article—he secured copies of paintings for publication in the magazine. His pieces on John Singer Sargent, George Inness, and Frederic M. Grant[40] suggest a mature appreciation for the artists as well as a sort of "Talk of the Town," cultural critic feel: "In the exhibits of the Chicago artists at the Art Institute in the last few years there have always been paintings which immediately attracted attention for their brilliancy of color—the paintings of Frederic M. Grant. Although it is a purely personal conviction, he seems, more than any of the other prominent artists to be destined for the permanence and greatness of Alexander, Sargent, and the other American masters."[41] Such urbane élan would not be out of place in *The New Yorker;* clearly, young Maxwell had found a role with which he felt comfortable and an environment that nurtured his intellectual and artistic growth. Without such opportunities—in the city, at school, at Bonnie Oaks—we can only speculate on how his path might have turned differently.

In the Senn yearbook one is surprised to find that sports-averse Maxwell also served as secretary and financial manager for the Student Athletic Association, undoubtedly inspired by his close friendship with sportsman Jack

Scully. The school art critic is easy to spot in the photo seated in the front row of team managers: the thin, slightly slouching boy, knees pinched together, hands folded in his lap, who sports the only light suit in a group of dark jackets, bulky sweaters, and a military coat. Looking at the picture, readers of *The Folded Leaf* might be reminded of a fictional boy: young Lymie Peters tending to the boxing gloves and locker room towels of his friend, Spud Latham.

Maxwell's early experiences at the Art Institute influenced his plans to study there after graduation from Senn. At the same time, his best friend, Jack, had enrolled at the University of Illinois in pre-medicine. When it came time for Jack to go to Urbana, he was recovering from pleurisy, and his parents thought he was not well enough to go to school, so Maxwell offered to go to campus with him and help him enroll: "We put up at my older brother's fraternity house, which I had stayed in before, until Jack found a room," he said, "and what with one thing and another, including the full moon, we both accepted pledge pins from the fraternity and I decided to spend a year at the U of I and then go to art school."[42]

Urbana and Harvard

In Urbana, Maxwell found a genteel, cultured, yet accessible academic community. Women kept monthly days "at home" to receive callers; dinner parties and afternoon teas were common. He recalls that the "men and women from the Romance Language and Philosophy and Classics departments...made up a delightful society, from which undergraduates were not excluded. I was never to meet anything like it. It constituted a large part of my education in manners, and was always there in my mind to draw on when I wanted a certain kind of dialogue, a lightness of tone."[43]

Two professors—Paul Landis and Bruce Weirick—helped change his art school plans. When Maxwell walked into his first freshman rhetoric class, his teacher read the names of those who were to be transferred to "star rhet" sections, and his name was not among them. To that point, he had not thought about becoming a writer, yet after publishing in the high school magazine and seeing his name in print, he was "a little disappointed." A day or so later, he learned that a mistake had been made and that he belonged in Paul Landis's "star rhet" class. "He cured me forever of purple prose by reading one of my themes aloud in class as an example of how *not* to write," he remembered. "As he was reading he stopped to point out here and there a phrase that was not hopelessly bad, and this helped me to live through it. Just." A big man with "an immensely tall forehead and a beautiful reading voice," Landis met Maxwell on the sidewalk a few weeks later and asked him to tea: "From that moment on, through all four years of college, he kept his eye on me. I couldn't have had a better mentor. He admired *Tom Jones* above all other English novels, and cautioned me that I ought not to read *Jude the Obscure* in any but the most cheerful surroundings." He also introduced his student to Virginia Woolf's *To the Lighthouse*, a book that influenced Maxwell's first novels, and "pulled strings" to get him into advanced English courses because he planned to stay in Urbana for only a year before going to the Art Institute. During this time, he was introduced to "Dr. Johnson and his Circle" by Professor Clarissa Rinaker, "a high-strung woman with a caustic tongue" who "scared [him] stiff." He remembered, "When I raised my hand and said that *Rasselas* was reminiscent of Oscar Wilde, her laughter at my misuse of the word reminiscent was not kind and unnecessarily prolonged." Even so, he came out of the class "loving Johnson and Boswell and Joshua Reynolds...and the whole opinionated crew."[44]

Maxwell's art school plans were ultimately changed when he took a course on the Romantic poets from Bruce Weirick, one of the most popular teachers in the English Department. He recalled that from the side, the professor looked like a "question mark. With his tilted cigarette holder, his eyebrows raised suggestively, his rasping ironical voice, his delight in wickedness of the milder kind, his stock of double-edged epigrams, he was catnip to the young." Weirick left his door unlocked so that students could play his records and read his books when he wasn't home. One day, he inquired into Maxwell's plans and told him he would "be happier and more secure financially" as an English professor. Maxwell was persuaded: He gave up the idea of becoming an artist and stayed in Urbana. Landis thought it would be useful for him to major in languages—"you didn't need to take a course in Shakespeare in order to read *King Lear*"—but guided him to English classes taught by professors he admired.[45]

Maxwell joined the Poetry Society, a group that met for readings on Sunday evenings at the home of Garreta Busey, a prominent local banker's daughter who taught in the English Department and had worked in New York on the staff of the *Herald Tribune* book section. Like Mildred Green, she became a mother figure to Maxwell, one with literary interests who provided him a place to live and write during the years between college and *The New Yorker*. Maxwell's poems imitated those of the lyric poets he admired—especially Elinor Wylie, Walter de la Mare, and Yeats. Indeed, his sonnets and lyrics share Wylie's and de la Mare's decorative images of nature; their themes of beauty, truth, death, and dreams; and, perhaps most obviously, their formal language. "I was saturated with lyric poetry, and I didn't mind if it showed," he told me.[46]

Wylie's notes to Zona Gale, which Maxwell read in Portage, originally piqued his interest in her poetry. He was particularly taken with her passion for moons, moonlight, and stars and a liberal dusting of gold and silver in her stanzas that critic Thomas Gray deemed "nearly obsessive." In "The Devil in Seven Shires," she writes: "The sixth is the shire of shadows / It shines within a cloud / Silver are all its meadows." "Madman's Song" describes "the sound of the silver horn," a "head on a golden pillow," and "the milk-white hounds of the moon."[47]

The young Maxwell contracted Wylie's penchant for such images. In an untitled poem, he wrote,

> One early morning as I lay in bed
> I looked out on a marsh that was all mist
> And silver. There behind the distant hills
> The cool gray sky held promise of the dawn
> That came in one great burst of glorious flame.
> It seemed as if the sky were all ablaze
> With fire of shining gold.[48]

This stanza, with its silver mist and golden sky, typifies Maxwell's Wylie-inspired verse.

As a college student, Maxwell must have embraced the theme of individuality coursing through her poetry as well, a concentration on the self over the masses, a celebration of identity and following one's own path. "The Eagle and the Mole," considered one of Wylie's best, had two messages for the budding writer: most obviously, that in solitude one may find the strength and freedom to accept one's own calling, and that the plane on which life is lived is not as important as its quality.

Similarly, her poem "Castilian," portrays Spanish painter Diego Valázquez, a man whose strength of character derives from his clear artistic choices, from his security in the knowledge that he is a master of his own canvas. Although Wylie's style and imagery became her most obvious influence on Maxwell's early writings, messages such as this must have appealed to him as well. The importance he placed on Wylie's work in college suggests that on some level her verse must have also encouraged his desire to develop strength from his individuality, to live and to write in his own way.

In Walter de la Mare's poetry, Maxwell found more natural imagery and a focus on the self journeying through a beautiful yet troubled world. His primary interests corresponded with de la Mare's: Dreams, death, childhood, and longing for a lost Eden not only dominated his early derivative verse but in later years became core concerns of his most powerful fiction. He first read de la Mare more than a decade before undergoing analysis, before his exposure to Freud's theories, yet even as a student he was naturally drawn to this poet fascinated with a dynamic dream life. For de la Mare, dreams were not only the source of art but the root of human imagination: a separate, unconscious state of being parallel, rather than subordinate, to the waking life.[49]

Maxwell's university verse captures this passion for dreams and the unconscious. Poems dashed off for campus poetry meetings on Sunday nights recall de la Mare's images of night and sleep, his references to gnomelike creatures found in the wooded forests of his dreams. This earliest of the writer's work also reflects de la Mare's belief in death as a "state of dreaming," his contemplation of beauty, and the search for a presence de la Mare calls the "impossible she," a mysterious, unattainable image of the ideal, a haunting female figure that embodies wholeness and goodness. The shadow cast by his mother's death undoubtedly contributed to his interest in de la Mare's view of the afterlife. While at the university, Maxwell dreamed that his mother was on the stairs of his rooming house. He awoke in the night calling out her name, only to realize that she was not there and never would be. In de la Mare's work there is no such finality: In *Behold, This Dreamer!* he suggests that life may in fact "prove to have been in the nature of dream, and death of an awakening."[50]

In his poem "Lyric," Maxwell's speaker is haunted by a dreamlike vision:

When twilight comes in stillness clad
  And fills my ears with music sweet,
Then beauty comes with shining eyes
  And crimson slippers on her feet.

She's sometimes dressed in cloth-of-gold
  With threads of pure fantasy
And sometimes in a shimmering robe
  Like silver mist upon the sea.
Her arms are whiter than the moon.
  Flame-coloured flowers are in her hair.

And when I close my drowsy eyes
   I see red slippers everywhere.
I know not why I turn away
   With aching heart, and dare not see
Where beauty dances with the wind
   Alone in white flamed ecstasy.

She does not tarry long, and yet—
   To me the thought is wond'rous sweet
That beauty came with shining eyes
   And crimson slippers on her feet.[51]

This lyric clearly suggests the literary influences that molded Maxwell's early writing. The unidentified beauty in his speaker's dream parallels the mythic, unreachable ideal of de la Mare's "impossible she." Seen only through the "drowsy eyes" of the unconscious mind, the image is fleeting: Like a mirage, its presence awakens desire, yet its impermanence renders heartache and yearning. Maxwell's inspiration here may be quite straightforward: The poem may simply echo one of his favorite poet's dominant themes or reflect the universal notion of beauty he absorbed from any number of writers who held his attention during this time. Yet it is reasonable to consider that the female embodiment of a lost ideal held particular resonance for him. His mother's death and interrupted childhood provided him with a mythic feminine figure of his own and a perfect past retrievable only through his fiction. The haunting absence of his mother produced in his own work the emotional power and unbearable longing he had found in de la Mare. At this early stage, however, his idyllic vision more closely mirrors the poetry he was reading, specifically de la Mare's notion of a higher beauty glimpsed in the state of dreams.

The poem typifies as well how Maxwell adopted the style and language of the lyric poets he encountered as a college student. It combines their romantic imagery, including plenty of Wyliesque references to silver and gold, with their antiquated syntax: "in stillness clad" and "fills my ears with music sweet," for example; "I know not" rather than "I do not know." Common to his student poems, the abundant metaphors and romantic personifications of beauty and nature also stem from these early influences and contrast sharply with the stylistic simplicity and spareness that became his signature. Yet if this collection of verse is a Maxwell anomaly, it is also a literary launching point, a small archive of his initial experimentations with the writing craft. From here, his inimitable style developed over decades and ended up in a very different place.

At the Poetry Society, he also met Robert Henderson, a graduate student in his first year of teaching who became his close friend and eventually followed him to *The New Yorker* as a fiction editor. Henderson remembered Maxwell as "very bright and successful at everything he wanted to do": a young man who liked to be different, who preferred a little black hat and turtleneck to the standard shirt and tie. As roommates, they discovered many of the same writers—both "loved Edward Arlington Robinson"—and shared an enthusiasm for opera. Maxwell had "some good records" they played on an old hand-wound Victrola.

One night, Henderson remembered, Maxwell invited a "lady friend" to the apartment and "put boards over either the bathtub or the toilet, and they climbed out onto the roof to see the chimney stacks as in Paris. And he came down and turned on the record of La Boheme." "I don't know how many sides there were, because it was long before long-playing," Henderson told me. "I guess they saw Paris out there....He just thought it was a good way to get to Paris, more or less." At this point, in the late 1920s, the two literature students had read of the expatriate writers in Paris, stories that further stimulated Maxwell's romantic vision of the city of lights he finally saw twenty years later.

During their summers home in Chicago, the two college friends saw live opera performances together, Henderson recalled, often standing at the rail at Ravinia: "And one time we went to the Chicago opera when it was in the old auditorium and sat way up in the balcony. But we put on our tuxedos"—the only black ties in a sea of less formally dressed patrons in the "cheap seats." Another time, they reversed their fashion statement: They sat in the orchestra section, where black tie was the tradition, Henderson remembered, but "we thought we'd be different than them and wear our jackets." Maxwell bucked convention on campus as well. Henderson often watched Illinois football games from the bleachers with Maxwell sitting beside him, lost in a book.[52]

From Urbana, Maxwell corresponded with Zona Gale, who returned his letters periodically; during this time, she was traveling extensively after her marriage to William Breese, a Portage businessman. Once he received a letter from Japan saying "that she had been the guest of honor at a dinner party and after dinner, for the entertainment of the guests, five hundred fireflies were released in the garden." When she came to lecture at the University of Illinois, she had a dinner for Maxwell and his friends in the upstairs dining room of a Chinese restaurant. "My friends took her simply as a visitation," he writes. "Which is what she was. I don't know which of the nine orders of angels she belonged to—was she a power, a dominion, a principality, an archangel? All I know is that when I was with her I had her undivided angelic attention."[53]

During his sophomore year, Maxwell's relationship with his closest friend, Jack Scully, reached a crisis with shocking consequences. A triangle had developed between the two young men and Margaret Guild, a fellow student Maxwell met in English class and the daughter of a celebrated English professor. Maxwell grew so distressed during this period that he attempted suicide by cutting his throat, a tragic moment that inspired the climax of his 1945 novel *The Folded Leaf*. While he was recovering in the hospital, his trusted friend Susan Deuel, invited him to her sorority's annual social. He replied,

> My Dear Susan,
>
> Having failed to discover whether the moon really was made of green cheese, I shall be delighted to come to the Spring party. As a tradition…there is something to be said for it. If I come on crutches and swathed in bandages I'm sure you won't mind.

The letter reveals a quiet grace and gentle humor even as he was healing from self-inflicted wounds. Sensitive and literary-minded like Maxwell, Susan also tried to cheer him with a loaned volume of Dante, for which he was grateful: "I know of nothing more genuinely unselfish than to surrender to one's friend, even for a few days, one's most cherished possession," he wrote her. "It is like gathering up all the most delightful part of one's personality and offering it. I have not read it, because I know it so well, already, but I hold it a long time on my knees, and wonder over it, and then run the tips of my fingers over it to see if it feels as exquisite as it looks."

The memory of Susan's kindness remained with him, and in *The Folded Leaf* she inspired a character that Maxwell named Hope. Their friendship lasted for more than sixty years. After Susan's marriage to Charles Shattuck, the couples remained close, and Maxwell, on more than one occasion, quietly helped them with financial loans. Decades later, in 1981, he wrote Susan that he had told his wife the story of the long-ago invitation:

> I was telling Emmy how you asked me to the Theta house dance when I was in the hospital with bandages around my neck, and how I borrowed a turtleneck sweater…and went, and the girls were so nice to me, all of them, and I had a wonderful time, and danced my head off, and Emmy remarked "For that you have no choice but to love her forever," and it appears I have.

A distance of sixty years allowed Maxwell to look back on the ordeal with some clarity. In part, he believed the poetry he was reading at the time gave him a "poetic idea of life after death"—a life in which he would be "reunited with [his] mother." Indeed, this is quite likely: At the time, he was reading and emulating de la Mare, whose verse resonates with ethereal images of an afterlife. One of Maxwell's own poems of the period describes the "sweet rest" that comes "to those whose lives are spent," and the "radiant soul" who dies young and finds "An exaltation born of ecstasy." He also felt—and attributes this feeling to Lymie in the novel—that he did not want to "live in a world where the truth has no power to make itself be believed." Later in life, he lost these feelings: "I have too much respect for the difficulty of arriving at the truth in the first place," he told me.[54]

Memorializing her friend in April 2001, writer Shirley Hazzard reflected on his attempt to take his own life: "Maxwell knew that quiet desperation can't be counted on to stay quiet, that heartbreak can grow irrepressible," she said. An attempt at suicide, "that extreme and most solitary experience must always be set, by survivors, as a measure against subsequent distress. I sometimes thought it a spectral presence in Bill's equilibrium and in his greatest pleasures. Photographs of Bill and Emmy when their daughters were small have the radiance of a reprieve, as though Bill marveled, like George Herbert, 'It cannot be / That I am he / On whom Thy tempests fell all night.'"[55]

* * *

Maxwell graduated from the University of Illinois in 1930 with highest honors and received a scholarship to Harvard graduate school. At Cambridge, he met Robert Fitzgerald, who, already a published poet as a sophomore, became a renowned scholar and lifelong friend. The two were initially drawn together because they were both Midwesterners—Fitzgerald was from Springfield, Illinois—and shared a love of writing and literature. At the time, Maxwell was still writing poetry, and he took his work to Fitzgerald, who would "criticize it patiently." Maxwell believed his friend was better educated and astute and "despised anything that wasn't first rate": "One day he looked at my poem and then he looked at me, rather in the way you look at children who present a problem, and he said, 'Why don't you write prose?' I was so happy that he thought I could write anything that I just turned to and wrote prose—as if he'd given me permission to try. The prose took the form of fiction because I do like stories and don't have a very firm grasp on ideas."[56]

Zona Gale came to see him again during his year at Harvard. She took him to a dinner followed by an informal meeting of young people where she spoke about writing. "What I remember," Maxwell writes, "is that an over-serious young man stood up and said, after she had finished speaking—he meant no offense: he was speaking as one writer to another—'Miss Gale, when you read something that you have written are you ever ashamed of it?' And she smiled mischievously and said, 'Not as often as I should be.'"[57]

Maxwell left Cambridge with his M.A. in 1931. He had wanted a Ph.D. from Harvard, with its scarlet-lined robes (his favorite color) and "snobbish" appeal. But a block on the German language held him back: "I think it was because when I was a little boy the papers were full of cartoons of Belgian women with their hands cut off and children on bayonets." Indeed, by the time World War I began, he was reading the *Lincoln Courier-Herald,* which carried daily political cartoons depicting gruesome "Huns." He might also have come across an editorial supporting the villagers of Brussels, Illinois, who refused to attend the Lutheran Church of a minister who preached in German. The paper supported even those with German names—Kulp, Goetze, Krause, Herrman, Wieneke—who participated in the "righteous wave of loyal American objection to anything German." Maxwell had no trouble with French, Greek, or Italian and only minor difficulty with Latin, but with German, he recalled "a total inability to memorize the vocabulary, so that every time I looked at a German word it was as if I'd never seen it before." After failing the German exam, he was put in an undergraduate class with a "wonderful" professor who, as a German, had had trouble with his colleagues during the war. Maxwell got through the year, but, knowing that sooner or later he would meet up with Old Norse and Middle High German, he headed back to Illinois.[58]

At Urbana, he found teaching composition "lovely when you found students who responded to things you were enthusiastic about. Teaching them to punctuate properly and to analyze the periodic sentences in Matthew Arnold's 'Gregarious and Slavish Instincts of Animals' was something else again." During his first year back in Illinois, he stayed with Garreta Busey and then at Sigma Pi fraternity, where he served as an academic advisor of sorts during the 1932–33 school year. His former fraternity was a bit deficient in academics and hoped that his presence would improve their reputation with the campus administration.[59]

Garreta Busey was quite influential in Maxwell's ultimate decision to leave the university and pursue a literary career in New York. While he was teaching in Urbana, a professor at Yale solicited her help with a series of biographical essays and sent her a two-volume life of Thomas Coke of Holkham, a leading agriculturist who introduced to Parliament the bill to recognize the American colonies. Asked to write a forty-page summary of the biography, Busey shared the job with Maxwell. "She wanted to save me from becoming an English professor," he said. "I was then twenty-three. She let me have all the big scenes.... I had so much pleasure in working with this material that I began to write my first novel, *Bright Center of Heaven*, because I didn't want the pleasure to end." About the same time, he was also reading a "silly novel" by Robert Nathan called *One More Spring*, about a group of people who live in a tool shed in Central Park: "I seem to remember that it encouraged the idea that life should be spontaneous and incautious. Anyway, I thought my life was foreseeable: I would advance through the academic ranks until I became a full professor (it did not occur to me that I might be denied this eminence) and then a professor emeritus, and then carried to the cemetery in a wooden box."[60]

In the depths of the Depression, with no job prospects in sight, he resigned from the University in 1933 to find his way as a writer in New York.

2

First Fiction:
Bright Center of Heaven
1933–34

MAXWELL HAD NO LUCK finding employment in New York, so he returned to the Greens at his beloved Bonnie Oaks. There, on the third floor of the renovated water tower, looking out over the trees, he sat at his typewriter composing his first novel, *Bright Center of Heaven,* as the sound of Josef Lhevinne's piano rose through the floorboards. All his life the writer appreciated this idyllic atmosphere and remembered Mildred Green as the charming, lively woman who provided him the space and unconditional support he needed to launch his literary career. "Some of the characters [in *Bright Center*] were derived from people living on the farm at the time, so it was a handy place to be," he remembered. "I would come for lunch and they would make remarks I had put in their mouths that morning. Which wasn't really mysterious, because if you are conscious of character—in the other sense of the word—you can't help being struck by how consistent people are in everything they do and say." Maxwell finished the book in four months, "with the help of Virginia Woolf, W. B. Yeats, Elinor Wylie, and a girl on the farm who was also writing a novel. When somebody said something good we would look at each other and one of us would say 'I spit on that,' meaning 'keep your hands off of it.'"

In the early years of their careers, Maxwell and Illinois friend Robert Henderson read everything they wrote aloud to each other. "So I heard most of his very first novel," Henderson said. But the final word came from Wisconsin: Maxwell brought the manuscript to Zona Gale to ask her whether he had written a novel. She told him yes but also mentioned that she had "read until four in the morning, and then gone downstairs to her study looking for the

last chapter." Maxwell remembered that he was "too thickheaded to understand what she was trying to tell me" and told her, "'No, that's all there is.'"
Two decades later, he realized what Gale found missing, but in later years he
could not recall the ending she had envisioned. After the novel was published,
Mildred Green found that her young friend's first book paid homage to her
twice: in her ebullient portrait realized through the character of Mrs. West
and in the dedication to "Baba, the most generous, the most beautiful, the
most astonishing of women."[1]

* * *

Bright Center of Heaven traces a single summer day at Meadowland, the pas-
toral haven of the widowed Mrs. West and the assortment of artists she wel-
comes each year to live and work in rural Wisconsin. While her houseguests
paint, write, and feverishly tackle the *Allegro con Fuoco* of the Tchaikovsky B
flat minor piano concerto in a renovated water tower, her two teenaged sons,
Thorn and Whitey, help with farm chores. Two lovers are in residence: Paul,
a newly reformed academician courts Nigel, an actress, who secretly fears she
is pregnant. A hypochondriac, Mrs. West's disgruntled sister-in-law, Amelia,
clings to social attitudes of her native South, and Johanna, the Bavarian cook,
privately ponders the fate of her ill mother back in the homeland. Mrs. West
directs Meadowland's coterie with an endearing exuberance that lends an
eccentric, even magical tone to the ordinary day. From the moment breakfast
is served, she anticipates the four o'clock arrival of Mr. Jefferson Carter, a
"Negro lecturer" and leader of his race who has accepted her invitation to
Meadowland after a meeting in New York. His impending visit strings the
work with subtle suspense as characters anticipate how Mrs. West's "socio-
logical experiment" will end.[2]

Bright Center of Heaven is primarily a gently humored novel of manners
structured as a series of interior monologues in repertory. Within its tight
scope, the narrative flows freely between the minds of the twelve Meadowland dwellers, focusing on their private joys and concerns while revealing
multiple views of their common experience. In lieu of formal chapters, the
breaks at the end of each section function as pauses between scenes in a play,
as transitions from one character's perspective to another's, from one of the
farm's settings to the next. These first scenes of Maxwell's career are highly
visual and contained within a well-defined setting and moment. Of all his
works, this one comes closest to approximating real time in its pacing and
duration. Here, he recreates a single day in 315 pages; fifty years later, *So Long,
See You Tomorrow* spanned a lifetime in only 135.

Bright Center of Heaven introduces literary traits Maxwell carried with him through decades of writing. Indeed, some of his most enduring qualities emerge in this first novel: his gentle humor and consummate empathy, focus on domestic life, concern with character, and facility with interior monologue. At the same time, it is the work of a young novelist who has not yet embraced his innate and most powerful material, whose unique voice has not yet crystallized. Its fundamental contrasts with the later fiction help illumine his development as a literary artist. For example, the narrative reflects neither the native language and landscape that will become his hallmarks nor the stark tone and dark undercurrents that infuse his subsequent works with pathos, with poignant apprehension of life's duality. In these pages readers will recognize some essential Maxwell qualities—his aesthetic sensibility and mature empathy for the human condition—yet also come upon passages that seem penned by another author altogether, that share neither the style nor tone of later novels such as *The Folded Leaf* or *So Long, See You Tomorrow*. *Bright Center* allows us to see how Maxwell made subtle and not-so-subtle narrative shifts at an early point in his career. Thereafter he gravitated toward a more natural, streamlined language; balanced characters' emotions with an intense yet wise objectivity; discovered that a traditional literary climax was not the only route to drama; and resolved to trust his own experience to guide his fictional world.

Naturally, Maxwell did not view the lessons of his first work as a personal *kunstlerroman*; what I see as evidence of his artistic coming of age he considered the literary indiscretion of his youth. The most positive comment he could muster in his signature to my first edition copy was, "You are right—it is a nice picture of the place, even if the story doesn't come off." In fact, of his six novels, *Bright Center of Heaven* remains the single one never republished; a thousand copies were issued in the first printing, and only a hundred of a second thousand sold despite positive critical reviews. At the end of his career, he relished the novel's scarcity and in several conversations shared his desire to "sweep it under a rug," to dismiss it as a derivative work written in a poetic style he later abandoned, as a case when he tried too hard for drama and missed the mark with his African American character. Indeed, it is hard to argue with his reservations about the book; certainly the poets and the modernist novelists he read at the University of Illinois served as his prime stylistic influences here. Readers who search out this rare volume will find lyrical embroidery that predates the straightforward simplicity and regional syntax that became his hallmark, forced conflict rather than a natural working out of events, and a stereotypic African American instead of the resonant, fully formed characters of his later work. Yet these early lapses in artistic judgment increase the importance of *Bright Center of Heaven* for a study of the author's development. Although glimpses of the mature Maxwell suggest aspects of his style and approach that were instinctive from the beginning, his moments of uncertainty and missteps on the way to mastery best reveal the pattern of his literary growth. It would be a mistake to look only at the highest-quality work of Maxwell or any artist, only to miss the work that helped it to become so.[3]

* * *

Maxwell returned to the Greens' Wisconsin farm in 1933, fresh from the reading of his formative years, which, in addition to classics of earlier eras, included contemporary poetry and fiction published in the twenties and early thirties. Woolf, Wylie, Yeats, and de la Mare remained his touchstones, and their voices reverberate in *Bright Center of Heaven*. Some of these influences worked their way permanently into Maxwell's own literary sensibility, shaped by his individual material and approach until they became his own (Woolf's use of interior monologue, for instance). On the other hand, de la Mare's high-flown language and flowery metaphor faded away. As Maxwell told George Plimpton in a *Paris Review* interview, "My first novel…is a compendium of all the writers I loved and admired….What I wrote when I was very young had some of the characteristic qualities of every writer I had any feeling for. It takes a while before that admiration sinks back and becomes unconscious. The writers stay with you for the rest of your life. But at least they don't intrude and become visible to the reader."[4]

With the benefit of reading his university verse, one can see how these influences made their way from his lyric stanzas to his first published novel. When characters at the Meadowland farm encounter nature or experience love, for example, they tend to think in metaphors and elevate the moment with images that seem grandiloquent by the standards of his later fiction. In several passages, celestial references specifically recall the poetry that filled his undergraduate imagination: "The night sky was opaque with invisible drifting clouds and gave back almost no planetary light, but only the reflected glow of the earth itself," he writes. "What few gray and tentative stars there were vanished as soon as the moon came out, yellow and subdued, from behind the clouds, like a night lamp burning at some heavenly bedside." Although loosed from the strict stanzaic forms of his sonnets and lyrics, sentences such as these retain qualities of his university poetry; in essence, they read like free verse versions of that earliest writing. Certainly Wylie and de la Mare peek through these passages: the moon and stars, the references to night and sleep reflect their stylistic and philosophical influence. Even with his shift to fiction, Maxwell continued to adorn his writing with poetic imagery: "Now the breakfast table was become like unto the earth itself, one half light and the other half darkness."[5]

The most extended example of such lyric narrative in the novel flows from the thoughts of Nigel, the actress, and Paul, the teacher. As they sit together in the woods, she becomes lethargic, her eyes closed; concerned, Paul realizes "how strange she had been all day, how like some one wandering continually back and forth between this world and a farther planet." Frightened, he shakes her:

> And when she did not speak, he took her face in his hands and called her by her name, over and over, until at last, far off in infinite space, she heard him and felt the pressure of his hands. Across all that distance it came to her, with the blinding clarity of truth, that her career, and all the things she had ever desired for herself, were as nothing beside her need of him, his need of her. Beyond the shadow of all doubts she was certain that if he let go, if he took his hands from her face even for a second, she would fall headlong. She would be bruised and battered against ten thousand unnamed stars.
>
> As they walked down the hill, now cloaked in the faint shadows of trees, unfolded and spread out upon the ground, and now exposed to the cool moonlight, this day, which had been a particular thing, separate and interminable, was joined to yesterday and tomorrow, and became a part of time.[6]

For readers of Maxwell's later work, this passage underscores the divide between the poetic style of this first novel and the sleeker, more realistic prose he soon adopted. Absent here is the understatement, the profound restraint that distinguishes almost all his subsequent fiction. By comparison, this scene feels overdramatized: The grand and romantic conceptions of nature—the "ten thousand unnamed stars" and "infinite space"—exaggerate the emotion. Images of the night sky and forest entwine with Paul's realization and Nigel's sudden epiphany about her need for him. Like speakers in de la Mare's verse, she finds "the blinding clarity of truth" while in a dreamlike state, and he envisions a sense of timelessness while "exposed to the cool moonlight." These similarities illustrate how deeply lyric poetry was embedded in the author's mind when he began his career as a novelist. For another writer such metaphoric language may seem natural, yet with the benefit of literary hindsight we can see that it does not suit Maxwell; his strength came through speaking plainly. As he told me, "The longer I went on writing the more of [the lyric poetry] I shed, until by the time of *So Long* and *The Outermost*

Dream all in the world I wanted was to say exactly what I meant, without lyrical embellishments."[7]

These "lyrical embellishments" also derive from Maxwell's exposure to the work of Virginia Woolf, probably the most influential author in his early career and certainly a central literary model throughout his writing life. As a complement to the verse he was reading at the time, Woolf's work became his paradigm for prose, a clear influence on the pacing and movement of his own fiction. Consider, for instance, the following sentence from the opening of her novel *To the Lighthouse:* "To her son these words conveyed an extraordinary joy, as if it were settled, the expedition were bound to take place, and the wonder to which he had looked forward, for years and years it seemed, was, after a night's darkness and a day's sail, within touch." Characteristic of Woolf's style, the mounting rhythm emerges from a series of modifying clauses; momentum builds through a sequence of brief suspensions in the narrative flow. The prose surges ahead then relaxes, surges and relaxes, until it reaches its destination. Maxwell's writing fell into the same cadence. Look again at the sentence that closes Nigel's scene in the woods: "As they walked down the hill, now cloaked in the faint shadows of trees, unfolded and spread out upon the ground, and now exposed to the cool moonlight, this day, which had been a particular thing, separate and interminable, was joined to yesterday and tomorrow, and became a part of time."[8] Clearly, the young writer's ear was tuned to Woolf's variable meter.

Ten years after *Bright Center of Heaven* was published, he found another unwitting link to Woolf's work: "I reread [the novel] and discovered to my horror that I had lifted a character—the homesick servant girl—lock, stock, and barrel from *To the Lighthouse,*" he said. "When I found myself writing about material that was my own, the echoes fell away."[9] Indeed, Woolf's poetic language and rhythm left him, yet her development of psychological life, her focus on character and the home fired his imagination in ways that remained with him throughout his career. These aspects of her work correlated with his own natural inclination as a writer; they suited his material and provided him a prototype for capturing interior spaces of mind and home. Consider, however, that although Woolf inspired his proclivity toward interior monologue, this was not a technique that could be appropriated as easily as other modes of style. Rather than merely imitate, he had to call on his own insight and empathy to probe the inner lives of his characters. This became one of his great strengths.

Maxwell grew to dislike the lyrical prose style he adopted early in his career, with its echoes of poets and novelists alike, yet his deepest regret about the novel remained the characterization of black lecturer and teacher, Jefferson Carter. As a first-time novelist, he had assumed that a good novel needed a dramatic climax followed by the requisite denouement, so instead of writing what actually happened when a racial leader visited the Wisconsin farm where he spent his youthful summers, he concocted a conflict. Maxwell told the story in 1991:

> In an article in *The New Criterion,* Bruce Bawer pointed out, correctly, that the black man in *Bright Center of Heaven* is totally unconvincing. The setting of that novel is taken from life, the characters largely but not wholly extensions of part of myself. Sixty-five years ago, at the age of seventeen, I worked on such a Wisconsin farm, and during the summer a black man, the National Secretary of the N.A.A.C.P., came for a brief visit. I had never sat down to eat with a black person before and I observed that my appetite was unimpaired and that the other people present appeared to feel that there was nothing unusual in the occasion. Which left me without any climax for my novel, so I invented one, unsuccessfully. I would have done better to stick to what happened, which was nothing much.[10]

The novel's climax does seem invented. Had Maxwell been content with "nothing much," *Bright Center* would have been more believable. In 1934, it might also have made a quiet yet poignant statement about race simply by depicting a "Negro leader's" visit to a Midwestern farm as uneventful, as easily accommodated in the flow of the family's daily life.

But instead we have this: Carter arrives in good cheer, greeting Mrs. West and her sons on the train platform. He is introduced as a black intellectual—as Bawer suggests, a bit stereotypic in this regard—and appears a deeply committed but reserved leader reminiscent of W. E. B. Du Bois. Back at Meadowland, Carter's private world is revealed when, alone in his room, he thinks himself a fool for coming, for taking time from his work when "there were plenty other folk who knew how to dance the social cake-walk to the white folk's music." He is haunted by the Scottsboro trial he witnessed months earlier in Alabama, the disturbing 1931 case involving eight black youths sentenced to death for rapes they did not commit against two white women. At the same time, he thinks of Mrs. West as "a kind of angel." He wonders what type of people he would encounter that evening: some, he knew, would be kind to him, while others might be intent on putting the "nigger in his place." He could abide the word "nigger," like a badge "dyed in honorable blood," yet was stung by the "*place* talk" that proliferated the class distinctions he was working to abolish. This self-observation proves accurate: Touched by the thoughtfulness of Mrs. West's younger son, Whitey, who gives him a tour of the farm, Carter overlooks the boy's unwitting use of the word "nigger" and, with utmost sensitivity, tries to ease his embarrassment. Using the word "place" in a derogatory manner, Paul, the teacher, faces a different reaction at the end of the evening.[11]

At dinner, Mrs. West's experiment turns out badly. Amelia refuses to acknowledge Carter when she is introduced at table. He graciously ignores her snub but becomes annoyed by the mannerisms and idiosyncrasies of the others. Wondering about their sanity, he notices a "violent chemical precipitation" beginning to take place within him. When the party adjourns to the outdoor screen tent, tensions flare: The man who came to Meadowland because "he found Mrs. West a kind of angel" suddenly cannot tolerate her rambling story of her grandfather's acquisition of Meadowland before the Civil War and imagines himself dragging her, her family, and guests "out of the half-darkness, seizing them by the scruff of the neck, shaking them till they listened to him." With "the blood...pounding...in his temples," he announces that men like her grandfather were "brutal" for making "farmland out of what the Lord intended to be forests." His festering emotions lead Paul to take up a debate on race, while Nigel, ignorant of what she is saying, comes to his aid. When Carter shouts at Nigel, Paul instinctively fires back a racial slur in her defense: "Until they have learned to behave like gentlemen, perhaps it is better that they be kept in their place." Infuriated, Carter beats down the screen and storms into the night.[12]

"I wish I could redo my first novel and make the Negro a more worldly character who would be beyond being upset by the scene in the screen tent," Maxwell told me. In interviews he did not infer that a racial slur does not merit anger but rather expressed disappointment in his own literary judgment, and in this regard the editor's self-critical eye does not fail him. Carter's weakness as a character derives from his being forced to fit the conflict the writer felt compelled to create, when, as a black intellectual experienced at maneuvering through a white world, he probably would not allow the trifles of some artists-in-residence to disturb him to the point of uncontrolled rage, "infuriated beyond the power of reason."[13] At the very moment Carter hears the word "place"—the one term we have been told he detests—he snaps, creating a moment that seems convenient and contrived. Here we see the fledgling novelist trying to summon racial attitudes he observed in childhood to portray the perspective of a black American. Despite such effort, the resulting scene is implausible: The dignified and sensitive leader of his race cannot be easily reconciled with the violently enraged man unable to maintain composure in the face of thoughtless comments and questions from a ménage of mostly comical characters. His sudden reversal in temperament sets up an explosive conflict at the expense of his credibility as a character. Given the sensitivity with which the writer portrays other characters in this novel and African Americans in later work, it is highly likely that he would have developed Carter more believably had he not been concerned with drama. For Maxwell, whose exceptional gift for empathy is otherwise certain and true from the beginning, this portrait becomes an aberration of his apprenticeship: Learning from this experience, he later created convincing, more fully developed black Americans using the same wisdom and sensitivity he brought to his other characters.

Zona Gale was keenly interested in the racial theme of *Bright Center of Heaven.* Decades ahead of her time, she wrote about race relations in a small Midwestern town and, consequently, was well suited to read and comment on the manuscript of Maxwell's first novel. Her 1915 story "The Reception Surprise" portrayed an interracial marriage. It was rejected by the *Atlantic Monthly* and by the editor of *Everybody's Magazine,* who told her that "as a nation we aren't quite ready" for the subject. As Deborah Lindsay Williams has noted, Gale "had the last laugh" when she published a version of the story under the title "Dream" in her 1919 collection *Peace in Friendship Village.*

The situations in "Dream" and *Bright Center of Heaven* are closely allied: In Gale's story, a highly educated couple moves to Friendship Village. One of the town's women plans a welcome reception but cancels when she learns that the wife is black. The story's title derives from the dream of another woman, Calliope March, who envisions a town where the races can live together as neighbors. Maxwell's Mrs. West shares Calliope's vision, her attempt to bring the races together, and her failure to convince others to her way of thinking. Gale wrote out of her desire for political change and commented on Maxwell's work from that perspective. Her words of endorsement appeared on the novel's back cover: "Here is the first human, laughing treatment of one of the most pressing of national problems, turned quaintly on its head."[14]

An enduring theme for Maxwell, Mid-American black experience in the early twentieth century eventually framed his body of work. *Bright Center of Heaven* initiated his literary interest in the subject; *Billie Dyer and Other Stories,* published nearly sixty years later, provided his final reflections on the small-town blacks beloved in his childhood. Between these poles, *Time Will Darken It,* his 1948 novel, portrayed minority families among the citizens of Draperville, Illinois, circa 1912. Here, race relations in the pre–World War I heartland conjure images of a conditioned, limited acceptance that belies the warm bonds between white families and their black household help.

The writer's evolving treatment of the subject glimpses the maturation of his insight and artistry: By the end of his career, his work preserved the memory of Lincoln's first African American physician and contemplated his own relationship with blacks using a spare style that relies on fact as much as fiction.

Maxwell's coincidental connection to the Springfield Race Riots of 1908 does not formally come into play, yet it is interesting to note that an incident that took place at the time and near the place of his birth ultimately instigated the formation of the NAACP, whose secretary he met while a teenager at Bonnie Oaks in Wisconsin. Notice, too, the similarity to the Scottsboro trial cited in *Bright Center:* Both involve black men wrongly accused of molesting white women. Clearly Maxwell was aware of these incidents; the Scottsboro case was being tried in Alabama as he wrote the novel. In *Bright Center,* Carter remembers the "courtroom lynching" of a Scottsboro boy on the stand whose healed scar drew up the corner of his mouth: "How strange a thing that a wound from the bayonet of a guardsman who was supposed to be protecting him from the mob should turn into a smile," he thought. He recalls the boy's testimony: "Yessuh, I was in the fight. I didn't do much fightin' myself because I had mah lil brother to take keer of, but I was in the car whar the fight was goin' on. . . . Nossuh, I didn't see no white girls. . . . Nossuh, I didn't do nothin' to no white girls. I was just in a rock fight, that's all."[15] In Maxwell's youth, as through much of the twentieth century, these words could just have easily been spoken by a boy in Illinois. The author, who held fond memories of black servants in the family household, remained deeply conflicted on this issue and found it difficult to write about. Yet all his life he was drawn back to the subject, and his later attempts to address race in early-century America proved more successful. With a tinge of irony, his Lincoln fiction yet to come portrays both the overt and subterranean racial discrimination that thrived in the only town named for the Great Emancipator before his presidency.

* * *

Despite the derivative language, regardless of the unfortunate mischaracterization of Jefferson Carter, *Bright Center of Heaven* has qualities that recommend it, particularly to anyone interested in the full sweep of the writer's career. Certainly it is pre-vintage Maxwell, a literary genesis that exhibits his early influences and, as a base point, helps to illustrate how his fiction evolved over a remarkably long life of letters. Here, through comparison with his later works, we see how he cultivated his natural reserve, cast off unnecessary flourishes, and rejected strictures of plot to dictate his characters. Although Jefferson Carter's visit is the centerpiece, the axis around which the novel turns, the work does not necessarily fall on the failed scene in the screen tent. Actually, Carter arrives quite late in the book, on page 223; as one reviewer pointed out, "the climax...is too long delayed to be really effective."[16] If this delay creates imbalance in the unfolding plot, it also gives Maxwell ample narrative room to experiment with his first ensemble of characters, the freedom to focus on nuances of both their interactions and private thoughts while he keeps the climax waiting. As a result, the novel is character-centered, like the rest of his work, despite the tacked-on feeling of the drama near the end. Before and after the Carter interlude—indeed through the majority of the novel—aspects of the mature Maxwell are already present: home life and gentle humor, a facility for character development and interior monologue, sensitivity to the connections between people, and a proclivity toward portraying the world of artists coupled with an awareness of language and dialect.

It is quite fitting that Maxwell's novelistic career opens with a scene in a kitchen—Mrs. West's in this case—the heart of the domestic life he embraced throughout his body of work. Just as he did fifty and even sixty years later, he lingers over its interior details and objects: the "gate-leg breakfast table by the window," knives and forks and spoons and china, yellow garden poppies, and the way the sunlight falls "upon the ledge of the east window, upon the polished floor, upon the broad oak table in the center of the room." For him, cutlery and glassware, pitchers and polished silver become talismans of a changeless paradise, the stuff of his mother's long-ago world. Part of the living, breathing fabric of home, they assume life as palpable as any character's: The room awakens from an afternoon nap as "the chairs stretched, the curtains stiffened."[17] In his second novel, *They Came Like Swallows,* he turns to the kitchen he remembers from his own childhood—for now he concentrates on Mrs. West's—yet his strong affinity for the domain of early-twentieth-century women, for the nucleus of home, emerges here in the opening pages of his first published fiction.

Against this backdrop, and particularly in the 222 pages that precede Carter's arrival, he molds the inner lives of his characters with much the same sensitivity and understanding of human nature that distinguishes his most mature work. From the beginning, he has the ability to project himself into others' worlds, to empathize with men, women, and children, with artists and farm crew alike. Based on Mrs. Green, Mrs. West becomes the novel's spark and central figure, an exuberant woman of fifty who, like Virginia

Woolf's Mrs. Ramsay and Mrs. Dalloway, manages the varied affairs of the house. Her ebullience is perhaps most palpable in her run-on biographical sketches of friends and acquaintances that break into multiple tangents before veering back on course, as well as in her ability to remain delighted with an elaborately orchestrated picnic that is rained on. She finds joy in getting drenched to the skin in a downpour (then "you needn't be afraid of getting wet"), and although she can no longer dance, "since neither time nor convention could bend or undo her delight, she danced with her mind."[18]

Maxwell also exhibits keen sensitivity in his portraits of artists' passions and thoughts while performing. Undoubtedly, his familiarity with Josef Lhevinne at Bonnie Oaks inspired his character Josefa, the pianist, who contemplates her own playing: "It was so strange a thing, this speaking even for a brief time through one's hands instead of one's mouth. One had to begin by placing one's whole life in one's hands, breaking them in, as one would a horse, to do work which was contrary to their nature, and dull, and beneath their dignity."[19] Although he took lessons in his youth, Maxwell was not dedicated to piano practice until decades later, when, in his fifties, he studied with a concert musician. He never considered himself a pianist, yet to witness him composing on his Coronamatic was to see an artist who, like Josefa, spoke through hands directly connected to his heart and mind.

Finally, it is worth noting that Maxwell intended *Bright Center of Heaven* as a comic novel. His gentle wit lightened a lifetime of literature yet to come, but this first fiction uncovers his sense of amusement unshadowed by the tragic scenes so vividly etched in his later work. Certainly characters here face private pains and challenges, yet when the cloud of sadness lifts, it lifts completely. Here, joys seem mostly untouched by the sorrow that cloaks even the brightest moments of his subsequent fiction. In essence, this is Maxwell's only truly light novel.

* * *

Soon after he completed the manuscript for *Bright Center of Heaven,* Maxwell took a freighter from New York down the Windward Islands toward Martinique in December 1933. Having read a book by Lafcadio Heran about St. Pierre, a city on the island that had been destroyed by volcanic eruption in 1903, he "thought it would be interesting to go there and perhaps write about it." He stayed in Fort de France and spoke rudimentary French to the islanders' patois, the first time he had the opportunity to use his second language in practice. A decade later, he began a novel based on this trip, but the work remained unfinished. "I had nothing to do all day except wander around looking at what there was to see," he said. "That month seemed as long as a year under ordinary circumstances in America." In Martinique, he received a letter from Garreta Busey saying that Harper was "seriously considering" his novel and waiting for Cass Canfield to return from Europe. "I thought I ought to hurry back and at least be nearby when he arrived at his decision," Maxwell remembered. "Which turned out to be favorable."[20]

3

Breakout Novel:
They Came Like Swallows
1934–38

AFTER RETURNING FROM Martinique, Maxwell stayed in New York until his first novel was published in 1934. "Although [*Bright Center of Heaven*] had two favorable reviews, it didn't cause any commercial excitement whatever," he wrote forty years later in *Ancestors*. "So I went home, and started another novel, and when that petered out I started another, and made my savings stretch as far as possible, and took help from friends. Not money. Room and board, in exchange for doing things for them that they were perfectly able to do for themselves. This was so I wouldn't feel obligated." He returned to the Greens' third-floor room on top of the converted water tower at Bonnie Oaks to begin a novel based on his own childhood and his mother's death. There, back in his peaceful post among the trees, he worked on the first part of *They Came Like Swallows*. He wrote seven versions—each about a hundred pages long—but was satisfied with none of them. "I needed to forget Virginia Woolf," he wrote, "and establish contact with a figure out of antiquity—the old, often blind, professional storyteller who made his living by standing on the riverbank by the ferry landing or by some crossroads, telling tales that began, 'Once upon a time.'" He "tried telling the story in the first person and in the third. Neither one worked. The omniscient author knew too much and at the same time too little."[1]

With his working manuscript in hand, Maxwell went to the MacDowell Colony in Peterborough, New Hampshire, where he stayed during the summer of 1935. American composer Aaron Copland was also there that summer, as was Maxwell's friend from Harvard, Robert Fitzgerald, who "added immensely" to his enjoyment of the writing community. However, Mrs.

MacDowell was another story. The widow of American composer Edward MacDowell and resident founder of the colony did not join the ranks of female mentors and maternal friends who enriched Maxwell's early writing life. In fact, she was perhaps the only elder woman who rankled him: "The MacDowell Colony was a beautiful place ruined by an accumulation of rules which it was virtually impossible not to break," he recalled. "Without meaning to I broke all of them.…Don't do this, don't do that, thank God I can't remember what they were." Mrs. MacDowell was "very old and had a toadying companion whose eye was forever out for infringements. Ordinarily I like old women, but Mrs. MacDowell and I didn't take to each other. I had the feeling that she didn't care all that much for anybody who wore trousers."[2]

On his twenty-seventh birthday that August, he bought tickets for Robert and him to see Martha Graham dance in the town hall, only to learn that Mrs. MacDowell was presenting a musicale the same evening and had invited people from the surrounding hills. The colonists, the majority of whom had tickets for Graham's performance, were expected to attend MacDowell's presentation. "One of them was a friend of Graham and got her to start her performance late," he recalled, "and the musicians who were to play for Mrs. MacDowell planned an intermission which would allow us to slip away unnoticed and go down to the village. In the intermission of Graham's recital (which struck me dumb with amazement) I was standing on the front steps of the hall with two girl dancers from Jacob's Pillow, when I saw Mrs. MacDowell drive by with her head out of the window counting the offending colonists." The rest of Maxwell's stay was "devoted to apologies," and in the fall, at a meeting of the MacDowell Association in New York, Mrs. MacDowell saw him and turned her back, he remembered, "releasing me forever from what would have been a considerable obligation."[3]

Despite such minor annoyances, Maxwell was able to make the first section of *They Came Like Swallows* work to his satisfaction while at the colony that summer, this time beginning the story through the eyes of a young boy. His eighth try with the material "stuck." "Looking at it now, I wonder what the difficulty was," he told me nearly sixty years later. "The difficulty was that I didn't know how to handle narrative, or what form the book would take. I spent a lot of time talking to other people, going swimming in a park in Peterborough, and even I once climbed Mount Monadnock, but the essential work got done. I mean I got past the block, into the second section."[4]

He finished the second section and wrote the third in two weeks in a room at Garreta Busey's house in Urbana. With his typewriter "beside a window looking out on a tin roof," the atmosphere was "perfect" for writing. "The roof was so boring it instantly drove me back to the typewriter," he said. Writing fifteen years after the "disastrous facts" of his mother's death, he still "hadn't achieved much distance from them," and so, more than at any other time in his career, he relived the experience as he wrote: "When I was writing the last section of *They Came Like Swallows*, I walked the floor in tears which I had to brush away with my hand when I sat down at the typewriter to write the sentence I had just written in my head."[5]

When Harper accepted his second novel for publication, he decided to job hunt again in New York and was hired by Paramount Pictures to read and summarize books for possible consideration for the movies. "The first book they gave me was long, seven hundred and fifty pages I suppose, a terrible, trashy novel called *Lady Cynthia Clandon's Husband*," he said. The studio asked for five copies of a twenty-five page synopsis that took him a full day to write; because the five copies were due the next day, he took his work to a typist, which cost him five of the seven dollars and fifty cents he earned for three days' work as a new reader. While he took on two more synopsis projects for Paramount, he received letters of introduction for interviews with *The New Republic*—who soon found out he "didn't know anything about politics"—and *The New Yorker,* which had accepted two of his stories, "A Christmas Story" and "Scotland's Burning." "Eugene Saxton at Harper's wrote to Katharine White about me," he said, "and she astonished him by replying that there were not many openings at *The New Yorker* at that time, but that she would talk to me. This was 1936—the Depression—and nobody had heard of an opening anywhere in years." During his interview, White asked him what salary he wanted. "Some knowledgeable acquaintance had told me I must ask for thirty-five dollars a week or I wouldn't be respected; so I swallowed hard and said, 'Thirty-five dollars,'" he remembered. "Mrs. White smiled and said, 'I expect you could live on less.' I could have lived nicely on fifteen."[6]

A few days after the interview, having returned to writing "those terrible things" for Paramount, he went to a Chinese restaurant where he was refused a table for one. The rebuff of this simple request represented a low point in the young Maxwell's quest to become a writer and make a living in New York's literary world. At that moment, he remembered, "the bottom dropped out of everything. I thought 'There's no place in the world for me. Absolutely no place.'" That evening when he returned to his rooming house on Lexington Avenue, he found a telegram from Katharine White under the door.[7]

The New Yorker

Maxwell began his career at *The New Yorker* the next Tuesday, November 3, at the salary he requested: thirty-five dollars a week. Originally, he was hired "not as a fiction editor but to 'see artists'—that is, to be a kind of front man between them and the Art Committee, which met on Wednesdays." Although he had strong literary credentials for an entry position at *The New Yorker*—with his first novel on the shelves, his second in Harper's hands, and a story that had already appeared in the magazine—he also had the fortune of good timing. Wolcott Gibbs, a fiction editor and frequent contributor to the magazine, had tired of "seeing artists" and believed it was someone else's turn to relay editorial decisions about cartoons and drawings, so Maxwell was given his spot. At the time, fiction, humor, and art were handled by the same editors; on Tuesdays, artists left their work with the office receptionist, usually in the form of a rough sketch, and it was considered the next day at the art meeting. Harold Ross, Katharine White, Rea Irvin, and Gibbs (until he gave up his place) attended the meetings, along with White's secretary, who took notes, and an office boy named Wilbur, "whose mind was on basketball." "The editors sat on one side of a big table, with knitting needles," Maxwell remembered. "The covers and drawings were placed on a stand by Wilbur; Ross would lean forward and touch the parts of the drawing that were unsatisfactory with the end of his needle. I too had a knitting needle, which I did not use for quite some time. Occasionally Mrs. White would say that the [cartoon] might be saved if it had a better caption, and it would be returned to the artist or sent to E. B. White, who was a whiz at this." On Thursdays, Maxwell returned the artists' portfolios to them and explained which ideas had been approved ("in which case they were to make a finished drawing") and which rejected. "The first time they paraded in one after another I was struck by the fact that they all looked like the people in their drawings," he recalled. "Some artists were too important to be entrusted to me. Peter Arno and Helen Hokinson were seen by Mrs. White. I noticed that they didn't look like the characters they drew."[8]

After Maxwell was with the magazine about three months, having spent many hours staring at a self-portrait of James Thurber on the wall above his desk, Gibbs handed him a manuscript and suggested he edit it. "He didn't explain what editing was, so I treated it as I would a manuscript of my own in an unfinished state—that is I cut and rearranged and put in or took out punctuation, and to my surprise he sent it off to the printer. The next time

I overshot the mark, and in the end it required a good deal of teaching and observing of his and Katharine White's editing before I began to get the hang of it."[9]

During these early days in New York, Maxwell worked five days a week at the magazine as an art and fiction editor and found life outside his job lonely: "When I got home at night I didn't want to have anything to do with people, having had so much to do with them all day long. I tried not to have a telephone, and when Mrs. White's secretary insisted, I had one put in but didn't answer it when it rang, which it didn't very often do. I didn't go to the theater or the opera or buy paintings or go to museums. I just was caught up in my job. I also had insomnia. And used to try and fall asleep between the passing of one Sixth Avenue L train and the next." Maxwell did have friends, however: "a brother and sister who were the children of a doctor who lived and had his office on upper Madison Avenue, and an actor/photographer, who later became a director for CBS." He spent every weekend with the actor's family in Elton, Connecticut, for about four years, an experience not unlike that found in his short story "The Patterns of Love," which appeared in *The New Yorker* in 1945.[10]

Harper published *Swallows* in 1937, and when it was chosen by the Book-of-the-Month Club, Zona Gale praised it in a glowing review that went out to subscribers. She had been distressed when Maxwell accepted the magazine position and encouraged his writing over the editorial work: "She didn't like *The New Yorker* particularly, and she thought I would stop writing, as indeed I did after three or four years," he said. His first payment from the Book-of-the-Month Club totaled eight thousand dollars, so much money that he "went into Wolcott Gibbs' office to tell him and could hardly walk, stunned by the overwhelming sum." Soon in New York, Gale asked him whether there was anyone there he would like to meet, and he answered, "Willa Cather." "At this period of her life Willa Cather was a recluse," he said, "and I had asked for the one person in New York that Zona couldn't take me to."[11]

Zona Gale died the next year. Although she only lived to read Maxwell's first two novels, she left a permanent impression on his thinking and writing. Her ideas about women in society influenced how he portrayed female characters in his later work, and her mysticism, her sense of life beyond what we know, remained central to his view of the human experience.

* * *

They Came Like Swallows details the day-to-day experience of the Morison family just as the Armistice is signed and the 1918 Spanish influenza epidemic has ravaged the country. Maxwell's first full treatment of his mother's death, it centers on the last weeks in the life of Elizabeth Morison, the pregnant mother of two boys who succumbs to the disease after she is weakened from the birth of her third son. With its measured, steady movement toward a family's devastation, the novel presents the most fatalistic view in the writer's body of work. Tragedy seems predestined from the outset: The father reads aloud newspaper reports about the epidemic as the flu creeps closer and closer. A sparrow flies into the home, a harbinger of death. And finally the disease overtakes them; they are powerless to avoid or to stop it.

As an illustration of Maxwell's literary beginnings, *Swallows* offers a clear view of the modernist influence that absorbed his early writing life, especially in its parallels to Virginia Woolf's *To the Lighthouse.* This connection is important to a study of his career not only for its implications for his first fictions but also as a touchstone for interpreting developments over the succeeding fifty years or more—for observing the literary directions he took as he matured and established his own style.

In essence, *Swallows* encapsulates artistic and experiential impetuses that compelled Maxwell as a young man to write: the novels of Woolf and the painful emotional legacy of his mother's death. In this second novel he introduces the early-twentieth-century Midwest that became his signature setting. As a foundation for his "Lincoln" canon, it originates themes, characters, situations, and images he refined throughout his career and initiates the fundamental family relationships of his fiction: a young boy's intense love for his mother, his resentment of his distant father, and the contrast between his older brother's robust physicality and his own sensitivity. *Swallows* establishes Maxwell as a writer of domestic fiction with a special affinity for childhood; among all his novels, it best illustrates his remarkable understanding of and ease with young minds and exudes a sense of pure, original feeling that distinguishes it as the prime example of his early work. Written before his foray into psychoanalysis, the novel presents experience and feeling untouched by Freudian investigations into inner life. Although psychoanalytic allusions added broader perspective to his later novels, *Swallows* deals in the pristine emotion of a writer reliving devastating events without having achieved distance from them.

Perhaps because he gave himself over so completely to the grief of his childhood tragedy as he composed this novel, Maxwell began to write more simply and directly, as if the words he typed on the page were his memories themselves. At this point, the poetic language, the early lyrical influences that had crept into *Bright Center of Heaven,* fell away in favor of the cadence of Illinois conversation. His sentences were unembellished, and the celestial, romantic imagery of the earlier novel ceded to a singular focus on the details of his Midwestern home: the flowing carpet patterns like rivers to a child's eyes, the window seat and sewing kit, the best blue china, a mother's voice wafting up the stairs. By now, Woolf had become an inspiration more than a model for his direct imitation: *Swallows* reflects her subject matter and insular, psychological focus yet also establishes an approach and direction that were uniquely Maxwell's. For the first time, his prose took on the refined restraint and spare elegance that distinguished his individual style. In embracing his native material, he found his literary voice, his own way of speaking through fiction.

Although *Swallows* marks the beginning of a distinctly Maxwellian mode, it also reflects the author's "intense admiration for *To the Lighthouse*" and his deep affinity for Woolf's young character, James. During one of our conversations, Maxwell's connection with Woolf's fictional boy came up when we discussed his 1976 story, "The Thistles in Sweden." In this short story, a small group of New Yorkers celebrates New Year's Eve with dinner and a parlor game: Between courses they take turns waiting in the bedroom until they are called out to answer such questions as, "If you were a school of Italian painting or a color of the spectrum or a character from fiction, what school of Italian painting or color or character would you be?" Nearly twenty years after the story appeared in *The New Yorker*, Maxwell answered the same question in one of our interviews. Without hesitation he replied, "a) Carpaccio, b) scarlet, and c) the little boy who was cutting pictures out of a catalogue at his mother's feet in *To the Lighthouse*. James I think his name was. The one who was unnerved by his father's loud quotations from Tennyson."[12] Those familiar with the writer's own childhood experience and catalogue cutting will understand the affinity he felt for Woolf's character. The young Maxwell sensed a kindred spirit in James, the quiet, sensitive, artistic boy who fears his father and, like the author, endures his beloved mother's death. From this very intimate identification sprang Maxwell's abiding connection to Woolf's work, to its characters and subjects certainly, but also to its sensibility, psychological insight, and narrative methods. Although Maxwell's first novel recalls Woolf's style—with its interior monologue, fluency with diverse perspectives, and precise renderings of home life—echoes of her work resonate most profoundly in *They Came Like Swallows*.

Maxwell first read *To the Lighthouse* as a graduate student at Illinois—an artistic epiphany of sorts for the young writer-to-be, who found in its pages a tragedy nearly identical to the one that had imprinted his own life and an inner world he recognized. His mentor, English professor Paul Landis, had picked up a copy of the Tauschnitz edition in Germany while on a round-the-world sabbatical trip during the 1931–32 academic year. "You may like this," he told his student. "I couldn't bring myself to finish it." Maxwell not only finished the book but also was deeply impressed. Landis may not have realized the service he had done: Woolf's novel proved to be the single most influential work on Maxwell's own writing, particularly during his formative years as a fledgling novelist. In his introduction to the 1997 Modern Library edition of *Swallows,* he recalls that "on the very first page" of *To the Lighthouse* he was struck by this paragraph:

> Since he belonged, even at the age of six, to that great clan which cannot keep this feeling separate from that, but must let future prospects, with their joys and sorrows, cloud what is actually at hand, since to such people even in earliest childhood any turn in the wheel of sensation has the power to crystallise and transfix the moment upon which its gloom or radiance rests, James Ramsay, sitting on the floor cutting out pictures from the illustrated catalogue of the Army and Navy Stores, endowed the picture of a refrigerator, as his mother spoke, with heavenly bliss.[13]

In this sentence, a stylistic prototype for some of his prose in *Bright Center of Heaven,* the twenty-four-year-old Maxwell saw a mirror image of his childhood self: the reflection of a boy who played imaginatively in his own world yet was ever mindful of his mother's presence. More than that, the passage recalls qualities he himself developed at an early age, qualities that both formed his own nature and later underscored his fiction. Three of these characteristics leap from Woolf's paragraph as particularly Maxwellian: a sense that both the future and past shadow the present, the tendency to consider life's emotional poles in delicate counterpoise, and the belief that small details of experience can have transformative power. Introduced in *Swallows,* all became central considerations of his fiction, developing in depth and complexity as his career proceeded.

Maxwell also recognized Mrs. Ramsay, James's mother, as reminiscent of his own. "Think what *To the Lighthouse* meant to me," he told George Plimpton. "How close Mrs. Ramsay is to my own idea of my mother... both of them gone, both leaving the family unable to navigate very well. It couldn't have failed to have a profound effect on me." Indeed, as a student Maxwell might well have taken Woolf's novel quite personally because its storyline and characters so closely reflect those of his own childhood. So when he wanted to write his own novel based on similar events, how could he approach the material differently? Like Woolf's, his work was intrinsically connected to autobiography yet molded by literary form. His also featured a boy who lost his mother to death after childbirth as the Great War drew to a close. In the end, *They Came Like Swallows* differed distinctly: Unlike Woolf, Maxwell did not incorporate the mother's viewpoint in his story but allowed her to be seen through the eyes of her family members, set apart as the lodestar of their universe. *To the Lighthouse* portrays a home overflowing with Mrs. Ramsay's attentive love and, after a symbolic (and literally parenthetical) mention of her death, depicts the hole she has left there. The circumstances surrounding her demise are, in effect, invisible. In contrast, *Swallows* focuses on the mother's passing specifically—the events leading to it, the jolt of the news, the tragic aftermath. As Maxwell wrote, "Because Virginia Woolf disposed of Mrs. Ramsay's death in a brief, terrible parenthesis, leaving the reader in ignorance of what led up to it, I felt my hands were not tied. I could go where she had chosen not to."[14]

Maxwell chose to portray the mother solely from the perspectives of her two sons and husband, creating characters based on his own child self, his older brother, Hap, and his father. Rather than shift frequently between characters' minds as he had in *Bright Center of Heaven*, here he more rigidly restricted the frame of reference by structuring the novel as a triptych. Each of three "books" filters exclusively through one viewpoint: first young Bunny's, then Robert's, and finally that of the husband, James.[15] Maxwell envisioned the novel as a set of three expanding concentric circles formed by stones cast, one after the other, on the surface of a pond. As he told Plimpton, each circle, each perspective had "ripples moving outward from inside the first ones but never overtaking them." This image must have been on his mind as he began to compose, for it sets Bunny's consciousness in motion in the novel's opening lines: As the boy awakens, "A sound…struck the surface of his sleep and sank like a stone."[16]

For critic V. S. Pritchett, Maxwell's three-part approach left the novel "technically weak": "The narrative disintegrates because you begin with little Bunny at his mother's knee, go on with little Robert who is 'father's boy' and then muddle along with father," he writes. "There is no unity."[17] Although his was the only such criticism at the time of the novel's publication, Pritchett's literary prominence prompts its consideration. For Maxwell, the novel's design was hard-won: After experimenting with various viewpoints, he settled on what was for him an unusual approach. It was modernistic, too, in that it filtered a single world through one consciousness at a time, juxtaposing three characters' perspectives as separate yet related spheres. Two elements,

I believe, actually produce the integrated effect Pritchett sought but did not find. First, as the central figure throughout the novel, the mother becomes a strong unifying element. Through their love for her, the three Morison males are brought together; their stories revolve around her. Second, the approach creates gentle momentum as one perspective layers the next. Rather than present three isolated sensibilities, Maxwell's method creates a set of related psychological experiences that build toward the final section. Bunny's ever-widening ripple of consciousness infiltrates Robert's perspective in the second section, and in turn the outlook of both boys becomes a subtext to the father's in the third. By novel's end, the father's inner world may be understood both individually and in light of what readers already know about his sons' emotional lives.

Part One, "Whose Angel Child," relives a Sunday in November 1918 through the eyes of Bunny, the younger Morison son, who becomes Maxwell's quintessential fictional child. Drawn most purely from the writer's own experience, he balances a nearly painful sensitivity with the sheer joy of seeing the world with a first, fresh view. Bunny embodies the fears and wonderment of childhood: the fragile happiness that can be shattered without warning and the youthful reverie that brings diversion and respite from situations that are too complicated. Like Woolf's little James, he creates an elaborate, imaginary existence among the everyday objects of home and a life that revolves around his mother, the reference point by which he judges everything around him.

Through Bunny's mind, Maxwell captures the acute visual sense of youth. "For [Bunny], to think of things was to see them," he writes, "schoolyard, bare trees, gravel and walks, furnace-rooms, the eaves along the south end of the building." From the opening scene, the boy sees so intensely, so intently that the most minute, homely details form cinematic daydreams that play before his mind's eye. As he opens his eyes from a nap, he first notices his eyelashes, like "spears" across his field of vision and entangled from sleep. Beyond them he views white woodwork unattached to the walls and the changing shape of chairs. Above him, on the ceiling, a water stain appears as a yellow lake, and "the lake became a bird with a plumed head and straggling tail feathers, while Bunny was looking at it." Maxwell does not write that the lake looked like a bird, nor that it seemed a bird, nor that he imagined a bird. Rather, the lake *became* a bird, transforming before Bunny's eyes. The author portrays the childhood mind as active, always creating: Bunny focuses intently on optical illusions and holds fascination for them much longer than an adult would. He becomes enthralled with the simplest image and prefers visually stimulating surroundings; for instance, he is disappointed when the castle-covered wallpaper in the dining room is replaced with a plain kind that gives him nothing to think about. But despite such setbacks, there is always new territory to explore. Looking through the window, he imagines himself out in the rain: "He was wet and shining. His mind bent from the wind. He detached a leaf. But one did not speak of these things." This is typical of the way Bunny projects himself into a scene: Rather than observe a leaf falling, he plucks it from the tree with his imagination. He assumes special powers of the childhood imagination and is actively engaged in fantasizing his surroundings. Even at the age of six, however, he understands that his imaginings are private, not part of the world at large.[18]

As a six-year-old, Bunny has a keen emotional barometer but is lost easily in a maze of words and situations he doesn't comprehend. Maxwell seems to know the exact point at which the child crosses from understanding to naiveté, as if remembering from his own childhood eavesdropping. Although Bunny is clever enough to feign sleep so he can listen to his mother and aunt talk about private matters, he naturally misinterprets what he hears on occasion. When he learns of his mother's pregnancy, he hopes she will "come around to his way of thinking"—that there is no reason to take on a new baby "at this time" and certainly "it was just as well that his father not be told." For Bunny, the end of the war in Europe does not register, and he imagines the "epidemic" only as "unpleasantly shaped and rather like a bedpan."[19] Such innocence furnishes much of the novel's gentle humor.

Bunny's "practically contemporary" interest in his mother's affairs further develops the focus on home life introduced in *Bright Center of Heaven*. The child can remember being in the kitchen "before he could remember anything else," with its old but clean-scrubbed comfort, its shiny metal and porcelain surfaces, its turnip tops in bowls along the window sill. This is where he goes for solace. When he is unhappy about the prospect of changing bedrooms when the baby arrives, he helps his mother polish silver at the counter: "As soon as Bunny took up a piece of rag and began to polish his mother's [engraved] name, the sadness slipped away." Unlike his older brother, he takes interest in the women's conversations about cooking: "I stir it," his mother said, "without ever changing the direction of the spoon." "In cold water," Irene said, "and then I let it come to a boil, slowly."[20]

Maxwell himself "always felt comfortable in the world of women":

> As a child I was often in my mother's bedroom when she and my aunt would be trying on clothes, and I was familiar with their corsets and the things on dressing table tops. Since I had no desire to kill animals, hunting and fish-

ing—the guns and tackle that were so conspicuously a part of the men's world, were not interesting to me. I think it is possible that the reason so much of what goes on in my novels is domestic is a reflection of all this.[21]

The author's memory of his mother's household adds rich texture and detail to his early-twentieth-century setting. An intricate network of activities and skills, the art of homemaking fulfills the family's emotional and physical needs and creates a sense of community and identity among the women. While at novel's end, childbearing threatens the mother's life, other aspects of home life provide fulfillment and joy, countering the uncertain world outside with a secure haven.

The reader leaves Bunny, who has come down with the Spanish flu, as he lays his head in his mother's lap. Now, Robert's perspective takes over, and in this center section crucial moments of the story unfold: The epidemic worsens, schools close, and his parents take a train to another town where she will have the baby. The writer understands the degree to which Robert, seven years older than Bunny, has developed maturity and awareness. Although he retains some of his childhood imagination, he has begun to unlock mysteries of the adult world. He has opinions about the ending of World War I and the Germans based on what he hears. Having listened to his father read newspaper accounts of the epidemic, he fears for the family when Bunny falls ill. Rather than retreat to his own world as Bunny does, he turns his eyes away in silent understanding: He knows his mother is pregnant and that the flu could affect her. He takes on the role of monitoring Bunny's room so that his mother does not enter and is plagued with guilt after she goes to the sickbed while he is busy killing the bird that has flown inside. He notices her expanding waistline and can see her embarrassment when he looks at her. Yet Maxwell knows Robert's limits and depicts his frustration when he falls short. After secretly locating the word "womb" in Aunt Clara's dictionary, he "read and reread, skipping the brackets and the abbreviations but with never a glimpse of meaning. The meaning was there, but he could not get at it. It was inside the words."[22]

Already at this early point in his career, Maxwell finds singular moments that intimately and indelibly capture his characters. Robert, who has lost his leg in an accident, is revealed in his daydreams: He concocts, in minute detail, a new procedure to regrow bones with a special cast of "elastic plaster." He envisions an elaborate treatment that would entail months of bed rest and medicines and imagines feeling with his hand for the new leg that might be under the bedcovers. Away from the neighborhood football lot, Robert is sensitive yet far from self-pitying. Like Bunny, he privately longs for love—from the roof, he imagines what it would be like to fall and have everyone come running—yet he courageously moves forward. At an early age, he has learned to keep fears to himself, ignore his physical loss as much as possible, and look ahead to all he *can* do. This loving portrait of Maxwell's older brother, with whom the writer shared little in common, reflects not only the inspiring fortitude of the young man but also the writer's sensitivity to a personal nature far different from his own. After the book was published, Hap did not relish his younger brother's portrait of him, and so Maxwell did not write about him again until after his death in the 1980s.[23]

Part III, "Upon a Compass-Point," brings the story inside the mind of James, now a grieving widower who returns home to face the devastating aftermath of Elizabeth's tragic death with Bunny, Robert, and the new baby born days before his mother's passing. Although James is not presented as extensively as the two boys, his excruciating pain chills the final scenes. In flashback, we see him lying in the hospital, two rooms from his wife, the sound of her "desperate suffocated breathing" coming to him as he stares at the rectangle of light projected through the transom onto the ceiling.[24] Later, he paces with Robert back and forth through the house until they come to the coffin in the living room (a scene that is repeated more than forty years later in *So Long, See You Tomorrow*).

Perhaps most memorably, he takes a long walk through snowdrifts on a frigid night before the funeral. Along the way, he struggles with the idea that his wife's death was part of a vast, ordered, and indifferent universe. As his late father-in-law once told him, "It's like this James.... There's the earth—the continents and the seas, and the moon revolving around the earth, and the sun beyond that, and all the constellations.... Somebody made it—some power—according to laws that can't be changed or added to" (ellipses Maxwell's). The family's fragile equilibrium has lost balance; here, no joy offsets the unpredictable, uncontrollable forces that penetrate the walls of the Morison home. James has reached a point beyond control, wandering the streets under the stars. Like characters in the naturalistic works of such writers as Stephen Crane and Theodore Dreiser, he perceives his plight in relation to a dispassionate world: "The snow dropping out of the sky did not turn when he turned or make any concession to his needs, but only to his existence. The snow fell on his shoulders and on the brim of his hat and it stayed there and melted. He was real. That was all he knew."[25]

The stunning scene ends with an image typical of Maxwell's approach: considering history not with a panoramic view, but through a "telescope," observing intimate, one-to-one moments that define the personality of the past.[26] Delirious with grief, James sees a carriage coming down the alley and believes for a moment that Elizabeth has come back to find him. He looks up to see his late wife in the wagon. Suddenly, the Spanish influenza James had read about just a month before, the epidemic that felled millions, has been reduced to two men locked in a gaze: The tear-streaked eyes of a new widower and the wild-eyed stare of a neighborhood man emptying trashcans on a bitter night. This is the first highly dramatic scene Maxwell handles with mature artistry. His narrative pacing and human understanding deliver a man's delusional crisis eclipsed suddenly by the recognition of a new and unacceptable reality.

It is not hard to imagine Maxwell's tears as he wrote this scene in the room at Garreta Busey's in Urbana.

* * *

Virginia Woolf surely influenced Maxwell's emphasis on inner life and the domestic sphere. Beyond his affinity with her story and characters, he also felt a kinship with her literary focus and concerns that so closely paralleled his own. *To the Lighthouse* may have given him confidence to write fiction in a way that came most naturally to him. Like Woolf, he was more inspired by the rhythms of ordinary life than by world events that marked his era: Although he was personally devastated by the influenza epidemic, for example, his writing is always restricted to its impact on the insular world of a single home. His focus on things he calls "small and unimportant" stems from his "distaste for the grandiose," a tendency that evolved from his early devotion to his mother and her world. This also corresponded with his own preference for enjoying people individually, on a one-to-one basis, rather than in large groups. Consequently, his work inclines toward the private realm, the details, both physical and psychological, that underpin home life, and the subtlest nuance of human interaction. "When I encounter something really grand, such as, for example, the last two pages of Tolstoy's *Master and Man,* I am overwhelmed," he told me. "The poet Louise Bogan was a friend, and lived decently, but frugally, in an apartment near the Washington Bridge. She used to say that the view of the Hudson River, between two bleak buildings, was all the view of the river she was intended to have. I feel my only chance to get anywhere near the vicinity of the grand and the tragic is through the modest means that have been given to me. This is not a feeling a major writer is likely to have." On the contrary, Woolf's proclamation in her essay "Modern Fiction" could have been his own: "Let us not take it for granted that life exists more fully in what is commonly thought big than in what is commonly thought small." Or, as Maxwell offered in Midwestern vernacular, "When you live on a prairie you see the whole of the sky. It is all there: and buildings, people, and trees, often ugly in themselves, have the saving grace of unimportance."[27]

This view carries through Maxwell's fiction, especially in the pages of *They Came Like Swallows*. A family's simple, tragic story, it captures the common cadences, the saving graces of home life in the heartland. With the Armistice as a backdrop, the Morisons' world is fully seen: From engraved silverware lovingly polished to a picket missing from the iron fence, the smallest details are intricately yet not overly detailed. For Maxwell, the home is universal center, the outward expression of human character and relationships. Within its walls crucial truths are learned, observations made, and core experiences realized. In essence, it becomes an extension of the inner life, a familiar space at one remove from the recesses of the mind.

Maxwell was gifted, as Woolf was, with the ability to project himself into the private worlds of diverse characters. Far less baroque than Faulkner's, more rationally ordered than Joyce's, his portraits of inner life are acute; their graceful yet barren quality can be searing. His interior monologues have a strong visual sense and depict both the subtle and obvious perceptual differences between children, adolescents, and adults. In *Bright Center of Heaven*, and again later in his career, he shifted from one consciousness to another in quick succession—the rapid movement itself a Woolfian trait. In contrast, *Swallows* maintains each perspective for a third of the novel, never returning to a character's viewpoint after his section has concluded. As the first autobiographical work based on his family, it challenged him to juxtapose the views of his child self with those of his older brother and father, and he does so with an exceedingly evenhanded, empathetic touch. The three carefully nuanced sections reveal his perfect sense of emotional pitch, his ability to depict the defining tragedy of his life as experienced by two family members who, from outward appearances, emotionally differed from him. Certainly the Modernists, and Woolf in particular, inspired this strong psychological emphasis, but for Maxwell it became a natural approach to fiction writing: "I guess I focus on what you call the internal landscape because I am aware, in myself, of a simultaneous double communication—the conversation I have with my wife at the breakfast table, for example, and the conversation I have with myself, that is so continuous and so fleeting often that I don't remember what I have said to myself from minute to minute. But there are places where the two conversations overlap and places where they cast light on one another because of the discrepancy, and this is interesting if you are writing fiction that you do not want to be superficial or on one level."[28]

The unusually real and natural children of Maxwell's fiction distinguish his focus on the "internal conversations" he describes and become a significant aspect of his literary achievement generally. Roger Angell finds the emotional connection to childhood a "powerful force…that worked in Bill Maxwell.…It's such an obvious thing to say. It is a cliché about him. But it remains true."[29] Indeed, Maxwell's singular ability to capture the inner workings of young minds with nuance and precision is an enduring characteristic of his work, realized first and most extensively in *They Came Like Swallows.* His portraits of early life have striking clarity and authenticity stemming from his ability to remember subtle shadings of youth often forgotten in adulthood. Through Maxwell's eyes, childhood remains unfiltered by memory's lens: He seems to render the actual childhood psyche, the pure experience itself, rather than interpret or rationalize it from a mature outlook. To read *Swallows* as an adult is to recall unexpectedly how a child's mind works, to recover its concerns, dark uncertainties, and vibrant imagination; to plunge into the first universe of experience—the intimate family home with a vast unknown beyond.

The writer's first decade of life, the years before his mother's death, represented a lost Eden, a childhood interrupted and encapsulated by a sudden, permanent separation. As a result, regaining this beloved past became a central mission in his work. Maxwell's memory had rare reach: He recalled his youngest years with unusual clarity and believed that, unlike most children, he did not go through a phase of what he called "infant amnesia," the forgetting of his earliest experiences by the time he reached age five or six. Instead, his first years were always accessible to him. He found he could assume a child perspective naturally, as if a line of communication between his child and adult selves remained open and fluid: "I think sometimes I call upon my child self, what I remember it to have been like, or some other child I knew when I was a child. But in general I don't think I have outlived any part of my life, it all seems to co-exist—childhood, adolescence, middle age, old age—no one of them any more remote than the other, or remote at all. It is easier for me to imagine what goes on in a child's mind while he is playing than it would be, for example, to imagine what is going on in Edmund Wilson's or George Bush's or Senator Moynihan's. In a pinch, though, I could do that, I think. Doing a child is easy as falling off a log."[30]

Some readers may miss the mother's perspective in *They Came Like Swallows,* yet in this case the absence of Elizabeth Morison's view is essential to the novel's tone and effect. Her story is told solely through the eyes of her two young sons—the father's perspective is not added until after her death—and so the book exudes the pure, unadulterated emotion of childhood. Casting a mystic aura about her, the writer depicts the sense of veneration and awe she inspires in her children; in their innocence, they would not see her as a woman but as a maternal figure. Consequently, we see her as they do—the utter core of existence—and can then feel the full weight of her death on those she leaves behind.

* * *

The 1918 influenza epidemic was the single global incident to assume sustained significance in Maxwell's writing, placing him among the few American authors who wrote about the effects of the disease. More deadly than any military aggression, the Spanish influenza eventually claimed 675,000 American lives and almost 30 million worldwide. As Alfred Crosby writes, far more Americans were killed by the flu in ten months than were felled on the battlefields of all wars of the twentieth century combined. Even so, while the Great War remained a permanent part of the nation's consciousness, the flu seemed to be forgotten as quickly as it had come. The "lost generation" that preceded Maxwell—writers who came of age during the Great War that shaped their lives and literature—did not focus on this tragedy that killed so many of their contemporaries. Consequently, Crosby has noted, some of the century's most important fiction leaves a gap in the era's national scene.

In adulthood, Maxwell met two other American authors who wrote about the Spanish influenza: Mary McCarthy, whose fiction he edited at *The New Yorker*, wrote of losing both her parents to the flu in her autobiographical *Memories of a Catholic Girlhood*. And Katherine Anne Porter, who was introduced to Maxwell in 1956 by their mutual friend, writer Frank O'Connor, lost her fiancé to the flu and nearly died herself. Although her employer, Denver's *Rocky Mountain News*, had already typeset her obituary, Porter survived to write about the experience in *Pale Horse, Pale Rider*, both a masterpiece of American short fiction and, as Crosby writes, "the most accurate depiction of American society in the fall of the 1918 in literature." She also lived to share a love of roses with William Maxwell, who sent her a Golden Damask rosebush, which she planted at her New England farmhouse.[31]

Maxwell belongs on the very short list of writers who captured the effect of the pandemic on wartime America. With Porter and McCarthy, he was among the American authors most affected by the influenza crisis. *They Came Like Swallows* directly tells the story of a family devastated by the disease, and a number of his other works—including *The Folded Leaf, Time Will Darken It, So Long, See You Tomorrow,* the nonfiction *Ancestors,* and the last stories—were born of the loss he endured, as was his literary career generally. While other novelists influenced by events of the early to mid-century found fame writing of combat—the slightly older Hemingway and younger Vonnegut and Mailer, for example—the less prominent Maxwell had no "gospel for America at war," as Edmund Wilson wrote in 1945.[32] Instead, in his own quiet way, he memorialized the devastation on the home front, focusing on family intimacies and aching personal loss. As a stay against oblivion, Maxwell wrote a gospel of his own—one of preservation and remembrance.

* * *

They Came Like Swallows received highly favorable reviews and earned the Friends of American Writers Award. David Tilden's piece in the *New York Herald Tribune* maintained that the novel's "simplicity reveals its distinction": "No one who was not a master of his work could have created its authentic pathos and humor, could so have given dignity and individuality and meaning to the every day life of a family." Fanny Butscher called the novel's children "as real as any children in literature."[33]

A fine novel in its own right, *They Came Like Swallows* has further value as a precursor to Maxwell's later work. Through the course of his career, most of the novel's characters recurred in other situations, under different names. The comfort and beauty of the overarching elms came to symbolize an era past, the family orchestra played again, and the boys continued to pace through the house with their father in moments of crisis. Even fifty-five years later, in the *Billie Dyer* stories, Maxwell continued to reexamine his mother's death and to bring new insight to the lives introduced here: a startling revelation about the older brother's "affliction," the moving story behind a visit to the fifth-grade teacher's home, and new understanding of the stern, business-driven father and the family cook. In *They Came Like Swallows,* the author first contemplated his life's material and explored its possibilities in literary art.

4

Mature Novelist I:
The Folded Leaf
1938–45

DESPITE THE CRITICAL SUCCESS and promise of *They Came Like Swallows,* Maxwell's literary production slowed in the years after its publication. His stories continued to appear in *The New Yorker,* yet as he assumed greater responsibility at the magazine, editing absorbed more of his time and energy. He was associated with some of the era's brightest new writers, including J. D. Salinger, who worked with him on his first *New Yorker* story, "Slight Rebellion Off Madison," about a boy named Holden Caulfield. As exciting as this work was, Maxwell continued to isolate himself after business hours in his Patchin Place apartment. He didn't answer the telephone and walked the streets at night trying to overcome insomnia. In his early thirties, he felt uncertain about his life's direction. "I didn't seem to be growing," he told Kay Bonetti. "I didn't have anybody to love, nobody to love me, and I had no wife, no child. I was just an incomplete person." Characteristic of his metaphoric thinking, he saw himself as a tree whose main stem had been cut out, so that it grew unnaturally wide but not tall; like the tree with its center missing, he felt he "couldn't assume [his] proper shape."[1]

Such severe self-doubts led to a turning point: The late 1930s to mid-1940s were defining years, as developments in both his professional and personal circumstances set him on a more positive, balanced course. During this time, he met three people who permanently imprinted his life: Louise Bogan, the highly regarded poet, fiction writer, and *New Yorker* critic; Theodor Reik, his psychoanalyst, a Freud protégé from Vienna; and Emily Gilman Noyes, the beautiful, artistic young woman from Portland, Oregon, who became his wife for fifty-five years, freeing him from what he considered a long, lonely bachelorhood and offering the home and family life he had yearned for since his mother's death.

* * *

Bogan had first noticed Maxwell in December 1937, when his story "Never to Hear Silence" appeared in *The New Yorker*. The brief piece captures the simmering conflicts between a young chemistry professor and his loquacious wife as they sit at the breakfast table with their children. A finely nuanced portrait of a couple's inner and outer worlds, it juxtaposes their stilted conversation with unspoken resentments that weaken the fragile fiber of their marriage. The scene opens as the wife complains about her husband's three-year laboratory experiment that has caused him to neglect his teaching and family, while unbeknown to her he has just discovered that the work has failed. Despite his urging to the contrary, she implores him to attempt the experiment once more, and her incessant badgering provokes the usually acquiescent man to explode in anger. When he asks whether she knows how it feels "never to hear silence," she ignores the question and inquires only whether he will be home for lunch. Bogan was so moved by the empathetic yet unflinching treatment of the troubled relationship that she wrote Katharine White, "May I congratulate the magazine on the terribly moving and well-written Maxwell story in this week's issue? It made me believe, for awhile, again, in the tenderness and strength of the human heart." At the time, she could not have known the supportive role she would play in the writer's future work. But the following June, *New Yorker* staffer St. Clair McKelway wrote to ask her for new poems on behalf of Maxwell, who had recently accepted responsibility for the magazine's poetry and wanted to make her acquaintance.[2]

Bogan, a *New Yorker* veteran, had contributed to the magazine since 1926—a year after its founding—first as a poet and then as the author of biannual reviews titled "The Season's Verse," a well-known series that continued to appear for nearly four decades. From 1925 to 1937 she was married to Raymond Holden, the magazine's managing editor and had a daughter by an earlier marriage. Her years with Holden were artistically productive yet rocked by devastating bouts with depression, which continued to plague her throughout her life. During the years 1930 and 1931, for example, she won the John Reed Memorial Prize for poetry, received treatment at the Neurological Institute in New York, and convalesced in a Connecticut sanitarium. Four years later, separated from Holden, she began a love affair with twenty-six-year-old poet Theodore Roethke and, according to Elizabeth Frank, provided him the literary guidance he needed: "Overhauling poems word by word and phrase by phrase," she "tested every poem he sent with her mind and ear."[3] Bogan demonstrated similar devotion to Maxwell's work, encouraging him to finish his manuscript of *The Folded Leaf* and occasionally calling his attention to passages that she thought could be improved.

When Maxwell met her in 1938, Bogan was forty-one, eleven years his senior, and her life seemed more settled. Recently divorced from Holden, she expressed renewed interest in writing her memoirs, accepted an invitation to contribute to *The Nation*, and promised Scribner's new poems for a collection by the fall of 1939.[4] Ironically, just as Maxwell expressed interest in publishing her poetry, she had a creative block; unable to write verse, she concentrated on critical pieces and lived a "life of responsible, acknowledged solitude" at Washington Heights, near Manhattan's northern tip. In December 1938, she invited him for a walk near the apartment on West 169th Street "with hamburgers to be picked up along the way," and the next spring they strolled Fort Tryon Park, where she began talking with him about her memoirs, work originally undertaken in the early thirties that later helped her assess his own autobiographical fiction.[5]

By 1940, Maxwell had "almost stopped writing entirely" because of his editorial work, but he took two steps that helped him regain his literary bearings: He showed Bogan what he thought was a short story about two boys in a high school swimming class and then acted on her suggestion that the piece should be developed into a novel.[6] With her encouragement and unflagging support, he struggled with the material for the next four years, composing his third novel, *The Folded Leaf.*

Based on his experiences at Chicago's Senn High School and the University of Illinois at Urbana-Champaign, the book develops the intensely personal psychological drama of Lymie Peters, a sensitive adolescent struggling for acceptance as he faces distress over his mother's death, his incommunicative relationship with his down-and-out salesman father, his inability to fit in with boys his own age, and, most significantly, his dependent and sometimes disturbing relationship with his best friend, Spud Latham. Tracing the boys' bond through their high school and college years, the novel continues Maxwell's exploration of the classic contrast between masculine sensibility and physicality, a theme that first emerged in *They Came Like Swallows* with his characterization of the Morison brothers. While this dichotomy was subtler in the earlier novel, a subtheme to the mother's death, here it becomes central to the boys' interdependence, to the complementary and conflicting aspects of their friendship.

From their first meeting in the opening swimming scene, Lymie's psyche is intrinsically linked to his physical inadequacies, to the comparisons he draws between his own underdeveloped physique and Spud's athletic build. Both boys' inner lives drive the narrative, but in the end Lymie's dominates: A motherless child too thin to wear knickers, he lives with his widowed father in a dingy apartment hotel and eats his meals in a diner. Isolated from the other Chicago high school students, he gazes through the windows of LeClerc's soda shop at the "wonderful tropical birds"—mascara-ed, bobbed-haired girls sporting clothes from Marshall Field's—but is too meek to venture inside. He finds comfort in his friendship with Spud, whose family becomes like his own. Together the boys leave Chicago for a Midwestern university where their friendship ultimately comes to crisis over their triangular relationship with a female student, a strain that leads to Lymie's unsuccessful attempt at suicide.[7]

Writing *The Folded Leaf*

Louise Bogan's influence at this critical moment in Maxwell's career helped him stay on course as a serious fiction writer. Even forty years later, he publicly acknowledged his indebtedness to her as he accepted the 1980 Howells Medal for *So Long, See You Tomorrow* before the Academy of Arts and Letters. He credited her with encouraging him to eschew full-time editing in favor of novel writing: She supported his 1940 leave of absence from *The New Yorker* to begin *The Folded Leaf,* a request general editor Harold Ross granted a second time in 1944 as he was completing the manuscript.

Bogan was well suited as Maxwell's mentor, especially as a critical reader of this particular work in progress. She shared his artistic sensibility, and, as Frank has noted, the two "lived in the same creative universe." Both had intense interest in the past, in mysteries of memory, time, and place, and a "wonderful eye" for domestic detail, for objects and interiors as touchstones of experience. Although primarily a poet, Bogan also wrote autobiographical fiction; most notably, she published three autobiographical pieces in *The New Yorker* in 1933 and 1934 and, as a result, understood the challenge Maxwell faced in exploring personal history. She wrote these stories with what her biographer called a "pure, disciplined attitude," which Bogan described to another young friend in 1943: "For as in all good art, the thing that is important isn't 'O, this all happened to me! How wonderful I and it were!' but 'Why did this happen at all? What is the mystery, that It happened, and I was there in the first place for it to happen to?'"[8] Bogan's ideas about autobiographical writing, developed through struggle with her own, might have influenced Maxwell as he wrote *The Folded Leaf,* helping him to refine and broaden his own approach during these years. In retrospect, Bogan's emphasis on moving beyond the merely personal supported his inclination to create new distance between himself and his characters at this point in his career, to separate his authorial self from the adolescent he had once been.

"Journey around My Room," the first story in Bogan's autobiographical trilogy, appears consanguine to Maxwell's work in its central attention to household effects, recollections of childhood, and dreams. The second and third pieces seem equally Maxwellian in theme: "Dove and Serpent" captures a mother's world and a child listening to her conversation with other women during tea, and, like *The Folded Leaf,* "Letdown" portrays a young person's tragedy, growth, and struggle toward maturation. Maxwell was quite taken with these stories and believed they were by far her finest fiction. Decades later, he concluded her 1970 memorial service with a reading of "Journey around My Room," his personal favorite, after asking the audience to imagine the sound of her voice instead of his own.

Written during one of Bogan's periods of depression, the story offers striking evidence of the two writers' literary and spiritual kinship. It opens with the author in bed reflecting on things in her bedroom—on its walls bounded by the kitchen, someone's bedroom next door, backyards, the Empire State Building, and Lexington Avenue—as well as on its wallpaper, mantelpiece, Japanese print, shells from a beach in Maine, "inadequately" varnished floors, and fireplace. She asks, "The initial mystery that attends any journey is: how did the traveler reach his starting point in the first place? How did I reach the window, the walls, the fireplace, the room itself; how do I happen to be beneath this ceiling and above this floor? ... Some step started me toward this point as opposed to all other points on the habitable globe. I must consider; I must discover it. And here it is." Suddenly, she journeys to her childhood past—to Ballardville, Maine, March 1909—and finds herself saying goodbye to her father at the train station. This particular day, she will not return as usual, for she has grown older and is headed for Boston. She mourns leaving behind the town's life and landscape, things she "shan't ever see again": the hydrangea bushes in front of Forrest Scott's house, the swing in the Gardners' yard, a bag of potatoes, a ten-gallon kerosene can, a black hound, a yellow cigar ribbon fluttering in the breeze. The past recedes as quickly as it appeared, and then, she is back inside her room. Why is she in this particular place at this particular moment in time? She seeks answers in the furniture, photographs, pencils, postcards, and books. Her journey ends with a troubling dream: She hears the mill dam foaming and must swim in its rapids. Her bedroom things—"the armoire, the green bureau, the lamps, the shells from the beach in Maine"—swirl in the waves and sink around her. "O death, O fear!" she cries.[9]

Maxwell must have felt an immediate sense of affinity for Bogan's work here: for her sanctification of everyday objects, the emotional force of her connections to them, and the profound sense of loss that accompanies her break from childhood. As he told me, "I am attached to countless objects and possessions. They are what make up my sense of home. Books, pictures, snapshots, clothes, classical records, the record player, the fireplace, the shapes of rooms, the light at various times of day. I could manage without any possessions, but I would be lonely. What this might indicate about me is that at some time I had had a home I was deeply attached to and had it taken away from me."[10] Like his mentor, he did not merely embrace the effects of home but rendered them inseparable from the inner life and personal identity. And, in a sense, Bogan's story predicts how he would venture past the perspective of childhood found in *They Came Like Swallows*—past young Bunny's very present connections to his beloved home—to capture images of lost youth through the emotion and memory of adulthood.

Indeed, *The Folded Leaf* shares the acute observations and psychological probing Bogan offers. Her story must have reinforced Maxwell's own sense of a personal journey, of the process of questioning and exploring characters' paths through life. In retrospect, it also suggests how the writers' worlds intersect: Both render dreams and memory with striking intensity and create fluidity between the past and present, the conscious and unconscious. Bogan's questions—What has brought her here? What is the meaning of her journey?—seem tuned to Maxwell's own inner dialogue at this point in his life and to his determination to explore those questions in literature.

Clearly Bogan's engagement with Freudian theory also provided her insight into Maxwell's state of mind and its effect on his writing process. She "viewed the ailments of civilization with a Freudian-Jungian eye" and "had come to believe in the unconscious as the source of human achievement and destruction." Among her psychiatrists over the years, two were prominent Freudians, and although she did not undergo psychoanalysis herself, she was encouraged to read psychoanalytic theory in order to understand her own depression. She absorbed the subject with intense curiosity. As Frank has noted, she wrote of her "Freudian discoveries" in 1936 and took extensive notes from her reading about "grief work," a therapy still under way when she met Maxwell. On the advice of a friend, Maxwell entered psychoanalysis with Theodor Reik while writing *The Folded Leaf,* an experience that both helped him to accept himself and influenced his novel writing. Bogan's intimate familiarity with the theory would have helped her to appreciate its interconnections with the writer's artistic impulses—how it influenced his heightened curiosity about the motivation behind characters' behavior. In particular, she was "interested in his time of life, fascinated by the unfolding evidences of human and creative growth she saw in his work." She wrote in her diaries that "the best time to write about one's childhood is in the early thirties, when the contrast between early forced passivity and later freedom is marked; and when one's energy is in full flood."[11] Maxwell must have made an ideal test case for her supposition.

By 1941 Maxwell and Bogan launched a lasting friendship. She invited him to her apartment to listen to records; he reciprocated by asking her to tea. She wrote to her close friend Morton Zabel in June,

> My pleasantest experience has been the renewal of a beginning friendship with Little Maxwell. I have seen him several times this winter. One afternoon he came up, and we played records, and he is the most wonderful record-listener I have ever met. He really breaks right up, and is shattered, and is frank, and is disapproving, and is delighted, so that it seems another *you* is involved: another expression of one's own taste, only fresher. [Schubert's] *Gruppe aus dem Tartarus,* for example, actually laid him out. "That was a terrible experience," he said. And, of the final record of [Mahler's] *Lied v. d. Erde,* he remarked: "That is a perfect expression of the romantic's yearning for the Infinite."[12]

Bogan's rare portrait of Maxwell not only dramatizes the intensity with which he experienced classical music but also characterizes his capacity for acute responses to art and life more generally; as Roger Angell has noted, he was sensitive to the point of "tearing up" at *The New Yorker* offices when something particularly touched him. The record-playing scene recalls similar sessions with university friend and fellow *New Yorker* editor Robert Henderson in Urbana a decade earlier and predicts the joy music brought Maxwell throughout his life. "I respond to music emotionally," he told me, "and get most pleasure from melody, being ignorant of the technical aspects of what I am hearing." He was partial to the pure, crystalline voices of lyric sopranos—German Tiana Remnitz, American Judith Raskin, and Spaniard Lucrezia Bori—and the English contralto Kathleen Ferrier. Although he had taken piano lessons as a boy, he had no patience for practicing until he took it up again in his fifties, when it became an obsession. "I stopped when my teacher had a heart attack and I had to face the fact that my time would be better spent at the typewriter, since I was a fairly good writer and a poor pianist."[13] As for his response to the Mahler song in Bogan's apartment, certainly the idea of "yearning for the Infinite" evokes analysis he might also have applied to the romantic poetry of Walter de la Mare in his college days.

Later, as Maxwell's guest, Bogan found the Patchin Place apartment charming: "Such a lovely little apartment you never saw: plants on the windowsills, and pale furniture, and faultless bibelots, and a fireplace and books." Maxwell thought the place "with low ceilings and little French windows…looked like something out of *La Boheme*" and tried to recapture the home atmosphere he cherished in his childhood. It must have seemed a step closer to Paris than the roof of his apartment in Urbana, Illinois.[14]

As Elizabeth Frank has explained, Bogan began to realize that the young writer's "spirit was in full harmony with her own." "Maxwell is really an exquisite human being," she wrote Zabel, "and I wish there was something between love and friendship that I could tender him; and some gesture, not quite a caress, I could give him. A sort of smoothing. I may be able to work out something along these lines later! Seriously, I simply love him like a brother." Frank maintains that Bogan's "love for him was by no means that simple. The possibility of danger existed, although she recognized it immediately and cut it short with her sense of humor." This humor was evident in her next letter to Zabel. In referring to Maxwell, she evoked the opening scene of Strauss's opera, *Der Rosenkavalier,* in which a princess, the Marschallin, carries on an amorous liaison with a younger nobleman in the enormous bed of her boudoir. Bogan admitted feeling "like the Marschallin, if you must know; but that is absurd, because there never has been, and never will be, of course, anything remotely resembling that Overture, in the M[axwell] business. No foamings of lace out from the big baroque (rococo, rather) bed; no scampering of slender young male legs around the boudoir; no large-bosomed breathings and swellings and flutterings and burnings.…Howbeit, I *should* feel like the Marschallin if I could!"[15]

Bogan resolved any uncertainty about a love affair when she sent Maxwell "an inscribed copy of *Dark Summer,*" her 1929 poetry collection, "saying that it was 'the least I could do for a person to whom one can say everything; and to a friend made in the non-friend-making-years.'" Shortly after Bogan's tea at Maxwell's, where she had left behind "a glove and small turban," she wrote him again:

> Something may have been garbled; in some way I have hurt you. That bothers me. Yes. In any acquaintanceship, even the most casual, one sooner or later

comes up against the submerged part of the other person; the two thirds of the ice-berg, existing under water. I did not think that this would happen, in the case of our friendship; but it seems to, there's nothing I can do, because I don't know what the obstacle is. Anyhow, dear young Maxwell, remember that you owe me nothing, not even that hat, which you may toss into the nearest ash-can. You will manage your own talent, and do your own work; and the decade from thirty to forty is a wonderful one, believe me. Everything becomes, in it, what it is born to be.[16]

As Frank has noted, Maxwell "had no idea what she was talking about" and called her to say there was no problem between them. Frank explains that Maxwell "was seeing for the first time...the inexorable pattern in Louise Bogan's life, according to which where she truly loved, she also expected rejection. The friendship weathered this sudden assault from the ghosts of Louise's [troubled] childhood, and entered a new stage."[17]

Maxwell kept on with his novel and sent the manuscript to Bogan "chapter by chapter, through four versions." He acknowledged that her "uncompromisingly serious attitude toward literature" helped him keep serious as well: "She never said enough is enough," he told George Plimpton more than forty years later. "From time to time I got a penny postcard from her with 'v. good' or something like that on it." In our interviews, he remembered, "The only two comments, apart from keep on going, that she ever made were a complaint that the physical description (which I rewrote) of Spud was too conventional, and once, when there was a gap between the arrival of chapters, 'Get that boy up off the sleeping porch.' (I was temporarily stalled)." Bogan's reservations about the depiction of Spud appear in her October 1942 letter to Maxwell: "The one thing I jibbed at a little was the description of Latham's physical set-up: 'wide in the shoulders and narrow hips like a boxer.' A little too easy? We've heard it before?" He listened to her counsel and wrote a less typical, more refined portrait for the published novel: "[Spud] was not quite handsome but his body, for a boy's body, was very well made, with a natural masculine grace. Occasionally people turn up—like the new boy—who serve as a kind of reminder of those ideal, almost abstract rules of proportion from which the human being, however faulty, is copied."[18]

Maxwell had difficulty writing The Folded Leaf in part because of the painful personal experiences it explored. Bogan sympathized with his task: "So nice to hear from you, and to get the MS pages," she wrote. "I truly think that the narrative goes, and interests. I can see the terribly tough job you have; but, after a month of absorbing the trials of Flaubert, year after year, book after book, as put down in his letters, I can see that no profoundly conceived idea can come through, in narrative prose, without the most grueling work." Maxwell also grappled with the notion that he was dealing with a small subject, that readers would not be interested in Lymie and Spud. "The whole time I was writing I had to struggle against the idea that this was a story that no one would want to read," he told me. "I had a strong temptation to burn it in the fireplace, perhaps because it revealed more about me than I was comfortable revealing.... It was also a difficulty for me that I was writing about adolescents, and who would want to read about *them?*"[19]

To help resolve these concerns, he replaced the first-person narrator he had originally used to tell his story with an omniscient figure whose intervening commentaries lend wider relevance to the boys' lives. Bogan concurred with this change, believing that the "I" was a difficult perspective to pull off. "As I see these paragraphs, you are right about shifting from the first person," she wrote:

> If the first person is to be the delicate observer, too much irony and sardonics have to be thrown in to keep "him" ("I") in his natural place. With the third person you can get more slight mockery in.... What I mean, and am trying to say is: that the sensitive observer has so much more insight than the other people, that one has to play him down a little, merely for proportion's sake, and that is difficult, working with "I." Proust was *out* to make the s. observer well above the bunch; but Proust is a special case; and even he gets terribly tiresome.[20]

The omniscient narrator allowed him to portray Lymie's relationships with the other characters more objectively and remotely, balance the novel's perspective, and capture Chicago and Urbana with a camera-eye view.

When his draft reached four hundred pages, he wrote her: "The problem of form in a long novel is frightening, and once you admit of length you also admit of a kind of insane inclusiveness. I find it hard to believe that I really know what I'm doing or that anyone else will know. New characters keep turning up and telling their life history, just the way they do actually in real life and I'm almost at the end of my patience." He asked Bogan to mark "anything that seem[ed] like cheap satire, or too easy writing, or just false; and sometime we'll go over it together, God willing." Although she gave few specific recommendations and Maxwell thought her too lenient, her approval and ongoing encouragement were critical to him. "From the criticisms that you do make I manage to construct greater severity for my own attitude toward what I am doing," he wrote. In August 1943, on his thirty-fifth birthday, she sent him a quotation from Marianne Moore's "In Distrust of Merits," which she thought he was "getting old enough to understand":

When a man is prey to anger,
  he is moved by outside things; when he holds
    his ground in patience patience
      patience, that is action or
    beauty . . .

He deeply appreciated her thoughtfulness and wrote her, "Thank you for realizing, in the midst of your own difficulties, that I would be waiting for your approval and unable to go on very far without it."[21]

* * *

At the time Maxwell was struggling with his novel about Midwestern adolescence, he was also writing stories for *The New Yorker* about young adults on the East Coast. This balance was forced by the magazine's restrictions: "The stories could be about Florida, they could be about Hollywood, they could be about the East Coast—wherever, presumably, *The New Yorker* readers went was what the fiction had to be about. Which rather tied my hands,"[22] Maxwell recalled of the magazine's years under Ross. As a result, the author's novel writing of the period was firmly planted in his Illinois past, while his short fiction dealt with contemporary life in and around New York. The magazine's constraints compelled him to broaden his scope, to write about the moment and place in which he lived. The pieces from his first decade at the magazine include some that reflect his bachelor years in the late thirties and early forties: Single men in their twenties and thirties find comfort in surrogate homes in Manhattan and New York's upstate countryside complete with the household detail and mother figure that mark his literary milieu. As in the rest of his fiction, these stories offer a celebration of everyday home life mitigated by unease or tragedy; at times the joy of an adopted family balances loneliness and angst about the future.

Among his stories of this period, "Young Francis Whitehead" (1939) and "Haller's Second Home" (1941) create stark portraits of American life as World War II approached. In "Francis Whitehead," we meet the title character, a twenty-year-old Cornell student from New Hampshire, who has decided to leave school without graduating to find a job in New York. When his widowed mother fails to convince him otherwise, she assumes that the two of them will get a small apartment together and is crushed when her only child announces in front of her guest, Miss Avery, that he will go alone. Mrs. Whitehead's grief, her fear of being without both her husband and son, becomes palpable when she continues serving tea as her tears overflow.

The plotline is no more complicated than this, characteristic of the era's slice-of-life *New Yorker* fiction, yet even in this brief encounter Maxwell etches a compelling character at a turning point. As is often the case, the author could have slipped easily into preciousness here, but already in this early story his tremendous reserve and the composed dignity he ascribes to Mrs. Whitehead do not allow it. Instead, we recognize a heart-rending moment both simple and monumental in a human life. What we expect to be the story of one character becomes the story of another, a characteristic shared by several Maxwell stories including "Haller's Second Home" and, later, "The Trojan Women." In the end, it is Maxwell's sympathy for Francis Whitehead's *mother* that creates the story's emotional high point: "'Francis is so young,' [Mrs. Whitehead] said. 'Just twenty, you know. Just a boy. And there's really no reason why he should be in such a rush. Most people live a long time. Longer than they need to.'"[23]

New Yorker readers met Francis Whitehead again two years later in a story titled for another character: Haller, a New York bachelor who finds a second home in the Mendelsohns' Manhattan apartment on East Eighty-Fourth Street. We learn that eleven years earlier, during the winter of 1930–31, Haller met the Mendelsohns on a visit with "somebody else's girl": a young woman engaged to the Mendelsohns' nephew, who was Haller's best friend from high school and college. Nervous about meeting her future relatives, the girl asked Haller to join her since he was down from Cambridge to attend the opera.

Readers of *The Folded Leaf* might sense that as Maxwell was writing about the college days of Lymie, Spud, and Sally, he was also working on a story that projects their potential futures. As is true of Lymie, "All in the world [Haller] wanted was to be loved"; here, however, "he had his hands full with the Harvard Graduate School, and a wife would have been more than he could manage." Indeed, Lymie seems to have graduated from his Midwestern college, entered Harvard, and gone to New York just as Sally was invited to meet Spud's relatives. As in the novel, there is an intimation of a triangle: as she took off her coat, the young woman explained to the Mendelsohns that if she hadn't been marrying their nephew, "she would have been marrying Haller," who, like the young writer, has been to the West Indies and to Santa Fe and enjoys classical music.[24]

After the opening scene, we hear no more of Haller's high school friend and the fiancé: the story advances ten years to 1941, the year it appeared in the magazine, and on to characters who have more recently entered Haller's life in New York. Since the original meeting, he has developed his own relationship with the Mendelsohns, who have accepted him as a son. He has also fallen for the Mendelsohns' daughter, Abbie, who is celebrating her birthday with a special family dinner. As the story unfolds, readers learn that someone is conspicuously absent. Francis Whitehead—adored by Abbie, Haller, and the rest of the Mendelsohns—has been drafted and sent to army camp. Selflessly, Haller has reminded him of Abbie's birthday so that he would remember to call or send a gift. Unbeknown to everyone but the cook, however, Francis has planned a surprise visit.

When Francis arrives, the household erupts with joy, and the group listens intently as he describes his experiences at camp while inhaling a home-cooked meal. Everyone goes to sleep after Haller leaves for the evening, and then, through the bedroom wall, Abbie hears Francis coughing. When she takes him a blanket, he awakens:

> He didn't seem to know where he was at first, and then she gathered from his sleepy mumbling that he didn't want her to go away. When she sat down, he wormed around in the bed until his thighs were against her back and his forehead touched her knee. There he stayed, without moving, without any pressure coming from his body at all. This time it was not the empty chair but a drowned man washed up against a rock in the sea.[25]

What began as an account of the comforts of "Haller's Second Home" ends with this haunting image of a young soldier's ultimate sacrifice, a sacrifice made by thousands of young Americans at the time Maxwell wrote this scene. To my knowledge, this is the writer's only allusion to an American soldier on the battlefields of World War II, a fact of some significance because his younger brother, Blinn, fought in Europe, writer friend John Cheever corresponded with him from the Italian front, and the author himself faced the possibility of entering the service.[26]

From a narrative point of view, the story reveals not only Maxwell's skillful storytelling but also how the shorter form helped him to refine his understated yet powerful style. The mode's requisite compression—and the appeal of a compelling twist—led him to draw readers quickly into his domestic scene, to create finely drawn characters and surroundings before taking a sudden, ghastly turn in the last line. Maxwell used a similar method to heighten the impact of certain scenes in *The Folded Leaf*—to dramatize the plight of Lymie's journey through his young life.

Within the span of a few pages, "Haller's Second Home" evolves from a story of friends and family to one of combat—from a birthday celebration to death on a foreign beach. The compelling, even shocking imagery at the end evokes the soldier's instinctual need for human touch and reassurance:

As he faces an uncertain future, he assumes a fetal position for comfort. Yet even here Maxwell chooses foreboding language: Francis "wormed around" Abbie, rather than curling around her or enveloping her with his body. The solace of home and love cannot protect him from imposing threats. Finally, we see Abbie's realization—or perhaps the narrator's prophecy—that Francis will not come out of the war alive. The temporary absence signaled by the empty chair might at any moment become a permanent loss. Unmentioned at the gathering, the future becomes a sinister presence at night, when dark realities eclipse the festive homecoming.

Though less celebrated than some of Maxwell's other stories, "Haller's Second Home" is among his most penetrating. It speaks powerfully about war's effect on the home front, contributing a painful glimpse of family sacrifice to the body of literature that deals with American life during this period. Like his other fiction to this point, it offers a rich home portrait: the Mendelsohns' apartment, which Haller loves despite its being furnished "with very bad taste or no taste at all," acts as a backdrop to strain borne with quiet dignity. Here, however, the writer explores new territory: He confronts the world as it is rather than as it was. Usually drawn to preserve the past, he breaks from this pattern to depict the historical moment in which he writes, even to predict an impending future. Perhaps we can thank Harold Ross and his strictures for compelling Maxwell to chronicle the present, even as he continued to explore the past.

Surrogate homes and families continued as a theme in Maxwell's stories as his work on *The Folded Leaf* progressed. "The Patterns of Love," published by *The New Yorker* the same year as the novel, relates a young bachelor's weekend visit with the Talbot family in the New York countryside. Written from the omniscient point of view characteristic of the author's 1940s work, this brief story details the nuance of the Talbot's daily interactions and inextricable bonds, casting their homestead as an idyllic refuge. Maxwell places Arnold, a young Manhattanite who longs to be entwined in the patterns of his own household, among the menagerie of Talbot children and animals: bantam roosters, baby ducks, a Great Dane. Details that go unnoticed by the family become "immortal" to him: the distinctive sound of the wood thrush and the Talbot boys' "Cain-and-Abel" relations marked by hostility as well as love.[27] Indeed, in Arnold we find a man poised to become the husband and father figure in Maxwell's later and more complex "Over by the River" (1974). Arnold personifies a young man who feels he may never have his own wife and children, who, like George Carrington in the later story, may be awed by his own family's natural rites of passage when they finally come.

"Patterns" is filled with familiar Maxwellisms: Arnold takes *Anna Karenina* off the Talbots' shelves and escapes to the little one-room house up the hill to read in seclusion. A glimpse of Mrs. West from *Bright Center of Heaven* appears. Like the matriarch of Meadowland, Mrs. Talbot oversees a country home while entertaining a literary bent—the intimate retreat Arnold enjoys was inspired by her reading Virginia Woolf's *A Room of One's Own*. Nothing too dramatic happens here: Young Kate Talbot's favorite hen is lost, probably killed by a rat, and two other families join the Talbots for a picnic with "hot dogs, bowls of salad, cake, and wine, out under the grape arbor."[28] Although for some this may seem more of a vignette than a story, it is crafted with a deft touch, with a gentle yet pressing momentum that leads to Arnold's eventual departure and return to his lonely city life. Even here Maxwell lends poignancy to this fleeting glimpse of a young man's unspoken yearnings: At the train station he listens again for the sound of the wood thrush, but realizes he has left it behind, along with the life he hopes for.

* * *

A series of letters Maxwell wrote to his father and stepmother beginning in 1941 offers more insight into his writing and the tenor of his life during this time. By then the geraniums in his Patchin Place windowsills had become so crowded that he moved to a "delightful" 1840 salt-box house in the country in Yorktown so he could garden.[29] For the rest of his life he had a house on Baptist Church Road, renting one after another until he bought the one he and Emily lived in for more than fifty years. As a single man in the early forties, he began to make the fifty-mile commute to the *New Yorker* offices in Manhattan on the Croton-Harmon rail line.

His correspondence home—which most often opens, "Dear Dad and Honey"—was saved from his stepmother Grace's personal belongings after her death in 1972 by the wife of Tom Perry, Maxwell's stepcousin who helped with historical research for *So Long, See You Tomorrow*. Although most letters focus on his family and friends, his writing, and *The New Yorker*, his observations about America during World War II enter intermittently and provide a backdrop for this period in his life as he shares with his father thoughts about the embattled world and the mood he observes in New York. Although his younger brother, Blinn, was sent to Europe, the writer explained that he had not been drafted because of health conditions: "Apparently they didn't care too much for what the x-ray of my chest showed," he wrote. "Also, I was below the weight standard.... Plus, general nervous condition, insomnia and what not, I guess they thought I'd be more trouble than I was worth. At first it seemed strange to be the last leaf on the tree, but now I've stopped thinking about it. Things are a little different from the last war, and people know that if you aren't in the army you have a good reason for not being." Decades later, Maxwell told Alec Wilkinson that he had been drafted: "I was a pacifist and I didn't want to get shot. The Army didn't recognize pacifism unless it was attached to some church. So I went to a psychiatrist and got a letter. What the letter said was that I had an anxiety neurosis. I waited around and nobody read it....Finally, when I was all but inducted, someone was willing to read my letter." Maxwell's papers were stamped, and he was excused. He told me in 1992, "I hate war. I hate the killing of young men, and, as it is now, everybody."[30]

His warm letters to his father have a tender tone that belies the father-son tension depicted in *The Folded Leaf* and other works. Yet the correspondence suggests that, in his thirties, he was still the artistic son seeking to be understood and respected by his successful corporate father. At times, he favorably compared the business practices of *The New Yorker* and Harper's to those of "the Hanover," the insurance company where William Maxwell Sr. spent forty-five years advancing through the ranks.[31] Appealing to his father's pragmatic nature, he presents his literary career in terms that would be appreciated by a businessman. Rather than share creative aspects of his work, he writes home about job security and longevity, company loyalty, work ethic, and reward for good service—perhaps in hopes of legitimizing his profession in his father's eyes.

By 1943 he had been working on *The Folded Leaf* for four years. Although his editing position allowed him to "pick up where he had left off with a fresh view of things," it continued to hinder his own writing. At this point, he took the second leave, telling Harold Ross that he was going to cut back to two days a week so that he could finish his novel, even though he would make only fifty dollars a week after taxes—not enough, he wrote his stepmother on September 3, "to keep an establishment in the country and a housekeeper on, but I thought I'd manage somehow." The letter contained more news, however: "Such a nice thing happened yesterday," he wrote,

> They called me in…and said that if I'd like to stay home from the first of October till Christmas, to finish my book, that they'd be glad to advance me the money to live on. That comes out of future salary, of course, but it will mean a great deal to be able to work uninterruptedly. And the way they did it was so nice. They said I'd been very helpful about filling in here, for people who were away, and they wanted to do something to show their appreciation. It sounded just like the Hanover.

In October, as he began the leave, he wrote his father:

> You go along with a firm, in a minor capacity as mine is now, and wonder
> sometimes whether they know you're there. But apparently they did all right,
> and were grateful for the work I do, especially filling in for people who are
> sick or away on vacation, and though I doubt if I'll ever be able to say I've
> worked 45 years for one firm, since I started later than you did, I have a feel-
> ing that so far as business is concerned my relations with them will probably
> be permanent.[32]

Indeed, Maxwell remained on *The New Yorker* staff for forty years and continued to contribute to its pages for two decades beyond his retirement in
1976, a record his father would have admired. He took such writing sabbaticals
periodically to work on novels and short stories throughout his tenure in the
fiction department. This particular leave was an especially welcome break
for him, and he made good use of his time away from the office.

Sequestered in Yorktown Heights, he wrote every day, stopping only to
eat and take periodic naps. In the country, he and his housekeeper, Fannie,
struggled with the wartime rationing books, he writes, "but we still eat better
than most of the population of the country, even though meat only turns up
on the table about twice a week and butter is more honored in the breach
than in the observance. About once every three weeks they give us a little
less gas than we had before, but we still get back and forth to the station and
to Peekskill to shop,…but won't it be nice when you can get in the car and
drive to New Mexico again and eat steak every night, if you feel like it?" After
a month out of the office he remarked, "I feel confident that the book will be
done by Christmas, which is the date I have set for myself. I'm enjoying it very
much, and work every day from about eight thirty till five, just long enough
to get a crick in my back from sitting at the typewriter." Genuinely fond of
Ross, Maxwell was grateful to him for the chance to accelerate progress on the
novel and remembered, "When [*Leaf*] was published and got good reviews,
[Ross] was pleased. He felt he had a stake in the enterprise."[33]

Maxwell completed the first draft while on leave and, in January 1944,
returned to the office for three or four days a week. During this period, he
reported doing "the good part of five people's work": bringing "a whole
suitcase full" of manuscripts home with him each evening, and reading until
eleven or twelve at night. "When you start at eight thirty in the morning and
have to get up at six the following morning that's some grind," he wrote his
father. "Actually though, I seem to be thriving on it. I weigh a hundred and
fifty pounds with my clothes on, and never have looked better." His hard

work seemed to be paying off financially as well. "Here I am, gradually a man of property, with a house, a housekeeper, and a dog. All that's lacking is a wife, and though there are no candidates at present, I feel somehow that even that will come in God's good time. Only I can't be sure how long I'll be able to hang onto the house, judging by the frequency and size of my income tax payments. Without noticing it, or meaning to particularly, on my three days a week last year [1943], I managed to make eight thousand dollars, and the income tax on that hurts." Even so, he was glad to pay income tax rather than fight with the soldiers "bogged down in the mud in Italy, eating out of a tin can and sleeping in what used to be a house."[34]

Theodor Reik

Maxwell shared the manuscript with his analyst, Theodor Reik, whose guidance significantly affected the novel's outcome. Born in Vienna in 1888, Reik was a student and lifelong friend of Sigmund Freud and a member of his group of pioneering psychoanalysts that included Carl Jung, Alfred Adler, Otto Rank, Hans Sachs, and Sandor Ferenczi. Among them, Reik was Freud's favorite, his chosen "Nachfolger," or successor. Erika Freeman has noted that, unlike the others, Reik "never broke with Freud" but instead "enlarged upon and deepened the area that Freud had explored." At the same time, Reik established his own groundbreaking work in the areas of masochism in human relations, the law of psychic potentiality, and the relationship between the psyche and art.[35]

When Maxwell met him in 1943, Reik was a sixty-five-year-old Jewish refugee and a relative newcomer to New York. After studying with Freud, he had established practice in Berlin and then the Netherlands before fleeing the Nazis in 1938. He left his money behind and started afresh and initially was barred from practice in the United States because he did not hold a medical degree. During this period, he founded the National Psychological Association for Psychoanalysis and turned to writing books, a number of which became classic texts in the field.[36]

The bald, bearded Reik was a quintessential Freudian with a Viennese accent as thick as his black-rimmed glasses. Like his mentor, he sat at the end of a couch above patients' reclined heads as they free-associated and recalled their dreams. He believed in a gentle, friendly approach with patients, not unlike Maxwell's own in working with writers as an editor at *The New Yorker*. As a result, Maxwell grew to trust and love him. From early 1944 until his marriage in May 1945, the author saw him five days a week, except in summer, at Reik's apartment on West Fifty-Eighth Street. He credited his analyst with setting him on a more positive course during the difficult period before he met Emily. Through the years, he returned for an occasional meeting. "Only a touch on his part could straighten me out," he wrote to Reik's granddaughter in 2000.[37]

Counting many writers and artists among his patients, Reik was originally attracted to psychoanalysis through his devotion to literature and relied heavily on his own creative intuition in his practice. His profound interest in the relationship between literature and psychology led him to work on a series of studies of authors and their works. After publishing a book on novelist Richard Beer-Hofmann, he completed the first doctoral dissertation with a psychoanalytic theme, a 1912 study of Flaubert's *The Temptation of St. Anthony*, which dealt with "emotional conflicts of the creative artist from a psychoanalytic point of view." He followed with a volume about Austrian writer Arthur Schnitzler as a psychologist and spent the next decade examining "psychological problems of writers and their works." As a result, he initiated the theory that authors' fictions derive from a wish to "undo the evil" they believe they have done. Maxwell acknowledged this desire: a need to assuage guilt about his mother's untimely passing that followed his unconscious death wish for her when he was a child. Reik's law of psychic potentiality recognizes this phenomenon by explaining literature as the story of the writer's "second self": the unconscious exploration and expression of possibilities in his life that were unlived or, as A. Bronson Feldman wrote, a "celebration of the might-have-been." In a sense, Maxwell's entire career was such a celebration: In *So Long, See You Tomorrow*, he describes the novel as a "roundabout futile way of making amends," as a stay against past tragedy where "what is done can be undone."[38]

Reik's kindly manner and literary sophistication made him particularly well suited as Maxwell's analyst. He believed that by reading a patient's creative work he could "get a first glimpse of what remained unconscious to the writer himself, when he tried to give shape to his experiences or to the experiences he imagined." As a matter of course, then, he read Maxwell's published novels, *Bright Center of Heaven* and *They Came Like Swallows*, as well as the work in progress, for which he suggested a change: Maxwell's original ending for *The Folded Leaf* occurred in the hospital after Lymie Peter's attempted suicide. Reik encouraged him to leave his protagonist in a more hopeful situation. He "wanted something more didactic, something that would make Lymie home free, those were the terms he thought in,"

Maxwell told me. "Actually, Lymie wasn't more home free, he remained Lymie."[39]

Reik's theoretical approach suggests why he advocated a more optimistic ending: As an analyst, he believed that literature could shape and direct the lives of writers and readers. Convinced that the particulars of literary works represent "potentialities of destiny in the poet's imagination," he may have reasoned that if *The Folded Leaf* depicted positive prospects for Lymie, then his patient would come to recognize promise in his own life.[40] Undoubtedly, Maxwell's self-portraits as the sensitive, submissive Bunny and Lymie revealed a great deal to the analyst, who believed it would be psychologically beneficial for the author to bring Lymie's childhood to a triumphal conclusion. Conceivably, Reik's goal was to render Maxwell, as well as Lymie, "home free."

The writer took his analyst's advice, and by March 1944 the fourth revision was under way. "Would love to pay you a visit this summer, providing I'm done with my book," he writes home. "Nobody can say your son is not a thorough painstaking writer, anyway, though they may accuse me of being a slowpoke. Actually though, there's no hurry, just so I get it done before I'm on my deathbed." During this period he continued to work at *The New Yorker* office two or three days a week and to fill in for vacationing *New Yorker* staff member Gus Lobrano, whom Katharine White had selected to inherit her editing duties: "I'll take over his job, for a few days, along with the other six I'm now doing. He's been wonderful to me, though, so it's a pleasure."

Around this time, Maxwell also received a call from *Harper's Bazaar* offering him the position of managing editor. "I didn't want a full time job," he wrote Maxwell Sr., "and I don't think I'd be as well-satisfied working there as I am at *The New Yorker,* but it kind of pleased me to have them consider me, anyway." Clearly, the demanding position at *Harper's* would not have allowed Maxwell several days a week at home to revise his novel. He cherished time for his own work and continued to put in full days revising. "Dear Pop," he writes, "Here it is seven minutes after nine and I've just knocked off work on my novel for the day, after starting in at nine o'clock this morning. Not as ambitious as it sounds, because there was time out for lunch and dinner and a nap. But a long day anyway, and fortunately it rained buckets all afternoon, so that there was no temptation to be outside."[41]

Throughout the summer Maxwell worked on a new final chapter. He abandoned his original intention to end the novel with Spud and Sally visiting Lymie in the hospital; instead he pictured Lymie about a month later stepping out of his room at a new campus dormitory. Wearing a turtleneck that covers his throat and wrists, he carries a bowl of straggly violets to the woods and plants them, a symbolic gesture of triumph over his childhood tragedies. In September Maxwell sent the revised manuscript to Louise Bogan, who "sat down and read the novel all through" on the night she received it. She was "impressed by the new largeness" yet she hesitated about the positive ending. "The last chapter I liked," Bogan wrote, "but I can see that you might want to give it more depth and sweep. And is it true that the boy actually gets rid of all his childhood, then?—Couldn't there be a loophole remark, in which it could be hinted that getting rid of one's childhood is almost a lifetime job; unless real steps are taken?" Ten days later she was still concerned: "Do write and tell me if you put in the loop-hole sentence."

Maxwell inserted the loop-hole in parenthesis: When Lymie "emerged from the sheltering trees and came out on the golf course there was a peculiar lightness in his step. Although he didn't realize it, he had left his childhood (or if not all, then the better part of it) behind in the clearing." As Frank has noted, the parenthetical disclaimer left "to implication all that Bogan had counseled about the battle for spiritual freedom." Indeed, Bogan offered wise counsel, yet Maxwell was most concerned with freeing Lymie from his demons as Reik advised.

Manuscripts of the additional final chapter reveal how earnestly Maxwell followed his analyst's counsel. A draft from late in the composition process—already with notes to the typesetter about font and spacing—suggests that even as publication neared, he continued to add and change sentences to give the final chapter a more positive slant. One of these late additions depicts Lymie's newly independent thinking as he enters the woods to plant the violets: "What I would like now, he thought suddenly, is something for me." Most telling, however, is a change in the final sentence: in a draft of the new last chapter, the author wrote that Lymie's childhood, having been left in the clearing, "would not trouble him any more." By the time the novel was published, he had pushed Lymie's new-found self-confidence further, changing this last pronouncement to the more melodramatic, "It would never rise and defeat him again." Certainly now there could be no question that Lymie was "home free": Not only would his childhood fail to trouble him, but it had been completely vanquished, rendered impotent in perpetuity.[42]

Reik's influence is also evident in the summary of the novel Maxwell wrote for Harper's sales staff five months before publication. Here the author recounts the boys' transition from high school to college, their misfortune in falling in love with the same girl, and Lymie's subsequent role as "devoted, unselfish intermediary. But working unconsciously, far below the surface of Lymie's mind, is the need to pay back a psychic defeat." He concludes,

Without meaning to, he arouses Spud's jealousy and when he cannot convince Spud of his innocence, Lymie tries to take his own life. The attempt at suicide is actually a psychological murder. Through his act of violence, Lymie finds his freedom from bondage and uncovers for Spud the gentleness in his own nature.[43]

The summary not only satisfied Reik's desire for Lymie's freedom but also grants Spud an epiphany the novel itself does not suggest. Having adopted Reik's vision for the novel, the writer struggles to make the new ending fit. He stretches to incorporate and to make sense of Lymie's sudden transformation—to reconcile the boy he originally created with the one who walks triumphantly from the woods.

* * *

Sensitive to his father's and stepmother's feelings, Maxwell wanted them to know what the novel was about before its publication, and he wanted to assure them that Lymie's downtrodden father was fictitious, not based on the senior Maxwell. He sent them a copy of the synopsis he had prepared for *Harper's* describing Lymie's psychological drama: the boy's isolation, his developing relationship with Spud, their love for the same girl, and the distress that led to his suicide attempt. "As you can see at a glance, it is highly personal, and presented many problems of taste and tact," he writes his father. "I could have done it as a sequel to *They Came Like Swallows* but most sequels aren't as good as the original book, and also, since Hap was distressed at being in the first one, I have tried to be more careful with living people, particularly with you and Grace. I live in a large place where most or practically all of the people I come in contact with don't know me or anything about me. You live in a small one and have a right to privacy."[44]

More than fifty years later, Maxwell recalled that his father and stepmother would have been upset had he written about his precise family background. "I tried this, in fact, and it worked, from the literary point of view, but I felt I didn't have the right to do it," he told me. "So I invented substitutes, made my father somebody he wasn't, and a widower." At the time of publication, he explained to his father,

> What I finally did was go back and reconstruct a character who might have been my father. He is made partly out of what might have happened to you if you hadn't been so lucky as to fall in love with Grace, and partly out of Ted Blinn [his Uncle who had difficulty making ends meet]. Nobody who knows you will be able to take it for a portrait of you, since it has none of your qualities but only here and there a detail. The other day I was looking through

some old letters and came upon the beauty you wrote me after the other book [*Swallows*], and realized that you would take this in your stride.

Yet despite his attempts to make Lymie Peter's father different from his own, family friends in Lincoln, Illinois, weren't deterred from making comparisons. On a visit home after the novel was published, the writer was asked by a Lincoln man, "Why did you make your father like that?"

"So much for invention," Maxwell said. Even late in his career he sometimes wished he had given Lymie Peters the father and stepmother he had had, yet in the final analysis believed he would not have written about them with as much understanding at that earlier point in his life, making for a novel that ultimately "wouldn't have been very good."[45]

The day before the 1944 presidential election Maxwell wrote his staunchly Republican father that it was "hard for [him] to work up much enthusiasm for Mr. Dewey." Jokingly, he reports that Wilkie was his choice, when, in fact, Wilkie had been the Republican presidential candidate four years earlier and was not slated in 1944. At this point in his life, Maxwell seemed to acquiesce to—as well as have a bit of fun with—his father's political position. His letter the next day—Election Day—suggests he was, at least temporarily, caught up in the infectious national spirit that swelled during the war. His mood is particularly notable because he had considered himself apolitical at the time, with "no real interest in politics until Adlai Stevenson." "I've just come back from the town hall with my convoy of voters," he writes,

> one octogenarian, Fannie, and a girl of twenty-three. There isn't a single person on the road so far as I can make out who isn't voting. Old Mrs. Tannehill's two daughters weren't going to let her get up this morning, because she wanted to vote for Roosevelt, but they relented, and the whole family drove off to the polls together. It's a moving thing to watch, because everybody feels so seriously about it, and, now that it's final and decided, and too late to change anybody's mind, the arguing and personal animosity of the last few weeks has subsided and the more usual neighborly attitude has once more replaced it.

Maxwell seems heartened by the rallying spirit in New York: "Somehow it gives me a feeling of faith in the future of the country, no matter what happens or who is elected. It's a wonderful world, and war, politics, and every unpleasant thing about it is really nothing compared with the pleasure of being alive."[46]

He finished the final revision on the book manuscript November 15, the date it was due. "So you see about vital matters I don't procrastinate," he assures his father. Pleased with the changes recommended by the editor, he was still unsure about whether the book would sell. "The three or four people I've shown it to seemed to like it but then you have to discount the opinion of your friends," he writes. "Mrs. Nyland in Brewster did the jacket for it, which is beautiful, and quite unlike the average bookjacket. I was very grateful to *Harper's* for letting me have my way about it. In general I am once more impressed in my dealings with them by their general fairness and lack of undue commercial interest. They're business men, of course, and have to make money. But there is nothing cheap or shoddy about the way they do things, and in some ways they remind me a little of the Hanover. A kind of decency and self-respect which is not too common in New York firms."[47]

Even late in the production process, the novel was still known by the unpoetic working title *No Word for Anybody*, a reference to Lymie's not leaving a suicide note. "After a novel is done, it is usually extremely difficult to find an appropriate title," Maxwell told me, "and you wish that you had spent a lot of time thinking about it earlier. Often the title isn't as good as it ought to be, because the author is tired and the publisher is breathing down his neck."

Louise Bogan came to the rescue. Maxwell remembered that after reviewing the final draft, she called him and said, "I have a title for your novel," and read him a passage from Tennyson's "The Lotos-Eaters":

> Lo! in the middle of the wood
> The folded leaf is woo'd from out the bud
> With winds upon the branch, and there
> Grows green and broad, and takes no care,
> Sun-swept at noon, and in the moon
> Nightly dew-fed; and turning yellow
> Falls, and floats adown the air.
> Lo! Sweetened with the summer light,
> The full-juiced apple, waxing over-mellow,
> Drops in a silent autumn night.

She had first seen the passage in a book on Shakespeare that used the words to depict "the sense of young beauty and doom" in *Romeo and Juliet*. She wrote Maxwell, "I think it has a real *adolescent* sorrow about it...the adolescent sorrow about growth; which always seems tragic to the young; and this is one of the moving themes of your novel." Grateful for her suggestion, Maxwell dedicated the novel to her. "In short, [the title] was a present from her," he said. "It was a beautiful image for adolescence and the emergence from it." After *Leaf* was published, Maxwell learned from a friend how much the acknowledgment pleased Bogan, who said, "His best novel is dedicated to me."[48]

*   *   *

As winter approached, Maxwell began making plans to return to the city full-time. He wrote to his father November 8, "I think I will close the house, the first of December, and move into town for the winter, if I can find any place to move into....I feel the need of a change, and of a little social life. I've been leading the life of a hermit the last year or so. And I think this is a good time to do it, before I get involved in something that requires solitude again." Although Maxwell's father and stepmother did not know until the next spring, Maxwell's move to the city was prompted by his courtship of Emily Noyes, a beautiful and vivacious young woman who had come to his office at *The New Yorker* looking for a position in the poetry department. After graduating from Smith College, she had worked for the Associated Press and a New York publishing house, and during their courtship she taught at a nursery school. Her large brown eyes resembled Maxwell's own and, as an artist and poet, she shared his sensibilities. In the fall, Maxwell had taken her to a party at a friend's house and afterward asked her to marry him. "He hadn't planned on saying it; the words simply came out of his mouth," Alec Wilkinson writes. "She said that she didn't want to get married and that she wouldn't be able to see him again until after the first of the year, but he could telephone her at the nursery school between four-fifteen and four-thirty....At four-fifteen Maxwell closed the door of his office and began dialing."[49]

Ironically, as he neared completion on a novel about his adolescent trauma, his life was taking promising turns: His courtship of Emily dispelled the loneliness that had troubled him since his arrival in New York eight years earlier, and a new sense of happiness complemented his success as a writer and editor. He left the country house for Manhattan the first weekend of December and moved into a small, ground-level apartment at 1160 Park Avenue, rented for fifty dollars a month from a captain in the Merchant Marines. During the holidays in Manhattan, he was caught in a "social whirl." But his life was not only social: In addition to editing at *The New Yorker,* he was working with Sally Benson on a musical titled "Memphis Bound" and correcting proofs of *Leaf,* which was scheduled for publication in early April. He spent Christmas in Oswego, New York, with the family of a friend who served as assistant director of a European refugee camp. The refugees were "pretty sad to talk to," Maxwell writes. "A thousand of them arrived, from a concentration camp in Italy, without a pair of shoes among them. The children were what got me down. They were so undersized. And you couldn't help thinking of all the ones who didn't get out."[50] Three years later, he and Emily visited the ravaged countries of Europe and saw first hand the aftermath of war.

Maxwell met Emily's parents in February 1945 when they visited from Oregon. Her father was a "well-to-do lumberman in Portland," where every morning of her childhood Emily looked to see if snow-capped Mount Hood "was there to see or hidden by clouds." On March 21 Maxwell wrote to his stepmother with news that he was getting married: "I want to tell you first because (a) you brought me up, and (b) I know how happy it will make you."

> Her name is Emily Noyes and she teaches in a Nursery School in New York City. She is twenty-three and (you can discount this, coming from me, but you don't have to discount it very much) as pretty as a picture. I met her about a year and a half ago and couldn't get her out of my mind. One night last October I sat up in bed, turned the light on, and went through the telephone book looking for her name. It wasn't there but I found her, and after one good look closed the house and moved into town, and have been courting her ever since. Yesterday she broke down and said yes.

The writer hoped to bring her to Lincoln as soon as they had a chance to settle into married life. With this news, he also mailed his stepmother a copy of *The Folded Leaf*, along with a positive review by Edmund Wilson scheduled to run in the next *New Yorker*. Ross had hired the legendary critic two years earlier. "The review isn't the result of my connection with the magazine," he wrote her, "they don't do things like that here. And Wilson is considered by many people to be the best literary critic in America, so I was and am very happy about what he said. But the book is unimportant compared to Emmy. I'm sure that you will love her and that she will love you."[51]

The Folded Leaf

The Folded Leaf stands as one of Maxwell's defining literary achievements: It marks a moment of transition in his writing and a distinct development in narrative method that distinguished his novel writing through *The Chateau* more than fifteen years later. Most notably, he introduces here a wise and empathetic omniscient narrator who allows him to intersperse intellectual commentary in his fiction. From this point on, his stories no longer are told solely through the consciousness of his characters; the addition of a narrator frees him to contemplate their predicaments openly, correlate their situations with others throughout history, and generally draw on his base of knowledge and experience to illumine their lives. Assuming a more prominent presence than in *They Came Like Swallows,* the narrator universalizes the boys' experience through philosophical, psychoanalytic, and anthropological allusions. With *The Folded Leaf,* Maxwell's fiction also takes in more scenery by venturing outside to glimpse Chicago's urban grit and the 1920s campus setting. As a result, his work acquires stronger affinity with the Realist tradition, extending the range of his detailed portraiture beyond the home and into the community. The author's work continued to deepen in the decades after *Leaf's* appearance in 1945, reaching full mastery thirty-five years later in *So Long, See You Tomorrow,* yet this earlier novel, particularly since a revision in 1959, represents the emergence of a distinct Maxwellian statement: a clear, refined, yet intense expression of the author's concerns and sensibilities. The power of Maxwell's style becomes fully realized here as his spare prose and prodigious restraint poignantly underscore his work.

To sustain his writing of *The Folded Leaf,* Maxwell conceived an image from nature, as he had when working on *They Came Like Swallows* nearly a decade earlier. This time he envisioned "walking across a very flat landscape toward the mountains," a notion that fostered a consistently stark tone and helped him build the controlled tension that drives the novel forward. The mountains in the distance derive from a trip he took to New Mexico during his early years at *The New Yorker,* and the protracted linear view recalls his Midwestern aesthetic—his native landscape and its connection to his narrative. Like the author, Lymie pictures himself traversing a flat expanse of land: In a dream "the field stretched as far as the eye could see, and he was still there, walking and walking, when the morning light awakened him." Here, Maxwell's style and imagery combine to reflect the strained psychological journey of Lymie's young life. In its bareness, his prose echoes the illimitable Illinois plain, a vista of isolation and exposure. At the same time, the visual impression—of endless walking, of traveling toward a destination ever out of reach—is equally austere. Like a sustained, unresolved chord, Lymie seems suspended on the brink of either resolution or jarring dissonance. Maxwell intended Lymie's attempt at suicide to furnish the tension-breaking climax; unsure when the event would take place, he allowed the landscape metaphor to guide him. "When I got to the mountains," he told Plimpton, "the necessary scenes would occur."[52]

The omniscient narrator views Lymie's walk with empathy and wisdom and lends wider relevance to the boys' lives. As in Maxwell's earliest work, the novel shifts between characters' minds freely yet intermittently preempts action with intervening commentaries. These meditations, much like dramatic asides to the reader, allow the author to philosophize about his characters from a distanced stance, to layer his portrait of the boys' inner lives with a removed, mature perspective, something he had not done in *They Came Like Swallows*. The commentaries take on several forms: At times the narrator universalizes the boys' experience with anthropological allusions inspired by Maxwell's reading of Frazer's *The Golden Bough*. He sees the boys' activities and emotions as part of an age-old continuum of human existence, as repetitions of behavior patterns that have endured for centuries. "The earth is wonderfully large and capable of infinite repetition," the narrator explains. "At no time is it necessary to restrict the eye in search of truth to one particular scene." In keeping with this philosophy, he compares Lymie's and Spud's world with that of primitive youths: When Spud fights another boy, their motions are described as "fixed and formal as the sexual dancing of savages." Later, when they participate in the initiation ceremony of their high school fraternity in a suite at Chicago's Hotel Balmoral, he compares the occasion to the ancient puberty rites of savages. Lymie and Spud are blindfolded, stripped naked, chased around the room with brooms, and forced to take a pill that turns their urine green. The narrator observes the perpetrators "re-enacting, without knowing it, a play from the most primitive time of man." "Torture is to be found in many places besides the Hotel Balmoral," he continues, "and if it is the rites of puberty that you are interested in, you can watch the same thing (or better) in New Guinea or New South Wales....The odor that you detect will be that which you were aware of in the Hotel Balmoral. The odor of fear is everywhere the same."[53]

Maxwell's exposure to Freud also influenced his decision to introduce an omniscient narrator at this point in his career. After his analysis in the 1940s, he often incorporated psychoanalytic references; for example, a Viennese analyst appears as a minor, recurring figure in some of his later work. Yet the extended ruminations in *Leaf* provided his first opportunity to engage theories he had learned from Reik, to interpret characters' lives, in part, through a Freudian lens. "Originally—because I rewrote the novel at least four times—it was simply a story about a boy who tried to commit suicide," he explained. "In analysis, I came to understand that man is his own architect, and that Lymie Peters was not pathetic but largely responsible for what happened to him, though often without being aware of it. This increased the dimensions of the book, and there was a further enlargement as I came to see what I had learned on the couch applied generally, and suddenly all people were interesting to me, more understandable, more human."[54] This interest extended not only to those he knew in life but also to the "imaginary," "partly imaginary," and "composite" characters who people his fiction. As a result, Maxwell's narrator here casts an analytic yet empathetic eye toward Lymie and Spud, lending a serious tone, a sense of grave consequence to their adolescent lives. Without wielding terminology, he draws on psychoanalysis to help illumine Lymie's inner life and his relationship to the world. He refers to complex, often troubling commonalities in human psychological experience and infers that in the unconscious—in the world of his dreams—the adolescent may begin to discover and understand the elusive truths of his young life.

In these meditations, the significant impact of the psychoanalytic experience on Maxwell's work first becomes clear in scenes that capture the crucial yet painful steps Lymie and Spud, as well as their tribal counterparts, must endure on the path from childhood to manhood. In the fraternity initiation scene, for example, the narrator has harsh words for fathers who neglect their adolescent sons in the modern, civilized world. In primitive society, "the dark impulses of envy, jealousy, and hate, are...eventually released through public ritual....The rites of puberty allow the father to punish the son, the son to murder his father, without actual harm to either." Lymie's and Spud's fathers are not present at the initiation ceremony to release them forever "from the basis of all [their] hostilities," to liberate them from their childhoods. Without such catharsis, the boys will struggle to leave youth behind; because of neglect, they "are in no way prepared to pass over into the world of maturity and be a companion to their fathers." As Diana Trilling observed, such commentaries do not involve "primitive psychoanalytical delving" but a "psychological attitude" that offers darker perspectives on father and son relationships, suicide, and masochism within the story of Midwestern youth.[55]

The narrator focuses more intently on Lymie as the novel progresses, connecting the young man's emotional life with the realm of dreams and the unconscious. Near the novel's end, as Lymie lies in the hospital healing from self-inflicted wounds, he comes to a realization: "The truth is that Lymie had never wanted to die, never at any time," the narrator reveals. "[The truth] is easier to get at in a lie than in an honest statement. If pursued, the truth withdraws, puts on one false face after another, and finally goes underground, where it can only be got at in the complex, agonizing absurdity of dreams."[56] For Maxwell, dreams served as a central image from his days as a college poet and—like those of early influence Walter de la Mare—most often evoked the search for a lost female figure, in Maxwell's case, a mother inextricably bound to a home she has nurtured. His analysis intensified his absorption with dreams, moving him to connect remnants of the unconscious mind with lives he created on the page. At the same time, Louise Bogan's use of dreams offered literary inspiration here; her "Journey around My Room," with its nightmarish loss of home, seems spiritually akin to Maxwell's work.

Characteristically, Lymie's dreams involve searching without finding, relentlessly pursuing a mother or a home to no avail. In one, he leaves Mrs. Latham during a parade to use the bathroom in a nearby hotel and returns to find that even his surrogate mother has been taken away, lost to him amid a thronging crowd. In another, in a place by the sea, he searches in vain for a particular house, number 28, to which he has been misdirected; he looks further and finds the right address, but as he stands before it, its number changes before his eyes. As agonizing and absurd as such dreams may be, they reveal an essential truth of Lymie's young life: He has lost his home, his mother, a part of himself left behind at their premature separation. Carl Jung might interpret the house as a symbol for the mother, for a womblike haven that had sheltered Lymie from the outside world.[57] The loss of this sanctum and the inability to retrieve it become the brutal blow, the recurring tragedy of the writer's body of work. In its longings and quest for a lost past, in its fixation on a specific dwelling, the latter dream is quintessential Maxwell. For the adolescent Lymie, the home and all it represents prove elusive, evanescent. Yet the possibility of regaining the past is already present here, if only partially: In a daydream Lymie imagines walking through the Victorian house where he was born, but, forgetting the layout of rooms, he must rearrange them and place furniture exactly in order to recall how they used to be.

Such active remembering provides but a glimpse of Maxwell's vigorous, even Proustian engagement with memory in his late fiction. In works such as *So Long, See You Tomorrow,* memory represents a viable realm of experience—a dynamic, sustaining, hypnotic force wherein the past and present mingle, life's losses are recaptured, and the child is again made whole. This opening up of memory occurred naturally as Maxwell aged and, in time, proved a primary source of inspiration for him. Images of home became increasingly entwined in these recollections and reveries: Thirty-five years later in *So Long,* a father and son still pace, trancelike, through the rooms of a beloved house they will abandon after a mother's death, and in the end, a skeletal house frame under construction becomes a metaphor for the very structure and subject of the author's final novel.

Maxwell's analysis also led to a surrealistic tone not present in his works before *Leaf.* Through Reik, he developed a quality of free association in his writing, a tendency to connect the situation at hand with extraneous images. Some of his narrator commentaries have the disorienting, hallucinatory quality of dreams: jarring with unexpected juxtapositions and producing irrational images connected to the story by chance. The most obvious and extensive example appears near the close as Mr. Peters visits his son in the hospital. When Lymie tells his father that he didn't think of leaving a suicide note, the narrator observes, "With that one remark the distance which had always been between them stretched out and became a vast tract, a desert country." The metaphoric desert that here divides father and son leads the narrator directly to a free-form discussion of the desert of the American West, indeed to a full chapter that flows from images of this landscape inspired by a trip Maxwell took to New Mexico during this period. Loosed from the confines of his story, he creates a sort of montage of experiences, observations, and ideas strung by the thread of his narrator's thought. In these disparate images we recognize Maxwellian themes: the difficulty of perceiving clearly, the ongoing search for love, the subtle strain of a flat landscape. He describes an old Spanish gardener with an adobe house, Spanish boys who in their goodness willingly share clothes and food with animals and strangers, and a windmill in the distance that revolves and slows and stops only to begin again. In this extended meditation, the novel's controlling metaphor returns as the narrator pictures Lymie walking on and on over the flat land toward the mountains. As on the Midwestern plain, in the desert "you can see a hundred miles in every direction," a view that creates "uncertainty." Here again the psychological strain of the endless horizon corresponds with Lymie's plight: "The desert is the natural dwelling place not only of Arabs and Indians but also of people...who, like Lymie Peters, have nothing more to say, people who have stopped justifying and explaining, stopped trying to account for themselves or their actions, stopped hoping that someone will come along and love them and so make sense out of their lives."[58]

Although Maxwell acknowledged that his use of Freudian themes was "partly the effect of [his] being in analysis" at the time he was writing the novel, he also suggested that he didn't want Freud's explanations to dominate: "I wanted to enlarge the experience by references to *The Golden Bough,* for example, and my own experiences from a later part of my life." The author's personal reflections, then, make up a good portion of the narrator's comments as well. For example, he proposes that "to know the world's injustice requires only a small amount of experience. To accept it without bitterness or envy you need almost the sum total of human wisdom, which Lymie Peters at fifteen did not have." Later, when Lymie and his father embark on their annual train trip to visit the mother's grave, the narrator begins an extended monologue on travel: "To live in the world at all is to be committed to some kind of a journey," the narrator remarks. "Neither the destination nor the point of departure are important.... What matters, the only sphere where you have any real choice, is the person who elects to sit in the empty seat beside you from Asheville, North Carolina to Knoxville, Tennessee":

> The great, the universal problem is how to be always on a journey and yet see what you would see if it were only possible for you to stay home: a black cat in a garden, moving through iris blades behind a lilac bush. How to keep sufficiently detached and quiet inside so that when the cat in one spring reaches the top of the garden wall...and disappears, you will see and remember it, and not be absorbed at that moment in the dryness of your hands.... Seeing clearly is everything.... You must somehow contrive, if only for a week or only overnight, to live in the houses of people, so that at least you know the elementary things—which doors sometimes bang when a sudden wind springs up: where the telephone book is kept.... Through all these things, through the attic and the cellar and the tool shed you must go searching until you find the people who live here or who used to live here but now are in London or Acapulco or Galesburg, Illinois. Or who now are dead.[59]

The mature judgment of Maxwell's late work is already apparent here. This meditation reveals sensibilities that not only shaped *They Came Like Swallows* years earlier but permeated his body of work: an intellectual yet always empathetic approach to people and their circumstances, the belief that central life truths are most often embedded in seemingly "small" aspects of life, and the recognition that although individual choice and will are limited, a window exists for influencing the human condition with vision and creative action. Recalling the domestic focus of *Swallows*, the narrator emphasizes the home as the most reliable evidence of how lives have been lived; a stay against the unpredictable, ever-present threat of tragedy; and a measure of individual spirit that outlasts the tenure, even the lives, of its occupants.

The passage also offers a view of the writer's methods of close observation: how he remains "sufficiently detached and quiet inside" to notice crucial details, to recognize significance in nuances of daily life. In retrospect, with knowledge of Maxwell's subsequent work, we encounter here the first subtle hint that artistic method will become a prominent subject for him. This meditation on seeing clearly later evolved to open contemplations on narrative writing in his fiction.

Louise Bogan's influence is evident here as well. Maxwell's favorite of her stories seems to have penetrated his thinking during this period; certainly his metaphoric journey and rapt attention to interior details mirror her own journey around her room. Yet there is more to this literary connection: The tone of the prose, the dead seriousness with which Maxwell examines life and its attendant objects, seems one with Bogan's sharp scrutiny, with her own emphasis on everyday effects as part of psychological experience. Like Bogan's story, Maxwell's traveling scene involves a search for answers to life's mysteries, to questions about the beginning and end of the human journey.

The meditation's final words—"Or who are now dead"—illustrate the Maxwellian balance between lovingly rendered home life and darker realities: the writer's ability to take a sudden turn, to arrest a gentle, straightforward passage with an inescapable chill. Although this quality is consistent with his approach since *They Came Like Swallows* and demonstrated clearly in "Haller's Second Home," it also suggests a parallel with Bogan. Maxwell might have been influenced by the sinister mood of her story, by the way its childhood memories so readily devolve into images of death. The passage also evokes the work of his *New Yorker* colleague E. B. White: A similarly abrupt change in tone distinguishes the final line of the classic essay "Once More to the Lake" (1941)—Maxwell's personal favorite—which recalls White's return to Maine with his son decades after a trip with his own father in 1904. At the close, his son decides to go swimming with some other boys: "Languidly, and with no thought of going in, I watched him, his hard little body, skinny and bare, saw him wince slightly as he pulled up around his vitals the small, soggy, icy garment. As he buckled the swollen belt, suddenly my groin felt the chill of death."[60] Maxwell admired these famous lines and, regardless of whether he took them as direct inspiration, felt a kinship with their subject and tonalities, as he did with Bogan's. About ten years older than Maxwell, both White and Bogan offered him touchstones of American writing that spoke to his own sensibilities and artistic temperament as he made his way in the New York literary world.

Finally, at the time Maxwell wrote this "journey" passage, he had already traveled a bit, lighting in a place long enough to live and write for a while. He had not yet gone to Europe, but he had taken many trips by train: from his room in the old Busey mansion in Urbana to Cambridge, back to the farm near Portage, Wisconsin, and off again to a summer of writing in Peterborough, New Hampshire at the MacDowell Colony. He had taken a freighter to the Caribbean, driven to New Mexico, and settled in New York. Little of this period in the thirties served directly as material for his fiction, but it provided him a broader context, a wider vision that deepened his writing about Illinois and beyond. Inspired by his reading, travels, analysis, loneliness, observations, and coming of age, commentaries in *The Folded Leaf* offer a glimpse of this maturation, of an expansion in perspective that informed his work for nearly five decades.

The narrator here represents the writer's first attempt to create a voice for his own observations and ideas; commentaries like the one quoted earlier contain the seeds of a distinct persona, the identifying characteristics and philosophies that formed the first-person narrator of his final powerful fiction. At the time of *The Folded Leaf*'s publication, Diana Trilling welcomed this first expression of authorial voice in his work: "In full control of his characters and situations, but not merged with them," she writes, Maxwell is "free to comment on their fates in his own person, so that we have the advantage of his intellect as well as of his creativity; in the degree that he keeps his personality clear of his people, he achieves a true distinction of personality."[61] This "distinction of personality" marks the most significant development in Maxwell's narrative since *They Came Like Swallows;* not only does it contribute a dispassionate intellect as Trilling suggests, but it also introduces a controlling presence, a guiding sensibility that developed to a fully formed character by the end of his career. Although it is usually unwise, even highly suspect to confuse a writer with his narrator, in this case Trilling rightly does so: Increasingly, Maxwell's sensibilities *are* the basis for his narrators' personalities, perceptions, and thoughts. At the same time, he forms his narrators based on the individual tone of each fiction so that they contribute to and enhance the particular work's literary effect. In *The Folded Leaf,* for example, the narrator's objectivity, his straightforward, understated remarks reinforce the story's grim, controlled drama. The far-flung connections drawn to the boys' lives—the New Guinea primitives, the Spanish boys of the desert country—and his observations about travel and truth are tangential yet highly relevant. They suggest that although adolescence is a life stage unto itself, its ramifications may be far-reaching, complex, subterranean. The narrator's sympathetic yet objective stance, his wisdom, worldliness, and philosophizing all invoke a subtle sense of foreboding, the notion that youthful experiences may haunt Lymie and Spud later in their lives.

Such objectivity does not supplant the pure, raw emotion of Maxwell's previous novel. Yet although the author continues to focus through his characters' eyes, to capture their inner worlds, he places them in broader context here through a detached viewpoint, a distanced, disembodied awareness. Critics generally believed the narrator's contemplations increased the novel's perspective, although one or two found them to be "intrusive," with a "blown-up quality" that "marred" the otherwise fine writing. Indeed, a case could be made that the experiences of Lymie and Spud do not need mythology, anthropology, or philosophy to heighten them, nor an all-seeing, all-knowing narrator to comment on them. Certainly, in the hands of another writer, such meditations could prove distracting, overblown, or overly didactic. Without moralizing or aggrandizement, the narrator's asides smoothly integrate characters' lives with other experiences and cultures. Looking back more than forty years later, Maxwell considered his own reasons for creating the omniscient interpreter: "I have all my life been an enthusiastic reader, and have read the same books over and over, and from the nineteenth century masters, especially the Russians, but also for example, *Tom Jones,* I felt that a commentator was called for. Really this stems from a fear, I am afraid well founded, that I was working with small scale things, and that if I didn't give everything I had to them, they would end up seeming trivial."[62]

The commentator certainly lends Maxwell an outlet for giving everything he had to the novel: The technique succeeds in universalizing the boys' lives; banishing any inkling of sentimentality with a sometimes haunting, ominous, and mysterious tone; and steering his narrative in a new direction. More than that, in a case when "half the book is stark simple autobiography and half is invention," the narrator provides the writer important psychological separation from the young men, a separation that had not been possible when he walked the floor in tears while writing *They Came Like Swallows* at Garreta Busey's in Urbana. With the earlier novel, he had achieved "no distance at all," he told me. "Now I try to do the same details but less personally, with my eyes on the other figures in the drama."[63] The commentary proves effective in helping him to establish this more detached perspective: The allusions and philosophical meditations add texture to characters and events, contributing a mood of sadness and tension. Clearly Lymie has exceptional difficulty finding his way, yet his problems, especially his palpable isolation, are sadly recognizable as central to all human experience.

* * *

Maxwell's quest to broaden the novel's subject matter had a second component: While he used the narrator's meditations to lend wider relevance to the boys' lives, he also grounded them in specifics. He believed that in order to "escape from Penrod" he must "place the story in a setting that was realistic, rather than *Saturday Evening Post*." So he created "the picture of the area in Chicago where Spud lives. And the details about the gymnasium, the house dances, the roominghouse." Although the writer continues to focus on the interior life, he sets the boys' experience against what he considered an "elaborate background"—two, in fact (Chicago and Urbana), that inspired his particular take on social realism of the period. With camera-eye precision, he describes the orderly urban classrooms, the teenage glamour of LeClerc's soda shop, and the bleakness of parts of Chicago. Through finely honed details, the genteel world of 1920s academe also comes to life: When Mrs. Forbes, Sally's mother, was "at home" the second Thursday of every month…Professor Forbes was on duty at the front door," while "Mrs. Forbes herself, always serene, always handsome, stood in the living room receiving." "Pouring tea at the copper samovar was…Mrs. Philosophy Mathews, so-called to distinguish her from the Mrs. Mathews whose husband taught animal husbandry."[64] Here we see the writer's quiet bemusement and his affinity for a gentler 1920s society over the more celebrated roaring variety. Although he admired Scott Fitzgerald immensely, Maxwell did not embrace his vision of the jazz age: Flappers had arrived on the heels of his mother's death, supplanting her halcyon world with frivolous decadence.

Maxwell's details are never tedious, nor do they overshadow his characters; rather, they create a sense of authenticity and place the boys in a historical context. As Trilling points out, the writer's "record of Middle Western American life in the '20s adds up to a more important social document than he was perhaps conscious of." Indeed, he offers cultural insight on a distinct American place in time, although his control of the composition suggests he was quite aware of what he was doing. Similarly, Edmund Wilson compared *The Folded Leaf* to earlier works of American literary realism and Maxwell to "certain American novelists who were working, against the popular taste, in the field of serious social realism at the end of the last century and during the early decades of this." He notes that Maxwell's unsentimental, detached portrayal of adolescence comes close to Stephen Crane's *Whilomville Stories* and Henry B. Fuller's Chicago novels. Although Wilson acknowledges that there is no evidence of Maxwell having been influenced by these writers, it does occur to him that in connection with Fuller there might be a "special kind of realism which is inevitably imposed upon a Middle Western writer by the landscape and life of his region. This realism may not be at all folksy; it may not be at all raw, like Dreiser's; it may be thoughtful, accomplished, and neat like the realism of Howells or Fuller." *The Folded Leaf,* he contends, is an example of the latter.[65]

Wilson's comments incite questions about the realistic dimension in Maxwell's fiction and how it compares with that of his fellow Midwestern writers. Without doubt, *The Folded Leaf,* like most of his fiction, finds its shape and substance in the prairie and people of his childhood. As Maxwell himself noted, "There is plenty of landscape and style in Central Illinois. The visual nature of an area and sense of place are a very important part of my writing." Yet even though Wilson recognizes this, his description of the writing in *The Folded Leaf* seems to shortchange Maxwell a bit, to overlook key aspects of his brand of realism. Certainly the author's approach is "thoughtful" and his prose style "accomplished," yet what makes his work reverberate with life is an engagement with pure feeling that, at some points, generates a raw intensity that Wilson overlooks.

In light of both Wilson's comparison to the realist William Dean Howells and the fact that Maxwell received the Academy of Arts and Letters Howells Medal in 1980 for *So Long, See You Tomorrow,* I asked the author about his literary forebear. "When I read Howells I always expect more than I get," he replied, "but I do recognize that we are working the same side of the street. I think my disappointment comes from the fact that he is (more than Henry James, say) limited by being a man of his period. As I am of mine." Maxwell missed something in Howells, "a sense of the tragic nature of life. Which may be nothing more than that he felt there were certain things that one couldn't write about, that he should have." In Maxwell's work, there is no such withholding of emotion: He deals plainly yet elegantly with inner life as if it were laid out, barren and exposed on the Illinois prairie. In capturing a tragic sense in his work, he does not set people against powerful and pervasive social institutions; the worlds of commerce, war, labor, and politics rarely clash with his characters' lives, as they do in Howells and Dreiser. Greater public movements and organizations become remote, even nonexistent, in the intense core of his characters; instead, the author is concerned with the subtle nuances of one-to-one relationships and the intimate implications of family intercourse. As mentioned earlier, at one of the most violent moments in world history, Wilson dubbed him a writer with "no gospel for Europe at war" and reviewed his novel favorably against *Age of Thunder,* a "phony" adventure story of a Frenchman parachuting into occupied France on a dramatic mission to the underground. Ironically, the release of *The Folded Leaf,* an austere ode to the psyche of Midwestern youth, was covered in newspapers headlined "U.S. Flyers Sink Japan's Biggest Warship."[66] Clearly, Maxwell's "imagination's home" and the world at large were poles apart.

MALE ADOLESCENCE

For all the insight *The Folded Leaf* provides for understanding Maxwell's writing, it is at heart an intense portrait of the male adolescent experience. In its opening scene, Spud, the new boy at school, saves Lymie from drowning in the class water polo game when Lymie is held underwater by a swarm of arms and thighs grappling for the ball he has inadvertently caught. After this dramatic, sudden meeting in the pool, Lymie appears at Spud's locker one afternoon; Spud initially rejects his friendship but later finds himself clinging trustfully to Lymie's fragile shoulder as they make their way through the dark fraternity initiation. Soon Spud begins to bring Lymie home for dinner regularly, encouraged by Mrs. Latham, who worries that Lymie is not being fed properly. In Lymie's presence, the Lathams' everyday dinner is transformed into a cheerful, *Saturday Evening Post* occasion: His "shyness and delight at being there had affected all of them, arousing their feeling for one another and drawing them temporarily into the compact family that he thought they were." Lymie's intense craving for family ties, for a sense of belonging, becomes a pathetic indication of his psychological neglect and fragility. Ironically, these needs become satisfied by way of his own desires: He perceives the Lathams as the perfect family he yearns for, and in turn, they fulfill his expectations by "unconsciously playing up to his idealization of them."[67]

Lymie and Spud's lives begin to form a synchronized cadence. After school and on weekends they sometimes go to the fraternity house—a one-room basement apartment secured through another boy's uncle in real estate— where members play the ukulele, wind and rewind an old Victrola, read a copy of Balzac's *Droll Stories* swiped from the shelf of an unsuspecting grandfather, smoke their first cigarettes, and waltz with Edith Netedu, who never gets dizzy no matter how many times she is twirled. By the end of the school year, when the fraternity house is lost to a tenant who can pay higher rent, Lymie finally feels comfortable venturing inside LeClerc's with Spud to have a malted milk after school. The relationship develops gradually and undramatically until one afternoon when its steady rhythm is disrupted by a physical, intimate, and somewhat obscure occurrence.

After counting the boxcars, coal cars, and oil tankers of a freight train in the pouring rain one day, Lymie and Spud return to the Lathams' in sopping clothes and shoes. "Noticing the hollows under Lymie's eyes," Spud decides that Lymie needs a nap, and proceeds to undo his tie and to unbutton his wet shirt in hopes of putting him to bed. Lymie, surprising both Spud and himself, puts up a tremendous fight, kicking, twisting, kneeing, and gouging "anything that he could lay his hands on." The raucous banging of furniture and jumping on and off the bed draws Mrs. Latham to Spud's room, but she is unable to stop them. As the struggle continues, Spud succeeds in removing Lymie's clothing piece by piece, and Lymie's fighting becomes fiercer: "Like a country defending itself against an invader,... he fought against being made to do something against his will, and he fought also against the unreasonable strength in Spud's arms." Suddenly, Lymie stops thrashing and lies motionless on the bed:

> As in a dream he let Spud cover him with a blanket. Something had burst inside of him, something more important than any organ, and there was a flowing which was like blood. Though he kept breathing and his heart after a while pounded less violently, there it was all the same, an underground river which went on and on and was bound to keep on like that for years probably, never stopping, never once running dry.
>
> He watched Spud pull the shades down and leave the room without having any idea of what he had done.[68]

Crafted with restraint, the scene captures a significant epiphany in Lymie's young life: his rejection and ultimate acceptance of love. Expressing Lymie's sensations directly without explication or sentimentality, the passage reveals the subtle and not-so-subtle ramifications of Lymie's isolation and parental neglect and suggests inextricable links between physicality and sensibility. Unaccustomed to receiving expressions of love, Lymie initially resists Spud's tenderness: He will neither relinquish his protective psychological distance nor willingly succumb to a greater physical force. When his endurance is exhausted, his emotional defenses also give way, and he accepts Spud's devotion, a devotion Lymie returns repeatedly and profusely in the years ahead.

Perhaps most striking about the scene is the sensitivity with which it captures raw, elusive emotion. "As in a dream," Lymie's feelings are not clear to him. He struggles against an enigmatic "something" that ruptures inside him and courses like a river. Unable to articulate what overwhelms him, he is aware only of intense sensation. The "bursting," "flowing," and "pounding" of his emotional release are acutely sensual yet controlled by a narrative voice that is objective, distanced, and wise. Maxwell, whose literary demeanor, style, and territory have been characterized as quiet and unassuming, here confronts strong, even violent reaction with fortitude and precision. As Bruce Bawer suggests, "few writers could manage such an episode without stumbling headlong into sentimentality, or, on the other hand, without making the whole thing seem merely a carnal encounter." Louise Bogan also singled out the passage: "After the scene of the pent-up boy taking it out in the fight, I think you can probably manage anything," she wrote him.[69]

Lymie's background may explain his powerful and somewhat mysterious response here—why the experience holds him with such gravity. The absence of love in his life stems from the death of his mother five years earlier, and like Bunny in *They Came Like Swallows,* his childhood happiness and security directly corresponded with her presence at home and his physical closeness to her. The bedroom scene at Spud's subtly alludes to such maternal love: Making Lymie undress for bed, tucking him in, and pulling down the shade for a nap suggest a mother caring for her child more than a sexually charged encounter. While Lymie flailed in protest, Spud remained "calm and possessed," as an adult "merely bent on making Lymie lie still under the covers and take a nap before dinner."[70] Lymie probably was not consciously thinking of his mother at this point, but buried beneath the affection for Spud, beneath the sudden capitulation to a stronger physical force, lies a motherless child still grieving for lost love. This past loss must course beneath Lymie's emotional surge on some level, just as it forms the undercurrent of his dreams. Spud's actions may have awakened in him the profound memory of being cared for, of being a nurtured dependent made to do things for his own good.

Viewing the scene retrospectively, with Maxwell's body of work as a context, this interpretation comes naturally not only because the mother's death becomes the central fact of his fiction, but also because the encounter corresponds with his understanding and conception of character. His later novel *The Chateau,* for instance, introduces Harold Rhodes, a man traveling in France with his wife, as a composite of all his former selves, including "the child his mother went in to cover on her rounds, the last thing at night before she went to bed."[71] The recurrence of this particular memory as a touchstone of maternal love in Maxwell's world supports the notion that Lymie may have associated Spud's attention with a motherly act. A part of Harold still waits in bed to be covered by his mother, just as Lymie unconsciously longs for the love prematurely wrenched from him. Lymie and Harold, indeed all of Maxwell's people, do not outlive their past lives; they live with them. Carrying their personal histories from childhood into death, they do not find clean-slate opportunities to start afresh but discover new ways to understand

and be at peace with what has gone before. Throughout the novel, Lymie does not grieve openly but lives with a vague yet deep-felt sense of loss; well behaved and quiet, he holds sorrow just beneath the surface. No wonder then that he would finally experience a wild outburst—a moment wound with love, loss, torment, surprise, and physical release.

The novel's critical history offers a continuum of views about this and other scenes that involve a sense of physicality between Lymie and Spud, particularly as the boys go to college and their relationship intensifies. While Bawer sees the friendship as "platonic," others interpret the sensual description—the "violent" heart pounding, the "flowing which was like blood"—as either overtly or unconsciously sexual. Maxwell himself used the latter term ten years earlier to describe Whitey's feelings for Nigel, the actress in *Bright Center of Heaven*. In his 1964 study *The Adolescent and the American Novel*, W. Tasker Witham recognized the love between Lymie and Spud as one of the novel's "chief themes": In his view, their "latent homosexual" "attachment" evolves into a "normal friendship, while the folded leaf of their undeveloped manhood unfolds into maturity." Later in the twentieth century, at least two critical volumes on gay literature discussed the novel and took issue with Tasker's take on the path Lymie ultimately followed. Roger Austen, for example, found that *The Folded Leaf* "reads like a genuinely gay novel" and that Lymie takes a sudden false turn to heterosexuality when he accepts a female student's invitation to a dance in the final chapter. James Levin has recognized that Austen's interpretation requires the reader to look "beyond the actual words of the text" yet sees this "generally dubious procedure" as appropriate here. He posits that while some readers might infer that Lymie merely goes through a temporary phase of infatuation with Spud, gay readers identify with Lymie and express doubts about his future adjustment in heterosexual life. Most recently, James Campbell has suggested that for the twenty-first-century reader, the boys' relationship seems "startlingly physical." For Campbell, writing more than fifty years after the novel's publication, *The Folded Leaf* offers scenes of male attraction that cannot be ignored: "While it is not quite established as the first post-war gay novel in American literature...the textual evidence is persuasive," he concludes.[72]

Maxwell vehemently rejected this idea and said he did not intend to portray homosexuality, latent or otherwise. From the beginning, however, he had been concerned about potential negative reaction from his University of Illinois contemporaries and wrote his trusted friend Susan Deuel Shattuck, who responded reassuringly. During one of our interviews, the writer recalled readers' inquiries about the boys' sexual orientation: During a cocktail party in his wife's native Oregon, for example, he was approached by a reader who had concluded that Lymie was homosexual and Spud bisexual. In response, the author insisted that this was not his intention. "Nobody now can quite believe how free from the explicitly sexual the friendship was," he said. "Open homosexuality, in the Middle West in the twenties, was extremely rare. They were spoken of, quite simply, by boys in locker rooms as cocksuckers, and this is not a term that Lymie would have found it possible to apply to himself. Or Spud either. I was writing about love, not sex, and if the reader doesn't believe me there is nothing more I can say about it." Maxwell described the scene at Spud's house as "the moment when Lymie, defeated in his will by physical strength he couldn't manage, became aware of the fact that he loved Spud—more than he ever had any other human being. More than life itself. The thing happened in the second that he admitted defeat and not in Spud's tucking him under the covers before he left the room. It was the loss of his belief that he couldn't be made to do anything he didn't want to."[73] As Maxwell implied, by relinquishing control, Lymie submits to Spud's love.

Critics concerned with the pure, enigmatic emotions Maxwell uncovers, who move beyond labels to explore the novel's nuanced portrait of adolescence, offer the most insight. For example, Witham recognized that *The Folded Leaf* captures the complexity and contradiction inherent in adolescent development: "The homosexual love and the heterosexual love and the self-sacrifice are all treated as aspects which normally appear, though in different guises, in the process of growing up." The most sensitive and discerning comments on this issue came more than thirty years later, however, from Paul Binding of the London *Independent:*

> To say that there is a strong homoerotic constituent in the boys' relationship is to state both the obvious and the ultimately irrelevant. Of course Lymie has physically registered responses to Spud; when, as they regularly and asexually do, they share a bed, Lymie likes his feet to touch his friend's. But we are concerned here with feelings that are too multi-layered to yield satisfactorily to labeling or even to overt analysis. They have to be presented in their often contradictory succession, and then viewed in the totality of a fiction to be understood. And maybe we never can finally understand, only empathise and acknowledge.[74]

Indeed, Maxwell's achievement here consists in his recreation of the overwhelming, often unknowable emotions surrounding a young person's coming of age. Perhaps we can also appreciate the novel's portrait of male adolescence by recognizing that, like many people's, Maxwell's early adulthood was plagued by self-doubt, loneliness, and the search for an acceptable role in his personal life that, in his case, led to psychoanalysis. This search fostered a courageous exploration of masculinity in his fiction, an attempt to depict an emerging manhood that differed from the more traditional examples offered by his father and older brother. As a result, his work challenges stereotypic images of the twentieth-century American male and explores the often unspoken emotions that line the road to maturity.

Love and longing, the idea of both platonic and sexual yearnings, coalesce in the experience of Maxwell's young people, suggesting how these emotions remain rife with complications, particularly in the formative years. And, as Maxwell suggests, love of any kind—especially when it has been lost in youth and not regained—has the ability to generate powerful physical response. The writer's analysis might have helped him to understand and accept such enigmatic emotion; from comments Theodor Reik made, we know that he and Maxwell discussed sexuality and love.[75] After *Leaf*, and after his marriage, Maxwell did not depict such acute though somehow vague sensuality. Yet, as in this novel, he never flinched in the face of difficult emotion nor did he edit the complexities, dark mysteries, and confounding uncertainties of the inner life.

* * *

From the scene at Spud's house, the novel skips ahead several years to the Midwestern college classroom of Professor Severance, who is reading and explicating poetry. Here, the boys' relationship becomes imbalanced and unsettling. A familiar young blond athlete with a block letter thrusts "one long, muscular, football player's leg into the aisle," while "in the row ahead of him, [sits] his exact human opposite—flat-chested with a long pointed face and straight dark hair that grew down on his forehead in a widow's peak." When Lymie is called on he can produce the correct answer out of thin air ("Wordsworth" in this case), yet he is flagged by a lack of self-confidence. Whether the hesitancy in his eyes stems from his early failures in the swimming pool and on the baseball field or the hesitancy caused these failures, the narrator is unsure. As a college sophomore he finds that his shortage of athletic talent no longer poses serious consequences, and the narrator posits that perhaps Lymie "attached too much importance to physical development. It is, after all, a minor barrier in the Grand Obstacle Race." Regardless, Lymie "still clung loyally to that one insurmountable barrier": "At nineteen he was almost painfully thin."[76]

When Lymie is invited to the home of Sally Forbes—a professor's unconventional daughter who, with her friend Hope Davison, is immediately drawn to Lymie's intelligence and individuality—he is again reminded of his role as foil to Spud's brawniness. Professor Severance, also a guest, points out the dichotomies of a beautiful, lacquered screen in the Forbes' living room with white flowers on one side and Chinese horsemen charging across the other: "The mutual attraction of gentleness and violence, don't you see, Mr. Peters? The brutal body and the calm philosophic mind." Lymie has always successfully played the white flower to Spud's horseman, but at the university the roles become exaggerated. Roommates and platonic bedmates in a campus boardinghouse, they continue to rely heavily on each other: "In the big icy-cold bed they clung to each other, shivering like puppies, until the heat of their bodies began to penetrate through the outer flannel of their pajamas and their heavy woolen bathrobes." Spud provides Lymie with a sense of security: Before Lymie goes to sleep he moves "his right foot until the outer part of the instep came in contact with Spud's bare toes, and from this one point of reality he swung out safely into darkness, into no sharing whatever."[77]

Lymie's demeanor becomes not only passive but also servile. Like a "faithful hound," he stands on the sidelines of the gymnasium to tie Spud's boxing gloves and holds the lever down for Spud to drink from the water fountain. In the locker room, when Spud dries off with a towel Lymie has set out for him, "his shoes and socks were waiting on the floor beside him, and the boxing trunks and jock strap that he had brought up from the shower room in his hand were hanging on a hook in the locker. It was not callousness that let him accept these attentions," the narrator maintains, because "he recognized that it gave Lymie pleasure to bend over and pick up the towel where he had dropped it, and to go off to the towel room and exchange it for a clean one." Even in fantasy, Lymie seems to revel in his servitude: In daydreams he takes the blame for Spud's unspecified crimes and jumps overboard from a lifeboat in which he and Spud find themselves with food enough for only one. When Lymie's friend, Sally, and Spud begin to date, Lymie accepts "the role of faithful friend, the devoted, unselfish intermediary" who accompanies them to the local hangout after class and is the courier for their love notes. Like a faithful spouse or doting parent, Lymie devotes himself almost entirely to Spud's needs and desires: He entertains Spud and Sally with his stories and anonymously gives Spud $100 to join a fraternity from which he himself is rejected.[78]

In his own undemonstrative way, Spud is devoted as well. He considers Lymie his best friend—"the only one, when you get right down to it"—but he is unable to express his feelings. After he moves out of the boardinghouse to live at the fraternity, Spud privately considers quitting the club so that he can live with Lymie again; he is unhappy separated from his friend, but without a formal grievance, he has no excuse to quit the brotherhood. The boys' relationship is strained when Spud becomes jealous of Lymie's attentions to Sally. Suppressed animosities in their friendship have been alluded to since the scramble in Spud's boyhood bedroom in Chicago: As Lymie angrily flailed about, the look on his "tormented face" had been "almost but not quite hate." Latent hostilities that have been building since the boys reached college surface now; the complexity and unhealthy nature of the relationship become increasingly clear. Although Lymie dances with Hope at the sorority dance, he clearly admires Sally and later innocently buys her violets when the two take the train to Chicago to see Spud in a boxing tournament. Spud's envy forces him to withdraw from and even become hostile toward Lymie, and a friend tells Lymie that Spud "talks for an hour at a time about how much he hates [him]."[79]

On a cold midnight Lymie puts a coat over his pajamas and crosses the campus to confront Spud about his jealousy. "What I came over to tell you, you have to believe," he says. "I'm not in love with Sally and she isn't in love with me." When Spud nods without answering, Lymie, "on a sudden impulse...knelt down and clasped Spud's knees.... 'Please listen to me,' Lymie said. 'Because if you don't you'll be very sorry.'" Silence hangs between them. As Lymie leaves, he turns on the foot of the steps with a final apology. Knowing that he does not forgive Spud, he walks into the night alone.[80]

At this point Maxwell ends his long, figurative trek across the flat plain toward the mountains he envisioned as he wrote. From the novel's conception, he had intended Lymie's personal crisis to provide the tension-breaking climax, and so he allowed the landscape metaphor to guide him toward the moment when Lymie, distraught and alone, attempts to end his life in the roominghouse bathroom. The nine brief chapters that close the book show the writer juxtaposing the extended, distanced perspective of the narrator with the hesitant responses of Lymie's father and friends who visit the hospital, as well as the boy's unspoken recollection of his own violent acts. Initially, Maxwell does not describe the horrific scene: Chapter 52 ends as Lymie walks home after his disturbing confrontation with Spud, and the next chapter moves directly to Lymie's father, who, after being summoned to the university, waits to speak with the dean of men about Lymie's condition. When Mr. Dehner, the landlord, calls a plumber to clean the bathroom after Lymie's trauma, Maxwell writes simply that Dehner "stood by while the plumber and his assistant had made the bathtub and the washbowl *useable* again, an experience that could easily have shattered a less nervous man."[81] The author does not describe a bloodied bathroom, the stark contrast of red stains on white porcelain, nor does he depict the plumber's horror upon seeing the room, his conversation with the assistant as they scrub the fixtures on their knees, the inevitable stains on the workers' own clothing, or their nausea as they envision the events of the previous night. This restraint focuses attention on the unspeakable, dreadful nature of Lymie's act and on the numb, almost stoic reaction of the landlord. In later fiction, particularly *So Long, See You Tomorrow* and "Love," Maxwell used this technique again to convey bitter sadness, yet at no point in his body of work does reserve heighten tragedy more pointedly.

Deriving its strength from what Maxwell leaves unexpressed, the scene also serves as a foil for moments of explicit description later in the novel. When Lymie awakens in his hospital bed and the night nurse leans over him to ask, "Why did you do it?" Maxwell spills Lymie's thoughts onto the page: "I didn't want to go on living in a world where the truth has no power to make itself be believed,"[82] Lymie answers, "without moving his lips, without making a sound." He replays the scene in his mind:

> There was a small bottle of iodine in the medicine cabinet in the bathroom in the second floor of Mr. Dehner's rooming house. I took the cap off and drank all of it. The iodine burned the lining of my throat on the way down and formed a solid knot of burning in my stomach. The burning got worse and worse until suddenly I flung myself on my knees in front of the toilet and vomited the horrible yellow stuff into the bowl.
>
> . . . I got up then and opened the medicine cabinet again and took out Mr. Dehner's straight-edged razor. With the warm water running slowly into the washbasin I began to cut my left wrist. The flesh parted with a stinging sensation and began to bleed. The blood turned pink in the lukewarm water and went down the drainpipe. . . . I cut my wrist again deeper. I made three separate incisions in my left wrist and each time the blood congealed, after a few minutes. So I transferred the razor to my other hand and cut wherever the veins showed through the skin.
>
> Finally (all this took a long time and I was very tired) I left the washbasin, knelt down beside the tub, and applied the edge of the razor to my throat. The blood flowed in a stream. The bottom of the tub was red with it almost immediately.[83]

Suddenly, without warning, we have been thrust into the bathroom with Lymie to witness each painstaking cut of the blade. Earlier, Maxwell magnified the tension surrounding Lymie's near-demise by withholding full information, by presenting the tragedy obliquely. Through indirect allusions, readers had felt the intense strain, sorrow, despair, denial, and even cool objectivity of Lymie's acquaintances; they had read the itemized bill for the plumber, a new razor, bathroom rug, and towel given Lymie's father by the landlord but were spared the sight of blood. Now, as observers of Lymie's self-mutilation, we confront first hand the arresting brunt of the heinous act. Maxwell's graphic description is particularly shocking for those accustomed to his bent toward understatement. In contrast to the indirect treatment of the landlord's experience with the plumbers, Lymie's vivid account seems highly brutal and unrelenting. This ability to alternate between what Maxwell called the "now direct and now indirect process...of literary art" is a major strength of *The Folded Leaf*. His meticulously orchestrated fluctuation between restraint and disclosure creates a charged rhythm that elicits both the seething intensity of repressed sentiments and the sudden shock of confronting a gruesome scene. This artful maneuvering suggests a writer in command of his craft, one who has taken painstaking care with language to "move the reader as [he has] been moved."[84]

The carefully paced narrative shifts to Lymie's hospital room where Sally delivers a note from Hope inviting him to the spring dance. When Spud arrives, he and Sally play together on the bed, creating an imaginary camping trip up and down the covers over Lymie's raised knees. For Maxwell, the scene's last line was important: "It was some time before the nurse came in and put an end to this childish game." With this, he "wanted to convey that the whole experience couldn't have happened to people older than the three of them were."[85] This image is reminiscent of Robert Louis Stevenson's "The Land of Counterpane," a poem about an ill young boy who invents a world of adventure among his bedcovers. The link holds particular meaning in light of Maxwell's affinity for the poet, whose Scottish roots he shared and whose published letters he reviewed for *The New Yorker* in 1993. Like Stevenson's child, Sally and Spud appropriate Lymie's knees as the hills of their fanciful landscape; their play evokes an earlier stage of their lives, suggesting that, while verging on adulthood, the three are still children, and their experiences and sentiments are those of youth. Stevenson's character recalls not only the kind of imaginative boy Lymie must have been but also the sensitive Bunny Morison of *They Came Like Swallows*, whose own world is filled with vivid fantasies and marred by serious illness. The "Counterpane" child personifies the prototypical Maxwell youth: physically weak yet sustained by considerable creative powers.

This characterization changes in the chapter Maxwell added on Reik's behest. The hesitant look in Lymie's eyes, present since his Chicago school days (and probably since early childhood) has suddenly vanished in the new ending. His shoes, which he managed to scuff on the way to the sorority dance, are now shined. Even his hair, at other times sticking straight up, now "lay smooth and flat on his head." Maxwell's Lymie had avoided his own reflection, standing "stiffly with his back to the wide gilt mirror"; now, he looks directly at himself in the glass, recognizing "the face he saw in the mirror as his own." Suddenly, his focus has shifted: Perhaps for the first time, he is acutely aware of himself as an individual. On his way to plant the violets, he walks by the place where he had once entertained Spud and Sally with his stories but does not stop because "What he was about to do now had no connection with either [of them]."[86] Never before have readers seen Lymie take action for himself: to this point, his life had been one of servitude to his friends:

> When he emerged from the sheltering trees and came out on the golf course, there was a peculiar lightness in his step. Although he didn't realize it, he had left his childhood (or if not all, then the greater part of it) behind in the clearing. Watched over by tree spirits, guarded by Diana the huntress and the King of the Woods, it would be as safe as anything in this world. It would never rise and defeat him again.

The small gesture of planting flowers becomes somehow grandiose as a metaphor for Lymie's discarded childhood "guarded by Diana the huntress and the King of the Woods." Typically, Maxwell's characters experience quiet epiphanies rather than ceremonious transformations heralded by mythological figures. By comparison, "Love" from the *Billie Dyer* collection also ends with a character arranging fresh flowers in the outdoors. In this case, however, a woman attends to the grave of a young teacher in a scene that is at once reserved and haunting, characteristic of the understated dignity the writer accords simple human acts, of the delicate counterpoise he creates between hope and despair. Indeed, "Love" and other Maxwell works—including the definitive version of *The Folded Leaf*—do not offer simple, absolute solutions to life's difficulties. Narrators of his later novels would laugh at the idea that childhood could be left behind in the woods, rendered powerless over one's later years. On the contrary, the continual presence of childhood throughout life is a predominant, recurring theme in Maxwell's work. And on a broader level, the ability of all past events to impose on the present is central to his view of the human condition. Even Lymie's father experiences the presence of his youthful self: When he sees "the bandages around Lymie's throat and wrists...the young man in [him] took his derby hat and departed." Childhood may not necessarily "rise up and defeat" Maxwell's adult characters, but it is understood and accepted as an ever-present, permanent component of their psyches.[87]

In the melodramatic swell of this final, first-edition chapter, one true note rings: Consider again the aforementioned narrator commentary: "If you live on a prairie you see the whole of the sky. It is all there; and buildings, people, and trees, often ugly in themselves, have the saving grace of unimportance." One would be hardpressed to find a more Maxwellian statement in such a decidedly un-Maxwellian chapter. The passage, later cut in the revision, reflects the landscape that inspired the author's imagination as well as his reverence for life at its most quintessential: inflated experience has no place in his world.

Maxwell's decision to add the chapter for publication—to change his original ending—clearly marks a moment when he veered from his natural inclinations. In retrospect, he told me that nothing could have made Lymie more home-free, "Unless you believe in the absolute efficacy of Freudian analysis. A boy who was no longer oversensitive, or subject to absolutes, subject also to neurotic, disguised, self-destructive or hostile impulses, would not be recognizably the same person." In interpreting Lymie's experiences, Maxwell observed that "the psychologist would bring up the word masochist, but I think we should shut the door on the psychiatrist and try to understand it without Freudian jargon." Instead, the writer seems in concert with his friend Louise Bogan's assessment of Lymie's emotional development: Out of dissatisfaction with the upbeat last chapter, she quoted Goethe as saying, "Maturity had to be achieved once more with every day we woke to."[88] More than ten years later, Lymie Peters would awaken to another day.

* * *

The Folded Leaf was published April 4, 1945 to positive, even glowing, reviews. Critics praised the book for its "fragrant authenticity," "true sympathy and understanding of human relationships," and "careful, unobtrusive art." Along with Diana Trilling's in *The Nation*, Wilson's was the most important notice the book received, and Maxwell stood up well to the formidable critic's standards. Wilson considered the novel in several contexts: in the larger tradition of Midwestern and realistic writing that preceded it and as a refined, intelligent departure from much of the contemporary wartime fiction of the 1940s. For him, Maxwell's account of adolescence in the Midwest seemed "moving" and "absorbing" compared with the melodramatic, "phony" books stimulated by the bombast in Europe. He recognized the writer's accomplished prose—"a style and a narrative skill which have been learned in the struggle with his subject" while observing a slight weakening of perspective and character late in the work.

Overall, *The Folded Leaf* was a resounding critical success, yet the final upbeat chapter disappointed even the critics who were most impressed with the novel. In her otherwise glowing critique in the *Saturday Review of Literature,* Sara Henderson Hay questioned how Lymie's suicide attempt "rather miraculously brings about an emotional straightening out of both boys, and leaves the reader wondering whether it could really be so finally resolved."[89] Edmund Wilson's single contention with the novel also revolved around the close: the fading of Spud's viewpoint and Lymie's sudden confidence. Maxwell remembered this critique years later: "I hadn't intentionally concentrated more on one than the other, but simply went where I felt most secure, and Spud was, I suppose, an extrovert and they not only don't say, as a rule, what they think and feel, they don't know, being as a rule predominantly physical." Yet Wilson found that the boy's leave-taking led to a poignant effect, as if we were "merely losing sight, at graduation, of two men we had known in college" and, in retrospect, realize the "grave implications" of this early period in their lives. In the end, however, he, too, was left "a little unsatisfied": "The author breaks off the story without quite having been able to persuade us to share Lymie's feelings of confidence." Diana Trilling came right to the point: "The resolution of *The Folded Leaf* is not only shadowy but fortuitous," she contended. "I completely doubt the independence which Lymie is supposed to have found so suddenly, and I look to the future of Spud with an uneasiness which his author gives us no evidence that he shares."[90]

Ironically, the disparaged first edition ending—the novel's single weakness according to numerous critics—was also the single aspect the author included at someone else's instigation. He wrote to his lifelong friend, Susan Deuel Shattuck, who served as a model for the character Hope: "I hope you like the book. The ending is weak but the rest, I feel, is as good as I could have done at the time." As the writer and his critics agree, Lymie's leap into maturity is not only psychologically implausible but artistically unsound, highly uncharacteristic of the control with which he molded characters' psyches to this point. Not since Jefferson Carter's unexpected eruption at the end of *Bright Center of Heaven* had a Maxwell character taken what seemed an unauthentic turn. The earlier aberration had been inspired by the young writer's eagerness to create a dramatic climax; this time, however, his first instinct was spot-on. He innately sensed the truth of Lymie's inner life, yet he yielded to the opinion of an authority figure. "I wished I had had the strength to stick to my original intentions," he said on recalling Trilling's dissatisfaction in her review. "When I finish a novel I am usually exhausted and wide open to suggestions from people I trust, when I shouldn't trust anybody but myself."[91]

* * *

Four weeks after the publication of *The Folded Leaf,* William Maxwell and Emily Noyes wed on Thursday evening, May 17 in the Alexander Chapel at First Presbyterian Church on Lower Fifth Avenue in New York. Gus Lobrano, Maxwell's fellow fiction editor at *The New Yorker,* and Katherine Noyes, Emily's mother, served as witnesses. Afterwards, the couple went home to Maxwell's place in the country where, Emily wrote, "we led a Wordsworthian sort of life, which suited both of us."[92]

Revising *The Folded Leaf*

"When I had a chance to revise the book, I did," Maxwell told me, "the first time for the Faber and Faber edition." For the 1959 re-release, the author reversed the first edition's overly positive close and reinstated his original ending in the hospital room. He not only deleted the ending Reik had suggested but also undid changes recommended by Harper editor Edward Aswell—the same changes the writer had thought "were sound, and [would] help the book" in 1944. More self-confident four decades later, he recalled that they "were neither necessary nor really helpful. I put almost everything back the way I originally had it." While Maxwell was making changes, writer Harold Brodkey brought him a marked copy of the book. "Mostly the things he objected to were ideas I had absorbed from Reik, rather than arrived at from my own experience, and I either cut or rewrote those sentences," he recalled. To recover the original, insecure Lymie, he deleted the last chapter added to the 1945 edition (chapter 62) while shifting one or two of its key plot elements into chapter 61, the new final chapter. In the description of Lymie contemplating the future from his hospital bed, he changed sentences originally published as "He *was going* to get well" and "He *would be able* to look into the faces of people" to "He *wanted* to get well" and "He *wanted* to look into the faces of people."[93] Here we see the writer fashioning a character less certain of the future: Lymie wants to become well and confident, but we are not assured that this will come to pass.

To the same end, the writer deleted the majority of passages in which Lymie thought about Spud and Sally when they visited him in the hospital. One seems especially significant: "Looking first at Spud and then at Sally, Lymie saw that they belonged together," Maxwell wrote in the first edition;

> They matched somehow. They were right for each other and for no one else. It was something that he had never realized before, but then his eyes were only now beginning to grow accustomed to the light, after the continual darkness and gloom of the hut in the forest.

Here, Lymie's sudden confidence and absolute certainty, his apparent awakening to new possibilities, had begun to satisfy Reik's desire for the youth's psychological emancipation. Yet the scenario contradicts one of the narrator's previous observations: Lymie has encountered no coming-of-age ritual; with his father largely absent, he has been denied the "presence and participation of grown men" in his formative years. Without guidance, he cannot achieve peace of mind or enlightenment; he cannot, in Reik's term, emerge "homefree." Rather, "what survives afterwards is merely the idea of exclusion or of revenge," the narrator explains. Untrue to the author's understanding of life and inconsistent with his sense of dramatic construction, this allusion to Lymie's edification was struck from the novel.[94]

Consider also the sentences that close the two editions. The first, "[His childhood] would never rise and defeat him again," is a grand pronouncement of absolute victory; the second, "It was some time before the nurse came in and put an end to this childish game," offers a straightforward statement of fact, a brief description of a simple action.[95] As mentioned previously, Maxwell considered the latter line important because of its reference to childhood. The tone it establishes is equally important; its matter-of-factness creates tension that swells beneath the action. Lymie has just survived his attempt at suicide, and Sally and Spud play a game to ease anxiety and awkwardness. At some point the nurse will come and calmly ask them to stop. The scene's composure starkly contrasts the event that has brought the friends together in the hospital room. Readers observe how Spud and Sally divert attention from the tragedy, how they cannot or will not cope with it head-on. Because the revised novel ends with an understated scene that presents emotion indirectly, readers do not leave wondering about Lymie's sudden turnaround. Rather, they close the back cover with a sense of the friends' feelings of sadness, disbelief, and inadequacy.

Maxwell took the opportunity to revise with an eye toward style and artistry as well. Comparison between the 1945 and revised endings provides insight into the development of his creative process: The revision reveals him reassessing and refining his fiction to include more indirect presentation, vivid imagery, and dramatic effects achieved through carefully controlled tension. In the later version, he writes more economically, banishes any remnants of sentimentality, and uses language and rhythm to portray psychological activity more precisely.

Consider again the sentences that begin "He wanted to get well" and "He wanted to look into the faces of people," as well as "He knew there were things he had not cared enough about." In the revision he makes the verbs parallel in these three consecutive sentences and identical in two. The new construction and the repeating verb *wanted* drive the prose forward and emphasize the mounting urgency of Lymie's thoughts and desires. Maxwell also improves the rhythm here by joining what were two sentences in the first edition to now read, "He wanted to look into the faces of people that he didn't know and might never see again, hear rain in the night, and sleep, and turn in his sleep and have dreams." By merging these sentences from the first edition, he portrays Lymie's emotionally charged state of mind more sharply here: Recognizing what he now desired for himself, the boy rapidly shifts from thought to thought and modifies his ideas without pause.

More changes: In the 1945 ending, Lymie reads Hope's invitation to the dance as he dresses in his new dorm room, while in the revised version, Sally delivers the letter to him in the hospital. A comparison of Lymie's internal responses in both instances reveals Maxwell's developing sense of narrative. The first edition reads,

> Lymie opened a desk drawer and slipped the note inside. If Hope had the courage to ask him to her house dance, if she wanted him, knowing that he'd have to wear a sweater instead of a white shirt, and that everybody there would know why he was wearing it. . . .
> The scars were almost healed. (Ellipsis Maxwell's)

And the revision:

> When he had finished reading, he turned, frowning slightly, and looked out of the window. He'd have to wear a turtleneck sweater instead of a white shirt, and everybody there would know why he was wearing it. . . . If Hope had the courage to ask him, if she wanted him, knowing that he . . .
> The pear tree was in full bloom. (Ellipses Maxwell's)

By adding the modifier "turtleneck" to "sweater," the author creates a much clearer picture of the circumstances in the revision: Lymie's neck still bears the self-inflicted wounds. The turtleneck becomes a sort of scarlet letter, a symbol of Lymie's deviation from acceptable society, a testament to his fragile mental state. Wearing a high-necked, winter sweater, he will be an anomaly in a crowd of young men in crisp white shirts and young women in spring pastels. With this one word, the author maintains tension by recalling Lymie's brutal, deliberate cutting of his own neck. And by simply transposing the last two sentences of the first paragraph, he heightens the drama: In the first edition, Lymie ponders Hope's courage in asking him to the dance and then remembers the sweater and how "everybody there would know why he was wearing it." In the revision, Lymie thinks first of the sweater and then recognizes Hope's fortitude: She has invited him despite "knowing that he. . . ." By breaking Lymie's thought here mid-sentence, Maxwell suggests his character's inability to articulate the painful experience, even in private reflection. Because readers are forced to complete the sentence themselves—"knowing that he . . ." had tried to kill himself—the violent act remains a menacing presence; it hovers like an ominous cloud over Lymie's world. The revision's two ellipses effectively portray the movement of Lymie's psyche, as if twice his thoughts break off just as he has made a painful mental connection. He is beginning to comprehend the ramifications of his attempt at suicide, of the invitation and the turtleneck.[96]

The one-sentence paragraphs that follow these descriptions deserve special attention as well. Clearly Maxwell had to change "The scars were almost healed," because in the revision Lymie would still be in the hospital at this point; his wounds would still be fresh. Although the earlier sentence depicts a positive development—Lymie's healing—it is still directly related to the tragic event. The substitute—"The pear tree was in full bloom"—turns attention away from his mutilation completely. Readers move instantly from a horrific image to a beautiful one. The sentence, which has a cadence nearly identical to the one in the first edition, provides a sense of hope to the definitive version, yet one more subtle, indirect, and realistic than was published in 1945.

In lieu of the dramatic transformation, Maxwell also added the "two or three sentences that give a clue how the two boys will turn out." Indeed, the revision offers several hints that indicate the boys will go their separate ways. When Spud enters Lymie's hospital room, he sits next to him on the bed opposite Sally. In the final lines, he rises to look at the violets, and "When he came back he sat on the bed again, beside Sally this time." Sally "took his hand in hers and Lymie's hand in her other hand."[97] These lines suggest that Sally and Spud will remain together but that the two boys will not be able to restore their damaged relationship. At the same time Sally will remain friends with both of them, but separately.

Most significantly, the definitive ending makes it clear that Lymie's problems are by no means over. Although his weakened state could account for his silence in the hospital, he is exceptionally passive, even stoic—"I'm fine," he replies to Sally's query about his health—and expresses no opinion when she discusses her mother's plans for his future in academe. Lymie remains in a subservient role: Spud "made [him] raise his knees" so that the couple could play their camping game. Yet Lymie makes no complaint about discomfort; rather than acting, he is acted upon. Through Sally's eyes, however, we glimpse what Lymie's future might hold: Looking at his gauze-covered wrists and throat, she reflects that there are "people for whom life just isn't going to be too easy, and that probably he was one of them and maybe she herself another."[98] Indeed, through the loss of his mother and the emotional distance of his father, Lymie experienced profound hurt at an early age; still, he was willing to risk further rejection and abandonment by giving profoundly in his friendship with Spud in hopes of being loved in return. A classic Maxwell protagonist, Lymie is a delicate survivor: He appears weak, yet his emotional reserves run deep. Had Maxwell stayed true to this characterization of Lymie in the first edition, Edmund Wilson and other critics may have found no weaknesses in the novel. For in its definitive ending (retained in all editions since 1959), he captures with utmost sensitivity the nuances of male adolescence, allowing no shortcut, no quick, triumphal emergence from the uncertainties of early life. Just as he recalls with amazing clarity the perspective of childhood in *They Came Like Swallows*, here he renders the fragile phase between youth and maturity with characters whose views of life are still forming, who are testing the waters of adulthood, by turns, with fear and courage. *The Folded Leaf* pictures both the freedoms and excruciating struggles of this time: the enigmatic yet overwhelming emotions that accompany physical and psychological growth, sexual awakenings, and the powerful desire to form adult relationships.

* * *

Maxwell said that when John Cheever first read the novel he observed "how much better 'fitted for life' Lymie was than Spud. I think he meant that one was open, an acceptor of people and experiences, and the other essentially closed by a sense of self-protection." Indeed, though certainly not "home-free," Lymie can look to his future with some degree of hope. Despite physical frailty and social meekness, despite his suicide attempt, he is unafraid to love and to be loved, to accept joy as well as pain, to observe, to learn, and to live fully. Perhaps this is the quality Louise Bogan saw in Maxwell's character even in the novel's early stages: Although the future may not be as bright as the full-blooming pear tree suggests, Lymie has the potential to endure, like Tennyson's folded leaf "woo'd from out the bud / With winds upon the branch, and there / Grows green and broad."[99]

5

Mature Novelist II:
Time Will Darken It
1945–48

IN SUMMER 1945, shortly after his marriage, Maxwell began writing *Time Will Darken It,* his fourth novel. "I had had the feeling that, for someone as happy as I was, writing was not possible," he wrote years later, "but one day, habit reasserting itself, I sat down at the typewriter and began describing an evening party in the year 1912. It took place in the house I lived in as a child. I seemed to have no more choice about this than one has about the background of a dream." Because his previous novels had been based on events from life, he had not faced uncertainty about the direction characters' lives would take, but with this book he said, "a set of characters seized me, and ran off with me. My function was simply to record what they said and did, rather than shape the goings on."[1]

Only in a few cases—in his fables and in the late story "Love"—did he describe writing as so actively passive, as a process in which characters' lives seemed to play out before him rather than being molded by him. Although an underlying motive revealed itself to him after he was well into the manuscript, at the outset he used no metaphor to conceptualize this work, no image to inspire structure or pacing as he had while writing *They Came Like Swallows* and *The Folded Leaf.* Rather, he wrote each morning of that summer, allowing the story to progress by characters' set conversations as if he were writing a play. When he started a new chapter, "it was a matter of figuring out which of them hadn't talked to each other lately." Usually around lunchtime, when he felt his "judgment faltered," he sat on the lawn behind his Yorktown Heights home and read what he had written that morning to Emily, who became the first and most trusted judge of his work. As Maxwell explained in 1992, "She reads it very slowly and carefully and more often than not smiles and says I think this is going to be one of your best stories. So I climb down from the euphoria and go back to the typewriter and eventually she smiles and says she likes it and then, and then only, do I know I have *done* it."[2]

The novel's 1912 party takes place in the home of Austin and Martha King, a young couple living in Draperville, Illinois, whose friends and neighbors have come to meet their houseguests from Mississippi, Mr. and Mrs. Potter and their young adult children, Nora and Randolph. Austin, an upstanding attorney who fulfills his obligations while naively overlooking the subtler aspects of personal relationships, has committed to host the relatives just as Martha begins a difficult second pregnancy. Beautiful but insecure, she is furious at his inconsideration yet attempts to be gracious to the visitors.

During the four-week summer visit, an elaborate web of relationships emerges: The Kings deal with marital discord behind their bedroom door while maintaining the appearance of decorum. Their neighbor, Mrs. Beach, cannily directs the activities of her two adult, single daughters, Lucy and Alice, while Mrs. Potter laments Nora's headstrong nature and unyielding distaste for cooking and sewing. Austin feels obliged to repay several friends who have made a bad investment misrepresented by Mr. Potter. And Rachel, the Kings' black servant, leaves Draperville when the drunken father of her children returns to town.

As in *The Folded Leaf,* the principal plot centers around a triangular relationship, this time between the Kings and Nora, who falls in love with Austin and stays in Draperville when the rest of the Potters return south. With Alice and Lucy Beach, she organizes and runs a Montessori kindergarten and then begs Austin to allow her to study his law books. Austin does not reciprocate Nora's feelings but allows her to read in his office each afternoon, prompting the "purveyors of local history" to spread rumors of adultery that severely damage his career. Nora's quest for an independent life in the North ends tragically after a disfiguring, dispiriting fire accident that prompts her abrupt return to Mississippi.

While writing the novel, Maxwell had trouble deciding whether Austin and Nora would consummate their relationship. "So I wrote it both ways," he said, "and continued to write it both ways, chapter after chapter. It was like a fork in the road. There was a chance, you know, I could do something experimental and publish them both, but it really wasn't what I wanted, so I faced the issue and decided that in the year 1912 he wouldn't have." That the author even considered publishing two versions of the story suggests his open attitude to new narrative methods, to varying his approach with each individual work. While his first two novels followed modes with which he was already familiar, he increasingly allowed his material to guide the structure of his fiction and experimented until he felt the inherent shape of his subject matter emerge. In this case, he threw away the more illicit account of the relationship: "It was a wasteful way of going about it," he said, "but I had to discover the form from the material." This process led him to more experimental novel writing later in his career.[3]

* * *

Time Will Darken It distinguishes itself from the author's five other novels as the least overtly autobiographical. Only limited details originate from unrelated events in Maxwell's family history: One summer during his early childhood, his Grandmother Maxwell's sister, who had married a Southern plantation owner, brought her Mississippi family north to Lincoln for a visit. As he writes in *Ancestors,* his Aunt Annette had been severely burned when she poured kerosene on a grate fire. And, before her marriage to Maxwell's father, his stepmother routinely walked door to door gathering children, including young Billie, for the walk to kindergarten as Nora does. As in *The Folded Leaf,* the narrator becomes a mouthpiece for the writer's observations and ideas; here, however, no character's life parallels his own. John Updike commended this approach, noting that characters who differ from an author are "the best realized in a way because you have to conceive them in the round. Your own self is kind of boundary-less....You don't really know what you're like. And so often things written out of the center of your experience are weaker than something written out of the margins. And that kind of reaching into the margins is something Bill did then, in *Time Will Darken It,* but he hasn't done a lot of it in later fiction."[4]

While Maxwell was writing the novel, "details flowed with absolute confidence through six or eight chapters," he recalled,

> Then, I had a dream that revealed to me where I was in fact going. The dream was close enough to what I was writing for me to grasp the fact that the husband in the novel represented my father and the wife my mother and the inadvertent troublemaker was the young woman who came to that last rehearsal [his stepmother]. And that it was because of what I had felt, long ago, sitting on the sofa beside my mother, that I had chosen to write about a triangular relationship that I knew instinctively would sustain me through the writing of the book, even though I had no idea how it would work out.[5]

Clearly, a psychoanalytic current was still coursing beneath his fiction. Through Theodor Reik, he had developed an acute awareness of the unconscious, which he used to explore character, experience, dreams, and time's passage. Without analysis, he might not have interpreted his latent emotional material in this way or been inspired to write this book at all. As he had envisioned traversing a flat plain while writing *The Folded Leaf,* now he followed internal terrain. His emotions surrounding the loss of his mother and the appearance of her replacement propelled his writing forward and, by novel's end, led him to restore his lost Eden by reordering the past.

As in none of his fiction before or after, *Time Will Darken It* undoes the tragedies of his early life: The mother does not die after childbirth, and she acknowledges emotional estrangement from the father. The "inadvertent troublemaker" who threatens to destroy the family's stability is defeated and banished. Although, like all Maxwell's fictional children, Abbey faces a world in which "the innocent and the young have to take their chances" against unforeseen tragedy, her childhood remains unshattered by disease, death, and irreversible change.[6] With her sensitive, introspective nature, she shares deep affinity with Bunny Morison in *They Came Like Swallows* and Lymie Peters in *The Folded Leaf,* yet, unlike them, she lives relatively undisturbed in an imaginative world, sequestered from adulthood yet aware of her place in the family and its circle of acquaintances. When awakened suddenly by grown-ups in the middle of the night, she is not terrorized with news of her mother's death like Bunny but relieved to overhear that her mother has made it through the operation and delivered her a brother. She is the child the author might have been, the one he would have chosen to be.

In this novel, Maxwell allowed a child respite from life-altering trauma just this once; as if in homage to Reik, his work here awakens "from a dream existence" the secret possibilities within his unconscious and celebrates what his analyst called the "second self," the life unlived.[7] Unlike *They Came Like Swallows* and the definitive version of *The Folded Leaf, Time Will Darken It* snuffs out completely the source of young Maxwell's debilitating pain and lifelong torment. It allows him to rectify wrongs, to create an altered version of his childhood beneath the surface of other characters' stories. In Reik's terms, Abbey need not struggle to be "home free" from past tragedy and grief like Lymie Peters, for she has been spared from disaster from the outset.

Critic James F. Maxfield recognized that with a basic knowledge of Maxwell's biography, "it is relatively easy to interpret the plot of *Time Will Darken It* as simple wish fulfillment"; more important to the success of the novel, of course, "the characterizations belie the simplicity of the underlying framework. Austin King, Martha King, and Nora Potter are all complicated human beings whose conflicts are brought to no more complete or satisfying resolutions than life normally provides.... Wherever they may have originated in the author's experiences and desires, he has conceived and presented them…with scarcely a trace of partiality or animus."[8] This even-handedness in depicting characters and circumstances with which he had close personal bonds was already characteristic of Maxwell. Indeed, one of his strengths as a writer was harnessing the unexpurgated core of his emotional life with objective detachment that afforded perspective and wisdom. Here, the novel's psychological underpinning becomes valuable as a source for understanding the author's latent motivations, how his analysis continued to influence his art, and, perhaps most importantly, how his exploration of the human condition became more complex through the decades. If his dream revealed suppressed desires that sustained his writing, his psychoanalytic experience offered a method for him to relate to, yet maintain distance from, his characters, to explore their inner natures while portraying the public moment that molded them. In short, he wrote a powerful novel with his own rewritten history submerged beneath lives fashioned from pure imagination. Aware of Maxwell's unconscious connections to the material—and of his working in the "margins," reaching beyond his own story—we gain a fuller sense of his creative life and can turn with new insight to the novel's people, historical perspective, human insight, and narrative art.

* * *

To this point, youth had been Maxwell's prime literary territory. Drawn instinctively to this stage of life, he had already distinguished his early career with truth-filled portraits of childhood and adolescence. Yet his vivid treatment of a grieving James Morison at the end of *They Came Like Swallows* predicted how he could bring the same insight to adulthood—a command of mature situations confirmed unequivocally in *Time Will Darken It*. One of Maxwell's most expansive novels, it shifts focus from childhood and adolescence to adult life, opening his work to a broader spectrum of perspectives, characters, and concerns. The Austin King family of Draperville, Illinois, the visiting Mississippi relatives, and a cadre of servants, neighbors, and townspeople create an elaborate network of relationships not found in his previous novels. Through adult eyes, Maxwell now explores intricacies of marriage and parenting as well as interactions between men and women, blacks and whites, and the middle class and its servants. His characteristic attention to the individual within a scene, his inclination toward interior monologue and character study, are balanced here with a detailed community chronicle, with his vision of a society that sprang from the broken prairie. For the first time in his career, he combines the subtle textures of daily life with a fuller view of the socioeconomic, psychological, and cultural dynamics of the early-century Midwestern town. Within this broader scene he develops the most complex, complete female characters in his body of fiction, an often-overlooked aspect of his work. And, after twelve years, he returns to the subject of African Americans in the heartland, writing of their lives in a more realistic mode and with greater authenticity than he had in *Bright Center of Heaven.*

Reading this novel as the fourth in Maxwell's sequence, one has the sense of hearing a familiar voice whose conversation has continued to evolve, mature, and crystallize. Its wise, compassionate, yet distanced tone emanates from the same sensibility as the narrator's in *The Folded Leaf;* its language and syntax share the same narrative style. In *Time Will Darken It,* for example, a reader comes upon this passage: "If you happen to be curious about the Indians in Venezuela, you can supply yourself with credentials from the ministry of Education and letters from various oil companies to their representatives in field camps. With your personal belongings and scientific instruments, including excavating tools for, say, a crew of twelve men . . . you can start digging and with luck unearth pottery and skeletons that have lain in the ground since somewhere around A.D. 1000." One is reminded immediately of the *Folded Leaf* narrator who similarly posed, "If it is the rites of puberty you are interested in, you can. . . ."[9] The sentence structure and anthropological references here are almost indistinguishable. Compared side by side, both narrators speak directly to the reader with a conversational but authoritative demeanor; they issue counsel confidently and interpret the human condition broadly yet incisively. These kindred voices not only provide transition from one novel to the next but also foster the impression of each as part of a larger, unified whole.

Like all his works, however, *Time Will Darken It* also suggests distinct developments. Its expanded scope prompts narrative adjustments that point his work in fresh directions. For one, the conversation-driven composition creates a looser, less studied structure than in his previous work. While reading *They Came Like Swallows,* for example, one is particularly aware of craftsmanship: the tripartite design carefully controls the story's advancement through strategic point-of-view shifts. By contrast, events seem to unfold naturally here; characters interact at a lifelike, variable pace, resulting in a longer, more expansive work that focuses with a wider lens. This broader concentration leads Maxwell to develop further the commentaries he introduced in *The Folded Leaf* by giving his narrator greater latitude to observe and philosophize. Although this change may seem natural and subtle, it becomes important to his evolution as a writer in that it allows him to interpret a fuller spectrum of human life and to articulate directly the body of ideas that shape his work. This time his meditations are less likely to be driven by the desire to universalize, to lend significance to characters' lives by juxtaposing their early-twentieth-century Midwest with ancient civilizations. Rather than serve primarily as a writer's tool that offers cultural context, the narrator becomes increasingly proactive. He not only advances opinions on everything from women and their relationships with men to gossip, death, and racial prejudice but also is the first to speak expressly about two of the author's most fundamental and related themes: the nature of history and the significance of art.

Here, through his narrator's words, Maxwell's ethos begins to solidify. His passion for preserving the past finds expression. Through reflections on storytelling, he explores connections between narrative and the human condition. Here, too, his intuitive yet intellectual understanding of life's delicate counterpoise finds voice. In short, this narrator makes primary statements on the core concerns of the writer's fiction and conveys the essence of issues and philosophical positions that will continue to develop throughout his career. Considered collectively, the interpretive asides in *Time Will Darken It* provide an artist's sketch of the ideas that underscore his body of work.

* * *

History, at least in a personal sense, has been a key motivation for Maxwell's writing since *They Came Like Swallows*. New to his work ten years later, however, is his narrator's direct discussion of history, both private and public. *Time Will Darken It* addresses the subject with straightforward, reader-directed commentary and wide-ranging interpretation of its complexity and value: What do we know of the past? Through what means do we understand it? How does it impinge on the present? Characteristically, his contemplation of history begins on home territory; for him, the greatest mysteries are the most elemental and personal. Particularly poignant is his narrator's meditation on parents—especially those who, like the author's mother, have died, and so are part of the enigmatic past. "There is nothing so difficult to arrive at as the nature and personality of one's parents," the narrator reflects:

> Death, about which so much mystery is made, is perhaps no mystery at all. But the history of one's parents has to be pieced together from fragments, their motives and character guessed at, and the truth about them remains deeply buried, like a boulder that projects one small surface above the level

of smooth lawn, and when you come to dig around it, proves to be too large ever to move, though each year's frost forces it up a little higher.[10]

The intimacy of this observation and the straightforward simplicity with which it inverts conventional thinking about the human condition are pure Maxwell. As is often the case in his work, the past's puzzles connect inextricably to maternal and paternal figures; a focus on the private realm reconsiders the import of life's most basic elements. Like the boulder pushing up from the grass, the narrator suggests, personal history reveals itself incompletely: For every fact unearthed, myriad truths lie beneath impenetrable soil. In this case, he maintains that the omnipresent mystery of death—the "grand" life question—is perhaps no mystery at all. More complex, more incomprehensible is the essential character of those with whom one shares the most fundamental, biological relationships. After *They Came Like Swallows,* such "smaller" realms assume profound significance in his work, overshadowing "larger" issues as the primary source for discovering history's texture and truth. The aspects of life closest to us, the narrator infers, may be more than they appear to be; they may be the most mysterious and perplexing of all. Zona Gale's influence resonates here: In their talks twenty years earlier, she had introduced him to her belief in a secret nature of things that are something more than they seem to be. Throughout his life, Maxwell remembered only this topic of their conversations, an idea so sacred to his mentor that it was etched on the flat surface of her own gravestone projecting above the smooth lawn of the Portage, Wisconsin, cemetery.

Another scene with Austin methodically pasting family snapshots into a big, black scrapbook becomes an occasion to universalize, to recognize that his volume was one among millions—"part of a set, of the great American encyclopaedia of sentimental occasions, family gatherings, and stages in the growth of children." Yet the moment also evolves into contemplation of the artifacts through which humans know history (photographs in this case), a meditation on the impulse to chronicle and construct what happened, and an acknowledgement of the ironies inherent in all historical knowledge. The narrator's list of forty of these "encyclopaedia" photos—"of statues in parks…children playing in the sand…girls with young men they did not marry…the cat that did not stay to have its picture taken…the son in uniform, standing beside the back steps, on a day when the light was not right for taking kodak pictures"—seem to capture private lives with camera-eye precision. On closer observation, they reveal people not necessarily immersed in the natural rhythm of living but in actively conserving and formulating a reality for future recollection. Seldom is there "any pretence that the subjects were doing anything but having their pictures taken."[11] Yet considered another way, preserving time through family photography itself becomes a natural part of living, from posing before the camera to pasting curling photographs on album pages. Saving the moment for posterity is a celebrated ritual, at times the central activity of the present.

Maxwell identifies intimately with this human affinity for preservation; the early loss of his childhood and desire to recapture that place in time motivates his narrator's commentaries here. Austin's photo album not only reveals a glimpse of the importance placed on constructing a record for the future but leads the narrator to question the reliability of these visual documents: Once a moment passes over into history, how do we know it? How may we be certain of the details that made up yesterday's world? Whereas many photos seem familiar, others, for whatever they explain, prompt further questions, including "who held the camera? ... What person voluntarily absented himself ... in order to preserve for posterity the image he saw through the [lens]?" What can one make of the photo of four women seated on a picnic blanket gazing at a young man at their side who appears to hold a revolver? Or of the picture "with the centre torn out of it, leaving an oval-shaped hole surrounded by porch railing, lawn, trees, a fragment of a woman's skirt, and the sky?" Captions scribbled beneath photos reveal little more: "Just after the smash upon the mountain" and "The Hermitage 1910" provoke questions of what, where, and when that cannot be answered. Like the ripped, ragged photo, the narrator implies, historical intelligence is fragmentary; as he reminds us later in the novel, "the truth is necessarily partial. Every vision of completeness is a distortion in one way or another, whether it springs from sickness or sanctity."[12]

Yet despite such mystery, the narrator suggests that static, fading photographs may subtly illuminate the sepia-washed tones of American prairie life before twentieth-century global conflict. In the faces, he finds a "strange absence of tension that exists in all casual photographs taken before the First World War."[13] The camera, then, may capture an unmistakable mood, a telling expression; its photos may reveal the face of a gentler, less complicated era. Or perhaps the narrator, influenced by the benefit of hindsight, finds in them a calm before catastrophe because he seeks it. Herein lies the challenge: Readers are reminded that historical clues in our personal scrapbooks—as well as in the metaphoric, collective one—are contradictory. At once, they reveal and mislead.

Venturing outside the King household, the narrator correlates the archeological excavation of Venezuelan Indian remains with his attempt to "arrive at some idea of the culture of a certain street in a Middle Western small town shortly before the First World War." This endeavor "is a much more delicate undertaking," he maintains, for "there are no ruins to guide you. Though the houses are not kept up as well as they once were, they are still standing. Of certain barns and outbuildings that are gone…you will find no trace whatever." Unlike the ancient Indian environ, the American neighborhood has inhabitants. Even so, "the people who live on Elm Street now belong to a different civilization. They can tell you nothing."[14] This stifling silence, this total break in generational communication suggests defeat for the curious cultural excavator. Yet although grief over collective memory loss is perhaps never stated more plainly in Maxwell's work, one can imply as the narrative continues that perhaps the silence is breakable. Perhaps, he suggests, story-telling can dispel mystery, abate the loss of personal and communal heritage, restore images ripped from photos of our private and public pasts.

In this spirit, and with true yet objective benevolence, the narrator recreates, interprets, and lends wider relevance to the community's historical layers. He remembers the pristine prairie that yielded to Draperville long before 1912 and foresees how modern life will derail "the gentle Calvinistic era" guarded by town elders. This broad historical view pairs with a celebration of the rich minutiae of early-century, small-town life: genteel summer parties, dusty carriage rides, and Draperville children who, like their German counterparts around the globe, pull parades of candlelit shoeboxes along the sidewalk. On-site practitioners of Draperville history conduct research—over the back fence, over the telephone, over the bridge table, in the back seats of carriages—in order to keep careful record of children born too soon after wedding ceremonies. Two miles south of town, at the wooded Chautauqua grounds, Draperville residents spend summers at cooking classes, light opera performances, lectures by William Jennings Bryan, and viewings of the local potter's bust of Marie Antoinette. An awareness of the passing generations, of the changing social landscape, underlies the town's psyche: Older citizens sit shocked and disapproving of jovial musical entertainment on Sundays, and the Chautauqua museum holds historical relics including "a gourd used as a powder flask during the battle of Fort Meigs." "Historically important objects useful in their own right are seldom found in museums," the narrator observes. The Chautauqua archive, for example, does not contain "the first hoe that shaved the prairie grass and so brought an end to one of the wonders of the world."[15]

Personal, emotional loss is heightened here by a foreboding sense that the country at large verges on upheaval. The narrator understands that the prairie town plowed under the prairie, that post–Civil War industry altered the agrarian society, and that international war looms on the horizon. He turns to storytelling, to the creation of narratives both formal and ordinary to excavate and preserve the nuance of passing eras, to rescue the past from collective memory loss without sentimentality.

This sense of mending, or at least offsetting, the ravages of time is suggested in the title Emily Maxwell found for her husband's novel. An artist herself, she had come upon the phrase "time will darken it" in the writings of painter Francisco Pacheco (1564–1654), who wrote an influential study of Spanish art in the seventeenth century and whose discussion of oil painting technique was excerpted for the novel's epigraph. On first consideration, the title words seem menacing, as if time will ominously shadow future circumstances. Taken out of context, they suggest nature's clock advancing heedless of humanity (as in *They Came Like Swallows*), the past languishing into oblivion. Yet Pacheco provides for a degree of human control in the face of time's passing. He describes how a painter's oils must be mixed with enough white to produce a bright tint: "It must not be dark," he writes. "On the contrary, it must be rather on the light side because time will darken it."[16] Indeed, time will fade a painting's colors, just as it will dim the details of memory. Yet Pacheco affirms the artist's ability to anticipate and compensate for time's effect on paint, just as the writer counters its passage by preserving the past with words. In essence, art can outwit hours, if only partially, and although nature may have the final word, artistic endeavor lends consequence, power, and grace to human life.

Maxwell took seriously the artist's role as preserver. Like Pacheco, he sought to neutralize time's effects through creative means, to safeguard the past and establish human significance amid a fleeting, uncertain existence. Certainly these aims are implicit throughout literature and the other arts, but for Maxwell they become particularly significant here. The narrator in *Time Will Darken It* provides the first direct discussion of storytelling in the author's work, the first allusions to the challenges and intricacies of artistic production and form. At this point his contemplations on the nature of fiction are brief and limited; nevertheless, they provide early hints of the author's self-referential prose and predict work still decades away in which imaginative writing becomes an increasingly important, and ultimately central, theme.

In one scene, the narrator's ruminations reveal both the author's philosophy about storytelling and, as Geoffrey Stokes has also noted, the ways in which stories expose their tellers. When mischievous Randolph Potter visits

Rachel, the Kings' cook, in the kitchen, he launches into a story about his friend, Griswold, a crippled boy from his Southern hometown who "notices everything," he says, "especially people's weak points, and that way, when the time comes, he gets what he wants. The other day. . . ." Here, the narrator interrupts briefly: "Most people, when they are describing a friend or telling a story, make the mistake of editing, of leaving things out," he explains. "Fearing that their audience will grow restless, they rush ahead to the point, get there too soon, have to go back and explain, and in the end, the quality of experience is not conveyed. Randolph was never in a hurry, never in doubt about whether what he had to say would interest Rachel."[17]

By the time Maxwell wrote this brief passage on storytelling, his ideas on the subject had crystallized: He had spent more than ten years publishing his own fiction and logged nearly that as a *New Yorker* editor poring over the pages of such modern masters as John Cheever and J. D. Salinger. He also remembered stories from his Lincoln childhood: anecdotes of his Aunt Annette's trips to Mackinac Island, Michigan; his brother's tragic carriage accident; and his Grandfather Blinn's ferret bite that caused fatal blood poisoning. From his perspective, for a story to capture the breath of life, it must neither omit detail nor be subjected to undue editing. Coming from an editor, this statement may seem ironic, yet it suggests the narrative balance he attempted. As a writer, he desired to include every necessary nuance while also striving for economy. This approach resulted in a style that became increasingly spare in the later decades of his career. Accordingly, as an editor, he proceeded with a light touch geared toward ensuring that the writer "said what he meant and meant what he said." Although, unlike Randolph, Maxwell had occasional doubts about the universal interest of his stories, he ultimately came to believe that if he was attracted to a topic, there were bound to be readers who were also.[18] And so, like his character, he created a narrative without slighting specifics, without rushing or backtracking. Particularly in *Time Will Darken It,* this approach creates a world that is fully seen—a textured portrait of the small-town Midwest circa 1912.

By the time Randolph finishes the story of his friend, Griswold, Rachel "had a very clear idea in her mind of the crippled boy who knew how to wait for what he wanted, and she also knew one more thing about Randolph Potter"—namely that he had hurt the Kings' dog before it bit him. As Stokes wrote in 1985, this scene "presciently conveys the risky path [Maxwell's] fiction has followed for more than half a century: Tell the story—tell it *all,* for otherwise there is no use telling any—but words are double-edged. At the end, they will expose *you.*"[19] Clearly, despite the autobiographical roots of much of his fiction, the author did not want to expose himself through words as Randolph does, but he knew that some level of exposure was inevitable. Even at this stage, long before Maxwell's late, more self-disclosing work, Randolph's circumstance suggests how a story and its presentation provide some essential knowledge of the teller, even if specific life events are not revealed. Through the decades, the author will continue to develop his own mode of autobiographical fiction, to create an imagined universe informed by his own experiences and insights, and, if the material demands, to enter the scene himself as a peripheral or central character. Here, however, he remains a behind-the-scenes philosopher, a guiding sensibility fronted by the narrator's commentary.

Maxwell's use of fiction as a subject develops naturally here in his narrator's discussions. Observations about Draperville turn easily toward ways people use language to preserve, explain, and interpret their lives—a matter at the center of his personal and literary concerns. Considered alone, these remarks might be viewed as mere footnotes that predict literary art as a major theme of his later work. In combination with Pacheco's words, they become a thematic underpinning built on the writer's ideas about the potential of fiction to rescue experience from time's plow; they reflect his interest in art as a source of strength in an unpredictable world. Emily Maxwell had a keen, sensitive eye in correlating her husband's work with Pacheco's instructions for landscape painting, for the artist's directions mirror the author's own novelistic modes and intentions. In the epigraph, Pacheco's words read in part,

> Once the sky, which is the upper half of the canvas, is done, you proceed to paint the ground, beginning with the mountains bordering on the sky. They will be painted with the lightest smalt-and-white tints, which will be somewhat darker than the horizon, because the ground is always darker than the sky, especially if the sun is on that side. These mountains will have their lights and darks, because it is the custom to put in the lowest part—after finishing—some towns and small trees. . . .
>
> As you get nearer the foreground, the trees and houses shall be painted larger, and if desired they may rise above the horizon. . . . In this part it is customary to use a practical method in putting in the details, mingling a few dry leaves among the green ones. . . . And it is very praiseworthy to make the grass on the ground look natural for this section is nearest the observer.[20]

Equally exacting in its perspective, the composition of *Time Will Darken It* seems to derive from this very method. From background to foreground, broad-sweeping horizon to family breakfast table, Maxwell creates a panorama of small-town Illinois with varying depths of field. Like a Pacheco landscape, the novel encompasses a series of minor scenes within its overall frame, some of which are left unresolved, and pictures the setting's multiple planes.

On Maxwell's canvas, the interior spaces seem nearest us, for they are described most intimately and meticulously and have the closest connections to the story's characters. In *Time Will Darken It,* as in his previous novels, these spaces become entwined with emotional life. As Bunny's imaginative visions of home create his sense of his place in the world, the Kings' kitchen and living rooms become integral to the way they interact with and understand each other. Painted with striking detail, the home constitutes a breathing presence in the family members' lives as they welcome visitors, live with servants, and contemplate privately their innermost thoughts and desires. Furniture, clocks, and other household objects again become animated as essential parts of a living household. Maxwell was a master at creating the texture of home life: Even a dry leaf that had "drifted in and was now resting on the edge of the rag carpet" appears, one of the very details Pacheco mentions in his discussion of painting a foreground.[21]

As the author wrote in his foreword to a 1992 edition of the novel, he believed that this story "needed things for the eyes to rest on. Houses all up and down a quiet street. Hitching posts. Elm trees arching over the brick pavement. Sounds, too: the ice cream wagon, the locust and the katydid. And smells from the kitchen or the pigpen." Here in the middle ground of his portrait, between barren skyline and individual intimacies, lie details that create a definite sense of time and place, talismans of a specific social moment: the wooded Chautauqua grounds, bay windows, broad porches, and Victorian carpenter's lace adorning the small-town architecture. However, Maxwell's prairie vistas provide the starkest, most breathtaking view: "The flayed landscape of the western prairie does little to remind the people who live there of the covenant of works or the covenant of grace," he writes;

> The sky, visible right down to the horizon, has a diminishing effect upon everything in the foreground, and the distance is as featureless and remote as the possibility of punishment for slander. The roads run straight, with death and old age intersecting at right angles, and the harvest is stored in cemeteries.[22]

The spatial depth here—the relationship between background and foreground, the optical effect of diminution—suggests the writer's keen awareness of the landscape's aesthetic composition and its psychological power. Like Pacheco's landscapes, the scene seems drawn in stages, from the furthest plane to the most immediate. It sweeps from the sky to the horizon below, then projects toward us, to forms attenuated by the backdrop of earth and sky, both vast and vague. Finally, with edgy, phantasmal imagery, the passage enters an internal perspective, a view not so much seen as hallucinated. Description yields to a sort of free association. The narrator's grim meditation, not uncharacteristic of those in this novel, creates a bleak, macabre mood on Maxwell's prairie; by the last sentence it turns surrealistic and nightmarish, as if combing the darker corners of the unconscious.

Artistic composition, then, both visual and literary, becomes an underlying motif in *Time Will Darken It*. Perhaps most obviously, the narrator comments on the human propensity for telling stories: "There is always a kind of truth in those fictions which people create in order to describe something too complicated and too subtle to fit into any conventional pattern," he observes. Francisco Pacheco searched for truth through his own medium: As the title-inspiring epigraph, his description of painting adds dimension to the theme and imbues the novel with a sense of artistic creation and unity. His assertion that "time will darken" paint not only provides insight into his technique but also incites the idea that art may have the power to outmaneuver time's hold on humanity. In his own descriptive passages, Maxwell appears to adapt Pacheco's words about the planes of a landscape, or, perhaps more likely, Mrs. Maxwell was reminded of her husband's verbal portraits when she read the artist's directives and so suggested the correlation. Regardless, the writer's awareness of the landscape's composition sends readers away with a strong visual impression—an impression, Pacheco might suggest, based on the execution of sound artistic method.

Certainly, in the context of the entire novel, this theme is a subtle one. Even so, it enriches both the work's content and form, lends a philosophic framework to Maxwell's character and community study, and provides insight into the development of his writing. Over the next thirty years, this fine thematic thread evolved into one of the major subjects of his late work; the nature of narrative became the axis around which his stories revolved. Indeed, Emily Maxwell did more than present her husband with a title for his novel. She deepened its artistry by connecting it to Pacheco's; she recognized the painter's ideas as a thematic subtext that both reflects the novel's literary intentions and extends its scope.

Maxwell and Gender

The novel's focus on adult life compels Maxwell to explore how men and women both relate to one another and function independently in the community setting, topics he had not considered expressly in earlier work. Here, he presents their respective spheres as separate yet equally significant: Austin's realm of business and law does not take precedence over the domestic domain sustained by Martha with the help of African American servants. Although both men and women make distinct contributions to life in Draperville, they are plagued by expectations that create a fissure between them on both collective and individual levels. The narrator observes that in 1912, "the split in the Republican Party was as nothing compared to the split between the men and women." During the opening Victorian party scene, women sit on one side of the room "with their tedious recipes and their preoccupation with children's diseases," and men defend their "favourite misconceptions" on the other. Only Draperville's young, "ready for courtship," and old, "bent on preserving the traditions of gallantry," speak to each other. "They met as ambassadors," the narrator suggests, "and kept open the lines of communication between the sexes." Perhaps the women's subject matter drives the men away, the narrator muses; perhaps the men, "knowing how nervous the women became when their husbands' voices were raised in political argument, withdrew of their own accord." In either case, Draperville women occupy themselves with cooking, sewing, meeting family emotional needs, and guiding community fellowship. With their self-worth and identity inextricably linked to the state of their home and family, they have neither inclination nor incentive to entertain intellectual, commercial, or political perspectives on the society at large.[23]

In this sense, Maxwell's portrait of women's dreams and frustrations, outlooks and socialization, shares close affinity with that of female authors a generation or so before him who were writing about the same general time period. Women characters in the novels of Willa Cather, Ellen Glasgow, Edith Wharton, Kate Chopin, and Anzia Yezierska, provide his Nora Potter, Martha King, and the Beach "girls" a spiritual sisterhood of sorts; despite diverse backgrounds, they are connected by the attitudes and obstacles of their era, by the "New Woman" movement that advocated female fulfillment beyond the home and challenged patriarchal order beginning in the late nineteenth century.

Regardless of such similarities, however, Maxwell's view holds key differences: Although, like the female novelists, he clearly illustrates limitations faced by the era's women, he simultaneously privileges the importance and value of home life. In contrast, the life of the American man seems dramatically overrated to him. Although he clearly contends that women should not be shackled by social expectations, he seems to warn that the world beyond the home may not be what they dream it to be. In his eyes, men occupy an even less enviable position: Taking an unexpected, unconventional stance, he implies that although their public preeminence may appear to serve them well, it actually may hinder their development as people, their ability to discern life and truth clearly. He sees men such as Austin King as unwittingly limited in their dominant roles as household heads and participants in the public exchange of ideas and capital. The trappings of their position—a sanctioned place at the civic table, confidence they are dealing in consequential matters—may render them blind to crucial nuances, may lead them to miss the merit of more "modest" aims and outlooks. As a result, their perception of reality may be partial, their quality of life and happiness diminished, and at times their judgment undermined. This view of the male condition runs throughout Maxwell's work. While his previous novels placed physical and cerebral males side by side, here he develops a man with conventional "sense" rather than sensibility—a continuation of his ongoing exploration of masculinity.

Meanwhile, the vital work of humanity takes place in the woman's domain, in the interior spaces of home, heart, and mind. This attention to home life continues to set his work in the domestic novel tradition and, especially in *Time Will Darken It*, lends historical and cultural value to his work. Such sensibilities remove him from the milieu of the stereotypic *New Yorker* writer preoccupied with postwar problems of the educated, male Manhattanite. Although the home environment had always been his natural territory, here he contrasts it directly with the male-dominated arena beyond the family sanctum.

Home becomes a primary focus for this narrator, a setting in which to explore female roles and life choices in the early twentieth century. Women in Maxwell's previous novels are viewed at some distance: In *They Came Like Swallows*, Elizabeth Morison is the pivotal figure, yet her story is told solely through the perspectives of her two sons and husband. Although *The Folded Leaf* introduces two interesting female students, the drama unfolds primarily through Lymie's and Spud's eyes; little is known about the women's own thoughts and reflections. In contrast, *Time Will Darken It* depicts a triangular relationship from the viewpoints of all three characters and focuses particular attention on the inner lives of the women involved. This change demonstrates how he gravitated toward creating realities far beyond his own and wrote from perspectives he could only imagine; here, female characters, both white and black, become fully formed. Scenes often filter through their perspectives, revealing how social situations shape their actions and attitudes.

Diverse women struggle with both public precepts and private circumstances in their attempts to direct their own lives. The novel's central women struggle in their community and family roles as well as in their relationships with men.

Among them is Nora Potter, the young, Southern interloper whose infatuation with Austin sets in motion the novel's central conflict. Restless, searching, naive, and highly inquisitive, she constantly absorbs herself with questions about society and her place in it. Because her parents believe that marriage, family, and entry into genteel Southern society should be their daughter's goal, they forbid her education. But to her mother's consternation, she reads voraciously and attempts to discuss her developing thoughts and philosophies with women who ignore her. Repelled by the traditional itinerary her mother imposes and by what she considers crippling nostalgia in the post–Civil War South, Nora imagines a life free from constraints. "Sometimes I wish I were a nigger or an Indian or anything that would keep me from having to be myself, Nora Potter, who goes to parties and pays calls, and sits by quietly, with nothing to say while Mama does all the talking," she tells one of the Kings' guests. "At home I wake up in a world that's always remembering something—the way things used to be. And trying to get back. And there isn't any getting back, so of course there isn't really any waking up." To counter this stagnation, Nora passionately explores spiritual, intellectual, professional, and romantic prospects, hoping to discover her personal calling. She perceives the prairie town as a fresh opportunity, a forward-thinking "foreign country" where she might finally exercise her mind rather than politely defer to her mother's idle, passive way of life. In the Midwest "the past doesn't hang over you" the way it does in the suffocating South, she observes upon her arrival. "You wake up in the morning and it's that morning you wake up to."[24]

Yet, as is often the case in Maxwell's work, things are not as they seem. Nora's impression of Illinois is an illusion; the interminable horizon signals neither a perpetual fresh start nor freedom from social strictures. Although the years between the Civil War and World War I have transpired less dramatically in Draperville than in the South, there is a past to wake to on the prairie. Indeed, Midwestern characters here become haunted, even debilitated, by their private pasts.

Despite her naiveté, Nora is a sympathetic figure. She refuses to compromise her ideals and stands firmly against her parents by staying in Draperville as a Montessori teacher. At the same time, however, she becomes loquacious, impulsive, and unbalanced. With her Southern family and community as paradigms, she can easily articulate what she does *not* want her life to be yet has difficulty defining what she *does* desire. Lacking any suitable role models, she cannot pinpoint a plan for her future; she cannot visualize what she wants. Without academic guidance, her intellect does not keep pace with her enthusiasm. Like other young, hopeful women of her time—in life as well as literature—she becomes frustrated by her lack of alternatives, the elusiveness of an existence that might expand her frame of reference, and the daunting, intense effort needed to pursue it.

In Draperville, Nora hopes to progress toward her aims. At the Kings' summer party her "blue-violet eyes were searching gravely for something that was not to be found in this living room or this town or perhaps anywhere, but that nevertheless might exist somewhere, if you had the courage and the patience and the time to go on looking for it."[25] But Nora has neither courage, patience, nor time: Rather than thoughtfully evaluate her new situation, she frantically flits from one incident to the next, from one person to another, in search of meaningful pursuits, rewarding relationships, and self-affirmation. Alone in her quandary, she often lacks the resources to make informed, rational decisions. Her desperation and inexperience result in indiscretions and misjudgments, both slight and serious, that intensify and complicate her confusion. She confronts Austin with her love for him and sneaks a personal letter from his bureau. Mindless of the aggravation and anguish she causes Martha, Nora attempts to engage her in inane philosophical conversations and through her daily presence chips away the Kings' fragile equilibrium and their relationship with the community.

To Maxwell's credit, Nora defies stereotypes: She is neither a dizzy, lovestruck ingénue nor a young woman of such exceptional strength that she can overcome forces beyond her control. Rather, he portrays the challenges, conflicts, and motives of an exuberant youth whose enthusiasm and curiosity are dampened by naiveté, misjudgment, and social attitudes. Each positive step she takes, each admirable quality she possesses, becomes thwarted by failings from within and without. Her refusal to capitulate to expectations, for example, suggests a degree of spiritual strength, yet her attempts to control the course of her life are capricious and misdirected. She is drawn to Austin, at least in part, because he is free from constraints that bind her: He possesses the autonomy, intellect, and public role that, in the abstract, she imagines for herself. Unfortunately, because she romanticizes and idealizes Austin, she can neither relate to him as a mentor nor pursue her goals independently. Her young life follows the tragic pattern with which Maxwell is concerned—ironically, her search ends when answers seem close at hand.

Even richer and more complex is the portrayal of Martha King, one of the most fully realized women in Maxwell's fiction. In this sensitive portrait, he focuses on the inner life of a married woman for the first time, poignantly depicting her perspective through courtship, marriage, and pregnancy. Martha has not actively piloted the direction of her life but has allowed it to transpire; she understands too late that, by allowing fate to determine her husband, she has not only failed to make the right decision but has failed to make any. As a wife and mother in a financially comfortable household, she exerts little if any control over her circumstances: Servants cook, keep the house, and tend to her daughter. Her husband decides to entertain the Southern houseguests. Feeling trapped and insecure, she can neither communicate with him nor find activity to fill her monotonous days.

Martha's personal contemplations and history first unfold in a scene in which she methodically cuts to pieces her party dress. The writer's technique is especially effective here: Juxtaposing images of her past and present and her own viewpoint with that of Austin and the omniscient narrator, he develops a textured account of her private and public personas. Moments when she snips, in stages, the garment's silk rose, sash, and lace inset interweave with flashbacks revealing her disdain for her Methodist upbringing and trepidation over Austin's awkward, relentless pursuit of her. As the narrative shifts between her thoughts of insecurity and Austin's, the narrator meditates on their behavior—as well as on the nature of the sexes in general—unifying and universalizing their lives.

Through disclosures about the Kings' past lives, the dress scene reveals how hurtful communication gaps in their marriage have evolved. Austin's clumsy courtship incites a relationship often marred by ambiguous, misinterpreted messages, both verbal and physical. Approaching life with separate perspectives and behaviors, the two young people are hampered by learned misconceptions and unrealistic expectations. The narrator observes, "Boys brought up the way Austin King was brought up are taught, along with table manners, to create a handsome high pedestal and put the woman they admire on it, for purposes of worship. What they are not taught is how to get her off the pedestal, for purposes of love." These notions put him at cross-purposes with Martha's desires. Raised in a strict Protestant environment filled with the "complacent, oversweet" smiles of people "singing their way to eternal salvation," she wanted to be neither saved nor worshiped. She longed for excitement, an end to composure and control: "Wasn't there anyone, she asked herself, standing on the church steps in the brilliant sunshine, or holding a plate of strawberry ice cream at a church social—wasn't there someone who would give her the sense of danger, a man who would look at her and make everything go dim around her?"[26]

Rather than search for an answer to her question, Martha becomes what the narrator calls a fish "with a hook in its mouth," attempting to escape yet being reeled in by her own destiny. She rebuffs Austin's proposal yet resists ending their relationship.[27] When he speaks of their joint future as a foregone conclusion, she does not protest. When he begins to invent children and a house with apple trees, she flees to Indianapolis. Ultimately, during her train ride home, she surrenders her future to fate. If Austin is waiting at the station, she will marry him; if he is not, their life was not meant to be. After accepting her conscientious suitor's proposal, she changes her mind, but the pinions of engagement have already been set in motion.

The narrator condemns neither party for Martha's predicament. Whether because of the society that molded her, her lack of resolve, or her inability to find an acceptable role for herself, Martha fails to direct her young life. Like Nora, she adamantly rejects her parents' views yet does not readily perceive satisfactory alternatives. Rather than explore options as Nora does, however unsuccessfully, Martha succumbs to an anxious, love-professing suitor despite her deep reservations. She accepts a life and love offered for the taking rather than make her own choices.

Martha's disillusion culminates in the bedroom, where her dress shearing becomes a metaphor for her frustration. As she begins her alterations, she seems absorbed in her traditional role, a woman contentedly contemplating the dress's effect in the mirror, refashioning it with carefully considered adjustments. But suddenly, "with reckless gleam in her eyes, burn[ing] her bridges behind her," she decides the dress is unattractive and cuts it to pieces; calmly, she folds and stores remnants "of what used to be Austin's favorite dress" among her sewing materials.[28] In light of her husband's particular fondness for the gown, Martha's drastic cutting signals a private declaration of independence of sorts—a quiet, clandestine act of free will. Her moment of resolve seems particularly poignant woven among memories of her restless youth and uncomfortable courtship. Seen in context with her past, it represents rejection of the man she believes entrapped her in marriage and regret for her early decision to relinquish her freedom. Her cutting reflects dissatisfaction with her circumstances, with her socially insulated and emotionally isolated role as a young, middle-class woman who craves a fuller, more daring life in the small, early-twentieth-century town. Although Martha's version of "burning her bridges" might seem tame to some readers, it does suggest her attempt to break free, to rip the seams of restrictive mores propounded by her church and the town "historians." Her actions and reflections in solitude, in this and subsequent scenes, are depicted with an acute awareness of female socialization, with a palpable, even biting sense of her disappointments, desires, and acquiescence.

Although a minor character, Martha's four-year-old daughter, Abbey, is particularly compelling not only as a female but also as the sole child in an adult-centered novel and the character with whom Maxwell felt particular affinity. Although more than two-thirds of *They Came Like Swallows* focuses exclusively through the eyes of the Morison boys, her reality is glimpsed only intermittently, yet in carefully chosen, vivid scenes. Here, through his narrator, the writer directly articulates his views about childhood. He believes that as for all children, the pattern of her future life will be determined by her own "incalculable strength and weakness" despite her seeming helplessness.[29] Clearly Bunny, Robert, and Lymie would harness their own strength to endure unforeseen tragedy, as did the author himself.

Yet Abbey may face additional stumbling blocks on her way to maturity. There is no indication that she will grow up more secure in her choices, more in control of her life than her mother was. At a very early age she learns that "her hair was too fine and too thin to be admired. Both of these drawbacks had been pointed out, not to the little girl but unfortunately in her presence." When she asks whether there will be children to play with at the party, Austin tells her, "No, this is a grown-up party and you mustn't interrupt people when they are talking, do you hear? Just be quiet and watch, and afterwards everybody will say, 'What a nice little girl.'"[30] Clearly a well-intentioned Austin hopes to foster in his young daughter qualities appropriate and beneficial for her future life. Before reaching school age, she understands that she will be judged by her physical qualities and praised for withholding her ideas. Even though the Kings' views on education and women may be more progressive than the Potters', Abbey's early conditioning plants feelings of insecurity and submission. Depending on the skills, talents, and interests she develops, she may, like Nora, become frustrated by the roles and sacrifices adulthood has in store.

For Lucy and Alice Beach, a life heavily supervised by their controlling mother has left them, at ages forty-seven and forty-three, the "Beach girls," the town old maids. Unlike other Draperville women, the Beaches have been exposed to music, art, and European travel. Lucy especially has shown keen interest in singing and for a short time took voice lessons from the teacher of the renowned Geraldine Farrar. "My daughter Lucy could have had a career on the concert stage in Europe but I wouldn't allow her to. I didn't want her to be subjected to unpleasant experiences," Mrs. Beach tells Mrs. Potter at the Kings' party.[31] Despite the narrator's hints that Mrs. Beach exaggerates her daughter's musical talent—it seems Lucy was actually dismissed by Farrar's singing teacher—the mother's comments may also suggest that even had Lucy been a fine singer, she would not have been permitted to use her talents outside the home. Ultimately, her music would be valued for contributing gentility and pleasantry to social life rather than for its artistry.

Ironically, despite their unusually broad cultural opportunities, Lucy and Alice find no more happiness or satisfaction than Martha or Nora, who, despite their own difficulties, did not allow their mothers to manage them. Although the Beach sisters become engaged with the possibilities of intellectual and artistic pursuits, they are neither expected nor allowed to participate beyond a social level. Mrs. Beach provides opportunities merely to enhance her daughters' standing and appeal, to promote their refinement. Once back in Draperville, they are expected to find suitable mates or, in lieu of that, to tend to their aging mother.

Unfortunately, although the Montessori kindergarten becomes a promising new outlet for their aspirations, it ultimately represents the submission and missed opportunity that has dominated their lives. After the school fire and closure, Lucy's knowledge of what she has missed leads to intense frustration; her education has become a cruel taunt, illuminating possibilities she will never realize, inciting ambition she must squelch. In the attic among the barely used kindergarten furniture, she suddenly finds the equipment "too bright and too fresh to be what it really was, the death of all her hopes." When the younger Alice remains optimistic about their futures, Lucy levels a disturbing opinion: "People call us the Beach girls but we're no spring chickens, either of us. We've had our chance and missed it, and I'm so tired I don't care anymore.... I don't know why people don't tell you when you're young that life is tiring." Knowing that her sister has not yet reached a similar state of resignation, Lucy offers to help her go abroad, overcome her mother's hold, and pursue whatever she wants to do even "if it's to be a bareback rider in a circus." Alice does not heed Lucy's appeal to ignore the bell that interrupts their discussion; she runs instead to her mother's aid, postponing forever the possibility of a personal turning point. The narrator observes, "These offers which come too late or at the wrong time, in words that are somehow unacceptable are the saddest, most haunting part of family life."[32] Indeed, the Beach sisters' spent promise and potential, though peripheral to the story, become a poignant image of tragic waste, suggesting that neither submission nor assertiveness, wifehood nor single life offered women fulfillment in the 1912 Midwestern town.

Maxwell's portraits of women went largely unnoticed throughout his career. Nearly fifty years after the appearance of *Time Will Darken It,* for example, Mary Flanagan's review of the author's collected short fiction in *The New York Times Book Review* stressed how his stories exclude and marginalize women, how he "is primarily interested in the mysteries of paternal rather than maternal power," and how his men are the "providers, materially and emotionally."[33] On the contrary, if Maxwell's fiction teaches anything, it teaches the power of maternal love. The mother figure, in both presence and haunting absence, is the central persona and most poignant inspiration of his work. The author said that his mother's death "made a novelist of him," and to suggest that his literary career was in large part an homage to her would not overstate the case.

Although Flanagan was writing specifically about *All the Days and Nights,* her views, which depart strikingly from other critics', do suggest that Maxwell's treatment of female characters remains under appreciated. This oversight is ironic given his intense attachment to his mother and the affinity for women and the home that permeates his fiction. After his mother's death, he developed close bonds with other older women: with Mrs. Green, Zona Gale, and Garreta Busey, all of whom nurtured his early literary pursuits; with Louise Bogan and Sylvia Townsend Warner at *The New Yorker;* and with Virginia Woolf, Willa Cather, Elinor Wylie, and Colette, whom he met in the pages of their books. He was aware that the writers who most influenced him often were female, a connection that affected the domestic quality of his fiction and its sensitive portraits of women's lives and psyches.[34] His friend Gale, of course, was among the most famous "New Women" of the era. Speaking with her regularly and intimately in his formative years must have influenced his thinking about women's lives in the early twentieth century. Although a close look at his novels reveals well-defined, respectfully depicted women—Mrs. West and the artists in *Bright Center of Heaven,* Madame Vienot and Barbara Rhodes in *The Chateau,* and Fern Smith in *So Long, See You Tomorrow*—his most pervasive and memorable female figure remains a guiding force in absentia, a powerful presence in her absence. As such, the mother is understood not through her own perceptions but through the eyes of those who knew and loved her. Over the course of the writer's work, she assumes nearly mythic status. Perhaps it is because this unforgettable figure recurs in his most widely read works that Maxwell has become known for portraying women at a distance rather than through their own points of view.

* * *

For this, we turn back to *Time Will Darken It*, which in viewpoint, subject, and structure is inherently, intensely conscious of the female condition. Fertility itself underpins the design: Framed by the onset of Martha's pregnancy and the caesarean delivery of her second child, the novel takes place over nine months and seeks to illumine the solitary sanctum of expectant motherhood. Although throughout his fiction Maxwell demonstrates an explicit interest in childhood, particularly in young children's idyllic relations with their mothers, he does not sidestep or downplay physical and psychological burdens surrounding childbirth. With awe and veneration, his narrator conceives of pregnancy as both mysterious and frightening and graphically describes his imaginings of it. He envisions "a country where women go when they are pregnant, a country with no king and no parliament," a kind of limbo where "the inhabitants do nothing but wait, and the present does not exist on any calendar; only the future, which may or may not come. Yet something is accomplished there, even so, and that inescapable tax which in the outside world is collected once every lunar cycle, in blood, is forgiven and remains in the hands of the taxpayer." The "country" the narrator imagines belies images of hopeful maternal bliss; its inhabitants, "often seized with cramps and vomiting," are controlled by oscillating physical symptoms and bitter, then vague emotions.[35]

Maxwell's narrative recognizes the possibility that some women may want to escape the "country" of pregnancy, and his narrator describes grotesque nightmares for those who seek respite from its bonds: "There is bound to be trouble at the frontier," he warns. "The roads, although policed, are not safe after dark. People are robbed of the calcium in their bones, and of their life's savings in dreams. The featureless landscape turns out to be littered with dirty things, maggots crawling, disgusting amoeba that move and have hairy appendages, or the bloated body of a dead deer."[36] Such grisly imagery startles in contrast to Maxwell's other portraits of a beloved mother figure devoted to home and family—especially to her second, sensitive son—and to his tender portrait of the pregnant wife in his later story "The Thistles in Sweden." To a reader now, these horrors might suggest a woman's violent visions of abortion. The reference to dark, unsafe roads might conjure images of back-alley operations performed in 1912 or in the mid-1940s, when the novel appeared. Strewn with gruesome, even decaying life forms, the barren landscape seems an infertile wasteland tormenting women who seek release from pregnancy, either physically or emotionally.

Looking back on the novel nearly fifty years later, Maxwell did not recall exactly what the imagery in this passage represents. He did not intend to suggest abortion, in any case, and believed he was free-associating, seeking to capture the human condition through the unconscious.[37] Still influenced by his analysis, he attempted to apply what he had learned from Reik to characters of his own creation, characters sprung more from his fiction writer's mind than from memory. In exploring the psychological life of a pregnant woman, he sought to grasp raw emotion, to arrive at fears that may surface only in dreams.

Perhaps not coincidentally, then, Maxwell closes *Time Will Darken It* as Martha drifts to sleep. She has come home from the hospital with the new baby and, after rocking the infant, slips back into bed with her husband "because it was cold, and she was not well and there was, after all, no place else to go." Asleep, Austin stretches his arm across her, which she removes, only to have him curl around her with his body "in a way that made her want to shout at him, and beat his face with her fists":

> She pushed the arm away, roughly this time, but he still did not waken. The arm had a life of its own. All the rest of him, his body and his soul, were asleep. But the arm was awake, and came across her, and the hand settled on her heart, and she let it stay there for a moment, thinking how hard and heavy it was compared to the child she had been holding, how importunate, how demanding; how it was not part of her and never would be, insisting on a satisfaction, even in sleep, that she could not give. She started to push it away once more but her own arms were bound to the bed. Only her mind was awake, able to act, to hate. And then suddenly the delicate gold chain of awareness, no stronger than its weakest link, gave way. Circled by the body next to her, enclosed in warmth, held by the arm that knew (even though the man it belonged to did not), Martha King was asleep.[38]

These final lines capture Martha's intense, unnamed frustrations. From her perspective, she suffers from her husband's demands, insensitivity, and emotional estrangement—"[he] was no part of her and never would be"—yet, with "no place else to go," she will ultimately stay in the marriage like many women of her time, trapped by prevailing codes of social behavior and financial dependence. Austin's arm seems to follow her, though, to plead with her for love and acceptance, as if some part of him unconsciously longs for the closeness they have been unable to achieve in waking hours. We leave them knowing there will be work to do and forgiveness to be granted if they are to remain together amicably. But Martha's lack of choices and Austin's hypnotic caresses suggest a shared future.

In a 1991 interview, Maxwell was faced with a reader who interpreted the final scene as Martha's revelation that she will leave Austin, citing its similarities to the ending of Joyce's *Ulysses.* He responded, "It was not my intention in *Time Will Darken It* that the reader would think Martha King was actually going to leave her husband, though I see now how you could think that. But I meant it as a kind of working out of her feelings in preparation for forgiving him. His happiness in having her home was a kind of affront in that it meant he had already forgiven himself. In spite of a certain incompatibility of temperament, they were tied together for life. As I had imagined them."[39]

Later, I asked his opinion about such discrepancies between author intent and reader interpretation. "I think often the reader reads because of a desire to live in another world than his own," he said. "He moves into the story, and becomes emotionally involved with the characters. If the writer has sufficient authority the reader doesn't question, or at least not very often, his account of what happened. But sometimes, if the emotions are touched on a deep level, the reader can protest and insist, no it was this way, not that." He believed that when there is such a misunderstanding, like the one about the ending of *Time Will Darken It,* "it is because the author has been over-subtle, or at least more indirect than some reader can accommodate. I think also that I meant to indicate something positive in Austin's arm, something beneath the ordinary level of thought that would hold the marriage together. I could have said this, but it would have been more didactic than I care to be."[40]

Maxwell's ideas here about characters and their effect on readers reveal much about his creative approach and outlook. He believed that an author brings characters to life "through his imagination, and sometimes through something like hallucination, and that once alive, they can go their own way (and did in *Time Will Darken It*) and that this leaves just as much room for differing interpretation and human behavior as actual life does." He paused. "Now that you speak of it, I can remember disagreeing with or disbelieving an author's statements about his characters. It is of course a proof of the validity of his art."[41]

Maxwell and Race

Finally, a discussion of *Time Will Darken It* must mention Maxwell's approach to African American characters, which, more than ten years after *Bright Center of Heaven,* has evolved somewhat. Here, the author intends a realistic view of black life in his signature time and place. The overly dramatized Jefferson Carter of the first novel gives way to more believable black characters and depictions of relationships between the races. *Time Will Darken It* discloses a conflicted chapter in the communal psyche: The middle class of Draperville—a post–Civil War town in the land of Lincoln—consider themselves enlightened on issues of race yet still harbor feelings of superiority. Embarrassed by the overt racism of the Southern guests, for example, Austin attempts to protect Rachel, the African American cook, by shutting the dining room door when they speak of "niggers" at the table. Despite this sensitivity, he and his family belong to a community amused by the fact that a black washing woman's son finished high school and went to St. Louis to study medicine;[42] where early one morning, Lucy Beach, the forward-thinking Montessori teacher, finds Rachel's artistic daughter in the kindergarten surrounded by crayons and paper, only to reprimand and send her home with her half-finished drawing as white children arrive to take "possession of the kingdom that was reserved for them."[43] For the first time, Maxwell attempts to capture how black Americans in heartland towns endured not only direct racism and poverty but also hypocritical and conditioned acceptance, genteel bigotry, and cordial condescension.

In Martha King's world, African American servants are an integral thread in the small-town fabric, providing significant support to the middle-class Midwestern family. Though intimate with their white employers, they remain detached; equal by law, they assume a wholly separate status and residential area. Elm Street, the site of the narrator's cultural excavation, is divided by a "great plane of glass, opaque from one side, transparent from the other." At the point where the street dips downhill and becomes dangerous to children riding bicycles, its dignified architecture and graceful elms give way to shabby houses with lawns of ragweed and dandelion. Here, on Lower Elm, Draperville's "Negroes" live with a few white families on terms of limited social intimacy. By day, Rachel occupies the Kings' kitchen on upper Elm yet after dinner walks down the sidewalk to a railroad caboose covered with black roofing paper that she has made her home. Resigned to "roofs that leaked, ceilings that cracked and fell, floors that were uneven, and the scratching of rats at night inside the walls," residents of Lower Elm live behind the opaque wall that separates their residences from their employers'.[44]

Personal and physical boundaries between the races exist in the Kings' household as well. When Rachel asks Martha whether her daughter can spend more time in their home, Martha agrees, yet she is blind to the possibility that Rachel's alcoholic, wandering husband has beaten the daughter. Like the "great plane of glass" that divides Elm Street, the door between the family dining room and the servant's kitchen establishes parameters that prompt unstated yet understood separation between "the front and the back parts of the house," a phrase that came to symbolize for Maxwell the general racial divide and the title for a late story that offers his most poignant writing on black Americans. Further discussion of his treatment of race requires consideration of this late short fiction. Indeed, the African American portraits in *Time Will Darken It* had surprising repercussions in his later life and work: In the 1980s, he returned to the story of Rachel's family in a way he could not have expected.

The Maxwells in France

Time Will Darken It was published on September 1, 1948, while the Maxwells were on a four-month excursion through France, Austria, and Italy. For Emily the trip was a long-awaited return to places she had seen with her parents when she was twelve, but for William, who would celebrate his fortieth birthday in Florence August 16, this marked his first time on European soil and was the culmination of a lifelong love affair with French culture.

They had set off from New York Harbor the morning of July 1, bound for Cherbourg on the Queen Elizabeth and packed with a four-month supply of everything they had been told was unavailable in Europe after the war, including a typewriter. Maxwell wrote his father that their cabin class reservations cost roughly the same as extending the living room six feet and building a terrace at their home in Yorktown Heights, but he figured they could manage on a budget of $15 a day once they reached the Continent. From Cherbourg they would travel to Mont St. Michel, then to the coast of Brittany for two weeks, then to Blois, where they had made arrangements to stay with a French family in a small chateau and "bicycle around through the Chateau country." The Salzburg Music Festival would hold them for another week before they spent a month wandering through northern and central Italy and then returned to Paris for a final month by way of Nice, Cannes, and Marseilles.[45]

More than four decades later he remembered that he had not expected to feel differently toward the country of France than he would toward the state of Texas. Although he loved to hear his friends Glenway Wescott and Janet Flanner talk about Paris during the prewar period—both were regular *New Yorker* correspondents on the subject—he hadn't been particularly conscious of the expatriates of the twenties and thirties. Unlike most writers, he hadn't "read and reread Hemingway," whose stories he admired immensely but whose "self-advertisement" and personal bravado were diametrically opposed to his more modest sensibility. Instead, he spent December 1933 in Martinique—a French-speaking island, appropriately enough—forgoing the European initiation of so many American-born writers his age and a bit older. Looking back, he was unsure why it didn't occur to him that he would love Europe. Perhaps, he said, he was so satisfied with books such as *The Counterfeiters* and *Le Grande Meaulnes* that he felt no need for anything more, or perhaps, as he told me, "when I had time I had no money, and when I had money, I had no time." Now, neither was an impediment: His savings account had been boosted by twelve years at *The New Yorker,* where he had a secure and flexible arrangement.[46]

To his surprise, when he peered out the porthole and glimpsed the first sight of coastline, he was awestruck: "Before I ever set foot on French soil," he writes, "I lost my heart."[47] Although he enjoyed time in other European countries—England and Spain, as well as Austria and Italy—France was the only place outside the Midwest to become the setting for one of his novels.

The trip there is well documented in a series of letters he and Emily wrote to his father and Grace from Europe, which were among those found after his stepmother's death. They read like a condensed version of *The Chateau,* describing many of the novel's key events, characters, and settings, including descriptions of the chateau, intimations of the Maxwells' relations with the French, and the tensions introduced by Berliners who stay with them in a Paris apartment. Unlike the novel, they also recount the couple's adventures in Italy and Germany, including the author's attempt to collect his overdue advance on the Italian translation of *The Folded Leaf.*

The letters stand as both private and public history, personal reflections as well as a first-hand account of postwar Europe, a quality shared by the novel. Maxwell's observations bring insights about French life after the German occupation and reveal both his concern for the Jews and his bewilderment over attitudes of some of the French who seem impervious to the atrocities of the Holocaust. The correspondence reveals an author who, even in France, delights in the everyday rather than the grand, who takes keen interest in new people and experiences, and has strong emotional bonds with his wife and family.

By the time Maxwell wrote his father and stepmother from the chateau on July 17, he and Emily had visited Mont St. Michel, embarked on a series of overnight stays in "queer places—Pontorson, Rennes, and Tours," and learned that outside Paris it behooved them to speak French or to "die in the attempt." The letter is written in scrawling script with a smudgy pen because the typewriter carried from New York had been stolen on the pier. Delighted with the French countryside, he was especially taken with the "miraculous" gardens, with how flowers and vegetables were planted together rather than separately as in America. His love for "anything old and run down" drew him to the villages and farms.[48]

Despite their adequate but limited facility with the language, the Maxwells found staying in a house with eight to twelve people speaking French to be an odd experience. After "sticking it out" for several days, they decided to take a three-day side trip to Paris and arrived on Bastille Day amid fireworks, street dancing, and illuminated buildings. Maxwell found the festival "enticing," and "Notre Dame with flood lights very beautiful," yet he had been more deeply touched by an intimate scene earlier in Blois, which he later recalled in *The Chateau:* "a group of children singing and performing folk dances in costume on a terrace." He and Emily had come upon them by accident, yet to him they alone were "worth traveling across the ocean for."[49]

Back at the chateau, Maxwell found the country pleasant. He describes the "beautifully furnished" residence with its guests of "considerable wealth and social pretensions" yet observes that "because of the war, side by side with the luxury and formality are certain real hardships." The French hosts were unaccustomed to doing without croissants and other foods basic to their cuisine; wheat bread was also unavailable, although it was promised after the harvest a month later. "In spite of government ineptitude," he writes, "the French people have made great strides—individually—at building and restoring farms and businesses and it is difficult to believe that the war ended only 3 years ago. Except for the towns that had some military objective, you hardly ever see a ruined building."[50]

After leaving the spot for good, the Maxwells returned to Paris for a ten-day stay in an apartment belonging to the chateau owner's niece, who was fond of Emily and whose husband worked on German affairs for the French State Department. When the doorbell rang one morning at 7 A.M., Maxwell answered it in his pajamas, "and there stood the concierge and 3 young, hollow sad Berliners, who had arrived in Paris, on their way to a conference in Rome, with no passport visa, and no money." For the next three days they lived together in the apartment—Emily cooking and catering to them—"with everybody talking in different languages, and getting along fine," he writes. "People everywhere have been so kind to us that we couldn't help being that way to the Germans, but gradually, although they were very intelligent and well-bred, the well-known qualities began to appear, like a cloud low on the horizon, and we felt sorry for them, but could not really like them." Still, after a month in France, the Maxwells were in love with the country, the people, the life, and the city of lights.[51]

They hated to leave Paris—as their French improved, their friendships flowered—but in early August they took what turned out to be a rough ride to Lausanne: The train went through tunnel after tunnel with the windows wide open, and their hair became matted with cinders. When they arrived beleaguered, they happened upon a deluxe hotel and decided to stay the night. "I thought I'd never get out with my shirt," Maxwell confessed, "but we were tired and dirty and there was a big moon looking over Lake Geneva to the snow capped mountains and there was a huge bathtub." The next morning he discovered how far the trip to Salzburg would be (having been misinformed in Paris), so they boarded an overnight train at 2 o'clock that afternoon and rode in a compartment with eight people, "six of whom couldn't stand fresh air…what a night and what a nightmare." Even so, the Maxwells savored their experiences, pleasant or not. He wrote to his father, "In a strange way the discomfort seems to alternate with the delight, making our life rich in contrasts, and never a dull moment.…We are both enjoying the trip so much more than we ever imagined we would, and I can't remember anything like it ever happening to me. When I went to the West Indies I traveled alone. This is a very different story."[52]

Finally in Salzburg, they found that the language barrier made them less comfortable than they had been in France, but they thoroughly enjoyed an opera August 7 and attended a play at an open-air theater before Cathedral Blanche the evening of the eighth. While in Austria, they surrounded themselves with an eclectic group of friends for dining, rowing, and going into town on the bus: another young couple from New York, an American soldier stationed in Vienna, his kindly Viennese wife, a former bar room dancer who had spent four years in a Nazi concentration camp in Czechoslovakia, and an American radio actor traveling with an Austrian boy. "In America, it would never work," Maxwell writes. "But here, it is fine."[53]

In Italy the Maxwells saw disturbing evidence of the war. "We look directly on to a row of ruins—18th century houses destroyed by the Germans as they retreated, and a terrible, hollow sight," Emily wrote her in-laws from the hotel in Florence. The scenery changed during evening horse and buggy rides: "All of Europe looks better to us softened by twilight." In Florence, William rented a "species of typewriter…with the W where the Z ought to be, and the M where the semicolon ought to be," and he began to compose regularly as well as to write more legible letters home. (Coincidentally, the misplaced letters were his initials. He hand-signed his letters, or the signature would have read "Zilliam ;axwell"). Emily recalled that her husband's early mornings were devoted to writing "the most *beautiful* short sketches of his impressions," while she did "laundry and a little sewing." "This is so necessary to us," she writes, "because neither of us enjoy sightseeing and leisure enough to live that way for 4 months." Here, Maxwell also found a copy of the Italian translation of *The Folded Leaf* and decided to go to Rome to see whether he could get payment from the Italian publisher, who owed him a three-hundred-dollar advance and six advance copies that had never materialized. "At the moment $300 would do wonders for our budget," he remarks, "which is still within a decent distance of $15 a day but could do with a blood transfusion."[54]

That morning, August 20, the Maxwells received a thank-you note from one of the Germans who had stayed with them in the Paris apartment. The letter tried "terribly hard to be nice," Maxwell writes home to Lincoln, "but it was quite clear that he had learned nothing from that war, felt sorry only for Germans, without realizing or admitting that the Germans were in any way responsible for their own condition, let alone the condition of the rest of the world. He doesn't want...Germany to have a democratic government like ours or like the Russians call a democratic government."[55] Clearly disturbed by the Germans' views, Maxwell later included a similar letter in *The Chateau* and, through the character of Harold Rhodes, expressed his outrage at their apparent disregard for Jews and his bewilderment over French criticism of American involvement in France.

Once in Rome, the Maxwells decided to stay longer than the five days planned. They found a "small, convenient, pleasant little hotel, with a double bed *at last*" and took time to linger in the shops and coffee houses, including one, Maxwell writes, "frequented by Mark Twain, Emmy, and me." Although the language barrier prevented them from making contact with Italians, they delighted in wandering through the streets, museums, and gardens past midnight, amid the "ghosts of the great writers of the past" and people singing in the streets. However, the songs were not what Americans might imagine, he wrote his father: usually "Bing Crosby's latest, and invariably off key." Here, too, he sought out his Italian publisher. After negotiation, a lawyer and the publisher's brother-in-law wrote a codicil to allow the payment to go to Maxwell, rather than to his agent in New York, and in lira, rather than in dollars as the original contract specified. The lawyer cashed the $150 check for him—half of the $300 he expected—but the author was finally able to buy a decent typewriter so he could continue writing.[56]

Word from Harold Ross awaited them in San Remo, Italy, where they arrived in early September: The editor enclosed a proof of Brendan Gill's review full of high praise for *Time Will Darken It* and a letter from a writer friend who had read an advance copy and was "wildly enthusiastic." Gill found the novel an advance over Maxwell's earlier ones and focused on its psychological exploration of "a catastrophic marriage" that transcends the small-town, prewar atmosphere: "As in all good novels, the place in *Time Will Darken It* turns out to be here and the time to be now," he wrote. His opinion of Maxwell's narrator commentaries is particularly revealing viewed in hindsight and with knowledge of the more self-conscious works to come: "Of the many pleasures to be found in this novel, I put high on my list the fact that the author makes no pretext of not having written it.…Mr. Maxwell unashamedly presides over his work…and I'm glad. Again and again, in the course of this book, I realized how old-fashioned those novels have begun to seem that affect to have produced themselves untouched by human hands." With this book, he wrote, "Mr. Maxwell enters his major phase." For the author in Italy, the early positive word seemed "like a good omen," he wrote his father, "though we won't know what is happening for a week or ten days probably."[57]

Within two weeks the Maxwells had traveled from the Italian Riviera back to Paris, where their adventure on the continent had begun. They arrived during the opening week of the United Nations session and found no rooms available in the city. They took one without a bath for the first night and then "tramped the streets," staying in "big hotels, little hotels, flea bags," until after four days they were happily settled in a little hotel on the Left Bank near the Luxembourg gardens and St. Sulpice, thanks to the help of a well-traveled New York friend whom they met on the street. While distractedly going from hotel to hotel, they sat at a sidewalk cafe on a noisy boulevard and read reviews of *Time Will Darken It* that had been forwarded by the publisher. "They went all the way from saying that I am the best American writer to the book was pointless, and were in general not very clear about what the book is about," he wrote his father. "I don't think it is going to have a popular sale, but it is still too early to tell. I've been rereading it here and am satisfied with it. By the time we get home it will be all blown over, for which I am thankful, because it is time to start on something new and different."[58]

Actually, critical reception was quite positive on the whole. Perhaps the negative response Maxwell mentioned came from *The Nation's* Ernest Jones, an admirer of *They Came Like Swallows* who found *Time Will Darken It* "the least satisfying of Mr. Maxwell's novels," with the same "power and the same faults" as *The Folded Leaf*. Namely, he believed that the "semi-philosophical commentary" was not "strictly relevant" to the fiction and that "the central figure is such a ninny that the importance of the theme is blurred." But this was a minority opinion. Others wrote that his "understanding of the mystical continuity of life, the sense of the spiritual relation of every moment of life to every other moment...gives his work mystery and beauty." The *Atlantic Monthly* noted his "rare powers of insight and evocation," and *The New York Times* described the book as "quiet, thoughtful, knowing," and "beautifully accomplished." And from the *San Francisco Chronicle*, "There are not half a dozen novelists writing today who can come up to Mr. Maxwell....If you do not read *Time Will Darken It*, you will have missed something rare in the way of experience."[59]

Two and a half weeks later, the author wrote his father again thanking him for a letter praising the book and sending better news home about its commercial success. He had heard from Harper that the novel was selling "way beyond their expectations" and was anxious to learn whether this was a sudden spurt—"1100 copies in one week is phenomenal these days"—or an indication that the book would continue to sell steadily. "If it does, I won't have to think about other work than writing," he glowed, "and you know how much that means to us."[60]

The highlight of their last weeks in Europe was an October 8 side trip to Chartres, which to Maxwell seemed "what all the other churches in the world had tried to be." When they climbed to the roof and into one of the towers, Emily scared him by leaning over the parapet to look down while he held her ankle. They came down in time to hear the end of a mass, wander through the streets, take tea, walk along a promenade, and return to the church at dusk, when "it was almost pitch dark, except for the candle light in one of the chapels, and the stained glass still held its colors." He describes the scene as "the most beautiful and moving thing" they had seen in Europe.[61]

The final week was filled with a trip to Versailles and visits from their French hosts from Blois, American and English friends, and Maxwell's French publisher. "I don't know how we are going to crowd them...and all the things still left undone—theater, museums, sightseeing and shopping—into one single week," he writes. But during the final two weeks he and Emily "had had enough and just waited for time to pass." Their last night in Paris they decided to see a movie, got as far as the box office, and then returned to their hotel room instead.[62]

On October 19 they boarded the Mauritania in Cherbourg for the crossing back to New York. Maxwell had not heard for several weeks about sales for *Time Will Darken It,* so he was anxious to get home. "I feel older and if not wiser at least better informed in the ways of the world," he wrote from aboard ship. They had promised their French friends that they would return in two years and hoped to see their favorite acquaintance from the trip, an Englishman with the United Nations Organization, when he visited America after Christmas. "The others we leave behind, reluctantly," he writes, "never having quite had a chance to get to know them."[63]

But Maxwell's time in France had just begun. He remembered, "I walked into our house on a country road forty miles north of New York City, put the suitcases down, and with my hat still on my head sat down to my typewriter and wrote a page of notes for a novel. I thumbtacked it to the bookcase behind me and didn't look at it again. For the next ten years I lived in my own private France, which I tried painstakingly to make real to the reader. It was my way of not coming home."[64]

Grace McGrath Maxwell, William Maxwell's
stepmother, in 1908, the year of his birth. She
married his father in 1923. Photo courtesy of
the late Dr. Robert Perry.

The Maxwell home on Park Place in Lincoln, Illinois, when it was new in 1922. William
Maxwell Sr. built the home after the death of the author's mother, and the author lived here
for one year before moving to Chicago in 1923. Maxwell recalled playing on the beams of the
house as it was being built in his final novel, *So Long, See You Tomorrow*. The house remains
in the family, currently owned by Ted Perry, the son of Tom Perry, who helped Maxwell with
research for the novel. Photo courtesy of the late Dr. Robert Perry.

Maxwell's senior class portrait from Chicago's Senn High School, 1926. Photo given to the author by the late Dr. Robert Perry.

As a senior in high school, Maxwell served as vice president of the Senn Athletic Association, handling the financial affairs of the group. He is pictured here in the Senn High School yearbook, the *Forum,* on the far right in the front row—the only light suit in the group. Photo used with permission of Senn High School, Chicago, Illinois.

Maxwell wrote his first novel, *Bright Center of Heaven,* in the third floor room of this converted water tower at Bonnie Oaks, the farm owned by Mildred Green, near Portage, Wisconsin. Photo by Barbara Burkhardt.

William and Emily Maxwell, in the late 1950s, with daughters Kate and Brookie. Photograph attributed to Consuelo Kanaga.

Maxwell with author and friend Eudora Welty at the annual spring meeting of the Academy of Arts and Letters in New York City, May 21, 1980. Welty presented Maxwell with the William Dean Howells Medal for *So Long, See You Tomorrow* that evening, twenty-five years after Maxwell presented her the same award for *The Ponder Heart*. The Howells Medal recognizes a work of fiction deemed by the academy as the finest in the preceding five-year period. Photo used with permission of the American Academy of Arts and Letters.

William and Emily Maxwell on the patio of their Yorktown Heights home after a day of interviews, August 1992. Photo by Barbara Burkhardt.

William Maxwell brought his typewriter outdoors to the patio at his Yorktown Heights home during an interview in August 1992. Photo by Barbara Burkhardt.

William and Emily Maxwell pictured with writer Stuart Dybek and Bernard Malamud's daughter, Janna Malamud Smith, at the Folger Shakespeare Library in Washington, D.C., December 8, 1995. Maxwell and Dybek both received the PEN/Malamud Award for fiction that evening. Photo by Gayle Krughoff.

William Maxwell and the author in the study of his Manhattan apartment, December 6, 1996.

Maxwell said that this photo captured the way he would like to be remembered. Photo by Dorothy Alexander.

6

Turning Point:
The New Yorker and *The Chateau*
1948–61

EVENTUALLY TITLED *The Chateau,* Maxwell's novel about France had a long gestation. He worked with the material over a twelve-year period, "remembering every town we passed through, every street we were ever on, everything that ever happened, including the weather. Of course, I was faced with the extremely difficult problem of how all this self-indulgence could be made into a novel," he later recalled.[1] Ultimately, he created a work of exquisite restraint, depicting the relationships between a young American couple, Harold and Barbara Rhodes, and the French people they meet during a trip abroad several years after World War II. The novel carefully details the intricate interactions between the Americans and their French host, Madame Vienot, who rents rooms in her family's faded, formerly grand Chateau Beaumesnil, a seventeenth-century estate one hundred miles from Paris. Maxwell masterfully captures the Rhodeses' American eagerness—the exuberance with which they set off on their European sojourn, their acute desire to love France and be loved in return—and their bewilderment in the face of situations in which they feel excluded or rudely treated. Despite their attempts to adopt the Vienot family's customs and etiquette gracefully and to speak and improve their French, they sense an undercurrent of tension beneath the dining room conversation. As a result, they find it unexpectedly difficult to penetrate a culture they long to embrace.

Along the way, they meet intriguing characters such as Madame Straus-Muguet, an elderly woman with "mouse-colored" hair, who immediately falls in love with them and insists on taking them to the opera and to restaurants, often footing the bill. She revels in her imagined intimacy with headwaiters, lead actresses, and the like, and when she attempts to make introductions, the Rhodeses realize she is only vaguely familiar to her glamorous idols or, in some cases, an unwelcome pest. Through their travels, the Rhodeses encounter such baffling circumstances: Why, they wonder, does Madame Straus-Muguet invent such stories? Why would an actress who sent her an affectionate note dismiss her so abruptly in front of them? And why does Madame Vienot's son-in-law treat them as intimate friends one day and ignore them the next? The novel's epigraph addresses such questioning from the outset in a quote from Elizabeth Bowen: "Wherever one looks twice there is some mystery."[2] The human impulse to solve such mysteries—and the ultimate futility in searching for definitive answers—becomes a central, unifying theme. In the absence of drama and climax, *The Chateau* explores the delicate dance of second glances and, in its own quiet way, suggests subtle interplay as the basis for human experience and the substance of narrative art.

Writer, Editor, Lecturer

SHORT STORIES

When Maxwell began writing *The Chateau* in fall 1948, *Time Will Darken It* was selling about four hundred copies a week: "Good for these times," he wrote his father, "but not enough to make any considerable sum of money....I'm glad not to be a young writer just starting out under such conditions. With the New Yorker and stories, we'll be all right."[3] So, while working on his novel, he also wrote and sold short fiction about Illinois, New York, and, for the first time, France. In particular, "The Trojan Women" (1952), "The Pilgrimage" (1953), and "The French Scarecrow" (1956) help to establish a more complete view of Maxwell's literary production and interests during this period. Representing his three primary settings, the stories offer continuity with previous work yet also reveal the author exploring new subjects and circumstances.

Readers of *Time Will Darken It* will recognize the setting of "The Trojan Women": 1912 Draperville, Illinois, where Mildred Gellert has left her husband to live in a cottage on the lake at the edge of town. One of Maxwell's shorter, simpler stories of this period, it opens as Adah Belle, Mildred's African American servant, returns from town with items from the house where Mr. Gellert is staying with his mother. It is September; all the other cottages have been boarded up for the winter. Adah Belle has brought two gift boxes for the children from their father: a set of blocks for the baby son and a handkerchief with an embroidered butterfly for the little girl. Intent on having the children forget their father, Mildred instructs Adah Belle to burn the girl's box on the trash pile.

First published four years after *Time Will Darken It,* the story shares a similar narrator, a voice that breaks in occasionally with commentary and touches on issues treated more fully in the novel: marriage and women's roles in the early twentieth century, the social climate of the small-town Midwest, and children learning to cope with adult failings beyond their control. Unlike Martha King, Mildred Gellert has taken steps to remove herself from a troubled marriage. Even so, Mildred is not as acutely sympathetic: Her personal history and the root of her unhappiness are unclear. However, we come to understand that it is probably boredom, a general ennui, that distresses her. As Maxwell glimpses the town's middle-class women—who feed on the gossip of Mildred's travails—we see that they, too, harbor feelings of emptiness kept hidden in the face of their friend's public ordeal:

> They were not, like Mildred Gellert, having trouble with their husbands. Their marriages were successful, their children took music lessons and won prizes at commencement, and they had every reason in the world to be satisfied (new curtains for the living room, a glassed-in sun porch), every reason to be happy. It was only sometimes when they woke in the middle of the night and couldn't get to sleep for a while, and so reviewed their lives, something (what, exactly, they couldn't say) seemed missing. The opportunity that they had always assumed would come to them hadn't come after all.

Draperville women have vague and not-so-vague dissatisfactions; like Martha King, Nora Potter, and the Beach sisters, they aim to toe the social line and are ostracized if they stray. Once again, card-playing historians sit in judgment. They initially support Mildred but become less loyal when there are no new developments. "The limit is boredom," the narrator explains. "Unless the tragic heroine can produce new stories, new black-and-blue marks, new threats and outrages that exceed in dramatic quality the old ones, it is better that she stay, no matter how unhappily, with her husband. So says the voice of doubt, the wisdom of fear."[4] Mildred, like several white middle-class women in Maxwell's world, finds the most unconditional comfort and friendship with her African American servant.

As "The Trojan Women" reinforces Maxwell's depiction of women's lives in *Time Will Darken It,* it also introduces a quality not seen in his previous young characters: a child who, in the face of family crisis, has learned strategies to cope. Unlike Bunny in *They Came Like Swallows* and Abbey in *Time*

Will Darken It, the little girl—a sort of "every child" whom Maxwell does not name—has found ways to protect herself within her limited means. In the final, poignant scene, she watches from beneath an oak tree as Adah Belle goes to the trash with the gift, sets a match to the pile, and returns to the kitchen. Once the woman is out of sight, the little girl runs to the fire and rescues the burning box. Inside it she finds a partially charred handkerchief with the butterfly still untouched by flames and hides it beneath the porch, where her mother will not go because of a resident snake. "When she came into the house, five minutes later, her eyes were blank and innocent. She had learned that much in a year and a half. Her eyes could keep any secret they wanted to." The young girl has begun to keep her own counsel, to adjust her behavior in a way that softens the harshness around her. At the end of a story that pictures parents' troubles and community scandal, the scene abruptly refocuses the reader on one of Maxwell's primary concerns: life's effects on children. The rather unexpected twist lends "The Trojan Women" emotional weight, centering and sharpening its impact. For in the end, the story is not about the adults' personal traumas but about the quietest presence in the scene: the child finding her way in a world where "the innocent have to take their chances."[5]

Maxwell published his first fiction set in postwar France a year after "The Trojan Women" appeared. In a sense, "The Pilgrimage" serves as an artist's sketch of the novel to come: It suggests the author experimenting with his new geographic territory, developing themes from his European experience. Like *The Chateau,* the story pictures American tourists—native Midwesterners living on the East Coast—who find both adventure and disillusionment abroad. Ray and Ellen Ormsby throw themselves into their travels in the spirit of the novel's Harold and Barbara Rhodes, yet their particular disappointment consists in their failure to recapture the past. The story follows their mission: to duplicate the perfect French meal, the gastronomic experience of some friends who have ecstatically recounted a dinner at the Hotel du Domino in Perigueux, where every course was "something with truffles" and the dessert combined "little balls of ice cream in a...spun sugar basket with a spun sugar bow." In their search for *the* restaurant, *the* roast chicken, and *the* sugar basket, the couple is never certain whether they have found the site so memorable to their neighbors. Once they are seated in the dining room, the waiter presents their menus with a flourish, but they have doubts: The space looks more like a coffee shop than the fine restaurant their friends described, the walls appear drab, the tables are bare, and the menu does not list the much-anticipated dishes. Thinking they have made a mistake, Ray insists they leave for another restaurant listed in the Michelin Guide that might be the right one, only to find on arrival that it does not serve chicken at all. They return, a bit sheepishly, to the Hotel du Domino, where the waiter seats them at the same table and presents their menus—this time without the flourish.[6]

Obviously, the clock cannot be turned back in Perigueux, France, any more than it can in Lincoln (or Draperville), Illinois. Although Maxwell's Midwestern characters fantasize about regaining a past plowed under by tragedy or loss—the mother's death, the elm-lined streets, the brother's "affliction"—the Ormsbys' quest, though trivial in comparison, originates in similar human desires to connect with what has been. In the Ormsbys' case, however, we suspect the couple is fixated on a past that might never have existed—at least not in the way described to them. The neighbors' recollections of a perfect evening, the best meal, "every" dish with truffles, were filtered through memory and emotion. Here Maxwell suggests, as clearly as he ever does, that the past is a moving target. It resists quantifying, offers mystery upon mystery, and, just as we think we have it in our hands, slips away: "It's very good," Ellen comments about the chicken casserole, "but I'm not sure I can taste the truffles. . . . With the roast chicken, it probably would have been quite easy." When Ray asks her whether she is certain the Richardsons had roast chicken stuffed with truffles, she replies, "I think so. Anyway, I know I've read about it." The Richardsons, Ray suspects, must have eaten in the garden. He decides they should not tell them that the dinner "as a whole" was not "all *that* good."[7]

Maxwell's stories of this period also suggest the continued influence of Theodor Reik. While in *The Folded Leaf* an omniscient narrator meditates on psychoanalytic themes, Manhattanites in the short fiction struggle with the past on analysts' couches. The analyst, at times an elderly Austrian with Reik's round face and thick glasses, more often becomes a disembodied, Viennese voice emanating from above characters' reclined heads.

"The French Scarecrow" deals in human fears, in the foreboding presence of potential hazards, both real and imagined. Here, Maxwell alternates scenes of bachelor Gerald Martin at the analyst's office in New York with those of his country neighbors, whose scarecrow, modeled on one they saw in France, represents the uncertainties and demons of all who encounter it. Its presence often takes the neighbors or their maid by surprise: Mistaken for a strange man, it momentarily terrorizes them. In the city, Gerald struggles with his own anxiety in analysis, pouring out his thoughts in free associations. He feels as though his sleeves and trousers are sewed to the couch, then moves on to Oedipus, bookcases, and, finally, dreams of childhood and his mother's dishes. He recalls, "And after she died, I could have thought that I did something I shouldn't have, and she died."[8]

Spending days each week reliving the past in analysis, such characters add new dimension to the theme of private history in Maxwell's work. While *The Folded Leaf* incorporates psychoanalytic concepts without labeling them as such—a feature the author acknowledged as "partly the effect of [his] being in analysis"—this and later work directly portray the patient in therapy.

THE UNFINISHED PLAY

Maxwell initially worked with material that became "The French Scarecrow" in the first scene of an unfinished, untitled play he wrote in the 1950s. The play offers not only a sense of the genesis of this and other stories but also a fuller understanding of the role psychoanalysis played in his fiction generally. The thick manuscript reveals him dealing directly, intently with ideas he learned from Reik—specifically, with the analyst's theories about traumatic shock and guilt. Though abandoned, the drama was fully conceived, a nearly complete draft in three acts with scenes already written and rewritten. For Maxwell readers, it can be a fascinating document that further illuminates the motivations of his work, predicts future developments, and deals with painful emotions in stark, bold terms. With the advantage of hindsight, we recognize scenes and images that recur throughout his body of fiction—as well as striking, singular moments in his writing life. Here, for example, he experiments with science fiction, with the technology of time travel, and transports a character based on his mother from the afterlife to contemporary New York and Illinois.

The play opens in the office of Dr. Weil, a Germanic analyst in session with Hugh Davis, a forty-two-year-old man who cannot resolve grief over his mother's death. Offering a fond portrait of Reik, the first scene contains lightly humorous dialogue regarding his fees, publishers, and cavelike office yet moves quickly to Hugh's dreams and past traumas: his near death after an attempted suicide, the loss of his childhood home, and his inability to get on with life three decades later. In conversation with his patient, the analyst introduces the play's premise: "With traumatic shock, the personality remains fixed in the moment of disaster," he explains:

> Grief is always, to some extent, like this, but with time most people get over their sorrow and go on living in the present. If they do not, they are brought to a standstill by the experience that was too much for them and that has

shaken the whole structure of their lives to the foundations. They give up all interest in the present and the future, and live permanently absorbed in the situation which they weren't able to deal with and which they go on trying to deal with, as if it were still confronting them. This is what happened to you when your mother died. It was too great a loss for you to bear...so you kept her alive, by incorporating her personality into your own....Instead of imitating your father's masculine qualities, and becoming forceful and direct, you showed an interest in the things that interest women....She lives on in you, but is not you....What you must do to get back your own personality is to bring her back to life and let her grow old gradually. And then you must let her die.[9]

Hugh does not believe he can do this, yet the analyst insists, "In the imagination anything is possible." The first scene ends, and the drama unfolds as a realization of the analyst's theory, an experiment in transcending past trauma through the imagination. Perhaps in his mind's eye, or in the world of his dreams, the grown son can bring his mother to life again so that as she ages and dies a second time, he can release his pain.

In scene 2, Maxwell enters territory that might surprise readers of his fiction: an airport control tower charged with coordinating high-tech flights from the afterlife to the present day. Hugh's mother—called both Blossom and Belle in the manuscript—has been summoned back to Earth because of her son's debilitating grief over her death. She has the option of declining the assignment but decides to stay. Traveling instantaneously and invisibly, she visits Lincoln, Illinois, to seek the counsel of her old friend Judge Gale, to whom she confides, "Once or twice very, very dimly, I let [Hugh] see my face. As if it came to him, like a memory, in his mind." In the Midwest, she also sees her husband with his new wife and witnesses "unsatisfactory" changes in the social mood since her death in 1919. In New York, she is appalled at discussions that transpire in analytic sessions with Dr. Weil (whose office she has visited while invisible) and then makes an appointment with him to learn more about her son's difficulties. She tries to smooth the strained relations between her older son and Hugh when they meet at the Waldorf-Astoria, a scene Maxwell later developed into the story "A Game of Chess." Here, too, the two women in Hugh's life meet as they could not in life: Spending time in their New York apartment, Blossom/Belle develops a relationship with Hugh's wife and learns how her son's devotion to her memory affects their daily lives.

Feeling unable to help, the mother returns to the airport, where she is refused a flight. As Dr. Weil tells her, she cannot choose the time of her return to the afterworld: "[Your son] brought you back, and you will go when he lets you go." Slowly, as the play progresses, she begins to age, to become older than she was at her death. Finally, one evening after work, the son tells his wife that "for the first time he forgot, since his mother was living with them, why she was there." He senses that he has released her as Weil predicted—that she is gone. "I feel I killed her," he cries to his wife. "Hold me." He looks for the analyst, who is no longer there, and the curtain comes down.

Maxwell's comments and summaries included with the manuscript suggest a writer striving to come to terms with the past, his mother, and death. Considering his play, he reflected: "If the dead came back it would be too painful to the living, because in one way or another they have failed the dead by accepting their death and making adjustments or transferences of affection, by managing at all. It would also be painful, and really unkind, to the dead, to bring them back." Perhaps for this reason, Maxwell never wrote from the mother's perspective in his published work but chose to see her through the eyes of other characters. "Oddly enough I never have considered writing from my mother's point of view," he told me. "When she was alive I saw things as she saw them, pretty much. And when she was dead I incorporated her personality into my own, so how I see things is (unconsciously) how she also would see them."[10]

This unpublished portrait is the closest the writer ever came to establishing his mother's point of view. In a sense, Reik's teachings gave him a framework for creating a more fully formed character in her likeness, for extending her presence into the present day of his work, and for exploring the process of overcoming grief. On some level, of course, the analyst's ideas about traumatic shock might have influenced his body of fiction more generally. Like the play, his novels and stories resurrect characters and settings from the past in an effort to resolve painful emotions. Maxwell said, "It has seemed to me that if I go on writing about the death of my mother, as I have time after time, somebody is going to rise up and cry enough." Indeed, the play's focus on catharsis parallels a similar search for peace found in the author's fiction, a hope for healing especially prevalent in his later works.

The manuscript, with its revisions and hand-written notations, also reveals Maxwell actively developing new narrative approaches. His experimentation with science fiction, for example, led him to treat time and space in new ways—to dissolve boundaries between the past and present, the living and the dead, and to deal overtly with the power of personal history. Here, for example, the mother figure takes a flight from the afterworld; in later fictions, narrators will move between different moments in their lives by way of memory and imagination.

Working in the dramatic form inspired a more visual approach to his material. For example, Dr. Weil, sitting in his chair, continues to be lit "from the knees down" throughout the play—an ever-presence whose ideas guide the action. In one case, Maxwell's work with staging influenced the imagery of his later fiction. He writes,

> There is no scenery in the ordinary sense—but the shapes of rooms, the location of a door or a window indicated as they are in a new house under construction, by upright and horizontal planking, the bare framework (see "The Palace at 4 A.M." in the Museum of Modern Art) which is moveable and combinable (and cheap). The whole back of the stage is taken up by a radar machine, which is not too obtrusive when the lights are on, but when the stage is in darkness, between scenes, it is dominant, giving a sense of time, the inexorability of time, to the action of the play.[11]

Here, readers of Maxwell's *So Long, See You Tomorrow* will recognize seeds of the novel's controlling metaphor, "The Palace at 4 A.M.," discussed in chapter 9. Although the author might not have remembered this reference when writing *So Long* about twenty-five years later, we can see retrospectively how the "bare framework" he describes will evolve into the structure of his final novel—how it will become a metaphor representing the artist's ability to transcend life's boundaries. Indeed, the "moveable" and "combinable" "Palace" of this set design suggests a sense of creativity that stands counter to the immovable radar machine, an ominous reminder of time's "inexorability." The "Palace" image also serves as a visual link between the author's adult world in New York and his childhood in Illinois—a connection first made in this unpublished manuscript and that proved critical in *Ancestors, So Long, See You Tomorrow,* and the late short fiction.

AT *THE NEW YORKER*

Although Maxwell did not publish a collection of his stories for two decades, he became involved in a joint project with some other *New Yorker* writers, an idea sparked during a cocktail conversation in the mid-1950s. One evening, writer Jean Stafford was at a party in Manhattan speaking with John Cheever over gin and water when someone unknown to them asked why they were so slow to bring out collections of their short stories. The two explained that aside from the indifference of publishers, to collect stories is "something like marrying many times and collecting all your wives under one roof on a rainy day." Besides, they had noticed that short fiction volumes were not often reviewed individually but rather "in tandem or four-in-hand and in an atmosphere of combativeness." Because they both wrote for *The New Yorker,* as did other writers they admired, they found such reviews driven by comparison, neglectful of the "exertion of uncommon cooperativeness" necessary for writers to make sense of life.[12]

Rather than create their own separate compilations, they decided to beat reviewers to the punch by placing *themselves* "four-in-hand": They approached fellow *New Yorker* writers J. D. Salinger and Daniel Fuchs about collaborating on a collection that would place their stories side by side, to be read in counterpoint. Salinger declined but recommended his editor, William Maxwell. Maxwell, who also served as editor for Stafford, Cheever, and Fuchs at the magazine, selected three of his own recent stories to be published with theirs: "The Trojan Women," "What Every Boy Should Know" (1954)—also set in familiar Draperville—and "The French Scarecrow." Unlike the *New Yorker*–published "Scarecrow," the two Draperville stories originally appeared in *Perspectives U.S.A.*: As Midwestern pieces, they fell outside Harold Ross's map of settings deemed suitable for the magazine's fiction. In retrospect, Maxwell saw these constrictions as a "good thing": By the time the magazine began accepting his Midwestern work under Ross's successor, William Shawn, the author thought he was "old enough to deal with the material."[13] Perhaps Maxwell was being too hard on his young self here. Certainly he had been writing novels about his native Midwest since the beginning of his career; among these, *They Came Like Swallows, The Folded Leaf,* and *Time Will Darken It*—written in the thirties and forties during Ross's tenure—rank among his strongest works.

In December 1956, the simply titled *Stories* appeared to reviews that recognized the four writers' distinct styles and approaches while also noting their commonalities: superb craftsmanship and "a certain…gloss and wit" that characterized *New Yorker* fiction at midcentury. According to one reviewer, the collection evinced the American short story's maturity: These writers were "now working in a form…quite individually its own," a form that had in large part been cultivated at the magazine.[14] Loosed from the strictures of traditional plot, the stories cast a dim view of society, a weariness of life in modern times. The last in the collection, Maxwell's work echoes strife and sadness, yet, not surprisingly, his voice is the gentlest among them, particularly when he deals with the world of children.

Throughout this period, Maxwell's editing career also thrived at the magazine, where he worked with some of the era's most prominent writers, including J. D. Salinger, Vladimir Nabokov, Eudora Welty, John Cheever, Mary McCarthy, and John Updike. His intense engagement with others' work—the constant reading, corresponding, querying, and negotiating narrative fine points—slowed progress on *The Chateau* yet also offered a rare, rewarding opportunity. In effect, his editorial position placed him at the center of a world-class community of writers on both sides of the Atlantic for most of his adult life. These intimate, long-standing associations formed one of the most extensive networks of literary friendship enjoyed by an American writer in the twentieth century. Maxwell was enriched both professionally and personally by the camaraderie he shared with the diverse range of authors, some internationally renowned, others accomplished but lesser known such as Nancy Hale and Natasha Stewart Ullman. Although Maxwell had established a number of these connections in the 1940s (with Cheever and Salinger, for example), key developments for his editorship followed in the fifties: Longtime friend Welty first published a story in the magazine, and notables Updike and Nabokov also entered his fold.

EUDORA WELTY

Maxwell had first met Welty during her visit to New York in 1940 and soon thereafter sent a letter to her Jackson, Mississippi, home soliciting short fiction for *The New Yorker*. She responded in December—having temporarily lost his letter in her unabridged dictionary—writing that she was "fresh out" of work that might be suitable. By 1951, however, she was at a crossroads: Her relationship with Harcourt Brace seemed "not too sympathetic," and Mary Lou Aswell, her editor at *Bazaar*, had left in an "editorial shake-up." Although Welty had misgivings about *The New Yorker*—in particular about Harold Ross's reputation for heavy-handed editorial "annotations"—Maxwell earned her trust as a "new ally," a sensitive editor with a light, steady touch who helped her achieve clearer prose without unnecessary tampering. In the early fifties, he stepped in to shepherd several of her manuscripts through the *New Yorker* editing process. The magazine published its first Welty story on December 1, 1951, eleven years after Maxwell's original solicitation. "The Bride of Innisfallen," for which she was paid $2,760, captured the record for the longest story to appear in the magazine at the time.[15]

The next May Welty brought her story "Kin" to Maxwell for an editorial conference. In June, after she had returned home, he sent her a copy of the story with suggested revisions. Only then did she decide "it sounded all right—the changes made that long day in Bill Maxwell's office were to the good and for clarity." That year Maxwell secured the magazine's acceptance of both "Kin" and "No Place for You, My Love."[16]

Welty returned to New York the next January with a new manuscript, *The*

Ponder Heart, which she read aloud to Maxwell and Emily in their Murray Hill brownstone apartment. With her smooth southern accent, Welty assumed the colorful part of Edna Earle Ponder, the narrator and proprietress of the Beulah Hotel in Mississippi, who speaks directly to readers as if they have just entered her establishment. Maxwell remembered that she read all day with only a break for lunch and that he laughed until he cried and then cried until no more tears would come. He must have laughed again on receiving a postcard from her picturing the revolving tables at the Mendenhall Hotel restaurant in Mendenhall, Mississippi, where, Welty wrote, bowls of "okra, corn pudding, butterbeans, turnip greens, beets, sweet potatoes, English peas, black-eyed peas, red beans, cole slaw, squash, fried chicken, fruit salad, cornbread, relish, iced tea, and pineapple betty" spun by diners lazy-Susan style.[17] "It would have been good in the Beulah," she observed, referring to her fictional *Ponder Heart* hotel. After the piece appeared uncut in *The New Yorker* in December 1953, Welty published it as a novella dedicated to Maxwell. *The Ponder Heart* received the William Dean Howells Medal of the Academy of Arts and Letters in 1955, an honor she presented to her editor twenty-five years later for his novel *So Long, See You Tomorrow.*[18]

VLADIMIR NABOKOV

Vladimir Nabokov came under Maxwell's wing in 1955 when Katharine White, his first *New Yorker* editor, moved from her editorial position to magazine policy because of ill health. Initially the Russian émigré was "distressed" at her departure: One of the magazine's creators, she had collected Nabokov's clippings from *The Atlantic* while at her home in Maine and rejoined the magazine in 1944 with the idea of soliciting his fiction. In White, Nabokov found a protective editor and a source of financial support; through her efforts he received monetary advances and funding for several trips to the Library of Congress. Certainly he had reason to dread the loss of such "kindness…generosity…and understanding."[19]

Nabokov found the same qualities in Maxwell. Their cordial professional correspondence grew warmer over their twenty-year relationship, during which Nabokov wrote *Pale Fire,* one of his most challenging works, and translated *The Gift* and *The Defense* from Russian into English, all of which Maxwell read in manuscript. By 1964, nearly ten years into their literary association, Nabokov had developed trust and admiration for him and had returned to Europe, where he and his wife Vera would live permanently. On March 5, ten days before he and Vera boarded *The United States* for a visit to New York, he wrote Maxwell about proofs for *The Defense,* which *The New*

Yorker planned to publish in two installments: "I have examined carefully and eagerly the proofs of the Luzhin Defense which I am now sending back with a few corrections and explanations. Let me add that I much appreciate your delicate and sympathetic touches. The thing reads beautifully."[20]

JOHN UPDIKE

In August 1954 Maxwell met John Updike, a recent Harvard graduate about to make a transatlantic crossing en route to a year at Oxford's Ruskin School of Drawing and Fine Arts. The young writer, who had already sold poetry and a short story to *The New Yorker,* had been invited to visit the magazine's offices before his departure.[21] Looking back more than forty years, Updike remembered the scene: "Maxwell, who emerged to shake my hand and usher me through the linoleum-floored maze to his own sunny office, conveyed a murmurous, restrained nervous energy and infallible grace; I was reminded of Fred Astaire." He recalled only one thing the editor said during "that first encounter, in which he was so deftly, patiently courteous and friendly and I was so bedazzled." That is, in response to a fear Updike expressed, Maxwell replied, "People imagine that losing your luggage is like death, but it isn't"—undoubtedly remembering his own European experience.[22]

After his year abroad, Updike returned as a member of the *New Yorker* staff, writing "Talk of the Town" columns and other pieces. When Katharine White left for Maine, Maxwell became his editor on a regular basis. "Our relationship in the many stories, well over a hundred, maybe approaching two hundred that he was the editor for, was just so amiable—it was a back and forth thing," Updike told me. "Bill is himself quite a clear and plain writer, deceptively so, at times. I'm not especially. So occasionally there would be a request for more plainness. But by and large, as he's said in interviews, he believes that the best editing is the least editing." Updike recalled Maxwell's style as "relaxed but perfectionistic, and that suited my mood exactly. He believed nothing was too much trouble" for even a slight improvement to a story. As a result, the two often had telephone conversations to make adjustments in the final stages of publication, even as stories were set in page format and ready for the printer. In particular, Updike recalled last-minute changes to "Who Made Yellow Roses Yellow?" and "Wait" during long talks that lasted "well into dinnertime."[23]

On another occasion Updike and general editor William Shawn agreed to kill the story "The Beloved" after it was typeset, and the writer felt uncomfortable having already received payment for work that would not be published. On his own volition, Updike remembered, Maxwell "extracted from the story's thirty or so pages six or seven that he felt would make a *New Yorker* story, and they were duly published—the one instance where I felt his contribution was so major that he should have co-signed the piece."[24] Among all Maxwell's writers, none could have been more steadfastly devoted than Updike, who sent congratulatory notes for his editor's late publications, confided in him when his own mother died, and corresponded with him to the end. Several days after Maxwell's death, Updike received a letter dictated by his editor on the last day of his life.

"THE WRITER AS ILLUSIONIST": THE SPEECH AT SMITH COLLEGE

In March 1955, Maxwell was invited to take part in a symposium at Smith College on "The American Novel at Mid-Century," joining Saul Bellow, Brendan Gill, and Alfred Kazin on the program. Although a Smith graduate, Emmy did not join him because she had given birth to their first child, Katharine, on December 19, 1954, an event they had dreamed about for nearly ten years. At last, after "recurring disappointment," the family life Maxwell longed for was fully realized: He now had a home, a wife, and a daughter to love. His circumstances had come full circle: What he lost as a child was now regained. Alec Wilkinson has noted that at this point Maxwell considered giving up writing to edit full-time because he thought he might be "running dry." Instead, he told Wilkinson, he just needed "a little public encouragement." He had "set his heart" on the Pulitzer Prize and the National Book Award for *Time Will Darken It:* "I wanted to be appreciated as a major novelist, and the book was respected, but not embraced. This was all because of Reik. He was Germanic, and had convinced me that I should be a person of stature in the world, and he was thinking of Europe, where it was possible to have that kind of career, but in America, if you insist on having it your own way, it takes a lot longer." Years later, Maxwell recalled that on the train ride to the Smith campus in Northampton, Massachusetts, he made notes for his talk on the novel. Wilkinson writes, "Some time before the train arrived he realized that he loved writing so much that he could never give it up."[25]

During our first meeting in 1991, Maxwell gave me a printed edition of the speech. The sensitive and passionate meditation on storytelling certainly suggests how, over the course of his train ride, he must have given up any thought of abandoning fiction writing. His handwritten notes from 1955 indicate that his ideas flowed naturally and easily; the comments he presented and subsequently published went almost unchanged from the moment they spilled onto the page as he traveled to Smith.[26] In retrospect, the lecture is the most important document articulating Maxwell's views about his craft: It provides insight into his process and approach generally and becomes particularly useful in understanding his ideas about fiction as he was composing *The Chateau.*

He opened his remarks by establishing magic as a unifying metaphor: "I prefer to think that it is with…the shoddy entertainers earning their living by the riverbank on May Day"—magicians, tightrope walkers, fortune tellers—"that Mr. Bellow, Mr. Gill, Miss Chase, on the platform, Mr. Ralph Ellison and Mr. Kazin, in the audience, and I, properly speaking, belong. Writers—narrative writers—are people who perform tricks.…The reader, skeptical, experienced, with many demands on his time and many ways of enjoying his leisure, is asked to believe in people he knows don't exist, to be present at scenes that never occurred, to be amused or moved or instructed just as he would be in real life, only the life exists in somebody else's imagination." To illustrate, he cites a number of illusionists whose sleight of hand "catches" readers in the opening passages of their works: Stephen Crane sets readers at sea "pulling at the oars in an open boat"; Melville introduces them to a stranger, Ishmael, with whom they have an immediate, personal relationship; Chekov etches in their minds an unforgettable lady and her dog walking along the seafront.

Maxwell catalogued the various tricks in the writer's repertoire: that of the opening sentence, of invoking a time and place, of detail ("If he is a good novelist, you can lean against his trees.…Ideally, you ought to be able to shake them until an apple falls on your head.") He also noted a "more general sleight of hand": "tricks that involve the whole work, tricks of construction." For example, in Elizabeth Bowen's *The House of Paris,* he finds none of the characters "as interesting as the way in which the whole thing is put together. From that all the best effects, the real beauty of the book derives." In a sense, he predicts here the achievement of his own late fiction, the care with which he tended to the construction of *So Long, See You Tomorrow* more than twenty years later. In our interviews, he ranked his final novel as his finest for the same reason he admired Bowen's.

Perhaps most entertaining that evening at Smith was Maxwell's simulation of how a writer—specifically, how he—begins a story with a mere detail, in this case a story about a ship voyage. He prefaced this section: "It would help if you would give what I am now about to read to you only half of your attention. It doesn't require any more than that, and if you listen only now and then, you will see better what I am driving at." And then he plunged ahead:

"Begin with breakfast and the tipping problem," he suggested. "Begin with the stealing of the marmalade dish and the breakfast tray still there." After a long list of potential scenarios and details that flow from the first, he then backtracks, choosing instead to "begin in the late afternoon with the sight of the English islands," and in quick succession returns to his original idea of beginning with the marmalade dish before changing his mind to "begin with the gate." At the end of the long process, he confides to his audience: "A writer struggling—unsuccessfully, as it turned out; the story was never written—to change a pitcher of water into a pitcher of wine."

Maxwell's playful yet realistic account of his creative process resonates in his fiction. His tone and attitude toward literature here are echoed in the dialogue of the authorial character who guides the final, experimental pages of *The Chateau*. Looking further ahead, the narrator of *So Long, See You Tomorrow* asks readers to "disregard" anything they find implausible, just as the author asked students to give him only part of their attention that evening in Northampton, Massachusetts. These parallels suggest that the experience of talking to a live audience at Smith was partially responsible for Maxwell's decision to address readers directly in his fiction, to step from behind the curtain to communicate more immediately with those for whom he wrote.

At Smith, part of this intimacy included discussion of how and why fiction can fall short—the obstacles to making narrative "tricks" work. The writer has "no enemy but interruption," Maxwell contends, explaining that this was the probable cause of Virginia Woolf's "only partly successful" trick in *Orlando,* that of the title character exchanging the mind of a man for that of a woman. "It would have been a great pity—it would have been a real loss if this particular book had never been written," he said. "Even so, it is disappointing." He shares that at times such interruptions are self-imposed, including "the most dangerous of all tricks in the repertoire": making "a few changes here and there, because what is behind [the writer], all the scenes that come before the scene he is now working on, must be *perfect,* before he can tackle what lies ahead....And tomorrow morning, with a clearer head...he will change back the changes, with one small insert that makes all the difference."

To stay focused, Maxwell himself wrote "in his bathrobe and slippers, unshaven, his hair uncombed, drinking water to clear his brain, and hardly distinguishable from an inmate in an asylum. Like many such unfortunate people, he has delusions of grandeur." All this he shared with students, faculty, and guests at Smith College. And then he closed, recognizing the mystery surrounding the desire to write:

The novelist's rabbit is the truth—about life, about human character, about himself and therefore by extension, it is to be hoped, about other people. He is convinced that this is all knowable, can be described, can be recorded, by a person sufficiently dedicated to describing and recording, can be caught in a net of narration....Why then should the successful manipulation of illusions be everything to a writer? Why does he bother to make up stories and novels? If you ask him, you will probably get any number of answers, none of them straightforward. You might as well ask a sailor why it is that he has chosen to spend his life at sea.[27]

The next day, the Smith *Sophian* described "Mr. Maxwell's beautiful and sensitive talk," which "gave new insight into how the artist creates and a new appreciation of the writer's role as the expressor of truth, as the man who observes and reinterprets society." It also reported a "battle of the books" during the panel discussion, a "cross[ing] of verbal swords" between Kazin and Bellow on one hand and Gill and Maxwell on the other. The argument centered on one of Kazin's major premises: that the novel had become "too self-conscious." Although Bellow agreed with Kazin that "a focusing upon the 'means' rather than the 'materials'...produced [an] objectionable style," Maxwell supported Gill's notion that the best writers were working in an "individual" rather than a "contrived" style, that even "the greatest writers work self-consciously," and that the important issue consists in "whether or not a quality of genius explodes through the writing."[28] Maxwell was moving quickly toward this "individual" style himself. In just a few years, he published his first experiment with self-consciousness, a move Gill supported and specifically commended in reviews of his friend's later work.[29]

THE CHATEAU AND KNOPF

By 1958, multiple drafts of Maxwell's new manuscript about France filled a grocery carton, while his other novels languished out of print. Publisher Alfred Knopf Jr. wrote him March 12 with an offer that would provide a home for *The Chateau* and new life for *They Came Like Swallows, The Folded Leaf,* and *Time Will Darken It:*

Dear Mr. Maxwell,
Brendan Gill tells me that all may not be well between you and Harper and Brothers. If this is in any remote way the case, we should be delighted, and indeed proud, to have an opportunity to talk to you about the possibility of your coming to Knopf. I find it hard to believe that your earlier books are out

of print, but if they are, I can well see how this might be a substantial irritant to an author who *is* an author.

Within a couple of months, Maxwell and Emily were lunching at Alfred Knopf Sr.'s home in Purchase, New York, and the two men quickly established a friendly rapport. "For some reason, I was as happy as a clam, the moment I set eyes on you," Maxwell wrote him afterwards. "As nearly as I can make out, the reason is that we share something—a pleasure in the pleasures of life." A contract was drawn that included reissuing his previous novels with Vintage—"part of the mutual understanding to bring happiness to the disgruntled author," Knopf reported—and bringing out the new book. Maxwell remained with Knopf for the rest of his career, which amounted to more than thirty years. He was always grateful to Brendan Gill for stepping in on his behalf and passed the favor on to his writer friend Natasha Stewart, who, at his suggestion, also received an invitation from Knopf.[30]

Soon after Maxwell signed, Knopf hosted a lunch for him and another of his authors, Frank O'Connor, who also contributed short stories to *The New Yorker*. Maxwell had first met the Irish writer in 1952, after several years of correspondence, and became his editor in Gus Lobrano's absence. The relationship proved mutually supportive. O'Connor appreciated a writer of Maxwell's stature reading his work and, in a successful role reversal, helped the editor get on with *The Chateau* when he found himself at a standstill. "I hadn't been able to make up my mind whether it should have an omniscient author or a first-person narrator, whether it should be told from the point of view of the French or the Americans traveling in France," Maxwell recalled. "I was afraid that it wasn't a novel at all but a travel diary."[31]

O'Connor visited his editor's country home in August 1958 and asked how the book was coming. Hearing about the carton filled with various "unreadable" versions, he insisted that he could read anything, and Maxwell was "horrified." At that stage in his career, he wasn't in the habit of showing anyone rough drafts, but he relented out of fairness: He had read early versions of O'Connor's *An Only Child*, which he considered a masterpiece. How could he refuse to reciprocate? O'Connor "went off with the grocery carton in the backseat of his car, and read through the whole mess." He concluded that it was actually two novels: one about the American couple and another about the French. "My relief was immense," Maxwell recalled, "because it is a lot easier to make two novels into one than it is to make one out of nothing whatever. So I went ahead and finished the book."[32]

In September, Maxwell thought he had found a way to write solely through the eyes of the Americans but by October realized it would not work: "I got to the last part and it just trailed off," he wrote O'Connor. "It wasn't a novel. All it proved was that I had been to Europe. It has to be counterpoint." In addition, he did not think the "psychological probing" of the Americans served a purpose as it had in past novels: "It isn't that nothing happens, so much as that I can't decide how much or how little to reveal, and that the less I tell the more it seems like, but will the reader stand for it? I tried having the French people reveal most of the things I had told as narrator, and you know, it was so un-French."[33]

Maxwell had not heard from O'Connor in a couple of months when he finally received a letter in late October. "Of course, it's not a novel," O'Connor wrote. "Novels were written exclusively by Jane Austen and Turgenev, and the secret died with them, but the substitutes have a lot to be said for them. I dread your counterpointing, not because I think you can't do it, but because I fear you won't let well enough alone. I wish, instead of re-writing immediately you felt dissatisfied, you had put it away for a few weeks, and re-read it some evening you were feeling really brilliant. You would then see what I saw; that the virtue of the novel was in its apparent thinness and ingenuousness."[34]

When Maxwell finished his final draft, he thought the novel left "all manner of threads hanging." Although it formally concluded with the Americans leaving Paris, saying goodbye to the old French woman, Madame Straus-Muguet, at the railway station, he saw that mysteries about the French characters remained. He was also concerned about his use of the French language: Although he was confident that he had succeeded in writing bad French dialogue for his linguistically challenged Americans, he wanted to ensure that his French characters were speaking as "French people would" and called on his friend Francis Steegmuller, the Flaubert biographer and translator of *Madame Bovary,* to read the manuscript. Steegmuller "tidied up the French where it needed it and was a great help," he recalled. The biographer also assisted with the matter of the story's "hanging threads" by making objections to the novel. In particular, he disliked the Americans, whom he found "foolish." Steegmuller's misgivings led Maxwell to create a new ending with an unusual narrative device: an epilogue that features an imaginary reader questioning a narrator who appears to be the author. "I answered some of his objections in this thing," Maxwell said, "but it also set up the idea of a dialogue."[35] In essence, Steegmuller became his imagined "every reader" in the novel's final pages, an anonymous character unsatisfied with the novel he has just read. Dialogue between the two flows, yet even as the author addresses the reader's questions, as he playfully fills gaps in the narrative, he also explains that mystery lies behind mystery, that "answers" about interpersonal nuance cannot lead to full understanding. As a narrative solution to reservations he and Steegmuller had about the manuscript, the epilogue lends a sense of experimentation to the novel. By allowing his material to dictate form, the author broke new ground on his literary path.

* * *

After a six-month extension to write the epilogue, Maxwell hand-delivered the manuscript to the Knopf offices on June 17, 1960. Mr. Knopf was out, hosting a lunch for Carl Van Vechten's eightieth birthday, but he wrote Maxwell the same afternoon to express his delight. Knopf editor-in-chief Harold Strauss and Maxwell's editor, Judith Jones, had mixed reactions, however. They found the American characters underdeveloped and thought answers to the novel's mysteries came too late. Both felt cheated by the "tricks" Maxwell played. "All I can say with assurance about this book is that no one will enjoy it," Strauss wrote, "but that some who persist in reading it through may admire it for what it is—an astonishing experimental novel. Not in style, which is pellucid, but in form. Maxwell has systematically expunged every narrative element from Part I (347 pages), and then supplied it in Part II (48 pages), in an astonishing dialogue between the novelist and the reader, in which he as much says, 'The story of what really happened isn't important; but if you, dear reader, insist on it, I'll tell it to you.' I'll say this much for Maxwell's method of mystification: if one gets this far, one wants to know." Even so, he continued, "One comes away with a vivid and profound knowledge of the French characters; Maxwell has created a dozen memorable people (among whom I do not include the Rhodes). Surely this is a literary achievement of some magnitude. He does it entirely without narrative, by sinking deeper and deeper into the situation, by deliberate mystification, by actions never explained until the disdainful second part." Strauss recommended replacing the epilogue with a prologue, so that readers would know from the beginning "what his people are up to," and drastic cutting of the "travelogue elements."[36]

Judith Jones concurred: "I can't think of any contemporary novelist who has succeeded so well in exposing the subtle vulnerabilities on both sides, the interplay of feelings and attitudes, and the irrational, overwhelming feeling of love that Americans will attach to Paris....Still the dissatisfaction with this as a novel persists, and one feels the 'elucidation' at the end more of an author's justification because the novel does not speak for itself....I think he could make it a stronger novel. If we go ahead as is, I think we must expect some disappointment both in terms of sales and critical reception." Mr.

Knopf noted on the manuscript record: "Curiously, I somehow react differently from HS and JBJ, for I find the last fifty pages the least interesting, almost unnecessary. While it's true that the book has no plot and is unlikely to reach a wide audience it does give a rare, charming picture of France and especially the Loire country. But of course I may be prejudiced because I know that country after a fashion."[37]

Maxwell met with Mr. Knopf and the editors to discuss cutting the epilogue. "I am always so tired out when I finish a book that I'm over susceptible to other people's ideas, and I didn't really know whether it was a good idea or a bad idea," he recalled. "Alfred Knopf was sitting in the room not saying anything, and I turned to him. He said 'Have it the way you want it.' So I did. Now, if I were to pick up *The Chateau* and that epilogue wasn't there, I think I would shoot myself."[38]

The Chateau

The publication of *The Chateau* marked the chronological and artistic midpoint of Maxwell's career. Now one of his lesser-known novels, it became his only book to hit the *New York Times* bestseller list, despite his editors' early concerns, and was nominated for both the National Book Award and the Pulitzer Prize. Thirteen years had passed since the appearance of *Time Will Darken It*. During this period *The New Yorker* achieved unprecedented literary and financial success, and Maxwell enjoyed a reputation as one of its leading writers and editors. Readers, it seems, had been waiting for a new Maxwell novel.

For readers of his Illinois fiction, of course, *The Chateau* may be intriguing as his only novel that ventures beyond his native territory. When a writer so intimately associates himself with a particular place in time—when, over many years, he claims it as his own—we may wonder what will happen outside the sanctity of his imagination's home. In other novels, Maxwell's sensibility seems to emerge organically from his Midwestern milieu; his tone and setting entwine seamlessly. Yet here, away from his established element, the strength of his observations and his sensitive approach to character become especially clear as we are encouraged to consider his view of the human condition from a new vantage point.

The Chateau's standing among twentieth-century American novels has never reached that of the critically acclaimed *They Came Like Swallows, The Folded Leaf*, and *So Long, See You Tomorrow*; even so, it contributes to a study of Maxwell's body of work on a number of levels. Valuable for its historical insights, it offers a vivid portrait of postwar France from an American perspective. With characteristic attention to subtle shadings of human interaction and domestic detail, the writer juxtaposes the Americans' thoughts and reactions with the sometimes mysterious behavior of the shell-shocked French and the ravaged countryside surrounding them—a theme that reminded some critics of Americans abroad in the Jamesian tradition. The novel also suggests two significant developments in Maxwell's writing: a deepening psychological insight that in some scenes exceeds that of the earlier novels and a more overt implementation of the self-referential narrative hinted at in *Time Will Darken It*. In essence, *The Chateau* bridges Maxwell's early and late periods by shifting focus from the story at hand to the storyteller's methods—to the very "tricks" he discussed at Smith College. In the novel's closing pages, his playful experimentation builds the relationship between creative writing and lived experience that emerges as a central subject of his later work.

MAXWELL'S POSTWAR DOCUMENT

Ironically, Maxwell's quietest novel is his only one that directly addresses the relevance of political circumstances in characters' lives and, in effect, offers a postwar document of some significance. Here, his characteristic focus on subtlety and inner life suggests how "small and unimportant" detail can poignantly reveal a historical moment. As Naomi Bliven noted, the novel has "the authenticity of a verified document, a history of what some citizens of the splintered world might say or mean to each other in our period."[39] Now, more than forty years after her review appeared in *The New Yorker*, Bliven's words seem prophetic, for *The Chateau* offers a rare window on the aftermath of the last world war and, in particular, an account of the first wave of American tourists to venture abroad three years after Europe's liberation. Maxwell captures the mixture of joy and tension that colors the Americans' travels and the conflicted emotions on both sides: The Rhodeses relish new experiences and people yet flinch at European views of American involvement and the plight of the Jews. By turns, the French seem both grateful and resentful, and Maxwell juxtaposes their hardships, indomitable spirit, and bitterness with the delight and disillusion of the touring pilgrims.

From the outset, we learn that "in the early spring of 1948 it had seemed to be a question of how long Europe would be [there]...in a way that was recognizable and worth coming over to see." Yet the Rhodeses go forward to find "ugly and pockmarked" buildings and the picturesque view of the Old Port at Marseilles "obliterated by the repeated bombings." Despite their sensitivity and sympathy for the French condition, conflicts arise that suggest how gulfs between people—gulfs of culture, language, and unshared experience—cannot always be bridged. In bed one evening, Harold asks Barbara, "Do I imagine it...or is it true that when they speak of the Nazis...the very next sentence is invariably some quite disconnected remark about Americans?" Harold's concerns are not unfounded. Shortly after their arrival, Mme. Vienot expresses her fear of war between the United States and Russia. "I blame your President Roosevelt," she says. "He didn't understand the Russian temperament and so he was taken in by promises that mean nothing....Never trust a Slav." Later, Harold is offended when Mme. Vienot complains that America expected too much in return for wheat provisions given to France under the Marshall Plan. And, while at the home of Jean Allegret, a well-to-do friend of the Vienots, Harold is forced to defend his country politely against the accusation that America "will bring another war down on us, just as Woodrow Wilson did." "What would you have us do?" Harold asked, "stay out of it next time?"[40]

In dealing with Germans, Harold feels even more bewildered. He oscillates between harshly, though privately, attacking their lack of concern for the Jews and feeling guilt for having judged them. After some Berliners stay with them in the Vienot's Paris apartment, they thank the Americans for their kindness while also taking "advantage of [the] opportunity to register with these two citizens of one of the countries that were now occupying the fatherland their annoyance at being made a political football between the United States and the USSR. *And the war?* Harold asked silently as they shook hands, *And the Jews?*" Late in their trip, Harold receives a thank-you note from one of the Germans and is depressed by their views about preparations for life under communism. "Our people need some decades of political education...and in the meantime it ought to get a strong government of experts assisted by a parliament with consultative rights only," the letter reads. "They haven't learned anything—anything at all," Harold tells Barbara. "He feels sorry for the German women but not a word about the others, all over the world. Not a word about who started it."[41]

* * *

In *The Chateau*, Maxwell continues his exploration of masculine sensibility and physicality. From the opening scenes, Harold measures his own inadequacies in light of this dichotomy. "Thin and flat-chested, narrow-faced, pale from lack of sleep, and tense in his movements," he views the French shoreline for the first time through a prism of tears, as if "some anonymous ancestor, preserved in his bloodstream…had suddenly taken over; somebody looking out of the porthole of a ship on a July morning and recognizing certain characteristic features of his homeland, of a place that is Europe and not America, wept at all he did not know he remembered."[42]

Harold's delicate nature and physical frailty suggest intimate connections with the sensitive boys of Maxwell's earlier novels; he obviously shares affinity with Bunny and Lymie rather than Robert and Spud. As an adult, Harold carries with him the child whose artistic interests and underdeveloped physique become alienating peculiarities: "A whole generation of loud, confident Middle-Western voices saying: *Harold, sit up straight.... Harold, hold your shoulders back.... Harold, you need a haircut, you look like a violinist* had had no effect whatever. Confidence had slipped through his fingers. He had failed to be like other people." Maxwell presents Harold's feelings of inadequacy and isolation as the result of experiences in early life, a theme that appeared in later fiction: The past constantly impinges on the present; individuals do not outlive, but live with, their former selves. Although painful childhood memories do not prevent Harold from becoming a productive, content, and compassionate adult, a cloud of melancholy subtly shadows his life, in part a result of the couple's inability to conceive a child. Like Lymie Peters, he still "avoids his reflection in mirrors and wants to be liked by everybody." Even his love for Barbara, undoubtedly the truest joy of his life, takes on a sense of poignant longing strikingly similar to Lymie's yearnings for his late mother: When Harold is "separated from her in a crowd he becomes anxious, and in dreams he wanders through huge houses calling her name."[43]

Such characterizations suggest that Maxwell's psychoanalysis continued to influence his writing. Here, questions he raises about motives and behavior stem directly from more comprehensive understanding of himself and new curiosity about others. After his work with Reik, an intensified focus on internal life led naturally to his consideration of the myriad personas within his characters. As the writer continues his focus on adulthood here, his ability to capture the psyche of youth—so powerful in *They Came Like Swallows* and *The Folded Leaf*—clearly informs his adult characters. Here, however, he does not use allusions to the external world to validate or enlarge characters' experiences. Instead, he delves further inward to reveal the multiplicity and complexity of human nature, calling on his facility with the childhood psyche to layer the inner lives of adults.

For example, Harold becomes "the sum total of his memories," at once "the child his mother went in to cover on her rounds, the last thing at night before she went to bed," and "a commuter standing on the station platform, with now the *Times* and now the *Tribune* under his arm, waiting for the 8:17 express. A liberal Democrat, believing idealistically in the cause of labor but knowing few laborers, and a member in good standing of the money-loving class he was born into, though, as it happens, money slips through his fingers." Not surprisingly, Maxwell privileges the childhood self as "in some ways the most mature of all these facets of his personality." To understand Harold, "it helps, of course, to know what happened when they were choosing up sides and he stood waiting for his name to be called." The "summer he spent in bed with rheumatic fever on an upstairs sleeping porch" claims a part of him, as does "the street he lived on—those big, nondescript, tree-shaded, Middle Western white houses, beautiful in the fall when the leaves turned, or at dusk with the downstairs lights turned on."[44]

"He's no one person," the narrator concludes, "he's an uncountable committee of people who meet and operate under the handy fiction of his name. The minutes of the last meeting are never read, because it's still going on." Here Maxwell suggests an essential relationship between childhood, adolescence, and adulthood, a timeless plane on which all stages of life, all aspects of self, exist. At once, Harold is each persona he has played as well as the sum of them. The committee members, who "know each other, but not always by their right names," represent internal contradictions: The bachelor who has resigned himself to loneliness knows the smiling bridegroom "with a white carnation in his buttonhole...aware of the good wishes of everybody and also of a nagging doubt in his mind."[45]

Although many of Harold's committee members seem to haunt rather than illumine his life, the novel also reveals his significant successes and strengths: He possesses a highly developed sensibility and intelligence as well as a lust for life and adventure. In effect, he resembles the gifted observer described by the narrator of *The Folded Leaf,* who understands that "the great, the universal problem is how to be always on a journey and yet see what you would see if it were only possible for you to stay home"; who keeps "sufficiently detached and quiet inside so that when the cat in one spring reaches the top of the garden wall...and disappears, [he] will see it and remember it." Harold takes this very approach to the people and places of France: He drinks in everything and everyone he meets, meticulously analyzing both the atmosphere and people at the chateau. On the professional front, despite "two false starts" in the business world, he now holds "a job with a future" at an engraving firm. His four months' leave of absence—"proof that his work is valued"—allows him to take an extended European sojourn with his wife, with whom he shares an emotionally, intellectually, and sexually satisfying marriage.[46]

Such circumstances suggest a future that readers of *The Folded Leaf* might wish for the struggling Lymie Peters: that as he matured he would retain his sensitive nature, create for himself a rewarding personal and professional life, and nurture a relationship with a loving partner. In fact, with each subsequent male protagonist in Maxwell's canon the weakness of self-doubt gives way to formidable yet understated inner strength, strength quite distinct from the physical prowess Lymie envied in Spud. Although Maxwell did not intend his novels as a series, Harold suggests a midpoint in the progression from the painful struggles of youth to the radiant, reflective maturity of the narrator in *So Long, See You Tomorrow*. Certain moments in *The Chateau* foreshadow this powerful work and reveal Maxwell's deepening insights.

THE EPILOGUE: "SOME EXPLANATIONS"

Though only fifty pages, the epilogue marks a turning point in the development of Maxwell's narrative art, adding new dimension to his technique and predicting the direction and concerns of his later career. Most notably, he introduces a first-person persona that resembles him in a novel for the first time. For the most part, an omniscient narrator interprets and offers perspective throughout part I (although the authorial figure sneaks in a comment here and there). In the epilogue, however, the first-person narrator takes center stage. Inspired by Francis Steegmuller's questions, the novel's final pages picture him stepping from behind the narrative to speak to an imaginary reader who can question and challenge his artistic choices.

The epilogue opens with the reader puzzling over the novel he has just read.

"Is that all?" he asks.

"Yes, that's all," the narrator replies.

"But what about the mysteries?" the reader persists, curious about the unexplained behavior of the French characters. Among other things, he wonders why "Alix didn't say good-by to [the Americans] at the station" and "why the actress was so harsh with poor Mme. Straus-Muguet, when they went backstage."

"I don't know that any of those things very much matters. They are details," the narrator says, and then asks, "You don't enjoy drawing your own conclusions about them?"[47] Readers can envision here the narrator and imagined reader deep in conversation, perhaps sitting side by side. Clearly, the narrator is no longer the eye viewing experiences with detached omniscience but the I behind the creation of the novel. The boundaries between the roles of author and narrator are beginning to blur.

The conversation continues. Despite his initial reluctance to solve the novel's mysteries, the narrator becomes increasingly playful in his attempts to satisfy the reader's curiosity. "Would you like to see [Eugene and Alix] sleeping together?" he asks. "It's quite all right. No trouble at all." And later, in answer to a question about Mme. Vienot, he writes, "Now suppose I pass my hand over the crystal ball twice. What do we see?"[48]

Maxwell's use of the magic metaphor stems directly from "The Writer as Illusionist," his Smith College speech. As an illusionist himself, he offers to perform tricks in hopes of appeasing his imagined *Chateau* reader. And, for the first time in his work, he openly discusses these illusions within the illusion of the novel itself. He tells his reader, "If you really want to know why something happened, if explanations are what you care about, it is usually possible to come up with one. If necessary, it can be fabricated." Here he provides a glimpse of the self-referential quality he developed further in his late fiction. In his own words, explaining away one mystery only "makes room for another," yet fiction lends meaning to experience beyond the questions we ask. Twenty years later, the author refers to his writing with increased complexity, sophistication, and seriousness in *So Long*; the art of fiction becomes a central concern rather than an afterthought. Yet even in this epilogue, his references to the creative process become explicit: "Every novel ought to have a heroine," he tells his reader, "and [Mme. Vienot] is the heroine of this one."[49] Although this may come as a surprise to readers who have followed Harold and Barbara Rhodes on their European trip, the sudden switch in emphasis draws attention to the writer's creative role. Through the "illusion" of fiction, he changes the focus, even the meaning of his story. Clearly, the epilogue illustrates Maxwell's experimentation with fiction as a subject for imaginative writing.

Maxwell understood well the reader for whom he performed. In the epilogue, the reader takes a particularly active role, at one point interrupting the narrator's description of Alix and Eugene's home with "swallows skimming the rooftops": "I've really had enough of those swallows," the reader says. Unfazed, the narrator maintains control: "For some reason, I never grow tired of them," he replies, and continues his story.[50]

Later, in the midst of a glowing description of the Palais-Royal and the Louvre, the reader again interrupts the narrator in midsentence: "Everybody feels that way about Paris. London is beautiful, too. So is Rome....What interests me is Mme. Vienot. It is a pity that [the Americans] did not bother to see her" on their return trip two years later. The narrator explains, "She was in the country. But just because the Americans didn't see her is no sign we can't....It is Tuesday" (ellipsis Maxwell's).[51] Here, the image of the two conversationalists becomes more vivid: The elliptical pause suggests the narrator taking a deep breath or giving the reader a knowing glance. Understanding that he must perform narrative tricks to satisfy his reader's curiosity, he describes Mme. Vienot during the Rhodeses' return trip, despite his insistence that they were unable to see her. This time, the reader character drives the narrative; or rather, the narrator, through the illusion of his narrative trick, allows us to believe that another, representative reader is controlling the novel's direction. In effect, the real reader is given a spokesperson who can discuss the story with the storyteller.

* * *

The epilogue also addresses Maxwell's interest in preserving the past and suggests the direction this theme will take in his future fiction. Clearly, he was concerned with safeguarding history from the beginning of his career, yet here, with the epilogue's new reflexivity, he explicitly suggests fiction as a means of coping with, and even controlling, the passage of time—a theme invoked earlier with Francisco Pacheco's words in *Time Will Darken It*. At one point, the narrator describes the circumstances of Frederic, Sabine's French fiancé, whose family home is occupied by Russians during the war: His "father arranged for him to escape in a Norwegian fishing vessel. Or perhaps it was on foot, across the border, with a handful of other frightened people."[52] This passage predicts Maxwell's later work by revealing his attempt to arrive at historical truth through narrative. By undercutting and amending his initial statement, he uncovers the problems associated with finding definitive answers about the past.

In a description of Mme. Vienot's home years after the Americans' visit, he becomes more explicit about "the relentless thieving" of time "that nobody pays any attention to; or, if they become aware of it, they try not to think about it." He elaborates: "If you are aware of a certain temperament, you do think about it, anyway. You think about it much too much, until the sense of deprivation becomes intolerable and you resort to the Lost-and-Found Office, where, by an *espece de miracle*, everything has been turned in, everything is the way it used to be." Certainly, the narrator accepts the passage of time as uncontrollable and history, in some sense, unknowable. However,

Maxwell offers meaningful connection with the past not only by preserving what was but also by creating what might have been, a realm of possibility to which he turned in coming years.

The "Lost-and-Found Office" becomes a metaphoric place in which the "thieving" of time can be halted, a psychological loophole through which the past can be recreated. It also serves as a forerunner to a similar, ultimately more successful image in *So Long, See You Tomorrow:* the "Palace at 4 A.M.," based on the Alberto Giacometti sculpture by that name. Like the "Lost-and-Found Office," the Palace becomes an imagined place where "what is done can be undone," where characters can change the past just as they make choices that affect the present and future. Of course, fiction itself is the literal "Lost-and-Found Office," where a writer can create his or her own vision free from the constraints of time, passing years, and death. Maxwell's move toward self-referential narrative seems a natural and logical development at this point in his career: If fiction provides a place where the past can be remade, certainly that place is an appropriate subject for a novel.[53]

* * *

Maxwell ends *The Chateau* with a poignant portrait of an aging Mme. Vienot, years after the Americans' visit, performing her nightly bedtime rituals. Having survived the devastation of her once satisfying life at the hands of both the Germans and her fortune-blundering husband, she has learned to rely on herself, to remain strong amid catastrophes beyond her control. As the head of a household of women, she lovingly puts her ailing mother to bed and mentally prepares herself to comfort her daughter, Sabine, who has recently lost her job. Seated at her dressing table, she removes her makeup, exposing the "gray underface": "She and it have arrived at a working agreement," the narrator tells us, "the underface, tragic, sincere, irrevocably middle-aged, is not to show itself until late at night when everyone is in bed. And in return for this discreet forbearance, Mme. Vienot on her part is ready to acknowledge that the face she now sees in the mirror is hers."[54]

Although Mme. Vienot knows she cannot stop the "thieving" of time etched in her face, she remains committed to maintaining control over her own existence in the restricted ways available to her. Before retiring, she finishes a letter and places it in a stack of several others she has written that evening. "The pile of letters represents the future," Maxwell writes, "which can no more be trusted to take care of itself than the present can (though experience has demonstrated that there is a limit, a point beyond which effort cannot go, and many things happen, good and bad, that are simply the work of chance)."[55]

Understanding intimately the limits of human effort, Mme. Vienot—like Maxwell himself—writes to fulfill the potential of that effort. Letters help her to control her own emotional and financial survival: they can ward off a lonely future by prodding forgetful acquaintances to remember her and to respond in kind, and because "paying guests...cannot be counted on to remember indefinitely what an agreeable time they had," letters remind them to return or to send other clients to her "pleasant, well-situated, wholly proper establishment."[56] The limits on human will that Maxwell suggests extend also to the illusion of fiction itself: As the reader character continues to question the novel's mysteries, the writer can foster understanding through his art. Even so, as the narrator explains, truth is difficult if not impossible to ascertain, and in the end human efforts to grasp the unknown, to recapture the past, cannot be completely satisfactory.

In the novel's final scene, Mme. Vienot, unable to sleep, reads the memoirs of Father Robert, an early-nineteenth-century Jesuit missionary. Snuggled in her bed, she "puts what happened to him, his harsh but beautifully dedicated life, between her and all silences, all creaking noises, all failures, all searching for answers that cannot be found."[57] In these last words, Maxwell again reminds readers that life, as well as art, offers infinite possibilities but no definitive solutions. Writing and reading become Mme. Vienot's means of coping with aspects of life she cannot control. For Maxwell, too, language is a means of agency in a world where unforeseen events can alter life suddenly, radically, and irrevocably. In essence, language serves as a central theme: first as a cultural barrier between the Americans and the French, then as a connection between the past and future, and ultimately as a subject for consideration in literary art.

PUBLICATION AND REVIEWS

The Chateau was published in March 1961. Louise Bogan wrote to him on the fifteenth full of appreciation for the work's experimental form and sensitivity: "You tell difficult truths, as the novelist must. And Part II breaks away from novelistic construction in, I think, an important way. Things slowly come to the surface, as they do in actual experience. And true virtue receives its due!" Preparations for a fourth printing were under way by May when Blanche Knopf, Alfred Sr.'s wife, wrote Maxwell with good news: "Congratulations! You are number seven on next Sunday's best seller list—I think that is absolutely marvelous and I am enchanted, and I hope you both will be." The author replied, "You were very kind indeed to write me about 'The Chateau' moving up to seventh place. What a cliffhanger it is. In order to fully appreciate a situation of this kind, one needs to have had a book disappear without a trace, a fairly good book, and I've lived through that, too. And so feel I have a right to be happy now." By October, Alfred Knopf reported, the novel had sold between seventeen and eighteen thousand copies.[58]

Indeed, *The Chateau* became one of Maxwell's most commercially successful novels at the time of its publication, yet reviews were unusually mixed. Overall, critics concurred that the story was beautifully told in a polished, straightforward prose, presented the intricacies of human relationships with keen sensitivity, and enhanced themes the author had explored in earlier novels. Several cited the artistry of the prose; as Naomi Bliven writes, "His style is a joy—exact, moderate, from time to time amused or amusing, always compassionate, sometimes as startling as lightning." Even so, some reviews found the novel too quiet and a bit too slow; at the least, several critics expressed empathy with those who found it tedious. *Time* blamed Maxwell's twenty-five-year tenure at *The New Yorker* for his "rueful resignation and wry disenchantment" and dubbed the book "precise, intelligent," though "slightly bloodless." Maxwell's "massive restraint sometimes brings his narrative to a dead halt," the *Time* critic continues. "His quietness of tone sometimes verges on the inaudible." Although Granville Hicks maintains that "the book belongs on a shelf that holds some of the most distinguished American fiction," and that some readers will "relish every word," he admits that it is "uncommonly quiet even for [Maxwell], quiet, slow moving, and perhaps at times rather dull." In retrospect, the most insightful review may have been Richard Gilman's in *Commonweal:* The critic acknowledges that although the novel is about the intricacies of relationships, it is also about the novel itself, "about the author's questioning of the novel as a source of accurate knowledge and solutions to problems. It is really an anti-novel," he writes, "and if you understand that there is no massive esthetic theory involved and that Maxwell isn't angry or jaded, you might appreciate and enjoy the kind of anti-novel it is."[59]

Nearly four decades later, British critic Miranda Seymour offered new perspective on the novel and its reception after Harvill of London released a new edition in 2000. In retrospect, and with a European sensibility, Seymour both assesses the work in terms of the historical moment in which it first appeared and comments on its permanent literary value: "*The Chateau* was first published in 1961," she writes. "Now, it is hard not to see it as a work of genius; at the time, it flopped." She attributes initial critical indifference to both the literary and social mood: "Novels were getting edgy and contemporary by 1961," she continues. "These were the years of Kingsley Amis and John Updike and Iris Murdoch." She posits that, at the time, Maxwell's novel "must have sounded dated and quirky, and...was imprudent enough, moreover, to contemplate the poverty of postwar France, as seen through the eyes of a couple of wealthy young American tourists. Not so much swinging as staggering back on to their feet, European readers of the early 1960s were not about to welcome what sounded like patronage. Neither were they ready for a book which, without making any fuss about it, subverts the idea of what a novel should be."[60]

In reality, however, most European readers of the early 1960s did not get a chance to judge *The Chateau* for themselves. Not that there was no interest by European publishers; on the contrary, Maxwell's reputation coupled with the novel's continental setting prompted early offers. By October 1960, for instance, French publisher Robert Laffont had already expressed "keen interest" in the French-language rights.[61] However, the author was concerned about the real-life family who lived at the chateau. "I refused to let the book be published," he remembered, "not only in France but in England because I thought English books would get across the channel so easily. I didn't want to hurt them." For many years, only one member of the French family knew about the book, a woman he had not met previously who visited America and saw the reviews. She called Maxwell, who extended an invitation for drinks. "She was only halfway through the book when she was [in New York]," he recalled. "She finished the book and went home, and never told anybody. Years and years and years passed....Eventually [the family in France] got hold of a copy and read it, and I had a letter from one of them. She said, 'It was very naughty of you. Could we please have a copy ourselves?'"

By the time the author and his wife returned to visit the French family, the book had been discovered. He recalled that the real-life counterpart of the deaf woman who appears in the novel was "by then very old, in her nineties and lying on a chaise longue in a Paris apartment—and I was very fond of her and I knelt down beside the bed to talk to her, and she said sweetly, 'You know you were very naughty to write that book. Because you didn't speak French, you didn't understand things.'" Not everyone in the family agreed with her assessment, Maxwell remembered: "Behind me I heard this whisper from her son-in-law, which was, 'He got everything right.'" The last time the author saw the family in France, he decided to make a final inquiry over dinner: "'A long, long time has passed,'" he remembered asking them. "'Is it all right to publish the book in France?' I'd had many offers for it. They said, 'We'll read it again.' So they read it again and the answer came back: 'No, not now. Not ever.'"[62]

How Europeans would have responded to *The Chateau* when the Occupation was fresher in their minds cannot be determined with certainty. Although Seymour thinks the work would have translated as "patronage," French and English readers, perhaps more than their American counterparts, might have appreciated the author's quiet sensitivity, his lingering over subtle nuances, and his manner of delicately revealing mysteries that lead to further questions without answers. In the present day, Maxwell seems to be an American writer with whom Europeans share particular affinity; his novels and story collections can be found prominently displayed in bookstores across the Atlantic, especially since their British reissue in the months before he died. His fiction, though deeply American on one hand, exudes a refined sensibility, a refusal to rush—what *Le Monde* called "La délicate élégance de William Maxwell"[63]—that European readers and critics embrace. In particular, Harold Rhodes offers direct counter to the stereotypic American often portrayed in the European press.

Consider, for example, a 2002 analysis published by London's *The Guardian*, headlined "The other side of America: In the U.S., not everyone is an overweight gun fanatic—and not everyone wants a war with Iraq." Perhaps it should not be surprising that the correspondent, Duncan Campbell, opens his commentary with a reference to *The Chateau*, specifically to Harold Rhodes as the sensitive, anti–ugly American who puzzles over why he and his wife are not uniformly embraced by the French, whom they so desperately wish to know. Indeed, Maxwell's Harold and Barbara embody the complexities and contradictions of the transatlantic relationship even today: America's love affair with the Old World and its self-image as "the nation that liberated Europe." Although Maxwell's work emanates, for the most part, from the heart of America, it also exudes a European spirit of refinement and reserve that in some cases plays against expectation. This quality becomes especially prominent in *The Chateau:* Like Maxwell's books, Harold serves as a literary ambassador, offering a fresh view of the American character to readers overseas. As Campbell implies in *The Guardian*, Harold contradicts a "monolithic impression of the US created in the European press: of a people wedded to guns, violence, the death penalty and over-eating." Maxwell, who until Adlai Stevenson viewed himself as apolitical, might be surprised to see Harold and Barbara cited so prominently in a political piece as representatives of a citizenry merely "anxious to connect," as evidence of an alternative American temperament. In retrospect, the writer who started a novel to keep his memories of France alive might well have achieved much more. Perhaps finally, as Campbell notes, the two young travelers offer a lesson "for Americans and Europeans alike, there are two words always worth remembering and always easy to forget: never assume."[64] Indeed, Campbell's conclusion echoes a central interest of Maxwell's novel: The mysteries of character and culture are best not guessed at, for they are layered with the past and present in intricate, often indecipherable ways. In the end, one must spend much time and thought in an attempt to understand and empathize with the essential character of another people—more time and thought than visitors are typically allowed—and even then, one will arrive at new questions indefinitely.

As a result of Maxwell's consideration for his real-life French hosts, Seymour's belated review of *The Chateau* is one of the first European responses to his only European novel. She views it as a work in which the author took chances, chances largely misunderstood at the time. This is particularly true of the epilogue, his "boldest section," according to Seymour, who writes, "The critics termed it an 'anti-novel,' and breathed a sigh of relief when Maxwell went back to a more traditional form nineteen years later with the novella *So Long, See You Tomorrow*. He was rewarded with the National Book Award and wrote nothing so perversely ambitious as *The Chateau* again."[65] Seymour's comments help us to understand Maxwell in the literary climate of the times as well as in light of critics' and readers' expectations of his work. She encourages us to reconsider *The Chateau*—to view it as a bold innovation rather than a mild tangent, as a novel that deserves to come out of the shadow cast by Maxwell's more widely recognized novels.

Indeed, *The Chateau* signals a major development in the arc of Maxwell's writing life and predicts the narrative innovations that became increasingly important in his work. Here, the author first reveals his beliefs about art in his fiction—a move to a more self-conscious approach that would allow him to bring fresh insights to his signature Midwestern material. Most significantly, *The Chateau* suggests a writer who is continuing to develop. As A. W. Phinney noted prophetically, "One is willing to place this on the shelf and await the wholly individual work which will illuminate Mr. Maxwell's other books and which seems very sure to come."[66]

7

The Novelist as Historian:
Ancestors
1961–71

READERS WAITED NEARLY TWO DECADES for the "wholly individual work" Phinney predicted. After *The Chateau* appeared, Maxwell
took a break from novel writing to focus on short fiction and nonfiction for
most of the 1960s and 1970s. He continued to work with Knopf on his next
book, *The Old Man at the Railroad Crossing*, a collection of fables, most of
which had appeared in *The New Yorker*. "Actually, they began because my
wife liked to have me tell her stories when we were in bed in the dark before
we were falling asleep," he told a National Public Radio audience in 1995.
"And I didn't know where they came from, but I just said whatever came
into my head and sometimes I would fall asleep in the middle of a story and
she would shake me and say, 'What happened next?' And I would struggle
back into consciousness and tell her what happened next. And then I began
to write them for occasions for Christmas and birthdays....And I would sit
down at the typewriter and empty my mind entirely and see what came out
on the typewriter, and something always did. And from the first sentence a
story just unfolded."[1]

Among them were "The Man Who Had No Enemies," "The Kingdom
Where Straightforward, Logical Thinking Was Admired over Every Other
Kind," "The Woman Who Never Drew Breath Except to Complain," and
"The Country Where Nobody Ever Grew Old and Died," which begins,

> There used to be, until roughly 150 years ago, a country where nobody ever
> grew old and died. The gravestone, with its weathered inscription, the wreath
> on the door, the black arm band and the friendly reassuring smile of the un-
> dertaker were unknown there. This is not as strange as it at first seems. You

do not have to look very far to find a woman who does not show her age or a man who intends to live forever.[2]

Like this one, the pieces can be other-worldly, yet they echo the sensibility and themes of Maxwell's stories and novels: fluidity between the past, present, and future; homes and mothers; and loss and recovery. Here, however, challenges are overcome and hardships reversed more often than in his realistic fiction. In "The Woman Who Had No Eye for Small Details," an unmarried woman takes her sister's children to live with her after their mother's death; "The Shepherd's Wife," who has difficulty conceiving, finally bears a child. Although a sense of life's mystery pervades these pieces, kinship with nature often offers solace and peace.

Maxwell considered the genesis of these fables to be quite different from that of short stories. "I think at the moment one has the idea for a story one has with it the time and place—which are, often not attached to it, but the source of it," he told me. "In writing the fables in *The Old Man at the Railroad Crossing* I was most of the time not anywhere. I was in the state of mind of storytelling. Though a number of them are based on actual experiences." Indeed, in writing these fables, he assumes affinity with the ancient storytellers he described in his speech at Smith College. He told his radio audience, "With real stories I feel responsible. I feel I must shape them. I feel they must be plausible….And these, no work is involved at all. I'm really a kind of medium to which they appear."[3]

* * *

Maxwell's short stories of the mid- to late 1960s evince a heightened awareness of time's passage, a bit more urgency in their retrospection. Although a desire to preserve the past inspired the author's fiction from the beginning, here he refocuses his attention on the process of retrieving, reconsidering, and reconstructing that past. Characters who return to scenes from their young lives celebrate memory yet also discover the ultimate futility in trying to relive it. The Midwestern homecoming, both real and imagined, developed naturally as a theme during this period. As the author aged, he wrote less as an omniscient storyteller capturing the essence of a beloved place and more through the eyes of characters immersed in careful, conscious scrutiny of the past—in momentarily suspending the present to explore private history and its connections to the settings of childhood.

The protagonist of "A Final Report" (1963) glimpses these emerging concerns in his work. Like other stories in this period, the piece offers loving

homage to figures from his youth occasioned by moments that bring characters face to face with their own history. The author uses such episodes as
links to a different time and place, as connections between seekers of the past
and those remembered. Setting memories of his own young life in Lincoln
side by side with stories of those who peopled the town, he begins placing
himself as a character among others, a technique he perfected in *So Long,
See You Tomorrow.*

"A Final Report" offers a loving yet clear-sighted portrait of a woman
Maxwell knew in childhood: his mother's best friend for many years and
next-door neighbor, who carried him on a pillow when he was an infant in
delicate health. Half a century later, her death and the final report of her estate
stir the narrator's remembrance of the woman he called "Aunty Cameron."
This connection—a prototype for others Maxwell made between his child self
and people he knew in Lincoln—inspires him to attempt new understanding of the past, to retrieve its joys and losses, and to contemplate beloved
objects as talismans of private history. The story explores the intersection
of the narrator's own child self with the world in which he lived with Aunty
Cameron—with what his memory tells him must have been so and what
must have actually been. For example, he tries to determine what it was that
made Aunty Cameron blame her husband for things and what happened to
a large picture that hung in the Camerons' spare room, a print of a man "in
a nightshirt on a tumbled bed, by a brook, over which red-coated huntsmen
are jumping their horses." Dr. Cameron had taken it to a club in Chicago,
but although he had promised it to the narrator, he never saw it again. The
narrator ponders, "And one night the club burned down, and then she had
something else to blame him for. One more thing. The truth is, he—The truth
is I have no idea what the truth is." Here, Maxwell's narrator begins to reas-
sess nuances of the past. Attempting to reconnect, he comes to understand
that ultimately he will fall short. He can venture a guess—"Perhaps he gave
the picture to the club, and would have been embarrassed to ask for it back,
and so pretended that he kept forgetting to ask for it"—but such guesses are
story, not history, and at this point Maxwell's narrator does not seem satisfied
with them.[4]

Characters also return to France to recapture the past. While in 1953 "The
Pilgrimage" offered a prelude to *The Chateau*—with its couple attempting
to recreate the dining experience of friends—"The Gardens of Mont Saint
Michel" (1969) offers a coda to Maxwell's novel of Americans in France
after World War II. In this story, a couple similar to Harold and Barbara
Rhodes try to share with their children the towering abbey they had visited

in 1948, eighteen years earlier, yet find it obscured by a new high-rise hotel and surrounded by a thousand parked cars. The medieval garden they remembered filled with flowers and vegetables has vanished. "Once in a while," the narrator comments, "some small detail represented an improvement on the past.... But in general, so far as the way people live, it was one loss after another, something hideous replacing something beautiful."⁵ Maxwell never stated more directly his disdain for the careless neglect of the past, a loss he felt deeply that seems to have led naturally to his next major project, a family history titled *Ancestors.*

Ancestors

In 1970 Knopf editor Judith Jones planned "a very special production job" for Maxwell's first foray into nonfiction. She wanted an "extra touch of elegance" befitting "a highly personal book by a beautiful writer and a real piece of Americana." Maxwell himself was involved in decisions about the book's design, from typography to photography and art. He and Jones agreed to include drawings of two family trees—one each for his mother's and father's sides—which they hoped would be "rather free-form, perhaps emerging out of a forest." "To keep it all very personal," Jones also thought the writer's younger daughter, Brookie, "might try her hand at drawing them." Although not wanting to personalize the book with a family portrait, they considered including an old print of Lincoln, Illinois, but in the end opted against pictures. Maxwell was also "very interested" in the book's typeface and was given sample pages for his approval. Ultimately, he settled on Caslon, a plain, distinctive font that gave the pages a historic feel that suited the material. Used in printing the first copies of the Declaration of Independence and the first United States paper currency, it became the font of choice for the writer's subsequent books.⁶

In his return to Illinois material, Maxwell was intent on preserving the sound of Midwestern speech as he remembered it and did not want copyeditors "correcting" prose that echoed regional cadence and grammar. His sense for the rhythms of common language was sure and did not always square with established rules of the English language adhered to by East Coast copyeditors (beginning sentences with "and" or "but," for example, or ending them with prepositions). Judith Jones treated his preferences seriously and carefully and, to forestall any tampering, established guidelines for working on Maxwell's manuscript: "No word changes or altering of syntax, the style is his, for better or for worse," she wrote in an office memo. And in matters of punctuation, it was "all right to question if he is really inconsistent about it (but don't let some fuddy-dud start querying about sentences that begin with And. He has his own kind of pacing and it shouldn't be touched)." She reported that the author did not consider himself a good speller and "would like to be checked on that. BUT in all quoted documents the spelling is as he has put it down." Her notes suggest she treated Maxwell with the consideration he afforded his own writers as a *New Yorker* editor. "Be sure he sees a sample of the first 50 pages of copy-editing," she wrote, "and that queries are made courteously and with discretion."[7]

* * *

As a nonfiction family history, *Ancestors* is not often mentioned among the novels and stories that built Maxwell's reputation as a distinguished fiction writer. Yet although it may seem a tangent in his canon, a documentary interlude, it actually becomes an artistic turning point leading directly to the complex and powerful fiction of his late career. In essence, writing nonfiction broadened Maxwell's conception of his craft. As a richly textured work in its own right, *Ancestors* also served as a narrative laboratory of sorts for experimentation with point of view, new self-consciousness, and a break from chronological storytelling. Here, he began to blur boundaries between fact and fiction; even as he wrote fully researched accounts of his ancestors, he acknowledged the limits of historical knowledge and documentation. Perhaps most notably, by juxtaposing his own history and literary intention, the writer intensified the relationship between his career-long explorations of self and art and made possible their interpenetration in *So Long, See You Tomorrow* and the subsequent *Billie Dyer* stories.

Maxwell opens *Ancestors* with a scene from his life in Greenwich Village in the late 1930s: the night his cousin William Maxwell Fuller, a Cincinnati financial broker, came to town on business and took him to dinner at an expensive restaurant on lower Fifth Avenue. Although Max Fuller shared little else with his younger cousin, he was also named for William Maxwell Sr. and spent his earliest years in Lincoln before attending high school in Chicago. What the writer remembered most about the conversation was Max's genuine interest in his New York life, the questions he asked, and the brief, unrevealing answers Maxwell offered in return.

Yet just as the author writes about his evening with Max—the actual event as he remembered it—he also questions how the meeting might have been different had he been forthcoming. He proposes what he *could* have shared, what he *would* have said had he been willing to put his "cards on the table." For example, he confides that he could have told Max about his interesting job that allowed less and less time for writing, or that his telephone rang unanswered because he was with people all day and needed quiet, or that nights often found him reading or walking the streets until he was "dead tired." He also failed to mention the tiny apartment in a Civil War–era building with a tree-filled courtyard, neighboring windows that framed his view of strangers' lives, and three experiences with unrequited love that left him sleepless because "there [wasn't] anybody in the bed beside [him]."[8] As autobiography, such rare glimpses of Maxwell's early New York life may prove interesting to his readers, yet the scene also has implications for his evolving art. Here, the writer begins to challenge the past: He offers Max's story as others told it to him, in effect making amends for having missed the chance to learn it first hand. Writing his family history becomes an opportunity to amend his own, to recast a moment from his younger life, making it more acceptable, more sensible to his older self.

Although neither could have predicted it that night, Max eventually made his own contribution to his cousin's career. Max was interested in genealogy and had spent a good deal of time gathering facts from several generations of Maxwell forebears. When he died in his early forties of Buerger's disease (a vascular disease), he left the work unfinished, but his mother updated facts about younger generations, and William Maxwell Sr. had it typed in Lincoln. Carbon copies, dated January 22, 1940, were sent to everyone in the family. At the time, William Jr. was not particularly interested in learning more about his ancestors, and his own copy remained in a desk drawer for fifteen years. "One day I came on it while I was looking for something else," he writes, "and I began to read it, beginning with my father's generation through the 19th century into the middle and early part of the 18th."[9]

The document proved more interesting than he had expected. His family roots traced to Henry Maxwell, a soldier with a Pennsylvania regiment in the Revolutionary War, born in Scotland about 1730, and to early Protestant leaders who helped shape pioneer life in the late eighteenth and nineteenth centuries. The writer decided to do some detective work of his own: He consulted family scrapbooks, far-flung relatives, regional histories, and biographies of Christian settlers to fill in the stories of myriad generations, mostly Scottish Presbyterians who lived piously, believing their dedication to the Lord's work on Earth would ensure their eternal reward. Piqued by this religious history, he decided to tell the ancestors' stories himself, to twine the migration of Henry's descendants from Pennsylvania to Ohio to Illinois with the movement of his Grandmother Maxwell's branch, which reached the prairie state by way of Virginia and Kentucky. In turn, this led him to write about his mother's family, the union of the Maxwells and the Blinns with his parents' marriage, and, finally, to stories within his own memory.

MAXWELL AND SOCIAL HISTORY

Ancestors places Maxwell, along with those he knew and loved, in a generational continuum, a cross-prairie movement that planted cultural roots in the nation's heartland. As a historical document, the book reveals both the pattern and evolution of social attitudes in a young mid-America as it endures Civil War, flocks to the World's Columbian Exposition in Chicago, moves from manual labor to office work, and embraces a religious fervor that fired passion into rural and town life. This long-ago world melds seamlessly with that of the New York novelist narrating his family history in the 1970s, creating the effect of lives lived on a single plane. The connections he makes between these worlds, and between his forebears over more than two centuries, offers a sense of perpetuity—a sweep of human experience that stretches back and then forward again to touch his own. Such fluidity figures prominently in Maxwell's late fiction, when the strictures of time lose their hold to powers of the imagination. Here in nonfiction he first loosens and dismantles chronology, using the novelist's prerogative to explore the material of the past.

Early in the book, the author recounts the social history of Presbyterian reformers known by their detractors as "Campbellites," particularly the intellectual and spiritual struggles of Barton Stone, who left the Presbyterians for the Christian Church, a sect that came to be known as the Disciples of Christ. This pioneer minister befriended the writer's great-great-great grandfather, Stephen England, who, after settling in central Illinois in 1819, preached the first sermon, organized the first church, and performed the first marriage ceremony in Sangamon County, Illinois—the future site of the state capital, just miles from Maxwell's native Lincoln. With characteristic candor and compassion, the author traces the Protestant beliefs that shaped his father's family through generations: While early church leaders such as Stone and England sought truth and faith through open discussion, a century later his Grandmother Maxwell had boiled down the doctrine to an unwavering preference for baptism by immersion over infant "sprinkling." In the next generation, his dogma-weary father abandoned churchgoing permanently and turned instead to truths published in the Sunday *Chicago Tribune*.

As in his fiction, Maxwell finds the nuance of history in everyday episodes and details. Yet in reviewing the lives of his ancestors, he also uncovers accounts of extraordinary endurance, hardship, courage, and faith: stories of a forgotten America, of visionaries who pioneered a young nation with actions and outlooks far removed from the world of twentieth- and twenty-first-century readers. Some episodes are moving, such as the experience of Robert Maxwell, Henry's son, who traveled west from his Pennsylvania home to find better farmland in Ohio and remained longer than anticipated when the new land had to be planted immediately. When he did not return to Pennsylvania on time, his wife left on foot, carrying a blanketed baby through the forest in search of him. Although injury, hunters, natives, or starvation could have killed her along the way, although she could have arrived in Ohio having missed him entirely on his return to Pennsylvania, she met her husband, the writer's great-great-grandfather, coming home. "The music of Beethoven's *Fidelio* always rises up in my mind," Maxwell writes, "when I think of that meeting in the forest."[10]

Picking up the westward journey two generations later, Robert Creighton Maxwell, who on his father's death was given to strangers at age five, walked six hundred miles from Ohio to Illinois alongside discharged Civil War soldiers and arrived near Lincoln, where he taught, farmed, and then practiced law from 1878 until his death. After traveling on foot for about a month, he must have remembered all his life his first sight of the great prairie, Maxwell writes, summoning a vision of the virgin land that charged his own literary imagination in the next century: The "vast illimitable plain spreading in all directions. Timber and grass, grass higher than his head and undulating in the wind like the long swells of the ocean. The Virgilian cloud shadows following one another. The meeting of earth and sky. The feeling of being exposed."[11]

MAXWELL AND AUTOBIOGRAPHY

As family tributaries flow toward the twentieth century, Maxwell blends his own story with those of previous generations; his experience, sensibility, and observation form the chronicle's core. As autobiography, the book becomes a window on the social forces that helped shape his philosophical, emotional, and intellectual nature; an illumination of his nascent sensibilities; and a view of his primary concerns as they developed from childhood to adulthood, ultimately becoming themes in his body of literature. Certainly, curiosity leads readers to note "real" experiences in nonfiction that have inspired a writer's novels and stories. Numerous images and scenes here have counterparts in Maxwell's fiction, including memories of his mother not recalled since *They Came Like Swallows* more than thirty years earlier. The author's look at his young life through matured eyes helps us understand how his artistic tendencies emerged at an early age, how particular subjects and outlooks became central to his work, and how the focus of his fiction evolved naturally from his childhood experience and sense of himself. As one critic observed, the book reveals the "unfolding of an original literary talent, planted in the past, firmly rooted in the present."[12]

For an author who so consistently inclined toward autobiographical fiction, whose own life usually provided the kernel from which novels formed, a book-length foray into autobiographical nonfiction allows him to speak directly to his reader without intermediary. The nameless, enigmatic commentator of previous works has been replaced by William Maxwell, the writer telling his family story.

Maxwell seemed to pass effortlessly from behind the omniscient narrators of his earlier works to his stage-center role. In his *New Yorker* review of *Ancestors*, Brendan Gill writes that the author has "contrived to outwit the difficulty that most autobiographers face when they pretend to have been thrust against their own will onto the stage at the very moment that they are making a leg on the audience":

> Not for him a tiresome display of false modesty; what is he writing his book for except to render himself visible? And knowable? He assumes his place in the spotlight as a matter of course, and with the audacious suavity of an expert magician continuously directs our attention elsewhere. Elsewhere is not, we may be sure, where the important action is to be looked for, and if we are diligent and alert what we are told about past Maxwells won't be a patch on what we deduce about the present one. How easy he makes his feats of autobiographical prestidigitation seem![13]

Gill's allusion to magic is apt: Although Maxwell writes *Ancestors* as history, he remains the "illusionist" he described fifteen years earlier when he shared the stage with Gill at Smith College. As historian, he uses the novelists' sleight of hand, the narrative "tricks" that bring meaning to facts; as novelist, he relies on the historian's documented accounts to provide authentic material.

This dual approach, this fluidity between genres, became increasingly central to the author's late work, which blurred boundaries between facts, fiction, and memory, between the author and his authorial presence in the narrative. As an editor, he worked with other fiction writers who published memoirs in *The New Yorker* during this period, most notably Vladimir Nabokov and Mary McCarthy, whose autobiographical pieces were collected as *Speak, Memory* (1966) and *Memories of a Catholic Girlhood* (1972). Such works attracted the attention of literary critics interested in the correspondences and distinctions between fiction and autobiography. As Timothy Dow Adams has noted, "Adventurous twentieth-century autobiographers have shifted the ground of our thinking about autobiographical truth because they readily accept the proposition that fictions and the fiction-making process are a central constituent of the truth of any life as it is lived and of any art developed to the presentation of that life....Autobiography in our time is increasingly understood as both an art of memory and an art of the imagination."[14]

Maxwell was among the twentieth-century writers whose body of work demonstrated this notion. In his own mind, he made a distinction between autobiographical fiction and what he called reminiscence, "writing in which there is no structure apart from I remember this and I remember that," in which interest develops mostly in places where "the writer's memories touch the reader's."[15] He believed that autobiographical fiction contrives to give experience form, to produce a literary effect. It may treat core experiences from actual life but emphasizes imaginative possibilities that lead to fuller understanding and truth.

Maxwell's novels and stories must be distinguished from his life, his male characters from his own self: Like any author, he molded his material to create art. However, after *Ancestors,* his fiction began to celebrate facts rather than to disguise them. What happened gained new importance. This change in his approach freed him to contemplate rich relationships between memory, reality, and fiction in his final writing years.

MAXWELL AND HIS CRAFT

Artistic developments in *Ancestors* seem both inevitable and groundbreaking for Maxwell: For example, the emergence of a fully realized first-person narrator appears a natural step in his literary growth after *The Chateau* yet also signals a shift in his technique. *Ancestors* marks the initial appearance of the "Maxwell" figure, who serves as mediating consciousness both here and in work to come. As a result, his fundamental relationship with readers changes. To this point, his narrative persona had not assumed a distinct identity; he had remained nameless. *Ancestors* ends this authorial anonymity: In the opening pages he introduces himself as William Maxwell, a New York novelist who spent his childhood in a "small town in the dead center of Illinois." As if to emphasize his newly disclosed identity, he opens chapter 2 with a meditation on his name: how he is fond of it, how it is neither common nor uncommon, how it is Scottish. In a moment, we see where he is headed: to the introduction of other Scottish surnames in the year 1100, and from there to the world of his forebears.

From such transitions, we understand quickly that Maxwell will become not only a subject among others in his book but the source of its creative control—the central, unifying figure as well as our guide through layers of historical record, memory, and conjecture. For the first time, he speaks directly to readers with the wise, sensitive voice that in large part defined the late, celebrated years of his literary life. Yet although the first-person narrator here becomes the template for a related persona in subsequent works, a few distinct differences exist: The nonfiction narrator in *Ancestors* documents his sources more formally, while the narrator character in the later fictions allows for hallucination and free association. Although the nonfiction narrator also finds pattern in experience and works with creative narrative structures, he takes as his primary aim the accurate reporting of experience substantiated by research.

Maxwell had made unsuccessful attempts to write from a first-person perspective earlier in his career. "The result was inevitably loquacious and without form," he said. "I think I learned how not to be loquacious, how to construct a self that would pass with the reader, from reading E. B. White, who is so candid, but also so, so disarming." He considered his *New Yorker* friend "an egoist—not an ego*tist*"—a writer whose work flowed from placing himself at the center of his observations—and an essayist who projected a self that was "never tiresome, usually amusing, always likable, always acceptable." Before *Ancestors,* Maxwell found himself unable to "rein in" his own attempts at creating such a presence: "I hadn't discovered how to treat myself in a way that wasn't the total interior life. The answer is to treat oneself as an outside person, as a character who therefore is manageable. And also not the center of the action and of attention."[16]

This change in perspective flows at least in part from his analysis with Theodor Reik, who helped him to shed the self-absorption that plagued his early adulthood and, in his writing life, to see himself as one among a cast of characters. In *Ancestors,* this outlook led him to layer stories of previous generations with his own, to develop an *I* that is at once a character, a person readers come to know intimately, and a trustworthy arbiter of experience. He creates this persona without handing over the whole of his life or producing the garrulous interior monologue he believed marred his early efforts at first-person narration. Recreated in his later fiction, this approach separated him from his modernist mentors—from the baroque thought processing found in Joyce and Woolf, and even from the intense insular world of his own Bunny Morison in *They Came Like Swallows*. Consider, for instance, how the first section of that early novel would read if told by young Bunny as narrator: The boy would relate family life solely through his child view, see his mother more as an extension of himself than as an individual, focus on the nuances of home that capture his incisive imagination, and leave us to infer the scenario at large.

By contrast, the *I* introduced in *Ancestors* looks outward: He not only shares his thoughts and personal history but also serves as interpreter and shaper of his ancestors' tales. In quoting an undated letter from his Aunt Maybel to his cousin about the Maxwell genealogy, he includes her words of wisdom about the grandson's "exema": "'I feel quite sure you never had anything like that but if you remember when you came home from Laurel, Mississippi, you had eaten so much salt pork, your stomach was upset and your skin was very rough but we soon cured that up with proper food.'" The narrator's reason for including this homespun diagnosis?: "My cousin's eczema is neither here nor there, but the very breath of [my aunt's] being is in that expression of concern and I could not bring myself to shut her up when I should have." With this disclosure, Maxwell invites us behind the writer's curtain. He brings us into his confidence and establishes the intimate tone and unvarnished approach that mark the last phase of his work. In sharing his methods with his readers, he writes,

> I know that it is possible to consider history wholly in the context of ideas....But that isn't the way my mind works. I have to get out an imaginary telescope and fiddle with the lens until I see something that interests me, preferably something small and unimportant. Not Lee's surrender at Appomattox but two men, both in their late thirties, whose eyes are locked, as if to look up at the sky or at an oak leaf on the ground would break the thread of their discourse.

Here, like the narrator in the *Chateau* epilogue, Maxwell becomes the book's own writer-in-residence, letting us in on challenges he faces, choices he makes, and ways he approaches this business of storytelling. Now, however, without facade or filter, such commentaries are simply presented as William Maxwell's own. As an author he had reached a milestone: Although it was "like venturing into cold water," he was pleased to have finally mastered the first-person perspective.[17] Now his own *I* was as identifiable and real as White's.

The essence of the *Ancestors* persona derives from the omniscient, contemplative narrators Maxwell first introduced in the mid-forties. Although transformed from a disembodied voice to an identifiable man, the nonfiction narrator shares the particular sensibility of his predecessors in *The Folded Leaf* and *Time Will Darken It*. Like them, he serves as an observer who brings wisdom and empathy to bear on characters' lives, yet with a more personal, less detached approach. For example, in his account of Alexander Campbell, the theologian whose founding of the Disciples of Christ figures prominently in his lineage, Maxwell relates how the young minister was trained by his father and correlates their relationship with one of a different culture and time, much as the voice in *The Folded Leaf* compares Lymie's and Spud's Midwestern adolescence with the puberty rites of young New Guinea primitives. He writes,

> When I think of [Alexander Campbell and his father] sitting side by side at a rude table in the backwoods in Pennsylvania, with the Bible and the Concordance open before them, and pen and ink and paper, I think of another scene that is superficially quite different but in essence identical: In Venice, in the Piazza San Marco, I saw a waiter showing his fifteen-year-old son—with the utmost professional seriousness and also with so much love that I felt obliged to look somewhere else—how the knife and fork should be placed and the only proper way to fold a napkin.[18]

The connections Maxwell makes here reveal both constancy and change in his writing since *The Folded Leaf*. First, and perhaps most obviously, the passage bears witness to his consistent sensibility and sagacity. The finely etched images of paternal love illustrate that in the transition from third- to first-person narration, from an omniscient to a very personal perspective, his rapt focus on nuances of human interaction, on one-to-one encounters, endures. He maintains his profound reverence for the practice of everyday life, whether on the American frontier, in a family restaurant in postwar Italy, or in the beloved Ninth Street home of his Lincoln, Illinois, childhood.

Yet there has also been a shift in his narrator's treatment of father-son relationships since 1945. In *Ancestors*, he centers on the love of fathers for their sons, of passing on family heritage, of tutelage and care. In contrast, the *Folded Leaf* narrator focuses on fear, on the darker psychology of coming of age, and has harsh words for fathers who neglect their adolescent sons in a civilized world. Maxwell's change in approach to this fundamental relationship could result from new perspective in his middle age, his own fatherhood, or higher regard for his own father years after his death. The outward-looking perspective that became a permanent result of his analysis may also be at work here. Generally, however, the first-person narrator seems less reliant on Reik's teachings: Preoccupation with specific Freudian theories loosened as the analytic experience became more remote.

As Maxwell told me, the overall effect of analysis on his work was a tendency to shift the emphasis from what happened to why it happened, which "inevitably brings the action to a dead stop." He had a hard time breaking himself of the "habit of looking for the why" but learned to make it an underlying element rather than a driving force. The *Ancestors* narrator reflects this change. Although both he and the *Folded Leaf* figure universalize characters' experience with connections to externalities, the earlier narrator's observations help explain *why* Lymie and Spud have emotional difficulties. Here, in nonfiction, commentaries reveal the Maxwell narrator's experience and character—the what rather than the why.[19]

*　*　*

As Maxwell's only sustained work of nonfiction, *Ancestors* is the novelist's single venture to "the other side"—to the world of facts, research, and documentation—and as such suggests his emerging focus on the artificial boundaries between nonfiction and imaginative narrative, between what happened and what might have been. He has arrived at the threshold where fiction borders "reality," history, and memory—the fertile territory he explored to the end of his career.

8

Maxwell's New York
1974–76

MAXWELL RETIRED FROM *The New Yorker* in 1976 and shortly after committed to publish his first collection of short stories the next year. Two decades had passed since the *Stories* volume with Jean Stafford, John Cheever, and Daniel Fuchs. A Maxwell compilation was overdue, and his formal departure from the magazine afforded a natural opportunity for a retrospective volume. *Over by the River* gathers thirty-seven years of his short fiction, written from 1939 to 1976. The first book to marry the major settings of his literary imagination, it offers stories with autobiographical roots that, like his novels, transcend reminiscence to become powerful fiction through his quiet wisdom, pinpoint observation, and command of storytelling.

Although *Over by the River* spans the breadth of settings in Maxwell's fiction, it also sustains a marked cohesiveness: a unity drawn as much from the distinct sensibility and raw life material underlying the collection as from common characters, relationships, and domestic concerns among the different pieces. Such connectedness is intrinsic to all of Maxwell's fiction, yet the correspondences threading through his canon become particularly apparent here. In essence, the juxtaposition of these dozen stories casts Maxwell's lexicon in relief. Touchstones of his fictional world become constants crossing boundaries of place and time within one volume, from Illinois to New York to France, 1912 to the 1970s, childhood to adulthood. Rather than appear in the order they were written, the pieces are organized in a form that underscores this seamlessness: As a set of frames within a frame, the collection opens and closes with two Manhattan stories. Moving inward, the pieces continue to be paired, with the second and penultimate stories set in Draperville, the third and tenth in France, the fourth and ninth in the New York countryside, and so on. Throughout, overarching themes and character traits recur and redevelop: the mother's death, Freudian analysis, aesthetic sensitivity, home life, quests to preserve the past. Specific moments, circumstances, even objects resurface in new contexts.

The earlier stories, first published from 1939 through the mid-1940s, reflect New York during World War II; later pieces are retrospectives, views of metropolitan married life in the fifties and sixties from a distance of ten or twenty years. Illinois stories evolve from portraits of Draperville in 1912 to the return of a native son from New York later in the century. In such stories, a new focus on memory emerges, as do increasingly fluid connections between the past and present. In essence, the volume functions not only as a cohesive work of fiction itself but also as a compendium of Maxwell's writing to this point in his career—an occasion to contemplate the development of his art. Prospectively, it also serves as a preamble to his final works, an assembly of stories that suggests his literary direction for the next fifteen years.

A number of these stories are considered in earlier chapters as they appeared chronologically in the author's writing life. Here, we pick up his short fiction in the 1970s, during which he published two of his best-known works: "Over by the River" (1974) and "The Thistles in Sweden" (1976), the collection's opening and closing pieces. The juxtaposition of this pair of stories offers a compelling illustration of the dualism in Maxwell's work—dark realities mitigated by hope and tenderness. To read them in tandem is to understand much of the author's world, for although they are not set in his native Illinois, they capture his view of the human condition as a state of delicate counterpoise. Taken together, their ending lines offer a vivid image of this central balance in Maxwell's work and a prelude to his final fiction.

"Over by the River"

For readers who missed these stories when they originally appeared in *The New Yorker,* the opening title piece offers the first and most compelling view of Maxwell's Manhattan: his quintessential New York story, republished in David Remnick's 2000 retrospective of the magazine's New York fiction. Those who know the author's Illinois work will discover that when his gaze shifts east he captures more conspicuously complicated lives, yet with the same sensitivity to human strength and frailty. As in his Lincoln writing, the focus remains on day-to-day rhythms of home life. Although he exchanges the rambling house on an elm-lined street for an apartment building with an elevator and doorman, the family space remains sacred.

"Over by the River" illumines the world of George and Iris Carrington, a couple grappling with the challenges of raising two young daughters in an urban neighborhood at Gracie Square. Although their building houses financially secure families with domestic help, dangers swirl outside: Desperate cries pierce the night, the neighbor's cook commits suicide, and an emaciated junkie with a switchblade lurks in the streets below. The setting lends immediacy and heightened urgency to the writer's concern with life's precarious balance, making the Carringtons' security and happiness seem especially fragile. At times, the edginess of modern urban life seems to penetrate the family enclave: The younger daughter suffers from recurring nightmares of ferocious tigers, and both girls endure persistent viruses. Still, George and other fathers earnestly rehearse "O Come, O Come, Emmanuel" for the school Christmas program, an event holding the same importance on the Upper East Side as it would in Draperville.

As in other Maxwell fictions, the story does not revolve around a traditional plot but allows the patterns of characters' lives to unfold. The writer approaches the piece chronologically, shifting quickly from scene to scene, not unlike the technique in his first novel, *Bright Center of Heaven*. The omniscient narrator returns, yet without the extended allusions to distant places and times. Here he plays a different role. Focusing solely on the family and city life at hand, he navigates between the Carringtons' private life and that beyond their doorstep—between the worlds of home and street, day and night, penthouse cocktails and trashcan scavenging. He witnesses all that the family cannot, from the bicycle theft at a neighboring building to the unopened society invitation that blew away, burned to ashes in the furnace at the Department of Sanitation, and floated down the East River on a garbage scow while the rebuffed sender wonders why lovely Iris Carrington ignored the attempt to become acquainted.

As in *Time Will Darken It*, the narrator catalogues elements in the neighborhood scene in Whitmanesque fashion: His attention to detail in public settings, to the objects, people, and vignettes that form community life, parallels his approach to the belongings he cherishes at home. He renders the view with reverence, unrolling it gingerly like a Chinese scroll that, right to left, reveals glimpses of life lining the river walk north from Gracie Square: "an old man sitting on a bench doing columns of figures...a Puerto Rican boy with a transistor radio...two middle-aged women speaking German...a paper drinking cup floating on the troubled surface of the water...a reception under a striped tent on the lawn of the mayor's house." Maxwell's eye searches out the intimate scenes within the scene, much as he does in his Illinois fiction. As he told me, "New York City is an amalgam of villages, and so to some extent, since my daughters walked to school, and to the places where their friends lived, it was like a small town." Indeed, especially within the walls of the Carrington apartment, basic family activities play out much as they would in Draperville: The children come home with colds, father goes to work in the morning, an African American maid cooks and cleans, and mother handles other home matters (which here include telephoning "Bloomingdale's, Saks, the Maid-to-Order service, the children's school, the electrician, the pediatrician, the upholsterer—half of New York City").[1]

Yet outside family quarters, Maxwell works with two very different worlds. His Illinoisans, for better or worse, are inextricably connected within their community; they know each other's comings and goings, their lives exposed for all to see on the flat prairie. Although his New Yorkers live directly above and below each other, boxed off in apartments stacked like blocks, their physical closeness yields emotional detachment rather than intimacy. Surrounded by skyscrapers, their lives are largely hidden from one another: They may hear activity outside but not be able to see it. From the street they observe people in windows whose names they do not know. The urban landscape promotes this cut-off, closed ambience: "We had to look for it," George says to a woman at a cocktail party, "the sky is so far away in New York."[2]

The flow of Maxwell's prose here reflects this life of limited vistas, of disconnected neighbors bound by proximity. Scenes are shorter than in his Illinois fiction, with frequent breaks in the narrative, as if the city's sheer congestion and compression permit only glimpses rather than sustained perspectives. Equally abbreviated scenes inside the Carrington household suggest that the family has internalized the density and pace of the outside environment: Fire engine sirens screech from Eighty-Sixth Street, a newspaper lies crumpled in the corner wastebasket, and George shaves before the bathroom mirror. Such vivid but fleeting moments subtly mimic the pulse, the multiplicity of the metropolis. In contrast, Illinois stories such as "What Every Boy Should Know" offer storylines with fewer interruptions, with narrative continuity that mirrors the prairie's illimitable views. In Draperville, old men sit at their front windows looking beyond "unpaved, nameless streets out where the sidewalk ended and the sky took over."[3] Although George Carrington shares the acute empathy and sensitivity of Maxwell's Midwestern males, he confronts an edgier society, a loaded landscape with little space to rest the eye and mind.

Rather than give a disjointed feel to the fiction, however, the series of city scenes creates a cinematic effect, forming an underlying pattern of relentless motion, a perpetual cycle of day and night that integrates the Carrington's insular home with the surrounding urban neighborhood. Dreaming and waking become the dominant unifying images: Between three and four in the morning, as the Carringtons dream, a night policeman watches the junkie contemplate possibilities of a plate glass window, and people walk their dogs in Carl Schurz Park. Like many dreams, George's are disjointed, yet they clearly suggest isolation, a disconnection with others: He dreams of people who "started out as one person and end up another" as he continues to pack his clothes even after the boat has left, and "what he thought was his topcoat turned out to belong to a friend he had not seen for seventeen years and naked strangers came and went." He wakens to what he thinks is the sound of one of the girls tapping on the bedroom door. Almost every night one or both of them are up with colds or nightmares. In the daytime, the tigers in Cindy's dreams appear to her on the street as she walks with her mother. Yet these connections furnish gentle humor as well: The morning after she dreams the tiger disappeared into the air conditioner, her mother, unaware of this development in her daughter's ongoing nightmare, announces, "I dreamt the air-conditioning in our room broke and we couldn't get anybody to come and fix it." The family members' inner lives—both their dreams and waking thoughts—touch and overlap in the author's intricate scheme.[4]

In this story, Maxwell focuses exclusively on everyday patterns of marriage and parenting for the first time. Although *Time Will Darken It* depicts the Kings' home life, Abbey, their daughter, is a minor, intermittent character; there is no daily routine, no full sense of the life shared by parents and their children. Roger Angell finds that in these later Maxwell stories, such fine points of family life have "a sense of wonder" about them: "They feel naïve—the details about marriage, about children, about making a household, about, also, I think, regular objects.... It's as if he felt he never would have these things—as if some miracle had come along and suddenly all these things happened to him." Maxwell's editor believes that the sudden, premature death of the mother influences these scenes as well: The devastation of the household he had known as a child makes everyday home life a longed-for treasure. As Angell says, "When Emmy comes along and they have a household of their own and children of their own, he reacts to these things in what is, not a childish way, but a child-*like* way." Maxwell's reactions, he suggests, at once make "very strong fiction, but again, are almost embarrassing in their innocence, in their clinging to what is going on."[5]

Angell makes a sound point: Some readers may detect a sense of "clinging" to family life in Maxwell's New York stories. Although the author revered details of home from the beginning of his career, the characteristic seems especially pronounced here. Even as urban dangers threaten outside, he recaptures what had once seemed irretrievable: a home with a mother, father, and children; a maid to cook and clean; toys, school programs, and stories. Here in New York, Maxwell's lost Eden has been found.

Yet even as the Carringtons represent family life recovered, the writer's sense of veracity does not allow the story to become sentimental. As in all his work, unforeseen dangers and disappointments balance moments of sheer joy; a darker side offsets delight in life. As Angell remarks, the stories are not "saccharin" precisely because "they really do reflect the way Maxwell feels." Indeed, the piece succeeds in large part because the author lays emotion bare, even when it is not especially flattering. While shaving, for instance, George looks at his lathered face in the mirror and thinks, "There was a fatal flaw in his character: Nobody was ever as real to him as he was to himself. If people knew how little he cared whether they lived or died, they wouldn't want to have anything to do with him." John Updike recalled another of the character's confessions: As much as George loves his family, he forgets them as soon as his attention is averted. "[Bill's] being more honest than most people there," he told me. Indeed, George's self-disclosures evince one of Maxwell's greatest strengths: his uncompromising insistence on emotional truth.[6]

One of Maxwell's finest stories and Emily Maxwell's favorite, "Over by the River" is a study in dualities, particularly in the connections and disconnections it finds between people. George is moved to tears at his daughters' grade school graduation. The girls, dressed in pastel costumes and "holding arches of crepe paper flowers," make their way to the stage as Class One becomes Class Two, and Class Two becomes Class Three. Wiping his eyes with a handkerchief, he realizes "it was their eagerness that undid him. Their absolute trust in the Arrangements." But, as Maxwell often reminds us, the Arrangements are fragile. In the final scene, the security of ritual, the human attachment, is lost: George thinks he hears a cry for help outside in the middle of the night. When he goes to the bedroom window, he hears the call again, but can see no one. The cries stop, and he anticipates reading about a rape or robbery or murder in the morning *Daily News*:

> But he forgot to buy a *News* on his way to work, and days passed, and he no longer was sure what night it was that they heard the voice crying "Help!" and

felt that he ought to go through weeks of the *News* until he found out what happened. If it was in the news. And if something happened.[7]

In these closing lines, Maxwell masterfully casts a net of uncertainty over the Carringtons' lives, balancing their joys with threats, both real and imagined. Yet, like most of his characters, they carry on, survivors poised between paper flowers and empty cries in the night.

"The Thistles in Sweden"

About a decade earlier, a couple in "The Thistles in Sweden" find a home in their Murray Hill brownstone apartment at Thirty-Sixth and Lexington. Paired with "Over by the River" in the volume's structural frame, "Thistles" becomes its natural complement: Its characters could be taken for George and Iris Carrington before they have children and move to the Upper East Side. More significantly, however, "Thistles" offsets the alienation that concludes the first story with a parting acknowledgement of life's wonder. Offering equilibrium between darkness and blessedness, it is one of Maxwell's most poignant and luminous short works.

As narrator, the husband frames the story with a street view of the nineteenth-century brownstone. Rounding the corner, he looks for its "romantic" windows that could be in "Leningrad or Innsbruck or Dresden (before the bombs fell on it) or Parma or any place we have never been to." Here, New York life is more welcoming and bohemian than it was for the Carringtons. Familiar with each other's lives, neighbors leave their doors open; the strictest boundaries consist of large pieces of cardboard preventing cats from descending the stairwell.[8] The story's intimacy derives from the husband's natural, conversational tone as he describes the beloved detail of their private world inside the apartment—the objects that make up an ideal, insulated space that envelops and ennobles them—then moves beyond it to glimpse shadows that threaten their happiness. In stages, he reveals their desperate longing for a child and his wife's unspoken sacrifices and desires, overlooked in an otherwise loving relationship. He tells their story in retrospect, yet in an intimate historical present, evoking both immediacy and the ongoing attendance of the past.

The story's top-floor walkup apartment offers Maxwell's fullest, most tender portrait of a home since the Midwestern Victorian in *They Came Like Swallows*. As in past works, the couple's things—furniture, draperies, paintings, and cabinets—assume sacred significance, indeed lives of their own, talking among themselves about the apartment and the couple with whom they share space. The husband imbues every item with love: a living room stairway to the roof that gives the cozy impression of a floor upstairs, the marble fireplace with a blocked chimney, the mural of a hexagonal tower in a kingdom resembling Persia, the gateleg table with four rather than the usual six legs, reminiscent of "Euclid's geometry." His spirit is nourished in this household as a plant rooted in black soil: "Since I was a child, no place has been quite so much home to me," he confides.[9] Here, everything is possible.

The title derives from another of the apartment's details: the heavy Swedish linen curtains in the living room with "life-sized thistles, printed in light blue and charcoal grey, on a white background. They are very beautiful (and so must the thistles in Sweden be) and they also have an emotional context; Margaret made them, and, when they did not hang properly, wept, and ripped them apart and remade them, and now they do hang properly." Through her husband's eyes, the curtains are endowed with Margaret's grace. They become inextricably connected to her, a physical manifestation of her love. A coalescence of wife and home, the title image encapsulates the husband's experience and happiness; his affection for her becomes nearly indistinguishable from his attachment to the domestic world they share. This perspective recalls the psychology of Maxwell's Lincoln children—including his own child self in *Ancestors*—who blur boundaries between a mother's identity and the household she nurtures, who do not notice where a woman ends and the stuff of home begins. We are also reminded of Roger Angell's notion that Maxwell's New York stories exude a "sense of wonder," a "child-like" view of home, as if, after years of longing, the bachelor in "The Patterns of Love" finally marries and establishes a household of his own. Introduced in "Over by the River," this worshipful tone becomes a bit more pronounced here. It also assumes new complexity as the husband's views of home are layered with his new understanding about the past, with realization about his wife as an individual and reevaluation of his expectations of married life.[10]

Living in "modest perfectionism," the "Thistles" couple entertain friends, care for their cats, and occasionally go to their place in the country. He works as a writer, and she stays home, a circumstance that makes him happy yet later becomes a source of regret: "Because I have not looked carefully enough at the expression in Margaret's eyes, I go on thinking that she is happy too," he says. When the two met, Margaret was employed by a publishing house and received an offer from the *Partisan Review* shortly after they were engaged. He remembers,

> When I was a little boy and came home from school and called out, "Is anybody home?" somebody nearly always was. I took it for granted that the same thing would be true when I married. We didn't talk about it, and should have. I didn't understand in her mind it was the chance of a fulfilling experience. Because she saw that I could not even imagine her saying yes, she said no, and turned her attention to learning how to cook and keep house. If we had had children right away it would have been different; but then if we had had children we wouldn't have been living on the top floor of a brownstone on Thirty-sixth Street.[11]

The story achieves emotional truth by speaking plainly about such insensitivities, by offering honest assessments of personal mistakes and lapses in judgment. Such passages offer a sense of catharsis that characterized Maxwell's fiction in his final years.

This recollection provides counterpoint to Maxwell's portraits of early-twentieth-century women—to feminine perspectives in *Time Will Darken It* and "The Trojan Women." In the novel, Martha King, Nora Potter, and the Beach sisters find themselves trapped by social expectations, unsuitable roles, unfulfilled desires, and vague feelings of dissatisfaction in the day-to-day rhythms of their lives in 1912. Ironically, nearly a half-century later, the husband of "Thistles in Sweden" unintentionally perpetuates this same pattern in his wife. Although unusually sensitive in other ways, he perceives marriage through the singular desire to regain his childhood home and the assumption that Margaret will play a prescribed role in his dream. Coincidentally, a breakthrough in their communication comes during a French lesson at Berlitz where they somehow feel freer to talk about what has gone unsaid between them. He learns that Margaret—who grew up in a big house with a rolling lawn, horses, and surrounding mountains—prefers the country to the city. She feels like a prisoner in the small apartment he loves. Because they are speaking in French, however, "nothing comes of it."[12]

Just as the couple finds an adoption agency to help them, they learn they are going to have a child of their own. Maxwell's descriptions of Margaret's pregnancy contrast sharply with Martha King's nightmarish experience in *Time Will Darken It:* "Margaret's face grows rounder, and she no longer has a secret that must be kept from me. The days while I am at the office are not lonely, and time is an unbroken landscape of daydreaming. When I get home at six o'clock, I creep in under the roof of the spell she is under, and am allowed into the daydream."[13]

Like all Maxwell's fiction, the story stands alone without consideration of its basis in autobiography. Yet those familiar with the author's life cannot help but read it as a moving tribute to his wife, Emily Maxwell. The inscrutably honest and self-critical narrative seems an apology to the intelligent woman who was his partner for fifty-five years, a painter who served as his trusted reader and offered him the life for which he had waited to the end of his young adulthood. In effect, "The Thistles in Sweden" becomes the first in a series of narrative apologies in Maxwell's late work. An unsentimental love letter, it expresses a husband's remorse for not seeing his wife clearly in all her aspects, for overlooking her needs in a desire to fulfill his own.

The story's closing paragraph plays like a film montage, a catalogue of scenes from the couple's life together in the apartment. As each replays before us, we remember the importance of the details and sense the narrator's appreciation for the woman who made this life possible. The final sentence reads,

> I think of that happy grocery store run by boys, and the horse-drawn flower cart that sometimes waited on the corner, and the sound of footsteps in the night, and the sudden no-sound that meant it was snowing, and I think of the unknown man or woman who found the blue duffelbag with the manuscript of my novel in it and took it to the police station, and the musical instrument (not a lute, but that's what the artist must have had in mind, only she no longer bothers to look at objects and draws what she remembers them as being like) played in the dark, over our sleeping bodies, while the children flew their kites, and I think if it true that we are all in the hand of God, what a capacious hand it must be.[14]

This may be Maxwell's purest statement on what he considered the "privilege" of living. In essence, "Thistles'" final line counters the vague and haunting end of the title story: The reassuring "hand of God" mitigates the screams George Carrington hears in the night and the unsettling mystery of what happened in the street, if indeed anything happened at all. As a result, Maxwell frames the collection with images that weigh unforeseen, unspeakable tragedy against simple, awe-inspiring wonder. Although his fiction may be best known for its darker moments, perhaps it is not coincidental that in this volume hope has the last word. In his final novel, he will reconcile these two extremes in an elegant, unified whole.

9

The Masterwork:
So Long, See You Tomorrow
1972–80

LIKE THE EARLIEST WRITINGS of most authors, Maxwell's university poetry and *Bright Center of Heaven* constitute his apprenticeship, the point at which his love for reading "moved" him "to emulation," toward establishing his milieu and honing his craft.[1] From here his career took a traditional path toward artistic maturity: a period of growth that by the mid-1940s resulted in strong command of his material and technique, refinement of his central concerns, and emergence of a distinctive style. Yet the works of this period, *The Folded Leaf* and *Time Will Darken It*, do not signal a singular apex in his writing. For unlike some authors' creative powers, Maxwell's did not wane as he aged, as he passed his seventieth or even eightieth birthday. On the contrary, his late work, particularly his 1980 novel, *So Long, See You Tomorrow*, suggests that he not only retained but heightened his technical skill and acute capacity for empathy, that he reached new levels of clarity, precision, and originality at an age when many writers produce works of diminished quality or have stopped writing altogether. As his last novel, *So Long, See You Tomorrow* attests to the major artistic developments he realized at a late stage in his career: He uses new techniques and makes fresh discoveries about issues that concerned him for a half-century.

So Long, See You Tomorrow can be a compelling introduction to Maxwell's work, yet read in order as his sixth and final novel it strikes me as a quiet yet breathtaking distillation of decades of distinguished fiction, the essence of a lifetime of literature and experience filtered through the wisdom of advanced age and maturity. Here, the writer's concerns, the aspects of life that most affected, haunted, and inspired him are concentrated to their most essential form, encapsulated by a simple, extended metaphor within a spare structure. While some of his earlier and more expansive novels may seem to take in more territory, to explore characters' lives more broadly or deeply, *So Long* evokes his enduring themes with quick, clear strokes, with lucidity that comes from culling the extraneous to expose the core. Like his earlier work, it revels in the everyday, preserves and undoes the past, contemplates the nature of memory and storytelling, images the Midwestern landscape, engages the psyche, and balances dark fatalism with trust in human resilience. In essence, it shares subjects and sensibility with earlier Maxwell fictions yet achieves new effects with innovative narrative modes and prose that has become increasingly yet still elegantly bare.

As Walter Sullivan wrote in 1980, "The novel is so soundly conceived and so brilliantly executed—I know of no narrative which has a structure quite like the one Maxwell employs—that theme cannot be separated from method."[2] Indeed, to relate the tale of *So Long, See You Tomorrow* requires a description of its technical design as well as its plot, for the two meld seamlessly. How the writer made his way to the facts included in the novel becomes part of the story itself. His frank discussions of combining these facts with both memory and fictional material reflect both the hybrid nature of his narrative and the very subjects it examines. At its most rudimentary level, the novel is based on a 1921 murder-suicide involving two tenant farmers in Lincoln, Illinois: Lloyd Wilson, who has an affair with neighboring farm wife, Fern Smith, is shot and killed one morning in the milking barn by Fern's husband, Clarence, his former best friend, who later turns the gun on himself. But the crime becomes only half of the storyline: By writing the novel, Maxwell tells his reader, he hopes to make a connection with the murderer's son, Cletus, who played with him on the beams of his father's unfinished house more than fifty years earlier. To accomplish this he becomes a character himself in the form of a first-person narrator who assumes his own personality and history; in light of this direct correlation, the character may be referred to interchangeably as both the narrator and Maxwell.

A man in his seventies, Maxwell has two stories to tell: that of his own childhood tragedy (the death of his mother) and that of the boyhood playmate, Cletus Smith, whose youth was also devastated by loss, first by his parents' divorce and then by his father's crimes of passion. After Maxwell moves from Lincoln to Chicago at age fourteen, he sees Cletus one day in the high school corridor but, surprised and not knowing what to say, fails to speak to him. Still ashamed of his behavior decades later, he describes the book as "a roundabout, futile way of making amends." "Except through the intervention of chance," he writes, "the one possibility of my making some connection with [Cletus] seems to lie not in the present but in the past. In my trying to reconstruct the testimony that he was never called upon to give." Fifty years later in New York, the narrator learns more about the murder from blurry microfilm copies of the *Lincoln Courier-Herald* sent from the Illinois State Historical Library in Springfield, thirty miles south of Lincoln. Where the news accounts leave off, he allows his fictional self to fill in the gaps of the family's tragedy, illuminating his characters' lives with both fact and invention.[3]

Writing *So Long, See You Tomorrow*

Maxwell had long remembered the actual murder committed by the father of the boy he knew in the early 1920s, yet not until the mid-1970s did he first write about the crime in a short story he planned to submit to *The New Yorker*. Titled "The Triple Murder" and "Bloody Murder" on varying unpublished manuscripts, the piece is most striking not for its potential literary merits but for the author's misremembering of the basic facts of the scandal. "It was not a thing you could easily forget," he wrote in 1992, but "the details floated around in my mind and were considerably altered, as is likely to happen with a memory carried over a period of many years." In the story, a boy wakens in the middle of the night to the sound of a gunshot inside the house followed by his mother's screams. Caught in bed, the mother and her lover are shot by the husband, who then forbids his young son to look in the bedroom. After fumbling through the house, opening and shutting drawers, the father leaves, and the boy summons the courage to telephone his grandmother. When she arrives, she opens the bedroom door against the boy's warning and finds a "sight that nothing in her whole experience had prepared her for." The story ends as the two are met by the morning milkman, who drives them to the grandmother's home to call the police.[4]

At the time, the scenario as Maxwell remembered it seemed very real to him. But when *The New Yorker* didn't "cotton" to his story, he "concluded that [he] didn't have the kind of literary talent that can deal at close hand with raw violence and put the manuscript in a drawer." Then one day, while sitting at his desk, he found himself thinking again about his classmate, the murderer's son: "The impulse that gave rise to the desire to write the novel was a sudden recollection of the meeting in the school corridor," he told me. To George Plimpton he explained, "Something made me think of that boy

I had failed to speak to, and thinking of him I winced. I saw myself wincing and thought, 'That's very odd indeed that after all these years you should have a response so acute; maybe that's worth investigating.' And so that's what I set out to do." He described the novel's two motivating elements as the murder of the father of someone he actually knew, "which may unconsciously awaken God knows what Freudian repercussions," and his "regret at not having behaved in a more human way."[5]

Although he had no difficulty imagining life from Cletus's perspective, the author was unsure about the boy's background. His father had owned two farms in central Illinois, and as a boy Maxwell sometimes saw the tenant farmers' children during visits there, but out of shyness he hadn't played with them. "When I found myself in a position where I lacked information and needed it, I fought my way to it," he said. He wrote to friends who had grown up on farms, read about farm life, and studied photographs by Wright Morris, among others. "After about a year I suddenly felt confident that I knew exactly what Cletus's life was like," he remembered, "and proceeded to write about it as calmly as I wrote about my own."[6]

In the novel, he reveals how his remembrance of the murder was very different from what had actually happened: "I might have gone right on thinking that Cletus's father had come home unexpectedly and found Cletus's mother in bed with a man and killed them both," he writes,

> but one day, as if I had suddenly broken through a brick wall, I realized that there are always sources of information about the past other than one's own recollection, and that I didn't need to remain in total ignorance about something that interested me so deeply. I wrote to my stepcousin Tom Perry and asked him if he could dig up for me those issues of the *Courier-Herald* that had anything in them about the murder of Lloyd Wilson.

Tom Perry was a devoted and enthusiastic aide in the writer's quest for information, and letters between the two cousins tell the story of their joint research. On November 2, 1972, Maxwell first wrote him in Lincoln after a rare visit home for his stepmother Grace's funeral. Perry was overseeing her estate, including two central Illinois farms, because the Maxwell brothers lived on the East and West coasts. "There is something of a literary nature that I need help on," Maxwell wrote upon his return to New York, "and maybe you can tell me what to do. When dad and Grace were building your mother's house, I used to play about in the scaffolding with a boy whose name I can't remember. I think this was sometime during the year 1922. But what happened was that his father came home one day and found his mother in bed with a man and shot them both, and was found three or four days later, having shot himself, and with his wife's lover's ear in his pocket. You know what Lincoln murders are like—few and far between but hair raising. Anyway, I wanted to try and use that situation for the jumping off place of I am not sure what, perhaps a novel."[7]

Perry sleuthed for local intelligence and wrote back within a week: "As far as the 'ear in the pocket' story; I also checked with the Library and they advised me that the copies of all the old Courier's and Star's were indeed sold or destroyed, but they were kind enough to call Springfield and enlist the help of the State of Illinois Public Library who informed us that they have micro-filmed copies of all the Lincoln Newspapers from July 1922 on." By making some general inquiries, he also learned the names of the murderer and his victim, as well as a few particulars, some accurate, others with facts interchanged, misremembered, or embellished by fifty years of Lincoln gossip. Perry heard that the man had been shot while milking a cow, and instead of being found in the murderer's pocket, as Maxwell remembered, Perry's source believed that the victim's ear was found in a mailbox by the rural postman. "I never meant you to go to all that trouble and I am amazed by the information you turned up," Maxwell wrote back. "The mailbox. Who could invent a detail like that?"[8]

As described in the novel, Perry arranged for the archive to send Maxwell photocopies of sixteen barely legible pages of the *Lincoln Courier-Herald* from January and February 1921. After Christmas, he wrote Perry to share his discoveries from the newspaper microfilm:

> [Smith] didn't murder his wife. I misremembered. And neither did he put [Lloyd Wilson's] ear in the mailbox—he put his own gold watch instead. But the murder was committed in the cowbarn, while [Wilson] was milking. When he didn't come back at the usual time his elderly housekeeper... sent the little boy, aged six, to see what was keeping him and the child came running back and said, "Papa is dead! Papa is dead!" ... It was the murderer who was found in the gravel pit about two weeks later, when they were dredging for gravel. He'd tied an anvil around his waist, tried to kill himself with a shotgun and when that didn't go off, he shot himself with the same pistol he had killed [Wilson] with. Apparently the ear was never found....At first there is no mention of the ear, then of a slight wound to the ear, then it is surmised that a rat had chewed it (or a cow!) and finally the bloody razor turned up in an overcoat pocket.

As Maxwell had remembered, the motive was Clarence Smith's jealousy over his wife's affair with the neighboring farmer, Lloyd Wilson, which had resulted in the estrangement of both families and the divorce of Cletus Smith's parents.[9]

Maxwell was astonished to discover how far he strayed from the facts in his short story, yet by writing the facts of the murder "wrong" in the earlier version he substantiates one of *So Long, See You Tomorrow's* central tenets: Memory, like newspaper reports and imaginary tales, is itself a fiction subject to myriad influences. Conflicting emotional interests, private prejudices, confusion, and plain forgetfulness conspire to alter perceptions over time. As he writes, "Memory...is really a form of storytelling that goes on continually in the mind and often changes with the telling....In any case, in talking about the past we lie with every breath we draw." At this point in his career, Maxwell increasingly placed more "trust in what happened," so as he wrote he maintained absolute fidelity to the newspaper, paying meticulous attention to its details and language. At times, passages from the reports are incorporated verbatim as he blends facts and quotes from different editions: the bloodhounds brought in from Springfield, the recovery of the .38 pistol in the gravel pit, the position of Wilson's body found leaning against a partition, the $9,000 divorce settlement he paid, and the only published statement by Fern Smith, the murderer's former wife: "I am the most miserable woman in the world." By novel's end all information packed into a week of *Lincoln-Courier* articles is incorporated into the story. "What I couldn't find in the newspaper account or what nobody could tell me, I have permitted myself to imagine," he writes years later, "but the reader is given fair notice I am doing this."[10]

Although Maxwell used the newspaper as a source for understanding what happened that early January morning in 1921, he acknowledged the limitations of such historical records as a source for discovering truth about the past. Like his novel, the newspaper is a text, a human construct that presents one version of reality. He explains that several newspaper stories about the murder were "repetitious and disordered" and "give the impression of being dashed off in the last minutes before the paper went to press." People are quoted as saying things Maxwell has trouble believing they actually said: "I am reasonably sure," he writes, "that Cletus's father did not say to a man he met on the street the day before the murder, 'I am broken and a failure and I have nothing for which to live.' Nobody I know in the Middle West has ever gone out of his way to avoid ending a sentence with a preposition."[11] Of course, the newspaper reports offered more than such amusing idiosyncrasies of early-twentieth-century, small-town journalism and tidbits of Lincoln history. Ultimately, the articles kindle much of the novel's power and complexity by providing the author with a reality to question, a set of "facts" to serve as counterpoint to his fictive world.

Attempting to weave the murder story with that of his mother's death proved challenging, however. Hoping to blend yet clearly delineate what was documented and remembered as well as imaginatively conceived, he knew of no literary model to use. He began by writing sections about the murder and farm separately from those concerned with his mother's death. Yet how could he connect Cletus's story with his own? He had "simply no idea" until one day, after getting up from a nap at his country house, he spied a book about artist Alberto Giacometti among the row on his wife's desk near the bed: "I opened it," he told me, "and read a letter from Giacometti to Matisse about the sculpture 'Palace at 4 A.M.,' and said, 'Oh! Now I have my novel.'" As he wrote years later, the letter contained both "a perfect metaphor" for what he wanted to say in the book and "a bridge between the two stories."[12]

The resemblance of Giacometti's sculpture to the skeletal house frame where young William Maxwell played with Cletus Smith in the early twenties provides the first and most evident connection between the novel's parallel stories. Soon after his remarriage, William Maxwell Sr. had built a new residence; like this house under construction, the artist's wooden sculpture has thin beams and uprights—no solid walls.

The "accident" of finding Giacometti's letter about the sculpture was indeed fortunate. Through the image, Maxwell brought structural and thematic unity to his novel and found a metaphor that encapsulated its central concerns. Ultimately, the metaphor took on such significance that he planned to title his novel *Palace at 4 A.M.* but didn't because Howard Moss, the poetry editor at *The New Yorker,* objected. "He himself had written a play with that title," Maxwell told me. "'How would you like it,' he said, 'if I wrote a play and called it *The Folded Leaf*?' He had me there. But I still prefer the title I didn't use because it says, or stands for, exactly what the novel is about." Fortunately, Maxwell's novel fared better than Moss's 1942 play, which was produced in New York to disappointing reviews.[13]

Maxwell completed *So Long* using the *Palace* image and then proposed the manuscript to *The New Yorker.* As originally submitted, the story was chronological, beginning with the death of his mother and introducing Cletus after his father and new stepmother began building the house. But the magazine wanted the order reversed: "*The New Yorker* has published so much reminiscence that the editors felt their readers would think this was one more 'I remember' piece, only of greater length, and simply never know what it was really about because they wouldn't read that far," he said. "So I rearranged the structure and put my cards on the table with the account of the murder from the very beginning."[14] Although the change did not reflect his original intention, it strengthened the novel structurally and thematically. With chronology dismantled—shifting freely between the late teens, early twenties, and mid-seventies—the past and present, the narrator's youth and old age, coexist on one plane. And with the murder disposed of in the first chapter, there is neither suspense nor traditional climax to divert attention from the focus on characters, from Maxwell's exploration of fact, fiction, and memory.

New Yorker editor William Shawn expressed further concerns about *So Long, See You Tomorrow* in a memo with thirty-three queries to Roger Angell, Maxwell's editor. At one point in the memo, Shawn objects to an expletive: At the moment when Cletus, whose parents had separated, timidly asks his father not to argue with his mother, Clarence replies, "Why, you little fucker!" and sends him sprawling to the ground. "We just can't do it," Shawn argues. "We've held out on this with every good writer we have. I know all the arguments. What I'd suggest here is just a dash. Not a dash representing a word but simply a dash to indicate an unfinished sentence." "Well, a dash seems better than any substitute word," Angell scribbled below. To which Maxwell replied, "Roger, OK, but exactly who are we protecting? At a dinner party two nights ago a young man in his twenties referred to a local character as an ass-hole and I noticed Emmy didn't turn a hair. Though she doesn't use the word herself, a younger woman undoubtedly would. This is not argument. The cut is better than a dash I think." The offending line is missing from the October 8, 1979, edition of the magazine but was reinserted by the author in the novel published the following year by Knopf.[15]

On other editorial issues, however, Maxwell would not budge. After all, he knew the way people spoke in 1920s Lincoln, Illinois. At one point, Shawn objects to the phrase "reason why"—"we try to avoid [it]"—insinuating that the addition of the word "why" was incorrect, or at least unnecessary. "Middle Westerners are partial to it," the author penciled in beneath Shawn's typed note, "and I would like to keep it here, mostly because it's found so commonly." Later, Shawn questions Maxwell's use of the word "that," suggesting instead the "exceptional restrictive 'which' to avoid ambiguity." To which Maxwell countered, "The gossips would say 'that' here, not 'which,'" and elected to keep it.[16]

Shawn's most vehement objections centered on Cletus's dog, Trixie, who has thoughts and emotions of her own; her point of view becomes as compelling as that of any human character. For example, Trixie does not raise her head when a Model T passes because "she is expecting a boy on a bicycle." After a run in the rain, she shakes water all over Cletus, but he doesn't hold it against her because "they both know it is something she has to do because she is a dog." At novel's end, left alone with the new tenant after Cletus's family vacates the farm, Trixie imagines hearing Cletus's footsteps: "He had heard her howling and come from wherever it was he had been all this time and was going to rescue her."[17] An innocent victim of human failings, the dog is a poignant indicator of the family's disintegration.

Shawn did not feel the same. When the dog "closed her eyes and went to sleep, and dreamed that she was chasing a rabbit," the editor had had enough: "Well, now, isn't this finally going *too* far?" he writes. "The author in this instance is omniscient, yes, and knows what the dog is thinking, but to know what the dog is *dreaming?* Again, all I can say is that it shakes my confidence in practically everything else." "I would omit the dream," Angell responded. But the dream remained. After Clarence leaves the farm, the dog "took note of the fact" that he didn't saw the fallen trees, split the logs, or fill the woodshed with wood as he usually did in winter. "Lord! We now have a dog taking note," Shawn raves. "There's no warrant in reality for any of this, is there?" "Yes, for all of it," Maxwell answers. Unable to resolve the dog's viewpoint with his perception that the story aimed for a "kind of realism," Shawn quips, "This goes farther than a Lassie picture." And later: "How can we believe what he tells us about the people? But I guess all this has been discussed with author and there is nothing to do but let it stand and not query." Ultimately, he reluctantly agrees to let Maxwell "have it the way he wants it."[18]

Looking back on the episode, it is risible to imagine a fiction editor several months shy of 1980, at the end of the experimental evolution in narrative theory and practice, having trouble accepting the characterization of a thinking, dreaming dog. "Only the old farts at *The New Yorker* did, clinging half to an obsolete aesthetic of 'realism,' half to the magazine's notorious and solipsistic editorial decorum," Robert Bray observed, in response to a talk I gave on the subject. Although John Updike has noted that the magazine did not receive due credit for publishing experimental work, in this case Shawn was clearly missing Maxwell's intention. The literary laboratories of Kurt Vonnegut, E. L. Doctorow, and John Barth had already turned realism on its ear with such postmodern innovations as *Slaughterhouse-Five, Ragtime,* and *Lost in the Funhouse* in the 1960s and 1970s. And Shawn had read manuscripts of Vladimir Nabokov's highly experimental *Pale Fire* (1962) and *Ada* (1963) when they arrived on his desk at *The New Yorker,* having been forwarded by fiction editor Maxwell.[19]

Shawn's objections belie his exposure not only to Nabokov but also to much of the period's important fiction. Yet perhaps he perceived Maxwell as too firmly entrenched in the realist tradition to accommodate suspension of disbelief. Perhaps he separated Maxwell so decisively from the mid–twentieth century's envelope-pushing raconteurs that he could not accept the unconventional in him. Perhaps he could not reconcile his view of the writer's earlier works with a novel that foregrounded his acts of creating. Or perhaps he *was* just being an old fart. Whatever the case, Maxwell held his artistic ground. His assured responses reveal confidence in his own literary judgment, command of his work and intention. The writer who had changed the ending of *The Folded Leaf* against his own propensity more than thirty years earlier had grown to trust himself.

So Long, See You Tomorrow

So Long, See You Tomorrow is Maxwell's masterwork. A slender volume, less than half the length of *Time Will Darken It* or *The Chateau*, it represents the quintessence of his literary career, the most compressed yet complete statement of his perennial themes. In these pages one finds his most mature expression of the tension between human choice and the control of outside forces, the tenuous balance that concerned him since his earliest fictions. Here, too, the parallel explorations of his career merge: His decades of experimentation with fiction writing dovetail with the continual reexamination of his life's material. His authorial presence has evolved from a disembodied voice to a full character, a first-person narrator who openly directs the novel's design while assuming a role in the novel's action. Through this persona, self-inquiry and narrative art meet, creating a seamless confluence of memory and method. Key to the study of Maxwell's narrative development, *So Long, See You Tomorrow* marks the final step in his transition from the modernist influences of his early work to fiction with distinctly postmodern sensibilities.

More than forty years after he introduced his childhood tragedy in *They Came Like Swallows*, the writer brings fresh perspective to his youth, taking full advantage of the more detached view afforded by passing decades, diverse life experience, and geographic distance. The strengths of his earlier work are heightened: the deceptive simplicity; the intelligent, straightforward style; the powerful understatement; the laying bare of tragedy and truth without sentimentality. Perhaps most significantly, *So Long* achieves complete synthesis of form and subject. The questions it raises, the human mysteries it explores are inseparable from its artistic framework. Its wise and empathetic narrator moves freely through time, from family tragedies in 1920s Illinois to his New York home five decades later. He contemplates the blurring boundaries among fact, fiction, and memory and, as an older man, perceives fluidity between youth, maturity, old age, and death. This final novel spans the poles of Maxwell's career: the Midwest and the East Coast; the simple, small-town upbringing and the culturally sophisticated Manhattan environ; the stern, Republican father and the Viennese Freudian analyst; the roles of grieving, motherless son and astute literary artist. Never has the author so tightly woven such diversity into so few pages: Murder and death combine with childhood play, rich metaphor with unadorned writing, and the narrator's point of view with that of almost every other character, both human and canine. At once, *So Long* displays his technical skill at its peak, intricately connects the art of fiction with personal history, and dramatizes his views about life and literature with deepened maturity and new authority.

At the time Maxwell began writing *So Long* in earnest, he had nearly concluded his forty-year career at *The New Yorker* helping other writers to streamline their prose. For decades, with a sympathetic yet astute eye, he had ensured that they "didn't use more words than necessary or reasonable." "Inevitably, this had an effect on my own work," he said, "and it became more and more concise. I also began to feel that to say precisely what you mean in the only exact way of saying it is a kind of bliss."[20] *So Long* stands as the prime example of his definitive spare style: Although clean and polished from the early years, his writing here is even more straightforward, more minimal, yet it still retains grace and warmth.

As his prose becomes sparser and more restrained, it more closely mirrors the prairie's stark symmetry: the plain, deceptively undramatic field of view that bares humanity to the surrounding sky. In essence, qualities of his signature setting merge with narrative style and structure, contributing to the novel's fully realized aesthetic unity. The unfinished house and *Palace* sculpture echo the equally spare language and Midwestern landscape. Like the skeletal image supporting the novel, the flat farmland results in "total exposure. Anyone can see what used to be reserved for the eye of the hawk as it wheeled in slow circles." Surrounded by "plowed fields or pastures, all the way to the horizon," the narrator's family carriage travels the champaign country. This geography becomes part of the narrative framework, reflecting not only unadorned language and the austerity of farm life but also the transparency of the author's process; his methods, like the Illinois carriage, are totally exposed.[21]

While writing *The Folded Leaf,* Maxwell had envisioned walking over flat land toward a distant peak. Here, however, he sees life's span on a level plane, the past and future extending before him over an illimitable vista. The Midwest of *So Long, See You Tomorrow* has no mountain to break its stretch, no climax to bring its characters to a turning point. Without the rise and fall of plot, people move toward but never reach the unbroken, ever-present skyline. This landscape lends an underlying, unrelenting tension echoed in one of the novel's central dichotomies: the determined nature of characters' lives and the freedom with which Maxwell molds their stories.

* * *

From a technical standpoint, Maxwell considered *So Long, See You Tomorrow* his finest novel because of its structure and "the fact that almost every sentence in it…was in eight or ten different places before it finally got locked into the place where it seemed to belong." This statement is only a slight exaggeration, he said, for when working on a novel he wrote much that was "flat" or "irrelevant" until suddenly a sentence, scene, or moment appeared on the page that he knew would stand. These he cut out with scissors and put in a folder so that he could find a place for them as the narrative proceeded. When the time came, he pasted the sentences one by one on pieces of paper that became his working draft. The *So Long* manuscripts, like delicately composed collages, consist of page after page of this cut-and-paste work. Here and there the effects of time have loosened or dislodged sentences from their original places; glue has become dry and paper brittle. Talismans of a meticulous yet tender approach to writing, the manuscripts underscore both the care with which Maxwell composed and the extensive narrative weaving needed to deal with fact, fiction, and memory on a single plane. As the author himself intimated, the novel's structure is perhaps its most distinctive characteristic: Its design binds diverse elements into a 135-page tour de force that establishes complex juxtapositions and intricately connects diverse aspects of language and life.[22]

So Long is packed with the kind of narrative "tricks" Maxwell described in his Smith College speech more than twenty-five years earlier. To achieve a unified work from such diversity, he relates the individual stories compellingly, modulates between them smoothly, and integrates them both thematically and technically. Four distinct threads of narrative weave through its pages: the narrator's boyhood memories, his present life as an adult New Yorker, the "facts" of the murder as recorded in the *Lincoln Courier-Herald,* and the author's fictional self, which fills gaps left by the news accounts. At a general level, these threads form two basic dichotomies—past and present, fact and fiction—and represent four ways of perceiving, interpreting, and understanding human character. More specifically, they embody various roles assumed by the Maxwell narrator, like the diverse "committee members" constituting Harold's persona in *The Chateau*.

The novel opens with a chapter titled "The Pistol Shot," in which the narrator recounts the tragic shooting death as reported in the newspapers, and follows with a second that introduces Maxwell's boyhood memories dominated by the devastating effects of his mother's death and father's remarriage. Chapter 3, "The New House," elaborates on these memories as the narrator recalls the building of his father's and stepmother's new home. Hearing the "pung, pung, pung, kapung" of the carpenter's hammering, he is drawn to the construction site and spends many days after school watching the framework of the house take shape. At this point memory is preempted by the emergence of another perspective: the narrator's present life. He introduces himself as an adult New Yorker rather than a grief-stricken, motherless child:

> When, wandering through the Museum of Modern Art, I come upon the piece of sculpture by Alberto Giacometti with the title "Palace at 4 A.M.," I always stand and look at it—partly because it reminds me of my father's house in its unfinished state and partly because it is so beautiful. It is about thirty inches high and sufficiently well known that I probably don't need to describe it. But anyway, it is made of wood, and there are no solid walls, only thin uprights and horizontal beams.[23]

The *Palace* metaphor visually connects the narrator's boyhood memories with his adult life in Manhattan by associating the house frame he played on as a child with the similarly skeletal sculpture he admires decades later in the art museum. In this passage, the *Palace* image bridges the narrator's youth and adulthood, and at a later point it also strengthens the relationship between the novel's two plots, the narrator's story and Cletus's. Here readers also become better acquainted with the voice of the narrator—clearly older and many miles removed from the murder and childhood scenes—that not only infuses the novel with particular sensibilities but also, like the *Palace*, relates the novel's diverse elements. Although the voice becomes important on a number of fronts, its technical role in fostering formal unity is crucial to the novel's structure.

In the next chapter, we discover the narrator's connection to the murder: Cletus Smith, the boyhood friend who walked with him along the beams of the house frame after school, is revealed as the murderer's son. Before leaving the childhood scene to discuss further details of the murder and the Smith's divorce, the narrator relates how he and Cletus would climb down from the scaffolding at suppertime, say, "So long," and "See you tomorrow," and part company until the next day. "One evening this casual parting turned out to be for the last time," he writes. "We were separated by that pistol shot." Recalling the title of the first chapter, this phrase connects the narrator's boyhood with the murder described in the novel's opening pages, smoothly linking his young self with his adult quest for facts about the murder. At this point, he also divulges the fated affair between Fern Smith and Lloyd Wilson, and describes his struggle to remember details about the case, his correspondence with Tom Perry, and his receipt of the *Lincoln Courier-Herald* reports.[24]

The introduction of Maxwell's real-life search for information about the murder and his desire to connect with Cletus clearly adds a self-conscious quality to the novel yet also functions as a further unifying element. To this point the adult narrator has been related to Cletus and the murder solely through memory. Now, historical documents in hand, he is actively and presently engaged in Cletus's world. His absorption with the boyhood friend and those involved in the murder fosters a story not only about the past and memory but also about the narrator's *responses* to the past and memory in the context of his current life. Connections begin to emerge: Memory and factual accounts function together as avenues toward understanding; qualities of the sensitive, motherless child begin to correspond with those of the adult narrator.

Chapter 4, "In the School Corridor," depicts Maxwell's move from Lincoln to Chicago, his chance meeting with Cletus in the high school hallway, and the ensuing, suspended guilt over his failure to acknowledge his former playmate. His remorse leads him to wind a final strand through the novel: his role as a fiction writer. "The reader will also have to do a certain amount of imagining," he forewarns. "He must imagine a deck of cards spread out face down on a table, and then he must turn one over, only it is not the eight of hearts or the jack of diamonds but a perfectly ordinary quarter of an hour out of Cletus's past life. But first I need to invent a dog."[25] The image of picking a card from a metaphoric deck creates the novel's key transition: Over several paragraphs, he passes smoothly from a reader-directed monologue to more traditional, third-person storytelling. From here, he explains, he will recreate the Smiths' and Wilsons' lives, relying neither on his memory nor on newspaper accounts; he will have to improvise. Assuming all liberties of the novelist, he shifts swiftly between the viewpoints of a striking number of characters (between seven and eleven per short chapter). Although this technique has been part of Maxwell's approach since *Bright Center of Heaven,* here it becomes more exaggerated. *So Long*'s four central chapters are devoted solely to the writer's improvisational self, to an illumination of his characters' lives through the art of fiction.

The closing chapter, "The Graduating Class," returns to the mature, first-person narrator as he recalls Cletus and continues to reexamine his youth. He remembers walking by his boyhood home on a return visit to Lincoln and back in New York dreams, like Lymie Peters, that his mother inhabits another, unfamiliar home where they could meet again if he were only to ring the doorbell. Lying on the analyst's couch, he relives grief over his mother's death and realizes that he still cannot bear the pain. He is reminded again of "The Palace at 4 A.M.," where "you walk from one room to the next by going through the walls....There is a door, but it is standing open, permanently. If you were to walk through it and didn't like what was on the other side you could turn and come back to the place you started from. What is done can be undone. It is there that I find Cletus Smith."[26]

Here in the *Palace,* at one point in space and time, multiple facets of the narrator converge: his youth, present life, historical inquiry, and imaginative powers. The image evokes his childhood beam-walking and adult museum-going, his curiosity about the "facts" of Cletus's tragedy and belief that fiction may pose a higher truth. As a stay against past tragedy, it also recalls Francisco Pacheco's notion that art may allow momentary control in the face of an indifferent world, an attitude that permeates Maxwell's own work. While in the first chapters the *Palace* serves only as a visual connection between the adult narrator and the house frame of his childhood, it now serves as a fictional place where the two boys meet outside the constraints of what was, where they may walk through a chimeric door to find misfortune "undone." In essence, Cletus has been transported from the realm of recollection to the world of the writer's creation. Here, Cletus's bond with Maxwell is cemented, and their stories become one.

In the final pages, the *Palace* image returns as the narrator depicts a scene in Aunt Jenny's house where Cletus, his mother, and his brother stay after the divorce. With his father still missing a week after the murder, Cletus lies on the bed "in the fetal position as if he is trying to get out of this world by the way he came into it." His books sit waiting on a chair, and he is already late, but knows that he "can never go to that school again. He walks in the Palace at 4 A.M....with his arms outstretched, like an acrobat on the high wire. And with no net to catch him if he falls."[27] At novel's end, the *Palace* unifies *So Long*'s principal themes and prompts reflection on the parallels between Cletus and the narrator. The image suggests both the young narrator playing with his friend on the unfinished house and the mature narrator joining Cletus—perhaps now aged himself—in the fanciful place where they might escape together from tragedies over which they had no control.

THE MAXWELL NARRATOR

As narrator, Maxwell guides readers through the novel's diverse terrain: happy as well as harsh memories of his Lincoln boyhood, encounters in the Museum of Modern Art and on the analyst's couch in New York, his search for the missing facts about the murder, and the creation of others' viewpoints as he imagines them. Through this montage of places, times, and psyches, he is the common denominator; his sensibilities constitute the novel's interpretive consciousness. In this role, Maxwell emerges as one of the most vivid characters in his body of fiction. His compassionate yet restrained voice makes him a vital presence on the page, "a person in whom the reader can at critical moments put his trust." "I felt that in this century the first-person narrator has to be a character and not just a narrative device. So I used myself as the 'I,'" he explained.[28]

His conversational rhythm and informal tone lend a new immediacy and intimacy to his fiction. Consider, for example, the pacing and mood of his description of Cletus's mother, Fern Smith: "She has—his mother has fits of weeping in the night"; and that of his revelation at novel's end: "Five or ten years have gone by without my thinking of Cletus at all, and then something reminds me of him—of how we played together on the scaffolding of that half-finished house." The dashes here add to the illusion that Maxwell speaks extemporaneously, that he addresses the reader directly—an effect he developed in *Ancestors*. Throughout the novel, he corrects himself or adds information in afterthoughts, giving the sense of a sustained, spontaneous monologue. Here, too, his voice echoes both the tone and spirit of the small-town Midwestern idiom and the intelligent compassion of a man who spent his life capturing subtle shadings of the human condition. As his literary run-in with William Shawn reveals, he took seriously the authentic language of his place and time. "It is not so much that the Middle West speaks to me as that it speaks through me," he said. "It is extremely important that a writer have a voice, and mine, in so far as I have acquired one, is clearly a reflection of the simple, direct, often humorous, emotionally charged speech of the people I knew when I was growing up in Lincoln. It has got me into no end of arguments with copy editors who have a vision of correctness that I subscribe to also, but not all that much, and certainly not at the risk of losing the effect of the human voice."[29]

In *So Long*, he comments directly on the language used by people he remembered from childhood. He writes, "He was simply my father, and I assumed that for the rest of his life he would be—'faithful to my mother's memory' is how I had heard grown people express it." And later, "I fancy, as people used to say when I was a child—I fancy that this was true of Lloyd Wilson's wife and that it was not true of Cletus's mother."[30] In earlier works, he would simply have incorporated such idiomatic expressions into dialogue. Now he not only uses the vernacular of his childhood but also explains it, makes it a topic of consideration. Language no longer functions solely to create literary effect but is examined and celebrated as a subject itself.

Looking back through the novels, one can see that characteristics of the mature Maxwell narrator have developed over decades. The persona shares the author's own attitudes and breadth of knowledge, and his storytelling incorporates narrative techniques that have evolved through previous fictions. In *So Long*, these qualities and methods condense to their purest form as natural, even implicit facets of Maxwell and his world. The narrator connects the primary preoccupations of the author's career and cements the relationship between his life material and his literary methods.

The *So Long* narrator shares affinity with the omniscient presence that observes Lymie and Spud in *The Folded Leaf*. Set apart from the boys' story, the meditations in the earlier novel often appear as separate scenes or chapters revealing the narrator's intelligence, empathy, and powers of observation. In contrast, *So Long* reveals such qualities subtly and gradually through the natural course of the narrator's conversation. Maxwell's concern with personality also takes new direction here: In *The Chateau*, he explicitly delineated Harold Rhodes's multifaceted persona through the "committee" metaphor, with members representing different traits or roles he had played in life. *So Long* seamlessly blends such varied aspects of character. Becoming acquainted with the story's "I," readers sense the narrator's multiple facets progressively, as if developing a relationship in life. By novel's end, the character embodies several Maxwells: the actual man and author, the personality projected through his writing, the creator behind the technical design of the novel, and Maxwell the child, fantasizer, researcher, and New Yorker. As he told me, "I don't think I have outlived any part of my life, it all seems to co-exist—childhood, adolescence, middle age, old age—no one of them any more remote than the other, or remote at all."[31] The consistencies of the narrator's sensibilities, the steadiness of his tone of voice, unite these distinct Maxwells and the worlds he perceives and imagines.

As a composite of previous characters the writer modeled on himself, the narrator is at once the child, the adolescent, and the adult—Bunny Morison, Lymie Peters, and Harold Rhodes—as well as the elderly man he has become. All have been shadowed by hardships: death and despair, feelings of inadequacy and isolation. Now, the *So Long* narrator struggles with his own past: After decades, he seems unable to forgive himself for slighting his friend and still grieves his lost mother. Yet this Maxwell character finds a way to cope: He writes his novel. He does so to connect with the past and to make amends yet, most importantly, to create a world of his own making where "what is done can be undone"—or, where what is done might at least be accepted, at last, with peace.[32]

AN UNLIKELY POSTMODERNIST

To read *So Long, See You Tomorrow* as the final novel in Maxwell's career is to find redevelopment of material originally introduced in *They Came Like Swallows* yet to recognize that forty years later he is working in a wholly different literary form. A major shift in his approach to fiction has resulted from a long series of small adjustments over a lifetime of writing that culminates here in the striking coalescence of fiction, memoir, and fact, in a more fully formed perspective on human limitation and possibility, and in dramatization of the relationship between literature and life. In retrospect, Maxwell had been moving away from his early modernist influences for years, yet here he takes the final steps in the transition to a postmodern mode. The author who began his career under the influence of Walter de la Mare, Elinor Wylie, and Virginia Woolf now shares common ground with Thomas Pynchon, Kurt Vonnegut, John Barth, and Vladimir Nabokov. For Maxwell, this is unlikely company; certainly he would have felt more at home with writers less extravagantly experimental, less brazen in their narrative trailblazing, in their efforts to push form to the limits of self-consciousness. Although Maxwell's intent and style may be significantly different from, and in some cases even diametrically opposed to, that of many midcentury postmodernists, his last novel is concerned with some of the very subjects and methods embraced by these celebrated innovators, albeit in a quieter, gentler, and less political way. Like Pynchon, Nabokov, and others, he began his career as a modernist and ended as a postmodernist.

Critics such as Brian McHale and Linda Hutcheon offer models for postmodernism that help place Maxwell in a broad literary conversation in the mid- to late twentieth century. Such studies lead us to distinguish a distinctly Maxwellian postmodernism that emerged from his own materials, intentions, and fictional practices, a mode that embraces highly personal connections to his past and the Midwestern milieu, an enduring focus on home life, and an increasingly layered perspective resulting from the opening of memory in advanced age. His work lacks the unbridled gusto of *Lost in the Funhouse* and *Slaughterhouse-Five,* with which Barth and Vonnegut attempted to break new literary ground. Indeed, while many postmodernists published increasingly showy displays of novelistic virtuosity, Maxwell moved in the opposite direction. His approach became even more natural and basic—striving for simplicity, for fidelity to language and actual experience—yet still questioned notions of history and its relationship to narrative and art. Essentially, *So Long* emanates from a world uniquely his own. Even so, a consideration of the postmodern moment in American literature helps to characterize the quality of Maxwell's particular achievements in his late career.

McHale observes writers who "travel the entire trajectory from modernist to postmodernist poetics" in the course of their careers, a notion that helps illuminate the pattern of Maxwell's own literary passage. To begin, McHale argues that the primary distinction between modernist and postmodernist fiction lies in the types of challenges emphasized in each mode, in the set of questions each asks about the human condition. Modernist work, he believes, is dominated by problems of knowing and understanding the world. It asks questions such as "'How can I interpret this world of which I am a part? And what am I in it?'" What are the limits of knowledge? And how do I understand the world in which I live? Postmodern fiction, on the other hand, favors problems that consider the nature of our *being* rather than our *knowing,* that deal with our existence within a reality. It suggests questions such as "What kinds of world are there, how are they constituted, and how do they differ? What happens when different [worlds] are placed in confrontation, or when boundaries between worlds are violated?" What is the very nature of a text and of the world projected in it?[33]

In Maxwell's work, the shift in emphasis from the nature of knowing to the nature of being, from a modernist to a postmodernist mode, becomes clear in a comparison between how he presents the same material—the story of his young life—in *They Came Like Swallows* and *So Long, See You Tomorrow.* In *Swallows* he depicts the last days of the mother's life through three discrete viewpoints. In essence, the author illustrates how different minds process the same set of circumstances differently: Characters are formed not only through their understanding and observations of their world but in equal part by the limits of that understanding and knowledge. In this early work, Maxwell embraced moderism: He dealt with the nature and limits of knowledge, with how characters understand and fail to understand the world around them.

In *So Long, See You Tomorrow* the unknown loses its hold. The Maxwell narrator hands over the story's outcomes at the outset—we know who shot Lloyd Wilson and that Maxwell's mother has died—and anything he does or does not grasp becomes inconsequential. Earlier in his career, he might have written about the Smith and Wilson tragedy with an element of the detective story, seeking to find out what happened, who knew about it, and what evidence existed to prove it. Instead of asking, "Who done it?" his questions now pertain to the relationships that precipitated the tragedy, how the families left behind managed day to day, and the connections he could create with his former playmate from a distance of fifty years.

At its core, this work does not focus on the boundaries of human understanding—although they are certainly apparent here—but on moving beyond limitation to improvise possibility. Stated another way, rather than be content to portray a character's awareness within natural restrictions, Maxwell turns to newspaper reports and his memory for answers. And then, when both of these sources of information come up short, he projects a world, his own version of what might have happened in the life of his long-ago friend, Cletus Smith. In leaving behind what was to consider what might have been, Maxwell makes the definitive crossover to the postmodern mode. Certainly modernist qualities are still present here: the extensive use of interior monologues, focus on memory and multiple aspects of the self, and what McHale calls the "multiplication and juxtaposition of perspectives, the focalization of all evidence through a single center of consciousness."[34] Even so, what is absolutely central to the novel, and indeed what is new to Maxwell's work, is the extemporaneous world of the writer's imagination. The unknown is no longer an impediment but a motivation for him to create, to fictionalize, his own universe. Like Pacheco, he sees human limitations but strives to mollify them through art.

Discussing his methods openly gives the author new narrative freedom at this point in his career. Twenty years earlier, the dialogue between a narrator and imagined reader in *The Chateau* epilogue served as the prototype for speaking directly about his intentions and methods, yet, at least in terms of its placement at the novel's end, it was a narrative afterthought. In *So Long, See You Tomorrow* this mode becomes a driving force: The subject of writing fiction is as fundamental to the novel as the murder, the narrator's childhood, and his quest for understanding. Throughout his work, Maxwell contemplated his life's material and the human condition while integrating thoughts and theories central to twentieth-century intellectual and cultural life: the interior focus of modernism, for example, the free association and unconscious realm associated with Freudian thought. Now, as he approached his fiftieth year as a novelist, these concerns joined with his overt exploration of literary art, adding a rich layer and texture to his work.

As narrator, Maxwell unveils his literary practices just as he did in his speech at Smith College. He portrays the challenge of capturing life with language, questions categories imposed on literature, and describes explicitly his struggle to make a meaningful connection with Cletus through imaginative writing. He often finds both his own words and those of the newspaper insufficient for depicting life truthfully and fully, yet he accepts them as the only means through which he might make sense of the past and present. Perhaps through fiction he may arrive at an understanding of both himself and his long-lost friend. He writes,

> Except through the intervention of chance, the one possibility of my making some connection with [Cletus] seems to lie not in the present but in the past—in my trying to reconstruct the testimony that he was never called upon to give. The unsupported word of a witness who was not present except in imagination would not be acceptable in a court of law, but as it has been demonstrated over and over, the sworn testimony of the witness who was present is not trustworthy either. If any part of the following mixture of truth and fiction strikes the reader as unconvincing, he has my permission to disregard it. I would be content to stick to the facts if there were any.[35]

Such candor might seem disarming or unusual: Not often does an author suggest that his words might not satisfy. Yet these direct appeals function much like dramatic asides; the free discussion of language and artistic intention draws readers closer to the narrator, to the mature Maxwell voice, and to the writer's craft.

The narrator continually reminds readers that he is in the process of literary composition: "This memoir—if that's the right name for it—is a roundabout futile way of making amends. Before I can go into all that," he confides, "I have to take up another subject." In addition to explaining that he will have to "invent a dog," he reveals that "Cletus Smith isn't his [friend's] real name," and at novel's end he contemplates his relationship as a writer to his own characters: "It is time to let go of all these people and yet I find it difficult."[36] The inadequacies of language, memory, and history become apparent through such intimacy with the writer's position. But Maxwell, aware that other avenues of knowledge or expression do not exist, forges ahead with a spirit of quiet perseverance. At once, his first-person narrator mourns the sadness of human existence and accepts the challenge of lending it meaning through artistic structure. While acknowledging the deficiency of language, he celebrates the writer's mind—its ability to represent and create. This dualism contributes to the dramatic tension that underlies his work; to his credit, he shares his struggles with these contradictions. Like his character Mme. Vienot writing letters to influence her future, like Francisco Pacheco painting oils brightly, his narrator composes fiction to compensate for losses that come with time's passage—to bridge the past, present, and future with his art. He understands the limitations of words but refuses to ignore their potential.

The postmodern sensibility of Maxwell's late work results as much from this self-reflexive narrative and historical documentation as from his setting a possible world alongside a known one. In this sense, *So Long, See You Tomorrow* shares complexities and challenges common to some of the twentieth century's foremost experimental fiction. For example, the narrator clearly separates sections that derive from the newspaper sources from those he fictionalizes, yet he blurs the line between the two by questioning the feasibility of one being more "true" than the other. At the same time, he challenges narrative form and the nature of fiction itself. Ultimately, the novel underscores Maxwell's attempt to absorb and make sense of historical data, acknowledges the truth as well the inaccuracies of the historical record, and provides a connection between history and literature by treating both as created texts. The narrator questions how one might come to terms with such a complex thing as the past—a historical, collective past, as well as a personal one. He suggests that history does not have the sole claim on the truth, which may best be explored and understood through art.

Linda Hutcheon offers insight about postmodern novels that challenge the boundaries between history and fiction. She maintains that such fiction questions but does not deny history or historical writing and "plays upon the truth and lies of the historical record.... As readers, we see both the collecting and the attempts to make order." According to Hutcheon, this type of fiction acknowledges the paradox that although the past existed in reality, it is accessible to us today only through texts, through its "traces" and "relics." Often incorporating "an overtly controlling narrator," it characteristically references other texts and artworks as well. In studying Maxwell, we should remember that he felt little affinity for others writing in this mode and had little use for theories and labels. Even so, for twentieth-century literature enthusiasts, *So Long, See You Tomorrow* fits Hutcheon's concept of postmodernism alongside Robert Coover's *The Public Burning*, Salman Rushdie's *Midnight's Children*, E. L. Doctorow's *Ragtime*, and Julian Barnes's *Flaubert's Parrot*, among others.[37] Although the Maxwell narrator resembles the "controlling" presence Hutcheon describes, he is also the product of the writer's own decades of writing and living, evolved from earlier Maxwell narrators and personas and called for by the material at hand. In a sense, he is postmodern yet "home grown." He melds newspaper facts and storytelling as the domain of imagination yet also calls on his Midwestern background to form the novel's essential underpinning—the parallel, childhood tragedies that compose its emotional center. Perhaps most importantly, the narrator attempts to connect to the past by confronting its inconsistent, elusive nature. The novel's essential story lies not in the history found in the *Lincoln Courier-Herald* but in the author's attempts to arrive at that history through "fact," fiction, and memory.

The close alliance between Maxwell's narrative and his authorial persona complicates the tension between reality and subjectivity: For example, are we reading something that William Maxwell the author really thinks? Did he actually research the newspaper sources with his cousin? Did some of this really happen, or is it all part of the fictionalized world he created? Although such questions may seem merely for literary curiosity seekers, they actually return us to the very nature of the novel, to the idea that *So Long, See You Tomorrow* concerns itself first with the conditions of human experience rather than our understanding of that experience—with modes of being rather than of knowing—and with specific attention paid to how that experience exists on different yet overlapping levels. That the novel provokes such curiosity about what is "real" and "made up" signals its success in blurring and complicating the boundaries life imposes.

The novel incorporates other texts and works of art, another tendency of postmodernism noted by Hutcheon. For example, the *Lincoln Courier-Herald* supplies the novel's historical, "factual" component, while Alberto Giacometti's sculpture *Palace at 4 A.M.* provides its structural form, encapsulating its central ideas within a single image. Countering the newspaper's historical compass, the *Palace* signifies the transcendence of history's boundaries through art. Maxwell also quotes extensively from a book titled *Artists on Art* in which he found Giacometti's description of the sculpture's genesis in a letter to Matisse. Both the book and letter provide additional narratives that enrich his own, narratives discovered serendipitously as he was writing the novel. Ultimately Maxwell's literary and artistic references celebrate what may be considered the very subject of the novel: the writer's mind and the ways in which he illumines the human condition.

I note consistencies between *So Long, See You Tomorrow* and other post-modern works to illustrate that although in many ways Maxwell took a distinctly individual literary path he also traveled in the general direction of a number of his contemporaries. A comparison with Vonnegut's *Slaughter-house-Five*, though counterintuitive, offers an example of my point. Although wholly dissimilar works in terms of intent, subject, and style, *Slaughterhouse* and *So Long* have several essential commonalities. First, both are piloted by strong first-person narrators who address directly the purpose and dilemmas of their fiction: Vonnegut describes his attempt to write his long-delayed novel about his experience at the apocalyptic bombing of Dresden at the end of World War II, an event so devastating that he was unable to finish the work until decades later. Maxwell proposes to "make amends" for his snub of Cletus Smith, yet we also understand that in doing so he attempts to address his own debilitating tragedy. Neither writer makes any effort to disguise the fact that the narrator's personality and life circumstances match his own. Although Vonnegut's zany forays into intergalactic love and war could not be farther from Maxwell's heartland homes and farms, both project worlds of the imagination so that they may come to terms with the past. In both cases, boundaries blur; the real and the imagined meld.

Maxwell had no intention of aligning himself with postmodernists such as Vonnegut. He believed that he arrived at the structure and methods of *So Long, See You Tomorrow* naturally and independently, by following his material rather than the prevailing literary trends. Indeed, the story of the novel's composition supports this idea: His writing over the years suggests a gradual inclination toward techniques used in the novel, toward revealing the mediating consciousness, incorporating facts, and creating a first-person narrator. As he read about the murder in the *Lincoln Courier-Herald,* unanswered questions naturally arose. At a dead end with nonfiction he decided to forge his own world, to create his own version of what might have happened in the lives of the Smith and Wilson families. Yet despite this self-directed development, Maxwell was not writing in a vacuum. Although he may not have picked up Vonnegut or Doctorow from bookstore shelves, he did read manuscripts of Nabokov's *Pale Fire, Ada,* and *The Gift.* About the latter he wrote to William Shawn, "The more I think about the rest of the book, the more excited I become. It is all but unreadable the first time through, and the second time through you hang on every word. It is such an anti-novel that it is almost hard to believe that it isn't, as Brendan [Gill] suggested, a spoof—that is, that he wrote it recently and is pretending that it is a translation. I'm not sure that it is a good novel, but I wouldn't have missed reading it for anything."[38] As an editor, then, Maxwell encountered some of the finest narrative experiments the century offered and responded with appreciation, excitement, and, at times, a bit of amazement. At the least, he might have been inspired by Nabokov's free-form narrative, by his willingness to suspend rules and boundaries of genre, to playfully manipulate language and form.

While going his own way, Maxwell contributed to the broader contemporary literary conversation, whether purposefully or not. His late work captures what Norman Mailer has called a "twentieth century mood," an inclination toward questioning the bounds of fiction and fact.[39] With *So Long* Maxwell creates a postmodernism distinctly his own, both gentle and fierce, with a domestic and interior approach that marries narrative experimentation with his signature territory: the Midwestern landscape, intimacies of personal relationships, the growth of the individual, and the private recesses of the mind.

* * *

In *So Long, See You Tomorrow*, the fragile balance that concerned Maxwell throughout his career finds a complementary metaphor: two boys walking the beams of an unfinished house, echoed in the skeletal sculpture *Palace at 4 A.M.* In retrospect, we know that the sculpture sparked Maxwell's imagination long before he used it as the central metaphor for *So Long*. Twenty years had passed since he evoked its image as the "bare framework" for the set of his unfinished play about his mother's fantastical return to Earth. Although it is not known whether he recalled this earlier reference to the sculpture as he composed his final novel, it held meaning for him through the decades: at once, it symbolized the rooms and walls of his boyhood home in Lincoln, the fragility of life, the relationship between past and present, and the hope of overcoming boundaries of space and time through creation and imagination. The unfinished play and *So Long* share these themes; in particular, they both aspire to triumph over tragedy, to dwell in the imagination where "what is done can be undone."[40] In the end, both offer a sense of resolution and release from grief. The play achieves this, in fantasy, through its psychoanalytic premise; *So Long* does so by connecting with the past through fiction writing.

In *So Long, See You Tomorrow*, the boys on the house beams and the structural sculpture image a tightrope walk between life's poles and choices; they signal the crucial point when one either maintains or loses control. For Maxwell, the *Palace* was a place where the narrator and Cletus have a second chance to overcome the tragedies of their early lives, where "there is a door, but it is standing open, permanently." In our interviews, he described the *Palace* as "the place where the two boys, each in his own way, struggled to find a way of balancing over an abyss. It is the place where the soul of the person is in jeopardy and his finding his balance will save him from disaster—or if he fails, not save him. It is the crucial experience."[41]

Most importantly, perhaps, Maxwell suggested that the *Palace at 4 A.M.* "does not shut off any possibility," just as his fiction was a refuge that never "shut off" possibilities denied by life. Indeed, the *Palace* seems akin to a place inside himself, where Maxwell composed his stories. "I think it is also possible that what the Palace means to me is the world of (exclusively) my imagination, where life can be and in fact has to be dealt with in the imagination's terms, not the reason's, or the heart's. It is therefore a construction, like the Piranesi prison, full of bridges in space overarching each other, above the empty and dangerous air. The danger of falling is ever present. The hope of safety is equally present. It involves an attempt at an acrobatic performance of a desperately serious kind, where failure would result in living death."[42]

And what is the palace in his mind like? "The closest I can come to describing the writing part of my mind is to say that in back of the house on Ninth Street, at the foot of a big elm tree there was a sandpile, which I used to play in by myself for hours," he told me. "What I built out of sand was whatever I wanted it to be. It was a world totally apart from the world of the house, or any other....It is a world I don't as a rule share until I have done what I meant to do, and am ready to tidy up the details. The idea that sustains me is a private one."[43]

Maxwell considered the writing part of his mind to be "largely imagistic"; unlike the reason and the heart, he believed his imagination created metaphors "to explain the situation and solve it."[44] The *Palace*, then, is a metaphor for the writer's art, the process by which he transcended life-imposed boundaries and created his own vision. In this way, *So Long, See You Tomorrow* reflects not only the lives of those he saved from the forgetfulness of the perpetual present but also the private, liberating domain that is the artist's true home.

Honors

At Christmas 1978, Maxwell wrote his friend, Charles Shattuck, in Urbana: "I am sort of in the neighborhood of finishing a novelette that I have spent two years on, but whether profitably I am far from certain." *So Long, See You Tomorrow* appeared in two *New Yorker* installments October 1 and October 8, 1979, before its publication by Knopf the next year.[45]

In May 1980, after a thirty-fifth wedding anniversary trip to the Philadelphia Art Museum and a weekend in the country, Maxwell accepted the William Dean Howells Medal from the American Academy of Arts and Letters, given to the most outstanding piece of fiction published in the preceding five years. In presenting the award, longtime friend Eudora Welty delivered a "beautiful speech" that Maxwell sent to Shattuck: "The most important facts in our experience, answerable or unanswerable, never go away," Welty said;

> William Maxwell has written his best novel out of his comprehension of this. A family tragedy, past or present, is a magnetic field of everlasting, imploring questions. The novel searches them out. It takes him back and forth in time; it does not waver, and it cannot flinch. It has its divining rod; it is direction and destination in one. *So Long, See You Tomorrow* is a vision which has taken on a verifiable construction, spare and plain, but no more simple than a house. In the writing, the novel's tension is finely strung and unremitting. Its quiet carries its own reverberations, so accurate and true that in the end they shatter the crystal: We are face to face with other people's mystery and with our own. There is nothing between us and the realization that without love and without death we should never have come into the presence of human mystery at all.[46]

Maxwell accepted the award with brief remarks that reveal his sense of whimsy. "Miss Welty has just slipped me an empty box," he told the crowd,

> The catch was broken and she thought it would probably fall on the floor—the medal, that is—and it's been in my pocket since ten minutes after three. When Miss Welty got the Howells Medal, a stranger came up to her afterwards and asked to see it and Miss Welty obliged and the stranger promptly dropped the medal on the floor, and it cost $50.00 to have the damage repaired. There is no empty box I could prize as highly as this one, because of what it stands for and because of those writers who have had it before me.

He devoted the rest of his acceptance to the memory of Louise Bogan more than forty years after their meeting:

I believe that it behooves the living, for our own sake, to keep the memory of the dead alive and vivid, and so I would remind you now of Louise Bogan, of her ravishing formal poetry and her literary criticism, so free from intellectual display and so on target. Because of her encouragement at a critical period of my life I stopped being a full-time editor and went back to writing novels and I therefore have her to thank for the fact that I am standing where I am this minute.

In closing, he quoted her "precise and moving" description of the creative process presented in a talk at New York University in the 1960s. "Actually, she is speaking of poets," he said, "but it applies equally to every artist who, after many years of effort and apprenticeship, has at last come into his own talent." He read her concluding remarks:

a poet can never be certain, after writing one poem, that he will ever be able to write another. Training and experience can never be completely counted on; the "breath," the "inspiration," may be gone forever. All one can do is try to remain "open" and hope to remain sincere. Openness and sincerity will protect the poet from...small emotions with which poetry should not, and cannot, deal, as well as from imitations of himself or others. The intervals between poems, as poets have testified down the ages, is a lonely time, but then, if the poet is lucky and in a state of grace, a new emotion forms, and a new poem begins, and all is, for the moment, well.[47]

Louise's words undoubtedly spoke to him. Twenty years had passed since his previous novel. He could not have known that he would publish another, let alone crown his career with a book of such acclaim. Yet decades after coming into his talent, he made a new statement, one that brings a sense of closure to his life's work, a fulfillment of his engagement with the stages of human growth over a lifespan. He had now come to the wisdom and perspective of age: Memory opened fully, and access to the remote past layered with the present, deepening the final impact of his literary contribution. His method and material merged into a unified artistic vision that not only took his fiction to a new plane but illuminated all his works that had come before.

10

Summing Up:
Late Short Works
1980–92

The Outermost Dream

AS AN OCTOGENARIAN, Maxwell continued to publish both fiction and nonfiction in *The New Yorker* through the late eighties and nineties with Roger Angell as his editor. In 1989 Knopf issued *The Outermost Dream*, a compilation of his reviews for the magazine that consider biographies, autobiographies, published letters, and diaries. Maxwell was not asked to evaluate fiction, and in his prefatory note he remarks that he would not have accepted the assignment in any case: "Too much of a busman's holiday. Also, after you have said whether [fiction] does or does not have the breath of life, what standards are you going to invoke when confronted with a thing that, like a caterpillar, consumes whatever is at hand?"

The author particularly enjoyed volumes of letters and diaries. On one of my visits to his country home, he was working on a piece about Robert Louis Stevenson's published correspondence and asked whether I would like to read excerpts of the letters, which he jumped up to retrieve from his study. His reviews of such biographical material gave him the opportunity to retell stories of literary and historical figures with the same combination of empathy and dispassionate observation he afforded his fictional characters. Here, however, he dealt with work that depicted actual events as they occurred, a proposition he embraced more and more as he grew older. As he wrote: "Looked at broadly, what happened always has meaning, pattern, form, and authenticity. One can classify, analyze, arrange in the order of importance, and judge any or all of these things, or one can simply stand back and view the whole with wonder."[1]

The Outermost Dream exudes this sense of wonder about its subjects, an attitude that came to Maxwell naturally. Since his days at the University of Illinois, he enjoyed contemplating interesting lives: The "rapture" he felt while condensing the multivolume biography of Thomas Coke for Garreta Busey led him to begin his first novel and, in effect, his writing career. Here, nearly sixty years later, the nineteen pieces serve as portraits in miniature of such historical figures as the Reverend Francis Kilvert, a nineteenth-century English curate whose startling "inner and outer dreams" inspire the title essay; Prince Marie Vassiltchikov, the daughter of an exiled Russian nobleman whose *Berlin Diaries* records the destruction of Berlin and the plot to kill Hitler during World War II; and Soviet dissident Andrei Amalrik.

In these essay reviews, Maxwell readers will recognize the insight and sensibility of his fiction, the familiar eye for the telling detail and the respect with which he treats his subjects' lives. They will also hear a voice that echoes the measured tones, empathy, and intelligence of his narrators in *Ancestors* and *So Long, See You Tomorrow*. At times, he breaks off for a paragraph or so to reflect more personally on the individual or event at hand, not unlike the commentaries in *The Folded Leaf* or *Time Will Darken It*. The literary pieces in particular become valuable to a study of Maxwell in part because they address the lives of authors who inspired him both artistically and personally. Perhaps more importantly, however, they offer a view of his attitudes toward his own literary calling, toward his choice of a career devoted to artistic pursuit. Essays celebrating authors he admired or knew reveal him not so much as critic but as devoted reader—as a steward of the dedicated literary life he shared with a number of the collection's subjects.

For example, we find his commentary on the lives of three women writers he admired from afar: Virginia Woolf, Isak Dinesen, and Colette. His description of standing "day after day looking up at the windows of that row of houses on the north end of the garden of the Palais-Royal, wondering which window was [Colette's]" serves as a compelling homage and testament to the deep connections he felt as a reader of her work. "Who she was, what she was, at all times lies open to you like a landscape when you read her," he writes. "She never describes anything she has not observed. Every important thing about her is there. Nothing is held back from the reader who may be curious about *her*."[2] Here, he captures the power of a profound reading experience: the intense hold literature can have on readers and the desire to connect with authors who inspire. As a writer of autobiographical fiction himself, he did not encourage close comparisons between his own life and literature, yet he appreciated and shared the natural attraction readers feel for writers.

He is drawn to empathize quite personally with Isak Dineson's loss of her father when she was ten. In conveying his own special understanding of this tragedy, he connects with her on a human level as well as on an artistic one—as a person who shared her experience and a writer whose work was also shadowed by bereavement. He writes, "If orphaned children were allowed to deal with their grief in an otherwise unchanged world, they would probably, in time, extricate themselves from it naturally, because of their age. But the circumstances always *are* changed, and it is the constant comparison of the way things are with the way things used to be that sometimes fixes them forever in an attitude of loss."[3] Of course, he and Dineson are both the orphaned children who share the "attitude of loss," a precise description of the tone that runs through much of his fiction. Such passages recall the compassionate yet distanced meditations of narrators in the fiction and reinforce our understanding of Maxwell's particular sensibilities.

The author devotes a number of the essays to books by and about friends and literary acquaintances: Francis Steegmuller's biography of "La Grande Mademoiselle" and James Lord's "A Giacometti Portrait," as well as memoirs by Eudora Welty and V. S. Pritchett. He admires Elizabeth Frank's biography of his friend Louise Bogan, whose letters he shared with the biographer, yet he also takes the opportunity to correct errors in other published accounts of his friends' lives. For instance, he defends Frank O'Connor against inaccuracies in his biography—"I see very little resemblance between the Frank O'Connor...presented in this book and the person I knew"—and comments in detail on its "misuse and misunderstanding of words and idioms."[4] Quoting numerous passages, Maxwell assesses awkward syntax, unfortunate word choices, and unsubstantiated claims. In doing so, he offers a rare glimpse of his literary judgment in action—of the precision, sensitivity, and seriousness with which he approached prose writing. Here we see his command of language and his willingness to challenge work and motivations that did not meet the standard and, perhaps most importantly, that unfairly disparaged the work and life of someone he held dear.

Judith Baumel of *The New York Times* noted that the pleasure of *The Outermost Dream* "is to see what engages Mr. Maxwell and how engaging he makes the material at hand....In this one wonderful volume we get Mr. Maxwell's clear prose, his magical narrative and the attractions of his quirky mind."[5] Indeed, to read the collection is to discover the kind of people, places, and situations that captured Maxwell's imagination and intellect, to get a sense of his personal taste and frames of reference. Consider, for example, the passage that opens his essay on V. S. Pritchett:

To resort to a parlor game: If Sir Victor were an instrument in a symphony orchestra, what instrument would that be? The answer is the bassoon. As a rule, it is off to one side and not in the front rows, which are hogged by the strings. It and the lyric-soprano voice seem made for each other, husband and wife, but for some reason this fact has largely gone unnoticed by composers. The bassoon cannot, even in the hands of a virtuoso, stand apart from or above what it is asked to play, like the violin, say, or the English horn, but to the ear bent on hearing it the pleasure it gives is very deep and satisfying."[6]

Here we recognize Maxwell as literary man: the genteel yet whimsical attitude; the playful, artistic mind that describes Pritchett by way of classical music. Daniel Menaker, a writer and editor who trained with him, once recalled, "The atmosphere at the dinner table in his apartment on East 86th Street could be so literary and artistic that it seemed to depart the hardscrabble world entirely."[7] Roger Angell also noted that the Maxwells insulated themselves from the popular culture, focusing instead on opera, classical music, poetry, and painting. In fact, Maxwell's devotion to high culture, his urbanity and inclination toward intellectual pursuit, inspired an essential quality of his fiction: the unsentimental tone, tough subjectivity, and distanced wisdom that balance his affectionate view of the heartland. Interplay between the cosmopolitan and regional, the erudite and emotional, generates a fundamental tension that distinguishes his work. In effect, *The Outermost Dream* invites readers to sit at the table alongside Menaker—to absorb the literary atmosphere and become familiar with the intellect that underlies Maxwell's fiction.

Billie Dyer and Other Stories

In his fiction of this final period, Maxwell returned almost exclusively to portraits of Lincoln, seven of which were gathered for *Billie Dyer and Other Stories,* a 1992 collection with novel-like unity. Told by a narrator familiar to *So Long* readers, the stories are complete fictions in their own right yet give the impression of a conversation continued, a reunion of sorts that yields new insights, even startling revelations, about people in earlier works. Supporting players from previous writings come into their own as fully developed characters, profiled compassionately yet unsentimentally by the Maxwell persona. Although *So Long, See You Tomorrow* offers the most powerful and fully realized adaptation of his life's material, this volume brings gemlike refinement, and at times a sense of closure, to some of the writer's major themes. Here we find the maturation of family relationships, fresh purpose for preserving history, an aged man basking in the wonders of long-range memory.

The author's most conversational work, these late stories so vividly recall the tone and rhythm of the human speaking voice, the patterns of oral storytelling, that at times we seem to be listening rather than reading. As a result, there is a purity about them: no obvious artifice, no pretension, no trying to be something they are not. A trustworthy, clear-eyed narrator relates lives simply, with dignity and love. Yet the purity here differs from that in *They Came Like Swallows* of fifty years earlier. *Swallows'* authenticity derives from the insular perspective of youth, from childhood emotion that is concentrated, heightened in the moment. *Billie Dyer* has a deepened vision: It speaks the basic truths of a man who sees the past as both remote and present, who views it as a distant land through a telescope yet through memory sees it closely, in every detail, as if it were there beside him.

In retrospect, for example, Maxwell returns to the life of his Uncle Ted in "The Man in the Moon," a sympathetic portrait and fuller story of his mother's brother, who had difficulty living in his father's shadow. Even more compelling, "The Holy Terror" discloses the full, shocking story of his older brother, Hap, familiar to readers as the boy who loses a leg in a carriage accident yet wins the singles tennis championship at summer camp. Hap's startling mistreatment at the hands of a morphine-addicted doctor haunts the narrator, who reveals the truth about the "affliction" after his brother's death.

Maxwell felt particular intimacy with the past when he wrote "Love," the collection's briefest story, which offers a portrait of Miss Vera Brown, his fifth-grade teacher who died of tuberculosis at age twenty-three. "It was a very odd experience," he told Linda Wertheimer of National Public Radio in 1995. "It's the only story I ever wrote that wrote itself.... It was as if it had already been written in my mind because one sentence followed another and I saw no way of changing or improving it. And I just stood back and said, 'Well, I've had a breakthrough. Now I know how to write and things are going to be easier from now on.' But I hadn't had a breakthrough. I didn't know any more about writing than I had before. It was just that that material, because it went way back to my boyhood, had settled itself in my mind into a permanent form and all I had to do was say it."[8]

The gemlike portrait is moving in its stark simplicity and bare yet restrained emotion and in the natural tone and rhythm of its narrative voice. Despite its brevity, the story recalls central themes of Maxwell's work: the past and present mingling on a single plane, a sense of communion between the living and the dead, and a central female figure, beloved by the narrator, who loses her life. At story's end, Maxwell closes in reflection: "But I know, the way I sometimes know what is in wrapped packages, that the elderly woman who let us in and who took care of Miss Brown during her last illness went to the cemetery regularly and poured the rancid water out of the tin receptacle that was sunk below the level of the grass at the foot of her grave, and filled it with fresh water from a nearby faucet and arranged the flowers she had brought in such a way as to please the eye of the living and the closed eyes of the dead."[9]

Two stories cast new perspective on the race relations that concerned the author since his first novel: The portrait of Billie Dyer in the title story uses fact and fiction to commemorate the life of a prominent African American from Lincoln, and "The Front and the Back Parts of the House" depicts Maxwell facing his own relationship with a black servant from his childhood and the inadvertent offense he has caused. He discovers that although writing may perpetuate the lives of those he knew in Illinois, it may also affect them in unexpected and unfortunate ways.

"BILLIE DYER"

In the title story, Maxwell returns to the theme he chose for his first novel in 1934: what happened when the races met in early twentieth-century mid-America. Whereas *So Long, See You Tomorrow* finds him ashamed of his own behavior in the high school corridor, he now turns his attention to a more public oversight. Dr. Billie Dyer—the first African American physician from Lincoln, who is named one of the town's Ten Most Distinguished Men at its centennial and honored by Lincoln College for his contributions to the field of medicine—is completely neglected in published histories of Logan County, Illinois. In "Billie Dyer" (1989) and later in "The Front and the Back Parts of the House" (1991), Maxwell depicts such inconsistent treatment of African Americans in his hometown. The Civil War, still within the memories of his oldest characters, signaled a time when many Illinoisans were staunchly anti-slavery; they or their ancestors hid and assisted runaway slaves heading north. Such conviction did not apply equally when it came to including minorities in the town's established social order; even in the Land of Lincoln, tolerance had definite limits. This state of affairs confused Maxwell as a child. In the story, he remembers hearing the adult conversation swirling above his head: "While they agreed it was quite remarkable that Alfred Dyer's son William had gotten through medical school, at the same time they appeared to feel that in becoming a doctor he had imitated the ways of white people, as darkies were inclined to do, and had done something that was not really necessary or called for, since there were, after all, plenty of white doctors."[10]

Maxwell seeks to make amends in a way that at this point comes naturally. He learns all he can about Billie Dyer—once again contacting cousin Tom Perry, his "one and only leg man"—and sets out to write a story. Through his research, he learns an amazing thing: In 1975, in a flea market in Canton, Texas, a Dallas real estate agent bought an army-issue shaving kit, a Bible, and a manuscript in a single lot in order to add to his shaving memorabilia collection. "On the flyleaf of the Bible was written, in an old fashioned hand, 'To Dr. William H. Dyer from his father and mother.' The manuscript appeared to be a diary kept by Dr. Dyer during the First World War." Maxwell writes that when the gentleman got around to looking at the diary, he read it three times in one sitting and decided to try to find Dr. Dyer or his heirs. Several years later he wrote the Lincoln Public Library, where a copy of the diary is now kept.

The diary, dedicated to Dyer's wife, recounts the doctor's war experience from commission to discharge in nearly one hundred pages of handwritten text with photos. In reading the account, Maxwell learned about Dyer's medical service at Camp Funston, his voyage overseas, and his time in France. Given his particular fondness for the country, the author must have been interested in the descriptions of Brest, Paris, and Marseilles circa 1918—places he had visited with his wife thirty years later under very different circumstances. In "Billie Dyer" Maxwell blends accounts from the diary with his memory and imagination to tell the story of this remarkable man, tracing Dyer's life from his Lincoln boyhood, through active duty in World War I and a distinguished medical career in Kansas City.[11]

As in So Long, Maxwell's narrative weaving is seamless. He brings us Billie's grandfather, Aaron Dyer: Born a slave in Virginia and freed when he turned twenty-one, he made his way to Springfield, Illinois, a station on the underground railroad (ironically, the later site of the 1908 riot and lynchings). His son, Alfred, moved to Lincoln, where for many years he cared for Maxwell's grandfather's horses and drove the family carriage. In Maxwell's boyhood, Alfred shoveled coal into the furnace of the family home on Ninth Street just around the corner from the Dyers' house on Elm—a block away, yet a different world. Here, Billie Dyer grew up in one of the modest homes that began at the bottom of the Ninth Street hill, a social demarcation depicted in a number of Maxwell fictions including Time Will Darken It. Dyer's close

friend, Hugh Davis, a white boy, raised eyebrows with his high school graduation address defending the "Negro" race, and another, John Harts, enjoyed
Billie's visits in the woods when John's doctor had advised him to live an
outdoor life temporarily on account of strained eyesight. Once, when Billie
visited John in his cabin at night, "there was a thunderstorm...with huge
flashes of lightning, so that for an instant, inside the cabin, they saw each
other as in broad daylight."[12]

Here, the writer's imagination comes into play: "There is no record of any
of this," he writes. "It is merely what I think happened. I cannot, in fact, imagine it not happening."[13] Where memory leaves off—both his own and that
of others—and where his historical sources fail him, the author again allows
himself to fabricate. As effective here as in *So Long*, the method encourages
portraits of two Billies—Dyer and Maxwell—both children of Lincoln who
found their way through different though no less real hardships, connected
by the natural links of an American town and, now, by Maxwell's fiction.
Indeed, the young Billie Dyer sets up a parallel childhood to Maxwell's own,
much as Cletus does in *So Long*. But for Billie Dyer, there is no single trauma
that we know of, just one climb after another over a lifetime of obstacles.

Another personal connection from life also links the two boys. Thanks in
part to the generosity of John Harts's father and Maxwell's grandfather, Judge
Blinn, Billie Dyer goes to medical school, in stops and starts, struggling with
money until he graduates. Just as he returns home ready to practice medicine in Lincoln, America declares war on Germany, and Billie answers the
call. The story is told with Maxwell's characteristic modesty, with calm and
understated tones, yet its subject clearly holds historical importance: "Billie
Dyer" presents a rare portrait of an African American officer in France during
World War I. Much is provided from the war diary: We learn about the racial
discrimination and humiliations Dyer suffers with dignity through his nearly
two years of service as a medical officer. Maxwell quotes Dyer: "From the
very start there was that feeling of prejudice brought up between the white
and colored officers, for among the first orders issued were those barring
colored officers from the same toilets as the white, also barring them from the
barber shop and denying colored officers the use of the ship's gymnasium."
"Negro" soldiers are asked to handle mustard gas cases because "they are less
susceptible than whites." A black boy convicted of rape is executed by the
military, a case so poorly handled that Dyer calls it a "lynching." Many of
his soldiers contract disease, probably the Spanish influenza, although Dyer
never identifies it as such. Still, there are lighter moments: He and his fellow
black soldiers are adored by the French, who perceive no color line.[14]

Dr. Dyer left no direct record of his forty-year medical career after the war, yet Maxwell is able to bring compelling insight to his character—a brief but telling view of his later years as an educated black man in mid–twentieth-century America. In this effort, the author writes, he is assisted by his younger brother, Blinn Maxwell, who met Dyer at a dinner in California in the late 1940s, and by Dyer's letters to mutual friend Hugh Davis, whose wife shared the letters with Maxwell. After the war, Dyer became head physician for the Santa Fe rail line. Blinn—in his only appearance in Maxwell's fiction excepting his birth on New Year's Day 1919—remarks on Dyer's need to discuss "the situation of educated Negroes in America—how they are not always comfortable with members of their own race, with whom they often have little or nothing in common, and are not accepted by white people whose tastes and interests they share." Clearly, as the color line has frayed a bit, other disturbing situations have emerged. At the same time, Dyer seems amazed at the turn of events: On several occasions he interrupts the dinner conversation to say, "I never expected to sit down to dinner with a grandson of Judge Blinn."[15]

As Maxwell writes, Dyer's letters to Davis are about "politics (he was an ardent Republican), the hydrogen bomb, various international crises, a projected high-school reunion that never took place, his wife's delicate health, and...the weather." They also reveal a seventy-year-old Dyer assuming positions never before held by an African American. Placed on staff at three major hospitals in 1956 while continuing to act as surgeon for the Santa Fe Railroad and the Kansas City police department, he works beyond his physical limits to "make good" on this new opportunity for his race, to keep "doors open" that had so recently been unlocked. Within a year, the *Lincoln Courier-Herald* reported his death. He had died in a car crash, having suffered an apparent heart attack while driving.[16]

The story accomplishes exactly what Maxwell set out to do: hold up a life that risked being forgotten, halt the thieving of time by conserving Dyer's legacy in a public and permanent way. The author must have felt satisfaction in having created such a fully resonant African American character, something he regretted not having done decades earlier in *Bright Center of Heaven* but that his long life afforded him time to redress. His maturity undoubtedly played a role in the quality of the later piece, yet the contrast between Jefferson Carter and Billie Dyer also suggests how changes in his writing technique led him to a more successful characterization. As the author's failure to portray Carter convincingly in *Bright Center* was driven by his attempt to create dramatic climax, his success with Billie Dyer derives in part from the narrative methods he perfected in *So Long, See You Tomorrow:* the blend of historical documents with memory and fiction, the unique authorial voice, the narrator as character, the writing process laid bare, the free passage between past and present. Evolved over decades, Maxwell's mode encourages a higher truth, a deeper understanding of his fellow characters and of himself. For although this is Billie Dyer's story, it is also certainly his own. The Maxwell narrator comes to Billie Dyer through their shared world, through the houses and people and elm-lined streets of Lincoln, Illinois, in the prewar era.

Maxwell's "Billie Dyer" captures a rich piece of American history and celebrates the legacy of an African American who quietly broke racial barriers in the first half of the twentieth century. To honor him as the first African American doctor from Lincoln underplays his significance, for he was one of only a few black physicians in the nation on staffs of major hospitals during his lifetime. His war diary is a rare primary source documenting the experience of a black medical officer in the Great War. Attending to thousands of injuries and cases of Spanish flu that raged through the troops, he did not enjoy the same privileges as his white counterparts. The power of Maxwell's story derives from a combination of authentic material and sympathetic imagination: Quotes from the recovered diary allow Billie Dyer to speak from the past, while the narrator, another Billie, reflects on their shared yet separate childhood worlds.

"THE FRONT AND THE BACK PARTS OF THE HOUSE"

Roger Angell remembers that when Maxwell submitted "The Front and the Back Parts of the House" to *The New Yorker,* the writer was asked to resolve attitudes he had about black servants in a revision. At the time the magazine was running the "Billie Dyer" stories, in the late eighties and nineties, assumptions made in the piece "seemed politically strange." "I thought about it afterwards," Angell says. "He was writing about himself then [as a child], when he didn't have those social/political things in mind, so he seemed unfeeling. Maybe he was unfeeling. But since, as a writer, he would be very hesitant to change something about his past self, he kept it."[17] As Angell suggests, writing about the past without a contemporary filter creates a sense of pristine, untouched experience yet risks the possibility of being misunderstood. Even so, Maxwell had the courage to stand by his sense of historical truth despite different times, changing standards, or new revelations. What was, was. Being true to the time and place he remembered entailed fidelity to past emotions and circumstances no matter how they looked in the light of the present. Maxwell gave "The Front and the Back Parts of the House" further consideration, as the magazine asked. Ultimately, he decided to include his own story of working through his relationship with Hattie Dyer, Billie's sister, and the family cook in the kitchen of his childhood. This became not only an important aspect of the story but, in effect, the story itself.

"The Front and the Back Parts of the House" revolves around a single event: In his early forties, Maxwell returned to Lincoln at his father's behest and naturally visited his Aunt Annette during his stay. "I have a surprise for you," she said. "Hattie Dyer is in the kitchen." On hearing this, Maxwell walked into the kitchen, cried, "Hattie!" and put his arms around her. "There was no response. Any more than if I had hugged a wooden post," he writes. "She did not even look at me. As I backed away from her in embarrassment at my mistake, she did not do or say anything that would make it easier for me to get from the kitchen to the front part of the house where I belonged." For Maxwell, this was a shock: He had fond memories of Hattie in the kitchen of his beloved Ninth Street home. Her mother had come to the rescue on many occasions after his mother died to care for the boys while their father was away. He ponders, "If I had acted differently, I asked myself later—if I had been less concerned with my own feelings and allowed room for hers, if I had put out my hand instead of trying to embrace her, would the truce between the front and the back parts of the house have held?"[18]

Years later, reading a Logan County history in New York, Maxwell found an interview with Hattie, who had been chosen as a "'respected citizen of the community' to give 'something of the history of one of our distinguished colored families.'" (Her brother, Billie, was conspicuously absent.) The writer continued to be curious about her, so he contacted Tom Perry to see what he could learn. Tom wrote back that it was too late, none of the living white people knew much about her, and the black people were hesitant to speak. The writer contemplated how he or someone in his family may have mistreated her. Perhaps overhearing racist remarks in Lincoln had made her wary of all white men, but he sensed her snub was more personal than general. He stopped thinking about it until Tom wrote a second time, still puzzling over the secrecy about Hattie. He then added in a P.S. that the elderly black man who took care of his yard was reading one of Maxwell's books, lent to him by another woman he worked for. In that instant, the author understood what he had done to offend Hattie so gravely.[19]

He tells the reader that in one of his novels set in Lincoln—we know it to be *Time Will Darken It,* although he doesn't name it here—he began with an evening party in the year 1912 hosted by Austin and Martha King in a house that bore striking resemblance to the Maxwells' own. It was "clearly our house," he writes, "to anyone who had ever been in it." Likewise, those back home might also have taken Rachel, the Kings' cook, as a stand-in for Hattie, particularly because he gave Rachel's daughter, Thelma, Hattie's own daughter's real name. To the author's later regret, he also portrayed Rachel's husband as a wandering, violent alcoholic who travels back to town from Indianapolis in a boxcar, wanted by police in both St. Louis and Cincinnati: "His eyes were bloodshot, his face and hands were gritty, his hair was matted with cinders." Rachel flees with her children, leaving her husband in a drunken stupor in a room filled with "dirty dishes, dried food, cigarette butts, and a small pool of vomit." Naturally, Maxwell concluded that Hattie mistook this portrait for her husband's own.[20]

The story of Hattie's rebuff and Maxwell's guilt over causing her grief with his own fiction has particular resonance in that it prompts rich ruminations and fresh insights on three topics that have always concerned him: his mother's death, the racial attitudes he observed as a child in Lincoln, and the writing that he made his life's work. All are bound up in his encounter with Hattie, for she was part of his original universe, his mother's world. Here she inspires his reexamination of racial issues and a realization that the art that helped him make amends could also inadvertently offend.

More than in any of his works, he seems to want to tear down any remaining barriers between himself and his reader. Here no metaphors impart artistic form and unity; no fiction stands in for things not known. Instead, the story offers explicit discussions of race and art, a feature that lends a sense of emotional purity and power to this short piece. For example, he tells us that before he uncovered what troubled Hattie, he searched his memory for how he might have offended her and reviewed his own family's relationships with African Americans in the early twentieth century. He describes his mother's natural easiness, her kindness to Hattie, but remembers overhearing his mother repeating into the telephone, "It just won't do!"—evidently pleading with a banker to prevent a black family from moving in across the street. "One of the things I didn't understand when I was a child was the fact that grown people—not my father and mother but people who came to our house or that they stopped to talk to on the street—seemed to think they were excused from taking the feelings of colored people into consideration. When they said something derogatory about Negroes, they didn't bother to lower their voices even though fully aware that there was a colored person within hearing distance."[21] "Front and Back" more closely binds Maxwell's ties between art and life while it clarifies his sorrow and guilt for racial offenses both intended and unintended.

The evolution of Maxwell's narratives about race from the 1930s to the 1990s suggests a white male writer's struggle to portray black Americans accurately and empathetically. Although he did not always succeed, he never excused himself from addressing difficult issues: the disgraceful past transgressions of his own townspeople or his own guilt for the plight of blacks he knew and loved. The strength of these late stories stems from his willingness to bare his own regret that as a white man he could neither fully comprehend nor adequately portray black experience. "I think a white writer writing about black Americans must call forth his utmost powers of sympathetic imagination, and even then the chances of success are not very good or are limited," he told me. "The great problem is unconscious complacency. It can only be done on one's knees to the subject. Sentimentality is also a danger. And ignorance of details, since our lives are so little shared with them."[22] As he drew back to the issue of race at the end of his career, Maxwell wrote his most powerful and distinctive work on the subject. His depictions of Billie and Hattie Dyer preserve their stories for the historical record and highlight the artistic process—the creation of a life he could hardly imagine and the desire to arrive at what must have been so. As an artist, he ponders the gap between the races of an earlier time and place while attempting, retroactively, to make amends in a small way through fiction.

Conclusion:
Stand, Accepting

SITTING OUTSIDE ON THE Yorktown Heights patio, I asked Maxwell about his legacy, about how he hoped to be remembered by readers: "When I think about future generations," he said,

> I think it would be nice, it would be a justification, among others, for my having lived the life I have lived, but I never imagine them thinking about William Maxwell the twentieth century novelist; only about this or that book, which it would make me happy to think that they are moved by, as moved as a present day reader, because that would mean I had got my hands on something that is a constant of human life.[1]

In the years after the publication of *So Long, See You Tomorrow,* retrospectives on Maxwell's work appeared: A 1980 profile in *Vogue* published an excerpt of *So Long* with a photo of a jaunty yet delicate Maxwell, and the author also sat for an interview with George Plimpton for *The Paris Review.* Bruce Bawer's "States of Grace: The Novels of William Maxwell," in *The New Criterion,* was the first essay to treat the full run of his novels, and Geoffrey Stokes's *Village Voice* piece, "The Gentle Man," sought to champion his work. *The New Yorker* published a montage from Maxwell's archive—including letters from Vladimir Nabokov and Mary McCarthy—and, on the academic side, John Paul Eakin used *So Long, See You Tomorrow* as a primary text in his study of autobiography.

Maxwell's eighty-sixth year was particularly notable. In December 1994, he published his collected stories, *All the Days and Nights,* which, more than any single volume, captures the dimensions of his fictional world and reveals his narrative development over six decades. The book was praised by critics, and honors followed in 1995: the Gold Medal for Literature of the Institute of Arts and Letters, the National Book Critics Circle Award for Lifetime Achievement, and the PEN/Malamud Award for short fiction, which prompted his reading with Stuart Dybek at the Folger Shakespeare Library in Washington. The collection includes all of the stories from *Over by the River* and *Billie Dyer,* plus a few additions, and closes with twenty-one of Maxwell's "improvisations." Like those in *The Old Man at the Railroad Crossing,* the fables here summon images of the traditional storyteller and recall the craft of fiction; as Maxwell described their genesis, they were not shaped with the writer's creative control but, like oral storytelling, are "in direct contact with the unconscious mind." They evoke his interest in memory and the fluidity between the past, present, and future he experienced late in life. Two have particular resonance: The title piece tells of a man who magically learns that all the days and nights of his life continue to be with him, each day "connected to the one before and the one that comes after, like bars of music." And in the hypnotic "the sound of the waves," a man and his wife listen as the sea's undulations seem to say, "this year, and next year, and last year, and the year before that, and the year after next, and before they came, and after they had gone."[2]

* * *

In the last months of Maxwell's life, he continued to write his friend John Updike in letters that reveal his mind undiminished, still sharp and engaged. For example, he lamented that the "text and advertising" of *The New Yorker* had become "too intensely married" after attempting to tear out all the advertisements in the seventy-fifth anniversary issue. He commented on new *New Yorker* books, complimented Updike on his recent reviews in the magazine, reminisced about golfing with his mother in Lincoln when he was a young child, and described Emily's courage in facing chemotherapy.[3]

His final days have been chronicled with exquisitely measured, affecting detail by Alec Wilkinson in *My Mentor,* a memoir published in 2002. The story is at once heartbreaking and somehow sadly fitting. As the Maxwells' failing health became known, guests came to pay their respects at the Upper East Side apartment. Poet Michael Collier, a friend of Maxwell, rode the train up from Maryland. The daughters of one of Emmy's childhood friends came from Oregon and New Hampshire. Wilkinson made special efforts to be with Maxwell almost daily. Maxwell's older daughter, Kate, moved back into the apartment, where she and Brookie attended to the last details of their parents' lives. Shirley Hazzard, one of Maxwell's *New Yorker* writers, came often. She had been married for years to Francis Steegmuller, who was helpful with *The Chateau.* Hazzard recalled that five days before Emily died, "the Maxwells, in wheelchairs, went to the Chardin exhibition at the Metropolitan Museum."

Three days later William Maxwell finished *War and Peace,* which he had been re-reading in his last year of life. He once wrote that he didn't mind dying, but found it "unbearable" that "when people are dead they don't read books," so he was hoping to re-read every book he had "deeply enjoyed."[4] Two days before Emily's death, Maxwell, their daughters, and friends, gathered around her bedside in the apartment to sing a favorite song from her Oregon childhood, "Don't Fence Me In." Emily suggested they open a bottle of champagne. With her eyes closed, she sang along, a moment Maxwell cherished.

Emily Maxwell passed away on July 23, 2000, in the middle of the night. Naturally, Maxwell had not expected his beautiful, younger wife to go before him and was not completely aware of the gravity of her condition until quite late. As Wilkinson has noted, Maxwell may have been under the impression that choosing against another round of chemotherapy meant a period of healing at home. When she died, he quit taking his medicine and became lethargic and dejected. More friends came and sat in their airy, book-lined living room in support. Kate Maxwell recalls that gradually, over the next week, her father "made the decision to carry on," to resume eating and seeing his doctor for his daughters' sake. Even so, "he continued dictating farewell notes and putting all his affairs in order." Kate remembers that on the night of July 30, Maxwell spoke of "going to a Kentucky farm where they put together old horses. At another moment he said he was going to 'saddle up and go [or 'ride'] south.'"[5]

Maxwell did not awaken the next morning. Unwilling or unable to go on without Emmy, he slipped away just "a few hours more than a week" after her passing. A couple of days later Updike received Maxwell's touching goodbye, dictated on his last day: "It's true that you are part of our family, and I wish I could tell you how much pleasure you have added to my life. Please go on being yourself."[6]

Two months later, in September, Kate and Brookie Maxwell held a memorial service for both their parents at the Cathedral of St. John the Divine in New York City. His brother Blinn, who traveled from California, was among the speakers. Afterwards, on the Cathedral House lawn, there was a pony for children to ride and balloons and ice cream for everyone.[7]

＊ ＊ ＊

During our first interview, Mr. Maxwell told me that in analysis he "came to understand that man is his own architect," a revelation that, during the

writing of *The Folded Leaf,* helped him to see that his charac
not pathetic but "largely responsible for what happened to him
without his being aware of it." Yet, "at the same time I say thi
also believe in the absoluteness of innocence."[8]

How did he reconcile these ideas in his own mind—respo
innocence, control and helplessness? Did he align himself with fellow Illinoisan Theodore Dreiser, who saw humanity as a wisp in the wind of an
indifferent world? Or did he believe we hold power to direct our own lives,
to overcome adversity and "go on . . . undestroyed by what was not [our]
doing?" Certainly this was the author's hope for Cletus Smith in the final
lines of *So Long, See You Tomorrow,* and for his own young self.[9]

"You could say I am of two minds about the matter of man's being his own
architect," he offered. In retrospect, his "two minds" seem key to the tone and
tensions in his work, the inspiration for a philosophy that underscores his
fiction. His world is one of dichotomies in delicate counterpoise: tragedy and
wonder, ugliness and beauty, safety and danger. Happiness is nearly always
shadowed by the possibility of sudden reversal. Likewise, he often portrayed
people who become disabled by external or internal forces beyond their control, yet these seemingly determined situations are balanced by a qualified yet
unmistakable affirmation of the potential for human will. For Maxwell there
was always a window, albeit a small one at times, through which life could be
reframed with creativity, intellect, perseverance, and humor. As his narrator
in *Time Will Darken It* contends, "The search is never hopeless. There is no
haystack so large that the needle in it cannot be found. But it takes time, it
takes humility and a serious reason for searching."[10] To be sure, the search
may take extreme dedication and endurance; still, Maxwell provides that in
exceptional moments we can circumvent forces that threaten to defeat us.
This philosophy seems inspired by his own hard-won survival: Ultimately,
he was able to recapture what was most precious to him, lessen the effects
of grief, and transcend past trauma with art and the love of family.

"I think it is somehow unimaginative to consider the universe as the product of chance," he told me. He paused a moment, looked over his tortoise
shell glasses, and then continued to type: "I am inclined to say that it is the
product of God knows. The evidence offered in Nature is so astonishing and
so consistently on the side of an Intention. I did not escape the influence of
seven or eight years of Sunday School, and believe we ought to help each other
when it is possible, that the self-centered life is a kind of living death, that life
on any terms is a privilege and that we ought to be grateful for it and use it
to our best ability, and not be frightened or frantic when we reach the end
of it. But instead stand, accepting, like a flower that has gone to seed."[11]

Notes

Meeting Maxwell

1. WM, *The Outermost Dream* (New York: Knopf, 1989), 173.
2. WM, Interview by the author, New York, New York, 23 November 1991.
3. John Blades, "Past Perfect," *Chicago Tribune,* 5 March 1992, sec. 2, p. 2.
4. John Updike to WM, 23 January 1992, WM Papers.
5. WM, Interview by the author, 23 November 1991 ("essential quality"); Roger Angell, Interview by the author, New York, New York, 4 October 1994 ("I think he was closer"); WM, Interview by the author, 27–28 August 1992, Yorktown Heights, New York ("in the only").
6. John Updike, to the author, 10 April 1997.

Introduction

1. WM, Interview by the author, 23 November 1991.
2. Roger Angell, Interview by the author.
3. WM to his father, 8 November 1944, copy in the author's files.
4. WM, "Imagining the Middle West: An Interview with William Maxwell," interview by Bill Aeul, Barbara Burkhardt, Bruce Morgan, and James McGowan, *Tamaqua* 3:2 (Fall 1992): 11.
5. WM, Interview by the author, 27–28 August 1992, 23 ("more important"); WM, "Imagining the Middle West," 9–10 ("My imagination's home").
6. WM, "Imagining the Middle West," 10.
7. WM, *Ancestors* (New York: Knopf, 1971), 190 ("I believe"); WM, "GLR Interview: William Maxwell," interview by Gerald C. Nemanic, *Great Lakes Review* 9–10 (Fall 1983–Spring 1984): 11 ("There must have been").

8. WM, Interview by the author, 23 November 1991.

9. Wright Morris, Letter to WM, 7 December 1969 ("fading"), 9 September 1969 ("What you 'av done").

10. WM, Letter to the author, 12 July 1995.

Chapter 1

1. WM, *Ancestors,* 266–67; Lynette Iezzoni, *Influenza 1918: The Worst Epidemic in American History* (New York: TV Books, 1999), 105–6.

2. Alfred Crosby, *America's Forgotten Pandemic: The Influenza of 1918* (Cambridge: Cambridge University Press, 1989), 18–19; Thomas D. Masters, "Springfield Newspapers Record the Influenza Epidemic of 1918," in *Practice and Progress: Medical Care in Central Illinois at the Turn of the Century,* (Springfield: Southern Illinois University School of Medicine, 1994), 58; Karen A. Walters, "McLean County and the Influenza Epidemic of 1918–1919," *Journal of the Illinois State Historical Society* 74:2 (Summer 1981): 132; *Bloomington* (Illinois) *Pantagraph,* 2 October 1918, p. 7, c. 2; Crosby, 38 ("the passage"), 21, 215.

3. Iezzoni, 66 ("There didn't seem"); Information on the effect of the influenza in Lincoln, Illinois, gleaned from *Lincoln Courier-Herald* (*LCH*) 1–7 October 1918 and Walters, 132.

4. *LCH,* 23 December 1918, 3; 27 December 1918, 3.

5. Crosby, 207; *LCH,* 18 December 1918, 8.

6. *LES,* 3 January 1919, 1; *LCH,* 2 January 1919, 1.

7. "Mrs. Will Maxwell Died Friday A.M. at Bloomington," *Lincoln Evening Star* (*LES*), 3 January 1919; WM, *Ancestors,* 182.

8. *LCH,* 6 January 1919 ("beyond description").

9. Ralph Gary, *Following in Lincoln's Footsteps: A Complete Annotated Reference to Hundreds of Historical Sites Visited by Abraham Lincoln.* (New York: Carroll and Graf, 2001), 82–83.

10. E. R. Pritchard, ed., *Illinois of Today and Its Progressive Cities* (Chicago: 1897), 125, ISHL Collections.

11. WM, *Ancestors,* 156–57 (William Maxwell Sr. attendance at Eureka College and return to Lincoln), 176–77 (Maxwell's parents' courtship and wedding): *Lincoln Daily Courier* (*LDC*), 12 August 1908, 8 ("merits the support"); *LCH,* 17 August 1908.

12. Roberta Senechal, *Sociogenesis of a Race Riot: Springfield, Illinois in 1908* (Urbana: University of Illinois Press, 1990), 25–46.

13. *LDC,* 17 August 1908, 2 ("Husky newsboys"); 19 August 1908, 3 ("in Springfield" and "It is well for the colored").

14. WM, *Ancestors,* 187.

15. Ibid.

16. WM, Interview by Kay Bonetti, printed transcript, copy in author's files, New York, New York, December 1997, 39–40 ("It was news to me"); WM, *Ancestors,* 269.

17. *LCH*, 15 January 1959 (father and rotary); WM, Interview by the author, New York, New York, 3 January 1993 ("from the 1900s"); WM, *Ancestors*, 279 ("Their relationship"); Interview by Bonetti, 23 ("trust in life").

18. Maxwell told me that his Aunt Maybel made a point of not buying his first novel in anticipation of the second: "I don't know how she arrived at this decision...but knew that she wouldn't like the picture of her [in *Swallows*]. But kept to my course, even so. I spoke to my father about it and he advised her not to read it, but she did anyway. Fortunately for me, she died before I saw her again."

19. WM, *Ancestors*, 211–14 (story of Judge Blinn).

20. WM, *Ancestors*, 223.

21. WM, *Ancestors*, 283–84 ("poison pen letters" story); The *Daily Pantagraph* (Bloomington, Ill.), 25 October 1992, C1 (Maxwell's staying with Aunt Edith in Bloomington).

22. WM, *Ancestors*, 286 ("faced with the prospect"); "McGrath-Maxwell Nuptials Held Wednesday Eve," *LES*, 6 October 1921; WM, *Ancestors*, 286 ("most of the furniture").

23. WM, "Imagining the Middle West," 17 ("I reached"); WM, Interview by George Plimpton, *Writers at Work: The* Paris Review *Interviews*, 7th ser. (New York: Viking, 1986), 50–51 ("an aristocrat").

24. WM, *Ancestors*, 288.

25. Ibid. ("stretched to three," "threw herself").

26. WM, Interview by the author, 27–28 August 1992.

27. Ibid.

28. WM, preface to *All the Days and Nights: The Collected Stories* (New York: Knopf, 1995), ix.

29. Ernest W. Burgess and Charles Newcomb, eds., *Census Data of the City of Chicago, 1920* (Chicago: Chicago University Press, 1920), 96; The East Rogers Park Neighborhood History Project, *Reading Your Neighborhood: A History of East Rogers Park* (Chicago: Loyola University Center for Instructional Design, 1993) ("Cosmopolitan community," "handsome buildings").

30. *A Souvenir Book of Lincoln, Illinois: Showing the Home and Industrial Advantages of Logan County's Leading City, and Containing Views of Business Houses, Factories, and Homes, the Portraits of Business and Professional Men* (Lincoln, Ill.: Courier-Herald Press, 1913); Board of Education, City of Chicago, *Report*, 1922–1923, 40–41; WM, Interview by the author, 27–28 August 1992 ("became more at home," "every conceivable opportunity"), 28; WM, Interview by Nemanic, 6 ("a stroke of fortune," "come-down").

31. WM, Interview by the author, 23 November 1991 ("He liked me"), 12, 2–3 ("stopped thinking").

32. WM, Interview by Bonetti, 10; Eleanor Green Piel, personal account of the history of Bonnie Oaks, *Annex A*, 11 May 1984, Wisconsin State Historical Society ("The summer months became legend").

33. Wisconsin State Historical Society, Madison, File on Bonnie Oaks, National Register of Historic Places Inventory—Nomination Form. Promising Wisconsin writer Margery Latimer, like many early-twentieth-century intellectuals, was a follower of Gurdjieff and, after her participation in what became known as the "Portage Experiment," married Toomer in her native Portage. She died in childbirth at age thirty-three.

34. WM, "Zona Gale," *The Yale Review* 76 (1987): 221 ("If you picked up a magazine"); WM, Interview by Nemanic, 9, 7 ("Oh, God, what a lovely creature"); Dianne Lynch, introduction to *Miss Lulu Bett* and *Birth* (collected), by Zona Gale (1920 and 1918; reprint, Oregon, Wisconsin: Waubesa Press, 1994), 8.

35. WM, "Zona," 221.

36. WM, Interview by Nemanic, 7 ("When I was talking to her"); WM, "Zona," 222 (remaining quotes).

37. Zona Gale, *Portage, Wisconsin and Other Essays* (New York: Alfred A. Knopf, 1928), 155 ("naturalistic"), 145 ("brighter"), 173 ("novel of tomorrow," "mysterious beauty"), 135 ("excitement in the presence of life"), 140 ("the growth of the individual").

38. Ibid., 167 ("special grace of seeing"), 119 ("new psychology").

39. WM, "Imagining the Middle West," 17 ("Once a week"); WM, "Vacationing on H.M.S. Pinafore," *The Forum* (Senn High School, Chicago, October 1925): 8.

40. The only three now found in the Senn Library.

41. WM, "Frederic M. Grant: The Fifth of a Series of Articles on American Artists," *The Forum* (Senn High School, Chicago, May 1926): 16.

42. WM, "Imagining the Middle West," 17 ("We put up").

43. Ibid., 22.

44. Ibid., 18.

45. Ibid., 19.

46. WM, Interview by the author, 27–28 August 1992.

47. Thomas Gray, *Elinor Wylie* (New York: Twayne Publishers, 1969), 30 ("nearly obsessive"); Elinor Wylie, *Collected Poems of Elinor Wylie* (New York: Knopf, 1932), 65.

48. Maxwell's unpublished college poetry is held at the University of Illinois English Department and Archives.

49. Doris Ross McCrosson, Walter de la Mare (New York: Twayne Publishers, 1966), 23; Coincidentally, de la Mare's view on the relationships between literature, dreams, and the self closely mirror those of Theodor Reik, Maxwell's analyst in later years—even though the fact that the poet rejected much of Freudian theory, and Reik had been Freud's protégé. Both men influenced Maxwell at different stages of his life: one on the page, the other on the couch. From their respective disciplines, de la Mare and Reik regarded literature as a product of the unconscious mind for writers and readers alike, as a dreamlike state in which one encounters a "second self"—a term used by both men to signify a life lived beyond the conscious, everyday world. More specifically, de la Mare regarded a dream as an appointment to meet a friend, a second collaborator in one's personality, and a way to access the unconscious. Reik

took the notion further by asserting that authors' "second selves," the unfulfilled potentialities of their lives, are realized not only in their dreams but also in their fiction. Theodor Reik, *Fragment of a Great Confession: A Psychoanalytic Autobiography* (New York: Farrar, 1949), 414–15 ("second self").

50. McCrosson, 24.

51. WM, "Lyric," unpublished poem, University of Illinois Archives.

52. WM, Interview by the author, 27–28 August 1992; Robert Henderson, Interview by the author, New York, New York, 4 October 1994.

53. WM, "Zona," 222–23.

54. WM, Letter to Susan Deuel (Shattuck), Undated (circa 1928) ("Having failed to discover", "I know of nothing"); WM, Letter to Susan Shattuck, 30 June 1981 ("I was telling Emmy"), Charles H. Shattuck Papers, University of Illinois Archives, Record Series #15-7-39; WM, Interview by the author, 27–28 August 1992.

55. Shirley Hazzard, "William Maxwell: 1908–2000," (Memorial speech delivered to the American Academy of Arts and Letters, New York, 3 April 2001). Reprinted in Proceedings of the American Academy of Arts and Letters, Second Series, Number 52, New York (copy in author's file), 91.

56. WM, Interview by Nemanic, 9 ("criticize it patiently"); WM, Interview by Plimpton, 51 ("One day").

57. WM, "Zona," 223.

58. WM, Interview by the author, 3 January 1993 (his favorite color); WM, Interview by Bonetti, 8 ("snobbish," "I think it was because," "a total inability"), 9 ("wonderful"); "German in Church," *LCH,* 5 October 1918, 4 ("righteous wave").

59. WM, Interview by Plimpton, 56 ("lovely when you found"); William Day, Interview by the author, Springfield, Ill., 4 February 1993.

60. WM, Interview by Plimpton, 51–52; WM, letter to the author, 27 October 1993 ("I seem to remember").

Chapter 2

1. WM, Interview by Plimpton, 55 ("Some of the characters"); Henderson, Interview by the author ("So I heard"); WM, dedication to "Baba," *Bright Center of Heaven* (*BCOH*).

2. WM, *BCOH,* 39.

3. WM, Book inscription to author's copy of *BCOH,* author's files; WM, Interview by the author, 23 November 1991 ("sweep it under a rug").

4. WM, Interview by Plimpton, 45–46.

5. WM, *BCOH,* 298 ("The night sky"), 9; ("Now the breakfast table"), 12.

6. Ibid., 301–2.

7. WM, Interview by the author, 27–28 August 1992 ("The longer I went").

8. Virginia Woolf, *To the Lighthouse* (1927; reprint, New York: Harcourt Brace Jovanovich, 1989), 3; WM, *BCOH,* 302.

9. WM, "Imagining the Middle West," 13.

10. Ibid., 15–16.

11. WM, *BCOH,* 234–36.

12. Ibid., 284 ("the blood"), 292 ("Until they have learned").

13. WM, Interview by the author, 3 January 1993 ("I wish I could redo"); WM, *BCOH,* 292 ("Infuriated beyond").

14. Deborah Lindsay Williams, *Not In Sisterhood: Edith Wharton, Willa Cather, Zona Gale, and the Politics of Female Authorship* (New York: Palgrave, 2001), 67 ("as a nation," "had the last"). Zona Gale, qtd. on back cover, WM, *BCOH.*

15. WM, *BCOH,* 235.

16. Theodore Purdy Jr. review of *Bright Center of Heaven,* by WM, *Saturday Review of Literature* 11:109, 15 September 1934, 110.

17. WM, *BCOH,* 2 ("gate-leg table"), 241 ("the chairs stretched").

18. Ibid., 155.

19. Ibid., 90.

20. WM, "Imagining the Middle West," 24.

Chapter 3

1. WM, *Ancestors,* 10; WM, Interview by the author, 27–28 August 1992; WM, Introduction to *They Came Like Swallows* (New York: Modern Library, 1997), xiv.

2. WM, Interview by the author, 27–28 August 1992.

3. Ibid.

4. Ibid.

5. WM, Interview by Plimpton, 53 ("beside a window"); WM, Interview by the author, 27–28 August 1992 ("disastrous facts"), 23 November 1991 ("When I was writing").

6. WM, Interview by Bonetti, 12 ("The first book," "didn't know anything"); Katharine White to Mary Leonard Pritchett, 30 October 1936, Maxwell Collection, University of Illinois (information on Maxwell's first stories); WM, Interview by Plimpton, 57 ("Eugene Saxton," "Some knowledgeable acquaintance").

7. WM, Interview by Bonetti, 13–14 ("the bottom dropped").

8. WM, Interview by the author, 23 November 1991; WM, Interview by Plimpton, 57–58.

9. WM, Interview by the author, 23 November 1991.

10. Ibid., 27–28 August 1992.

11. WM, Interview by Nemanic, 8 ("She didn't"); WM, Interview by Bonetti ("went into Wolcott Gibbs' office"); WM, Interview by Nemanic, 9 ("At this period").

12. WM, Interview by the author, 23 November 1991 ("intense admiration"); WM, "The Thistles in Sweden," *Over by the River and Other Stories* (*OBTR*), (New York: Knopf, 1977), 232; WM, Interview by the author, 3 January 1993 ("a) Carpaccio").

13. Martha Landis, Telephone interview by the author, 8 October 1996; WM, "Imagining the Middle West" 18 ("I couldn't bring myself"); Virginia Woolf, *To the Lighthouse* (1927; reprint, New York: Harcourt Brace Jovanovich, 1989), 3.

14. WM, Interview by Plimpton, 46 ("Think what *To the Lighthouse*"); WM, Introduction to *Swallows*, xii ("Because Virginia").

15. Perhaps Maxwell deflects comparison with Woolf's little James here by using the name for the father figure rather than for the child.

16. WM, Interview by Plimpton, 50 ("ripples moving"); WM, *Swallows*, 3.

17. V. S. Pritchett, review of *They Came Like Swallows*, by WM, *The New Statesman and Nation*, 28 August 1937, 312.

18. WM, *Swallows*, 32 ("For Bunny"), 3 ("the lake became a bird"), 11 ("He was wet").

19. Ibid., 19 ("come around to his way"), 15 ("unpleasantly shaped").

20. Ibid., 10 ("practically contemporary"), 48 ("As soon as Bunny"), 33 ("I stir it").

21. WM, Interview by the author, 27–28 August 1992.

22. WM, *Swallows*, 116.

23. Ibid., 85; WM to WM Sr. 8 November 1944 (Hap's response to *Swallows*).

24. WM, *Swallows*, 140.

25. Ibid., 165 ("It's like this James"), 166 ("The snow dropping").

26. WM, *Ancestors*, 46 ("telescope").

27. WM, Interview by the author, 23 November 1991; Virginia Woolf, "Modern Fiction," *The Common Reader* (New York: Harcourt Brace Jovanovich, 1925); WM, *Leaf* (first edition) (New York: Harper: 1945), 308.

28. WM, Interview by the author, 23 November 1991.

29. Roger Angell, Interview by the author.

30. WM, Interview by the author, 27–28 August 1992.

31. Crosby, 315–16; WM, *The Happiness of Getting It Down Right: Letters of Frank O'Connor and William Maxwell*, ed. Michael Steinman (New York: Alfred A. Knopf, 1996), 49; George Hendrick, *Katherine Anne Porter* (Boston: Twayne Publishers, 1988), 5; Crosby, 317–18 ("the most accurate").

32. Edmund Wilson, "Faintness of the 'Age of Thunder' and Power of 'The Folded Leaf,'" review of *The Folded Leaf*, by WM, *The New Yorker*, 31 March 1945, 73.

33. David Tilden, "Memory, as a Star to Steer By," review of *Swallows*, by WM, *New York Herald Tribune*, 2 May 1937, 2; Fanny Butscher, "A Poignantly Etched Portrait of a Woman," review of *Swallows*, by WM, *Chicago Daily Tribune*, 1 May 1937, 15.

Chapter 4

1. WM, Interview by Bonetti, 43.

2. Elizabeth Frank, *Louise Bogan: A Portrait* (New York: Alfred A. Knopf, 1985), 328 (account of Bogan-Maxwell meeting); Louise Bogan to Katharine White, 30 December 1937, Amherst, also reprinted in *What the Woman Lived: Selected Letters of Louise Bogan 1920–1970*, ed. Ruth Limmer (New York: Harcourt Brace Jovanovich, 1973), 178n.

3. Frank, 140 (account of Bogan's depression), 228 ("overhauling poems").

4. Ibid., 287 (memoirs), 290–91 (*The Nation*), 302 (new poems for Scribner's).

5. Ibid., 327–28 ("life of responsible"), 329 ("with hamburgers").

6. WM, Interview by Plimpton, 64 ("almost stopped writing entirely").

7. WM, *The Folded Leaf,* (1945; reprint with revisions, Boston: Godine, 1981), 15 ("wonderful tropical birds").

8. Frank, 332 ("lived in the same creative universe," "wonderful eye"); Bogan, quoted in Frank, 215 ("For as in").

9. Bogan, "Journey around My Room," *The New Yorker,* 14 January 1933, 16–17 ("The initial mystery"), 18 ("the armoire," "O death").

10. WM, Interview by the author, 3 January 1993.

11. Frank, 273 ("viewed the ailments"), 238 ("Freudian discoveries"), 328 ("grief work"), 332 ("interested in his time of life"); WM, Interview by Bonetti, 44 (entered psychoanalysis); Bogan, *Journey around My Room: The Autobiography of Louise Bogan: A Mosaic* by Ruth Limmer (New York: Viking Press, 1980): 9 ("the best time to write"—undated diary entry).

12. Frank, 329 (account of friendship); Bogan to Morton Zabel, 2 June 1941, *What the Woman Lived,* 218.

13. WM, Interview by the author, 3 January 1993, 27–28 August 1992.

14. Bogan to Zabel, 2 June 1941, *What the Woman Lived,* 218 ("such a lovely"); WM, Interview by Bonetti, 22 ("with low ceilings").

15. Bogan to Zabel, 2 June 1941, *What the Woman Lived,* 218 ("Maxwell is really"); Frank, 330 ("spirit was in full harmony," "love for him"); Bogan to Zabel, 4 June 1941, *What the Woman Lived,* 218 ("like the Marschallin").

16. Frank, 330 ("an inscribed copy"); Bogan to WM, 22 August 1941, quoted in Frank, 330–31 ("Something may have").

17. Frank, 331 ("had no idea," "was seeing for the first time" [all Frank's words]).

18. WM, Interview by Plimpton, 64; WM, Interview by the author, 3 January 1993 ("chapter by chapter"); WM, Interview by Nemanic, 9 ("uncompromisingly serious"); WM, Interview by Plimpton, 64 ("From time to time"); WM, Interview by the author, 3 January 1993 ("The only two"); Bogan to Maxwell, 9 October 1942, *What the Woman Lived,* 227 ("The one thing"); WM, *Leaf,* 5 ("[Spud] was not quite").

19. Bogan to WM, 9 October 1942, *What the Woman Lived,* 226–27 ("So nice"); WM, Interview by the author, 27–28 August 1992 ("The whole time").

20. Bogan to WM, 9 October 1942, *What the Woman Lived,* 227 ("As I see").

21. WM to Bogan [n.d.], quoted in Frank, 331 ("The problem," "anything that"), 332 ("From the criticisms," "Thank you for realizing"); Marianne Moore, "In Distrust of Merits," quoted in Frank, 332. As Elizabeth Frank notes, the quotation from Moore's poem is itself a quotation.

22. WM, Interview by Bonetti, 17.

23. WM, *Over By the River and Other Stories* (New York: Knopf, 1977), 132 ("'Francis is so young'").

24. Ibid., 152 ("All in the world"), 151–52 ("she would have").

25. Ibid., 169 ("He didn't seem").

26. Two decades later, his novel *The Chateau* glimpsed the war's aftermath in France, yet in that work the interactions between two American tourists and their French hosts, rather than the war itself, were the predominant theme.

27. WM, *Over By the River*, 78 ("Cain and Abel").

28. Ibid., 82 ("hot dogs").

29. WM, Interview by Bonetti, 22 ("delightful").

30. WM to WM Sr., 1944, Copy in the author's files ("Also, I was"); Alec Wilkinson, *My Mentor: A Young Man's Friendship with William Maxwell* (New York: Houghton Mifflin, 2002), 64 ("I was a pacifist"); WM, Interview by the author, 27–28 August 1992 ("I hate").

31. After the senior Maxwell's 1923 promotion to vice president in Chicago, he was offered a higher post in the New York office in the 1940s, but did not accept it partly because of failing eyesight.

32. WM, Interview by Plimpton, 67 ("pick up"); WM to Grace Maxwell, 3 September 1943, copy in the author's files ("to keep an establishment"); WM to WM Sr., 4 October 1943 (postmark), copy in the author's files ("You go along").

33. WM to WM Sr., 4 October 1943 (postmark), copy in the author's files ("but we still"); WM, Interview by Plimpton, 67 ("When [*Leaf*] was").

34. WM to WM Sr., 4 March 1944, copy in the author's files.

35. Erika Freeman, introduction to *Insights: Conversations with Theodor Reik* (Englewood Cliffs, N.J.: Prentice Hall, 1971), 1; "Dr. Theodor Reik, Freud Protégé, Is Dead at 81," *New York Times*, 1 January 1970, 22; Freeman, 1 ("never broke with Freud").

36. Freeman, 1.

37. Theodor Reik, Interview by American Academy of Psychotherapists, volume 22, printed transcript (copy in author's files), 15; WM to Loretta Butler, 18 February 2000, WM Collection.

38. Bronson A. Feldman, "Reik and the Interpretation of Literature," *Explorations in Psychoanalysis: Essays in Honor of Theodor Reik* (New York: Julian Press, 1953): 97; John C. Gustin, "On Theodor Reik," *Explorations in Psychoanalysis*, xi ("emotional conflicts"); Reik, *Fragment*, 25 ("psychological problems"); Feldman, 104 ("celebration"); WM, *So Long, See You Tomorrow*, (New York: Knoft, 1980), 132 ("roundabout futile way").

39. Reik, *Fragment*, 414–15 ("get a first"); WM, Interview by the author, 27–28 August 1992 (confirmed Reik read his first two novels); WM, Interview by the author, 27–28 August 1992 ("wanted something").

40. Reik, *Fragment*, 415 ("potentialities").

41. WM to WM Sr., 4 March 1944 (postmark), copy in the author's files ("Would love"); WM, *Outermost Dream*, 168 (Lobrano inheriting Katharine White's editing duties); WM to WM Sr., Spring 1944, Saturday ("I'll take over," "I didn't want"); WM to WM Sr., ca. 1944 ("Dear Pop").

42. Bogan to WM, 18 September 1944, Amherst ("sat down"); Bogan to WM, 28

September 1944 ("Do write"); WM, *Leaf* (first edition), 310 ("emerged from"); Frank, 333 ("to implication"); WM, *Leaf* (first edition), 309 ("What I would"); WM, manuscript of *Leaf,* WM Collection, 373 ("would not trouble"); WM, *Leaf* (first edition), 310 ("It would never").

43. WM to WM Sr., 8 November 1944, copy in author's files.

44. Ibid., 8 November 1944, copy in the author's files ("As you can see").

45. WM, Interview by the author, 27–28 August 1992 ("I tried this"); WM to WM Sr., 8 November 1944, copy in the author's files ("What I finally"); WM, Interview by Nemanic, 7 (""Why did you"); WM, Interview by the author, 3 January 1993 ("wouldn't have been").

46. WM to WM Sr., 8 November 1944, copy in the author's files ("hard for"); WM, Interview by the author, 27–28 August 1992 ("no real interest"); WM to WM Sr., 7 November 1944, copy in the author's files ("I've just come back," "Somehow it gives").

47. WM to WM Sr., 27 November 1944, copy in the author's files ("So you see").

48. WM, Interview by the author, 3 January 1993 ("After a novel"); Bogan to WM, undated, Amherst ("I think it has a real"); WM, Interview by the author, 3 January 1993 ("It was a beautiful," "His best novel").

49. WM to WM. Sr., 8 November 1944, copy in the author's files ("I am doing"); Wilkinson, 67 ("He hadn't").

50. WM to WM Sr., 19 January 1945, copy in the author's files ("social whirl," confirms publication date); WM to Donald Sheehan, 14 February 1955 (confirms Emily's graduation from Smith); WM to WM Sr., 19 January 1945 ("pretty sad").

51. Emily Maxwell, "EM: A Statement about herself and her work," n.d., reprinted in program of the Maxwell's memorial service 8 September 2000 (copy in author's files) ("was there"); WM to Grace Maxwell, 21 March 1945, copy in the author's files ("I want to tell you"); Ben Yagoda, *About Town: The New Yorker and the World It Made* (New York: Scribner, 2000): 215–16 (Ross hired Wilson); WM to Grace Maxwell, 21 March 1945 ("The review").

52. WM, Interview by Plimpton, 50 ("walking across"); WM, *Leaf,* 191; WM, Interview by Plimpton, 50 ("When I got").

53. WM, *Leaf,* 51 ("The earth"), 36 ("fixed"), 48 ("re-enacting"), 51 ("Torture is").

54. WM, Interview by the author, 27–28 August 1992 ("Originally").

55. WM, *Leaf,* 52–54 ("the dark"), 54 ("from the basis"), 53 ("are in no way"); Diana Trilling, review of *Leaf,* by WM, *The Nation,* 21 April 1945, 467.

56. WM, *Leaf,* 270.

57. Thanks to Dr. Jana Van Fossan Dreyzehner for sharing her thoughts on Jung.

58. WM, *Leaf,* 265–66.

59. WM, Interview by the author, 27–28 August 1992 ("partly the effect"); WM, *Leaf,* 66 ("to know"), 77 ("To live in the world").

60. E. B. White, "Once More to the Lake," *Essays of E. B. White* (1977; reprint, New York: Harper Perennial, 1999), 256.

61. Trilling, 466.

62. Ernest Jones, review of *Time Will Darken It*, by WM, *The Nation*, 25 September 1948, 353 ("intrusive," "blown-up quality"); A. W. Phinney, "Maxwell's New Novel," review of *The Chateau*, by WM, *Christian Science Monitor*, 30 March 1961, 7 ("marred"); WM, Interview by the author, 27–28 August 1992 ("I have all").

63. WM, Interview by the author, 27–28 August 1992 ("half the book"), 23 November 1991 ("no distance at all").

64. Ibid., 27–28 August 1992 ("to escape, "elaborate background"); WM, *Leaf*, 112.

65. Trilling, 466; Wilson, 74 ("certain American"), 73 ("special kind").

66. Gordon McKerral, "Novelist Preserves Youth," *Decatur* (Illinois) *Herald and Review*, 28 February 1981, F9 ("There is plenty"); WM, Interview by the author, 23 November 1991 ("When I read Howells"); Wilson, 73; "U.S. Flyers Sink Japan's Biggest Warship," *New York Times*, 8 April 1945, 1.

67. WM, *Leaf*, 72; Sara Henderson Hay, "The Magnetism of the Opposites," review of *Leaf*, by WM, *Saturday Review of Literature*, 7 April 1945, 9 ("unconsciously playing").

68. WM, *Leaf*, 96–97.

69. Bruce Bawer, "States of Grace: The Novels of William Maxwell," *The New Criterion*, May 1989, 32; Bogan to WM, 17 May 1943, Amherst.

70. WM, *Leaf*, 96.

71. WM, *The Chateau*, 59.

72. Bawer, 32; W. Tasker Witham, *The Adolescent in the American Novel: 1920–1960* (New York: Frederick Ungar Publishing Co., 1964), 127; Roger Austen, *Playing the Game: The Homosexual Novel in America* (Indianapolis: Bobb-Merrill, 1977), 100 ("reads like"); James Levin, *The Gay Novel in America* (New York: Garland, 1991), 65 ("beyond the actual"), 66 (gay readers identify with Lymie); James Campbell, "Secrets of the Confessional: William Maxwell, Novelist and Revered Fiction Editor of *The New Yorker*, Suffered Early Personal Tragedy," *The Guardian* (London), 11 January 2003, 34.

73. WM, Interview by the author, 27–28 August 1992 ("Nobody").

74. Witham, 265; Paul Binding, "Mismatched Buddies Probe the Deep Heart of Man: *The Folded Leaf* by William Maxwell," review of *Leaf*, by WM, *The Independent* (London), 27 December 1998, 10.

75. Theodor Reik, Interview by Academy of Psychotherapists, volume 22, printed transcript (copy in author's files), 22–23.

76. WM, *Leaf*, 100–102

77. Ibid., 136 ("The mutual"), 131 ("in the big," "his right foot").

78. Ibid., 221 ("faithful hound"), 119–20 ("his shoes"), 154 ("the role").

79. Ibid., 222 ("the only one"), 96 ("tormented"), 241 ("talks for").

80. Ibid., 245.

81. Ibid., 253.

82. Lymie's words about his attempt at suicide closely mirror Maxwell's own in an interview with the author in August 1992. In speaking of this experience, Maxwell

said, "I didn't want to live in a world where the truth has no power to make itself be believed."

83. WM, *Leaf,* 257–58.

84. WM, Interview by the author, 23 November 1991 ("now direct," "move the reader").

85. WM, *Leaf,* 274; WM, Interview by the author, 27–28 August 1992 ("wanted to convey").

86. WM, *Leaf* (first edition), 308 ("lay smooth"); WM, *Leaf,* (1945; reprint with revisions, Boston: Godine, 1981), 140 ("stiffly"); WM, *Leaf* (first edition), 308 ("the face"), 309 ("What he").

87. WM, *Leaf* (first edition), 310; WM, *Leaf,* 248 ("the bandages"); WM, *Leaf* (first edition), 310 ("rise up").

88. WM, *Leaf,* (first edition), 308; WM, Interview by the author, 3 January 1993 ("Unless you believe"), 13 ("the psychologist"), 42 ("Maturity").

89. Trilling, 466; Hay, 9; Wilson, 73 ("careful unobtrusive art," "moving").

90. WM, Interview by the author, 27–28 August 1992 ("I hadn't intentionally"); Wilson, 73; Trilling, 467.

91. WM to Susan Deuel Shattuck, 3 April 1945, University of Illinois Archives; WM, Interview by the author, 27–28 August 1992 ("I wished").

92. First Presbyterian Church, New York, Marriage Record, 17 May 1945; Emily Maxwell, "E.M.: A Statement about herself and her work."

93. WM, Interview by the author, 27–28 August 1992 ("When I had"); WM to WM Sr., 27 November 1944, copy in the author's files; WM, Interview by Nemanic, 10 ("were neither"); WM, Interview by Plimpton, 65 ("Mostly"); WM, *Leaf* (first edition), 303 ("He was"); WM, *Leaf,* 271 ("He wanted").

94. WM, *Leaf* (first edition), 304 ("Looking"); WM, *Leaf,* 53 ("presence," "What survives"); WM, Interview by the author, 27–28 August 1992 (Maxwell discussed with me the novel's dramatic construction).

95. WM, *Leaf* (first edition), 310; WM, *Leaf,* 274.

96. WM, *Leaf,* 271 ("He wanted"); WM, *Leaf* (first edition), 308 ("Lymie opened"); WM, *Leaf,* 273 ("When he had").

97. WM, Interview by the author, 27–28 August 1992 ("two or three"); WM, *Leaf,* 274.

98. WM, *Leaf,* 274 ("made him"), 272 ("people for whom").

99. WM, Interview by the author, 27–28 August 1992 ("how much better"); Alfred Lord Tennyson, "The Lotos-Eaters," *Selected Poetry of Tennyson,* ed. Douglas Bush (New York: Random House, 1951), 58.

Chapter 5

1. WM, preface to *Time Will Darken It, The Chateau, So Long, See You Tomorrow* (collected edition) (New York: Quality Paperback Book Club, 1992), v ("I had had"); WM, Interview by the author, 27–28 August 1992 ("a set").

2. WM, *Time Will Darken It* (New York: Harper, 1948), preface, v ("it was a matter," "judgment faltered"); WM, Interview by the author, 27–28 August 1992 ("She reads").

3. WM, Interview by Bonetti, 19.

4. John Updike, Interview by the author, Springfield and Urbana, Ill., 24 April 1997.

5. WM, *Time,* preface, xx.

6. Ibid., 174.

7. Reik, *Fragment,* 414–15.

8. James F. Maxfield, "The Child, the Adolescent, and the Adult: Stages of Consciousness in Three Early Novels of William Maxwell," *The Midwest Quarterly* 24 (1982–83): 334.

9. WM, *Time,* 20; WM, *Leaf,* 51.

10. WM, *Time,* 222.

11. Ibid., 186 ("part of a set"), 186–87 ("encyclopaedia"), 188 ("any pretence").

12. Ibid., 188 ("who held"), 204 ("the truth").

13. Ibid., 188.

14. Ibid., 20–21.

15. Ibid., 154–55.

16. WM, *Time,* epigraph quoted from Francisco Pacheco.

17. WM, *Time,* 115.

18. WM, Interview by the author, 23 November 1991 ("said what"), 27–28 August 1992 (Maxwell believing readers would be interested in what he was).

19. WM, *Time,* 115; Geoffrey Stokes, "The Quiet Man," *Voice Literary Supplement,* December 1985, 27.

20. WM, *Time,* epigraph.

21. Ibid., *Time,* 21 ("drifted in").

22. Ibid., preface, vi ("needed things"); 248 ("The sky").

23. Ibid., 43 ("the split"), 44 ("They met").

24. Ibid., 80.

25. Ibid., 31.

26. Ibid., 97 ("Boys brought up"); Zona Gale might have influenced Maxwell's thinking here. As Deborah Lindsay Williams wrote, "Like many early feminists, Gale realized that putting women on a pedestal was only an excuse to exclude them from their own lives, and in no way prevented exploitation." In 1922, Gale observed, "The pedestal does not seem to be high enough to prevent a husband from scaling it to collect his wife's earnings." 96 ("complacent," "Wasn't there").

27. Ibid., 105 ("with a hook").

28. Ibid., 101.

29. Ibid., 74.

30. Ibid., 14 ("her hair"), 18 ("no, this").

31. Ibid., 30.

32. Ibid., 343–44 ("too bright"), 344 ("People call us"), 346 ("if it's to be"), 347 ("These offers").

33. Mary Flanagan, "Quiet Dramas of Reconciliation," *The New York Times Book Review*, review of *All the Days and Nights*, by WM, 22 January 1995, 3.

34. WM, Interview by the author, 3 January 1993 (expressed awareness that he was most influenced by women writers).

35. WM, *Time*, 267.

36. Ibid.

37. WM, Interview by the author, 5 December 1996.

38. WM, *Time*, 367–68.

39. WM, "Imagining the Middle West," 15.

40. WM, Interview by the author, 3 January 1993.

41. Ibid.

42. Maxwell told the story of such an African American physician in his late story "Billie Dyer."

43. WM, *Time*, 230.

44. Ibid., 54 ("great plane"), 255 ("roofs").

45. WM to WM Sr., 23 June 1948 (postmark), copy in author's files.

46. WM, *Time*, preface, vii (state of Texas); WM, Interview by the author, 23 November 1991, 27–28 August 1992.

47. WM, *Time*, preface, vii ("Before I ever").

48. WM to WM Sr. and Grace Maxwell, 17 July 1948, copy in the author's files.

49. Ibid.

50. Ibid.

51. WM to WM Sr. and Grace Maxwell, 8 August 1948, copy in author's files.

52. Ibid.

53. Ibid.

54. WM to WM Sr. and Grace Maxwell, 20 August 1948 ("all of Europe"); WM to WM Sr., 20 August 1948 ("species of typewriter"); WM to WM Sr. and Grace Maxwell, 20 August 1948 ("the most"); Ibid. ("This is so"); WM to WM Sr., 20 August 1948 ("At the moment"), copies in author's files.

55. WM to WM Sr., 20 August 1948, copy in author's files.

56. WM to WM Sr., August 1948 ("small, convenient"); WM to WM Sr., 25 August 1948 ("ghosts"), copies in author's files.

57. WM to WM Sr., 4 September 1948, copy in author's files ("wildly enthusiastic," "like a good omen"); Brendan Gill, "A Delicate Undertaking," review of *Time Will Darken It*, by WM, *The New Yorker*, September 1958, 78–79.

58. WM to WM Sr. 20 September 1948, copy in author's files.

59. Ernest Jones, review of *Time Will Darken It*, by WM, *The Nation*, 25 September 1948, 353; Horace Reynolds, "A Novel of Character," review of *Time Will Darken It*, by WM, *Christian Science Monitor*, 9 September 1948, 11 ("understanding of the mystical"); Review of *Time Will Darken It*, by WM, *Atlantic Monthly*, December 1948, 120; Richard Sullivan, "Life in Draperville, Illinois," review of *Time Will Darken It*, by WM, *New York Times Book Review*, 5 September 1948, 4; Henry Joseph Jackson,

"Mid-U.S.: 1912," review of *Time Will Darken It,* by WM, *San Francisco Chronicle,* 3 September 1948, 16.

60. WM to WM Sr., 9 (?) October 1948, copy in the author's files.

61. Ibid.

62. Ibid. ("I don't know"); WM to WM Sr., October 1948, Saturday ("had had enough").

63. WM to WM Sr., October 1948, Saturday.

64. WM, *Time,* preface, viii.

Chapter 6

1. WM, Interview by Plimpton, 47.

2. WM, *Chateau,* 106 ("mouse-colored"), epigraph quote from Elizabeth Bowen.

3. Alfred Knopf Collection (four hundred copies a week); WM to WM Sr., 27 October 1948, copy in author's files ("Good for these times").

4. WM, *OBTR,* 56 ("They were not"), 58 ("The limit").

5. Ibid., 61 ("When she came"); WM, *Time,* 74 ("the innocent).

6. Ibid, 63 ("something with truffles").

7. Ibid., 71 ("but I'm not sure," "I think so"), 72 ("all *that* good").

8. Ibid., 114.

9. WM Papers, University of Illinois at Urbana-Champaign.

10. WM, Interview by the author, 27–28 August 1992.

11. WM, Interview by the author, 23 November 1991 ("It has seemed"); WM Collection ("There is no").

12. Author's note to *Stories,* by Jean Stafford, John Cheever, Daniel Fuchs, and WM (New York: Farrar, Strauss and Cudahy, 1956).

13. Ben Cheever, *Letters of John Cheever* 191; WM, Interview by Bonetti, 17 ("old enough").

14. Paul Engle, "Superb, Brief Tales by Four American Writers," review of *Stories,* by Jean Stafford, John Cheever, Daniel Fuchs, and WM, *Chicago Sunday Tribune,* 23 December 1956, 5.

15. Ann Waldron, *Eudora: A Writer's Life* (New York: Doubleday, 1998), 114; Michael Kreyling, *Author and Agent: Eudora Welty and Diarmuid Russell* (New York: Farrar, Straus and Giroux, 1991), 159 ("not too sympathetic," "editorial shake-up," "new ally"), 155 ("annotations"); Yagoda, 223 (information on "The Bride of Innisfallen").

16. Kreyling, 159.

17. The Mendenhall Hotel and Restaurant finally closed its doors at the end of 2001. Owner Natalie Morgan remembers Ms. Welty being driven from Jackson, about thirty miles away, to eat at the revolving tables regularly. (Telephone interview, 11 October 2002.)

18. Kreyling, 163–64 (Maxwell remembered Welty reading *The Ponder Heart* aloud); Eudora Welty to WM and EM (postcard), 1955, WM papers.

19. Brian Boyd, *Vladimir Nabokov: The American Years* (Princeton, N.J.: Princeton University Press, 1991), 293 (came under Katharine White's wing, "kindness"), 73 (Katharine White rejoined the magazine with the idea of soliciting Nabokov for stories).

20. Vladimir Nabokov to WM, 5 March 1964, WM Papers.

21. The story, "Friends from Philadelphia," was edited by Maxwell (personal interview, 24 April 1997).

22. John Updike (speech presented at the University of Illinois at Urbana-Champaign honoring William Maxwell at a celebration of his gift of papers), 24 April 1997, reprinted in *More Matter: Essays and Criticism* (New York: Knopf, 1999), 780–81.

23. William H. Pritchard, *John Updike: America's Man of Letters* (South Royalton, Vt.: Steerforth Press, 2000), 22 (Updike as *New Yorker* staff member); Updike, *More Matter,* 781 (Maxwell became Updike's editor); Updike, Interview by the author ("Our relationship," "relaxed"); Updike, *More Matter,* 782 ("well into").

24. Updike, *More Matter,* 782.

25. WM, Interview by the author, 27–28 August 1992 ("recurring disappointment"); Alec Wilkinson, *My Mentor: A Young Man's Friendship with William Maxwell* (New York: Houghton Mifflin, 2002), 77–78 ("running dry," "set his heart," "I wanted"), 81 ("Some time").

26. WM's handwritten notes from the symposium's panel discussion are located in the Smith College Archives, Northampton, Massachusetts.

27. All quotes from speech taken from WM, "The Writer as Illusionist: A Speech Delivered at Smith College," 4 March 1955 (copy in author's files and in the Maxwell Collection at the University of Illinois Rare Books and Special Collections Library).

28. "A. Kazin Occasion," *The Sophian* (Smith College, Northampton, Mass.), 8 March 1955, 2 ("Mr. Maxwell's beautiful"); Harriet Wise, untitled report, *The Sophian,* 8 March 1955, 1–3 (balance of quotes in this paragraph regarding symposium).

29. Gill and Maxwell countered the other two again on the issue of perceived homogeneity in *The New Yorker*'s fiction. From Maxwell's perspective, there was "a great variety" of work published in the magazine, whereas Kazin maintained that there was "a formula that people tr[ied] to live up to." Maxwell's literary taste also showed itself that evening: *The Sophian* reported that "Mr. Gill and Mr. Bellow affirmed Faulkner as the greatest contemporary American novelist while Mr. Maxwell emphasized that the field was wide enough for all types of writers."

30. Alfred A. Knopf Jr. to WM, 12 March 1958, Knopf Collection, Harry Ransom Center, Austin Texas; WM to Alfred A. Knopf Sr., 27 May 1958, Knopf Collection ("For some reason"); Alfred A. Knopf Sr., office memo, Knopf Collection, HRC ("Part of the mutual").

31. WM, Interview by Plimpton, 63 ("I hadn't").

32. WM, Interview by Bonetti, 31 ("unreadable," "horrified"); WM, Interview by Plimpton, 63 ("went off"), 64 ("My relief").

33. WM to Frank O'Connor, October 1958, *The Happiness of Getting It Down Right: Letters of Frank O'Connor and William Maxwell,* ed. Michael Steinman (New York: Knopf, 1996), 92 ("I got to the last part"), 15 October 1958, 94 ("It isn't").

34. Frank O'Connor to WM, 1958, *Happiness,* 95.

35. WM, "Imagining the Middle West," 14 ("All manner"); WM, Interview by Bonetti, 332 ("French people would"); WM, "Imagining the Middle West," 14 ("foolish"); WM, Interview by Bonetti, 32 ("I answered").

36. Harold Strauss, office memo (critique of untitled novel by William Maxwell), Alfred A. Knopf Collection, HRC.

37. Judith Jones, office memo, Alfred A. Knopf Collection, HRC; Alfred A. Knopf, note on manuscript record, Alfred A. Knopf Collection, HRC.

38. WM, Interview by Bonetti, 32.

39. Naomi Bliven, "Brief Encounter," review of *The Chateau,* by WM, *The New Yorker,* 25 March 1961, 163.

40. WM, *Chateau,* 7 ("In the early"), 9 ("ugly"), 31 ("obliterated"), 100 ("Do I imagine"), 55–56 ("I blame"), 199 ("will bring"), 201 ("What would you").

41. Ibid., 282–83 ("advantage of"), 327 ("Our people"), 329 ("They haven't").

42. Ibid., 4.

43. Ibid., 6 ("A whole generation"), 61–62 ("avoids"), 64 ("separated from her").

44. Ibid., 59 ("the sum total"), 60 ("in some ways"), 57–58 ("summer he spent").

45. Ibid., 60.

46. WM, *The Folded Leaf,* 79 ("The great"); WM, *Chateau,* 60 ("two false starts").

47. WM, *Chateau,* 357.

48. Ibid., 362 ("Would you like"), 397 ("Now suppose").

49. Ibid., 357 ("If you really"), 358 ("makes room"), 378 ("Every novel").

50. Ibid, 363.

51. Ibid, 394–95 ("Everybody feels"), 385 ("She was").

52. Ibid., 370.

53. WM, *So Long,* 132 ("what is done").

54. WM, *Chateau,* 401.

55. Ibid.

56. Ibid., 401–402.

57. Ibid., 402.

58. Louise Bogan to WM, 15 March 1961, Amherst; Blanche Knopf to WM, 16 May 1961, Alfred Knopf Collection, HRC; WM to Blanche Knopf, May 1961, Alfred Knopf Collection, HRC; Alfred Knopf to WM, 5 October 1961, Alfred Knopf Collection, HRC.

59. Bliven, 6; Review of *The Chateau,* by WM, *Time,* 14 April 1961, 112, 115; Granville Hicks, "A Quiet Sort of Magic," review of *The Chateau,* by WM, *Saturday Review of Books,* 18 March 1961, 116; Richard Gilman, "The Anti-Novel of a Trained, Cool-Tempered Sensibility," review of *The Chateau,* by WM, *The Commonweal,* 7 April 1961, 50.

60. Miranda Seymour, "A Young Man with Money and a Wife," review of *The Chateau*, by WM, *Times Literary Supplement*, 7 April 2000, 28.

61. William A. Koshland to Milton Greenstein, 24 October 1960, Alfred Knopf Collection, HRC.

62. WM, Interview by Bonetti, 36–37.

63. Josyane Savigneau, "La délicate Élégance de William Maxwell," *Le Monde*, 3 July 1987, 11.

64. Duncan Campbell, "The Other Side of America: In the U.S., Not Everyone Is an Overweight Gunslinger Fanatic—And Not Everyone Wants a War with Iraq," *The Guardian*, 25 October 2002, 22.

65. Seymour, 28; Although I agree with Seymour on this point regarding *The Chateau*, I respectfully question her characterization of *So Long, See You Tomorrow* as a novel with "traditional form." Although its effects are not as obviously experimental as the epilogue in *The Chateau*, like the earlier novel it marks new narrative developments for Maxwell, most notably a subtler yet more thorough questioning and blending of the boundaries between fact and fiction, life and art.

66. A. W. Phinney, "Maxwell's New Novel," review of *The Chateau*, by WM, *Christian Science Monitor*, 30 March 1961, 7.

Chapter 7

1. WM, Interview by Linda Wertheimer, *All Things Considered*, National Public Radio, 8 February 1995 (transcript in author's files).

2. WM, *The Old Man at the Railroad Crossing and Other Tales* (New York: Knopf, 1966), 27 ("There used to be").

3. WM, Interview by the author, 27–28 August 1992 ("In writing the fables"); WM, Interview by Wertheimer ("With real stories").

4. WM, *OBTR*, 137 ("in a nightshirt"), 139 ("And one night," "Perhaps").

5. Ibid., 164.

6. Judith Jones to Betty Anderson, office memo, 18 August 1970, Knopf Collection, HRC.

7. Judith Jones to Judy Pomerantz, office memo, 21 August 1970, Knopf Collection, HRC.

8. WM, *Ancestors*, 10 ("cards on the table," "there [wasn't] anybody").

9. Ibid., 18.

10. Ibid., 28.

11. Ibid., 38–39.

12. Ruth Cobbett Biemiller, review of *Ancestors*, by WM, *Saturday Review*, 24 August 1971, 20.

13. Brendan Gill, "The Past Regained," review of *Ancestors*, by WM, *The New Yorker*, 21 August 1971, 89.

14. Timothy Dow Adams, *Telling Lies in Modern American Autobiography* (Chapel Hill: University of North Carolina Press, 1990), 15.

15. WM, "Imagining the Middle West," 11.

16. WM, Interview by the author, 27–28 August 1992 ("The result," "I think I learned"); WM, Interview by Bonetti, 37 ("never tiresome," "I hadn't discovered").

17. WM, *Ancestors,* 81 ("I feel quite sure"); WM, Interview by Bonetti, 37–38 ("like venturing").

18. WM, *Ancestors,* 115.

19. WM, Interview by the author, 27–28 August 1992.

Chapter 8

1. WM, *OBTR,* 43–44 ("an old man"); WM, Interview by the author, 3 January 1993 ("New York"); WM, *OBTR,* 11 ("Bloomingdale's").

2. WM, *OBTR,* 32.

3. Ibid., 88.

4. Ibid., 14 (description of night policeman, junkie, people walking dogs), 24–25 ("what he thought"), 17 ("I dreamt").

5. Roger Angell, Interview by the author.

6. Ibid.; WM, *OBTR,* 23 ("There was"); John Updike, Interview by the author.

7. Emily Maxwell told me that "Over by the River" was her favorite of her husband's stories as she drove me back to the Croton-Harmon train station, 27 August 1992; WM, *OBTR,* 49.

8. WM, *OBTR,* 219.

9. Ibid., 223 ("Euclid's geometry"), 219 ("Since I was").

10. Ibid., 220 ("life-sized thistles"); Roger Angell, Interview by the author.

11. Ibid., 225 ("modest perfectionism"), 227 ("When I was").

12. Ibid., 237.

13. Ibid., 239.

14. Ibid., 242.

Chapter 9

1. WM, Interview by Plimpton, 45, Maxwell quotes Saul Bellow, who, as a fellow panelist at the Smith College Symposium, said, "A writer is a reader who is moved to emulation." WM was fond of this statement and believed it applied to himself.

2. Walter Sullivan, "The Feckless Present, the Unredeemed Past: Some Recent Novels," review of *So Long, See You Tomorrow,* by WM, *The Sewanee Review* 88 (1980): 441.

3. WM, *So Long,* 56 ("Except through").

4. WM, *So Long,* preface, viii ("It was not"); WM, "Bloody Murder" (manuscript), WM Collection.

5. WM, *So Long,* preface, ix ("cotton"); WM, Interview by the author, 23 November 1991 ("The impulse"). WM, Interview by Plimpton, 50 ("Something made me think"); WM, Interview by the author, 23 November 1991 ("which may unconsciously").

6. WM, Interview by Nemanic, 6 (WM's reference to his father's farms); WM, Interview by the author, 27–28 August 1992 ("When I found myself," "After about a year").

7. WM, *So Long,* 33 ("but one day"); WM to Tom Perry 2 November 1972, copy in author's files.

8. Tom Perry to WM, 8 November 1972, copy in author's files; WM to Tom Perry, 28 November 1972, copy in author's files.

9. WM to Tom Perry, 2 January 1973, copy in author's files. Note: To avoid confusion, I have used the character names Maxwell gave to those involved with the murder rather than the real names from the *Lincoln Courier-Herald* when discussing the actual history of the case.

10. WM, *So Long,* preface, ix (WM astonished to discover he had strayed from facts of murder); WM, *So Long,* 27 ("Memory"); WM, Interview by Plimpton, 45 ("trust in what happened"); *LCH,* 8 February 1921, p. 1 ("I am the most miserable"); *LCH,* 20 January–February 15 1921; WM, *So Long,* preface, x ("What I couldn't find").

11. WM, *So Long,* 34.

12. WM, Interview by the author, 23 November 1991 ("I opened it"); WM, *So Long,* preface, x ("a perfect metaphor").

13. WM, Interview by the author, 23 November 1991 ("He himself"); information on Howard Moss's play "Palace at 4 A.M." in Berg Collection, New York Public Library.

14. WM, Interview by the author, 23 November 1991 (*The New Yorker*").

15. William Shawn, "Mr. Shawn's Queries on William Maxwell's *So Long, See You Tomorrow* (Part II)," to Roger Angell, WM Collection, 1; Roger Angell, notes on Mr. Shawn's query; WM, "So Long, See You Tomorrow (Part II)," *The New Yorker,* 8 October 1979, 58; WM, *So Long,* 102.

16. Shawn, "Mr. Shawn's Queries," 1.

17. WM, *So Long,* 57 ("she is expecting"), 69–70 ("they both know"), 123 ("He had heard").

18. Ibid., 118 ("closed her eyes"); Shawn, "Mr. Shawn's Queries," 2; WM, note on Mr. Shawn's query, 2 ("Yes, for all of it"). Incidentally, the thinking dog here had precedent in Maxwell's 1974 *New Yorker* story "Over by the River": The Carringtons' dog, "on good terms with everybody," is not "intimidated" when Iris is frustrated with her. The dog is "in agreement" with her owner that "it is a crime against Nature to keep a hunting dog in the city," "though only one of them could have put it in words" (23–24).

19. Robert Bray, response to "The History of an Illinois Novel: William Maxwell's *So Long, See You Tomorrow*" (paper presented by the author at the Illinois History Symposium, Springfield, Ill., December 1995); Updike, *More Matter,* 783 (Updike noted that *The New Yorker* did not receive credit for publishing experimental work).

20. WM, Interview by the author, 23 November 1991.

21. WM, *So Long,* 57 ("total exposure").

22. WM, Interview by the author, 27–28 August 1992 ("the fact").

23. WM, *So Long,* 25.

24. Ibid., 31 ("So long").

25. Ibid., 56.

26. Ibid., 131–32.

27. Ibid., 132 ("in the fetal position"), 133 ("can never go").

28. WM, Interview by the author, 27–28 August 1992 ("a person"); WM, Interview by Plimpton, 44 ("I felt").

29. WM, *So Long*, 66 ("She has"), 134 ("Five or ten"); WM, "Imagining the Middle West," 10 ("It is not so much").

30. WM, *So Long*, 14 ("He was simply"), 37 ("I fancy").

31. WM, Interview by the author, 27–28 August 1992.

32. WM, *So Long*, 132.

33. Brian McHale, *Postmodernist Fiction* (1987; reprint, New York: Routledge, 1989), 11 ("travel the entire"), 9 ("How can I"), 10 ("What kinds").

34. Ibid., 9.

35. WM, *So Long*, 56.

36. Ibid., 28 ("This memoir"), 132 ("It is time").

37. Linda Hutcheon, *A Poetics of Postmodernism: History, Theory, Fiction* (New York: Routledge, 1988), 114 ("plays upon"). Hutcheon uses the term "historiographic metafiction" to describe this type of fiction.

38. WM to William Shawn, office memo, *The New Yorker*, WM Collection.

39. Shelley Fisher Fishkin, *From Fact to Fiction: Journalism and Imaginative Writing in America* (Baltimore: Johns Hopkins University Press, 1985), 209.

40. WM, Unfinished Play ("bare framework"); *So Long*, 132 ("what is done").

41. WM, *So Long*, 131 ("there is a door"); WM, Interview by the author, 27–28 August 1992.

42. WM, Interview by the author, 27–28 August 1992 ("does not shut"), 16 ("I think it also").

43. Ibid., 16.

44. Ibid., 17.

45. WM to Charles Shattuck, 25 December 1978, Shattuck file, University of Illinois Archives, Urbana.

46. Eudora Welty, Speech delivered to the Academy of Arts and Letters, New York, New York, May 1980, Academy Archives.

47. WM, Speech delivered to the Academy of Arts and Letters, New York, New York, May 1980, Academy Archives. Excerpt of Louise Bogan speech quoted by Maxwell also appears in *Journey around My Room: The Autobiography of Louise Bogan*, 120–21.

Chapter 10

1. WM, *The Outermost Dream*, viii ("Too much of a busman's"), ix ("Looked at broadly").

2. Ibid., 173 ("day after day"), 177 ("Who she was").

3. Ibid., 31.

4. Ibid., 148 ("I find very little"), 145 ("misuse").

5. Judith Baumel, review of *The Outermost Dream,* by WM, *The New York Times Book Review,* 14 May 1989, 23.

6. WM, *The Outermost Dream,* 49.

7. Daniel Menaker, "The Gentle Realist," *The New York Times,* 15 October 2000.

8. WM, Interview by Linda Wertheimer, *All Things Considered,* National Public Radio, 8 February 1995 (transcript in author's files).

9. WM, *Billie Dyer and Other Stories,* (New York: Knopt, 1992), 39–40.

10. WM, Ibid, 9.

11. WM to Tom Perry, 21 July 1987, copy in the author's files; WM, *Billie Dyer,* 16–17.

12. WM, *Billie Dyer,* 15.

13. Ibid., 15.

14. Ibid., 20 ("From the very start"), 25 ("they are less"), 27 ("lynching").

15. Ibid., 30–31 ("the situation"), 31 ("I never expected).

16. Ibid., 31 ("politics").

17. Roger Angell, Interview by the author.

18. WM, *Billie Dyer,* 86.

19. Ibid., 96–97 ("respected citizen").

20. Ibid., 104 ("clearly our house"); WM, *Time,* 231–32 ("His eyes"), 295 ("dirty dishes").

21. WM, *Billie Dyer,* 101.

22. WM, Interview by the author, 3 January 1993.

Standing, Accepting

1. WM, Interview by the author, 27–28 August 1992.

2. WM, Interview by Linda Wertheimer, *All Things Considered,* National Public Radio, 8 February 1995 (copy of transcript in author's files); WM, *All the Days and Nights,* 364.

3. WM to John Updike, 24 February 2000 ("text and advertising"), WM Collection.

4. Hazzard, 92 ("The Maxwells"); WM, "Nearing Ninety," *The New York Times Magazine,* 9 March 1997, 76 ("unbearable," "deeply").

5. The Maxwells' last days are lovingly rendered by Alec Wilkinson, *My Mentor,* 139–66; Kate Maxwell commented on her father's last days in a note to the author via Michael Steinman, December 2003.

6. WM to John Updike, 31 July 2000.

7. Wilkinson, 166–67.

8. WM, Interview by the author, 27–28 August 1992 ("came to understand"), 3 January 1993 ("at the same time").

9. WM, *So Long,* 135.

10. WM, Interview by the author, 3 January 1993; WM, *Time,* 86.

11. WM, Interview by the author, 3 January 1993.

Index

Adams, Timothy Dow, 214
Adler, Alfred, 96
The Adolescent and the American Novel (Witham), 119
A.E., 34
"All the Days and Nights" (WM), 271
All the Days and Nights: The Collected Stories (WM), 158, 270–71; honors for, 271
Amalrik, Andrei, 258
American Academy of Arts and Letters, 182, 255
Amis, Kingsley, 202
Ancestors (WM): and autobiography, 210, 212–14; and history, 211–12, 216; influence of Reik/psychoanalysis on, 215, 217–18; Maxwell persona in, 214–18, 259; midwestern speech in, 208–9; mother in, 78, 213; narrative technique/style in, 12, 209, 211, 214–18, 244; Ninth Street home in, 25–26; as precursor to *So Long* and *Billie Dyer*, 209; reference to *Bright Center of Heaven*, 61; reference to Edith Blinn, 28; reviews of, 213
Anderson, Sherwood, 14, 31; *Winesburg, Ohio*, 14
Angell, Roger, 9, 76, 85, 223–24, 226, 236–37, 261; as editor, 3, 257, 266
Anna Karenina (Tolstoy), 93
Armistice, The, 65, 75
Arno, Peter, 64
artistic development, 11–13; and *Ancestors*,

209, 217–18; and *Billie Dyer* stories 262, 266; and *The Chateau*, 204; and short fiction, 220; and *So Long, See You Tomorrow*, 229–30, 238–41, 245; and the unfinished play, 178–79
Associated Press, The, 103
Astaire, Fred, 183
Aswell, Edward, 129
Aswell, Mary Lou, 181
Atlantic Monthly, 169, 182
Austen, Jane, 189
Austen, Roger, 119
Austria: travels in, 163–64; Salzburg, 166; Salzburg Music Festival, 163; Vienna, 166
autobiographical fiction, 10, 146–47, 213–14

Ballardville, Maine, 83
Balzac, Honore de, 116
Barnes, Julian, 251; *Flaubert's Parrot*, 251
Barrie, J. M. (James Matthew), 37
Barth, John, 237, 246–47; *Lost in the Funhouse*, 237, 247
Bates, Annette Blinn. *See* Blinn, Annette
Baumel, Judith, 260
Bawer, Bruce, 54, 118, 119, 270
Beer-Hofmann, Richard, 97
Beethoven, Ludwig van, 212
Behold, This Dreamer! (de la Mare), 41
Bellow, Saul, 184, 185, 187, 293n1
Benson, Sally, 103
Berlin, Germany, 96

Berlin Diaries (Vassiltchikov), 258
"Billie Dyer" (WM), 13, 262–66
Billie Dyer and Other Stories (WM), 9, 78,
    126, 260–69, 271; racial theme in, 56–57,
    262–69
Binding, Paul, 120
Blades, John, 2
Blinn, Annette (maternal aunt), 21, 27, 28;
    fire accident, 137; and "poison pen let-
    ters," 29; trips to Mackinac Island, 146;
    visit from WM, 31
Blinn, Annette Youtsey ("Nettie," maternal
    grandmother), 25, marriage to Judge
    Edward Blinn, 28; and "poison pen let-
    ters," 29
Blinn, Edith (maternal aunt), 21, 27, 28; and
    education, 34; young WM's visit to, 29
Blinn, Judge Edward (maternal grand-
    father), 23, 25, 27–28; and Billie Dyer,
    264–65; death of, 146; marriage to Nettie
    Youtsey, 28; and Ted Blinn's bet on
    airplane, 28
Blinn, Ted (maternal uncle), 28, 100, 261
Bliven, Naomi, 192
Blois, France, 163, 165, 169
"Bloody Murder" (WM), 231
Bloomington, Illinois, 21, 29
Bogan, Louise: and autobiographical
    writing, 83; background of, 79, 80–81;
    comment on *The Chateau*, 200; *Dark
    Summer*, 86; and depression, 80; "Dove
    and Serpent," 83; and Freud 84–85; as
    friend and mentor, 74, 85–87, 158, 255–56;
    and John Reed Memorial Prize, 80;
    "Journey around My Room," 83–84, 108,
    111; "Letdown," 83; as literary inspiration,
    108, 111; and *The New Yorker*, 82; "The
    Season's Verse," 80; support for writing
    The Folded Leaf, 81, 82–89, 99, 102–3, 118,
    127, 134
Bonetti, Kay, 79
Bonnard, Henri, 16
Bonnie Oaks (farm, Portage, Wisconsin),
    32–36, 48, 51, 54, 57, 61. *See also* Portage,
    Wisconsin
Book-of-the-Month Club, 65
Bori, Lucrezia, 85
Bowen, Elizabeth: epigraph for *The Cha-
    teau*, 172; *The House of Paris*, 185
Bray, Robert, 237
Breese, William (husband of Zona Gale), 43

Brennan, Maeve, 2
Brest, France, 263
Bright Center of Heaven (WM), 48–60; Afri-
    can American theme in, 49, 50–51, 53–57,
    140, 161, 266; as comic novel, 59; dedica-
    tion to Mrs. Green, 49; domestic life in,
    50, 58–59, 71; as first novel, 50, 57–59, 229;
    and *The Folded Leaf*, 119; influence of
    lyric poetry on, 51–53, 66–67; influence
    of Virginia Woolf on, 51, 53, 58–59, 68;
    narrative technique/style in, 11, 51–53, 75,
    128, 221, 243, 265; as novel of manners, 49;
    and "The Patterns of Love," 93; plot of,
    49; publication of, 61; reviews of, 61; and
    Theodor Reik, 97; women in, 158; writing
    of 47–48
Brittany, France, 163
Brodkey, Harold, 129
Brothers Karamazov, The (Dostoevsky), 32
Bryan, William Jennings, 144
Busey, Garreta (Illinois friend and mentor):
    as mentor, 46–47, 60, 158, 258; as poetry
    society host, 39; WM writes *They Came
    Like Swallows* in her home, 62–63, 74,
    112, 113
Bush, President George Herbert Walker, 76
Butscher, Fanny, 78

Cambridge, Massachusetts, 112. *See also*
    Harvard University
Campbell, Alexander (ancestor), 217
Campbell, Duncan, 203–4
Campbell, James, 119
Campbellites, The, 211
Canfield, Cass, 60
Cannes, France, 163
Cathedral Blanche, Salzburg, 166
Cathedral of St. John the Divine (New
    York), 272
Cather, Willa, 15, 34, 65, 150, 158
Chardin, Jean-Baptiste-Simeon (exhibit at
    Metropolitan Museum), 271–72
Chartres, France, 169
The Chateau (WM): as anti-novel, 201,
    204; art of fiction as subject in, 204;
    comparison to *The Folded Leaf*, 9, 118;
    comparison to other Maxwell novels, 9,
    191–92; comparison to *So Long, See You
    Tomorrow*, 191–92, 238, 292n65; delivery of
    manuscript, 190; epilogue of, 186, 189–91,
    196–200, 216, 249; European response and

publications, 201–4, 292n65; French family that inspired, 202; French language rights of, 202; influence of Reik/psychoanalyis on, 194–96; and Knopf, 187–91; language as theme in, 200; masculinity in, 194–96; narrative technique/style in, 12, 104, 214, 241, 245; "The Pilgrimage" as sketch of, 174; plot of, 171–72; publication of, 191, 200; reviews of, 192, 201–4; sales of, 200–201; women in, 158, 199–200; World War II references in, 164, 171, 192–93, 198–99, 283n26; writing of, 170, 171, 172, 181, 188–90; youth in, 194–96

Chautauqua Movement, 23, 144. *See also* Lincoln, Illinois; Lincoln Chautauqua

Cheever, John, 91, 133, 146, 179–81, 219

Chekov, Anton, 33, 185; *The Cherry Orchard*, 33

Cherbourg, France, 16

The Cherry Orchard, (Chekov), 33

Chicago, Illinois: attends Lyric Opera, 43; attends Ravinia (summer classical music venue), 43; Chicago Public Library, 36–37; experiences at Art Institute of Chicago, 37, 39; Marshall Field's, 82; Michigan Avenue, 31; move to, 30–32; rides the "El" with father (public transportation), 32; Rogers Park neighborhood, 31; as setting in *The Folded Leaf*, 82, 88, 105–6, 114–16, 123; World's Columbian Exposition, 211; years at Nicholas Senn High School, 31–32, 36–38

Chicago Tribune, 2, 32, 211; influenza epidemic coverage, 19; WM obituary, 8

Chopin, Kate, 150

Christian Church, 211

"A Christmas Story" (WM), 63

Civil War, 152, 211, 262

Cohen, Sol, 13

Coke, Thomas, of Holcomb, 46–47, 258

Colette, 1, 158, 258

Collier, Michael, 271

Commonweal, 201

Connecticut, Elton, 65

Conrad, Joseph, 37

Coover, Robert, 251; *The Public Burning,* 251

Copland, Aaron, 61

correspondence, 2–4

The Counterfeiters (Gide), 164

"The Country Where Nobody Ever Grew Old and Died" (WM), 205–6

Crane, Stephen, 73, 114, 185; "The Open Boat," 185; *Whilomville Stories,* 114

Crosby, Alfred, 77

Crosby, Bing, 167

Croton-Harmon, New York, 2, 93

Davis, Hugh (Lincoln friend), 264–65

de la Mare, Walter: *Behold, This Dreamer!,* 41; as literary influence, 39–40, 41–42, 45, 51–52, 86, 108, 246; parallels with Theodor Reik 278–79n49

Der Rosenkavalier (Strauss opera), 86

Deuel, Susan. *See* Shattuck, Susan Deuel

Dewey, Thomas E., 101

Dineson, Isak, 259–60

"Disciples of Christ," 211

Doctorow, E. L., 237, 251, 252; *Ragtime,* 237, 251

domestic fiction, 15–16, 58–59, 66, 71–72, 75, 110, 220, 222–28

"Don't Fence Me In" (song), 272

Dostoevsky, Fyodor, 33; *The Brothers Karamazov,* 32

dreams: and de la Mare, 41–42; in *The Folded Leaf,* 83–84, 107–9, 117; and Louise Bogan, 84; in "Over by the River," 223; and *Time Will Darken It,* 137–38

Dreiser, Theodore, 73, 114, 115, 273

Dresden, Germany, 225, 252

Droll Stories (Balzac), 116

DuBois, W. E .B., 54

Dybek, Stuart, 4–5, 272

Dyer, Aaron (Billie's grandfather), 263

Dyer, Alfred (Billie's father), 263

Dyer, Billie, 27, 262–69. *See also* "Billie Dyer"

Dyer, Hattie (Billie's sister), 27, 267–69

Eakin, John Paul, 270

Ellison, Ralph Waldo, 185

England (WM's travel to), 164

England, Stephen (ancestor), 211

Eureka College (father's alma mater), 23

Faber and Faber (edition of *The Folded Leaf*), 129

fables (WM), 205–6, 271. *See also* individual titles

Faulkner, William, 75

Feldman, A. Bronson, 97

Ferenczi, Sandor, 96

Ferrier, Kathleen, 85

Fidelio (Beethoven), 212
"A Final Report" (WM), 206–7
First Presbyterian Church, New York (wedding), 129
first story, 30
Fitzgerald, F. Scott, 114
Fitzgerald, Robert, 2, 45, 61–62
Flanagan, Mary, 158
Flanner, Janet, 163
Flaubert, Gustave, 87, 189; *Madame Bovary,* 189; *The Temptation of St. Anthony,* 97
Flaubert's Parrot (Barnes), 251
Florence, Italy, 163, 166
The Folded Leaf (WM), 9, 79–134; artistic method as subject in, 110–11; as autobiographical novel, 3, 32, 38; comparison to *Bright Center of Heaven,* 50; comparison to *The Chateau,* 191; domestic life in, 110; ending of, 126, 238; first edition of, 127, 128, 129, 133; as gay/homosexual novel, 119–21; influence of Louise Bogan on, 81, 82–89, 99, 102–3, 118, 127, 134; influence of Theodor Reik/psychoanalysis on, 96–100, 106–9, 121, 126–27, 129–30, 273; Italian translation of, 164, 167–68; and Knopf, 187; Lymie's attempt at suicide in, 44, 100, 105, 106, 123–25, 128; male adolescence in, 116–21, 133, 138, 194, 196, 217; manuscripts of, 99; as midwestern novel, 107, 114–16, 114–16, 127–28, 180; mother's death in, 78, 108; narrative technique/style in, 11, 104–16, 137, 217, 229; narrator in, 107, 195, 217, 218, 245, 258; plot of, 81–82; publication of, 127; publisher's summary of, 99–100; as realistic novel, 104–5, 113–16, 127–28; reviews of, 104, 107, 112, 114, 127–29, 133; revision of, 105, 129–33; setting of, 105–6, 113–16; title of, 102, 235; women in, 151; writing of, 82–89, 94–103, 105, 135, 240
Folger Shakespeare Library, Washington, D.C., 4–5, 271
Forster, E. M., 8
Fort de France, Martinique, 59
Fort Tryon Park, New York City, 81
Forum (Senn High School literary magazine and yearbook, Chicago), 32, 37
France: affinity for culture, 30, 163; and Billie Dyer, 264; Blois, 163, 165, 169; Brest, 264; Brittany, 163; Cannes, 163; Chartres, 169; Cherbourg, 163; correspondence from, 164–70; German Occupation of, 164, 203;

Marseilles, 163, 264; Mont St. Michel, 163, 164, 207–8; Nice, 163; Paris, 1, 43, 86, 163–64, 168, 193, 197, 202, 263; Pontorson, 165; Rennes, 165; as setting, 11, 164, 174–75, 187, 191, 192–93, 202; travels in, 163–70; tours, 165; Versailles, 169
Frank, Elizabeth, 80, 82, 84, 86, 87, 99; WM review of Bogan biography, 260
Frazer, Sir James, 106
Freeman, Erika, 96
French language, 59, 189
"The French Scarecrow" (WM), 5, 172, 175–76, 180
Freud, Sigmund: analysis and theory, 36, 41, 66, 106–9, 127, 215, 217–18, 220, 232, 243–44, 272; and Theodor Reik, 96
"Friends from Philadelphia" (Updike), 290n21
"The Front and the Back Parts of the House" (WM), 13, 262, 266–69
Fuchs, Daniel, 180, 219
Fuller, Henry B., 114, 115
Fuller, William Maxwell (cousin), 209–10

Gale, Zona, 33–36; and *Bright Center of Heaven,* 48–49, 56; correspondence with Elinor Wylie, 40; death of, 36, 65; "Dream," 56; grave of, 142; home (Portage, Wisconsin), 36, 108; literary influence on WM, 15, 142, 158, 287n26; *Miss Lulu Bett,* 33; *Peace in Friendship Village,* 56; *Portage Wisconsin and Other Essays,* 35; and psychology, 36; "The Reception Surprise," 56; *Romance Island,* 34; and *They Came Like Swallows,* 65; University of Wisconsin, 34; visits WM at Harvard 45–46; visits WM in New York City, 65; visits WM in Urbana, Illinois, 43–44; wins *Delineator* contest, 34
Galsworthy, John, 37
"A Game of Chess" (WM), 177
"The Gardens of Mont Saint Michel" (WM), 207–8
German language, 46
Germany, 68, 265
Gershwin, music of George and Ira, 26
Giacometti, Alberto, 199, 235, 241, 252; *Palace at 4 A.M.,* 179, 199, 235, 241, 243–44, 251
Gibbs, Wolcott, 64–65
Gide, Andre: *The Counterfeiters,* 164
Gill, Brendan: and Nabokov, 253; refers WM

to Knopf 187–88; review of *Ancestors,* 213; review of *Time Will Darken It,* 168; at Smith College 184, 185, 187, 213, 290n29
Gilman, Charlotte Perkins, 34
Gilman, Richard, 201
Glasgow, Ellen, 150
Godine Press (Boston), 7
Goethe, Johann Wolfgang von, 127
Golden Bough, The (Frazer), 106, 109
Gold Medal for Literature of the American Institute of Arts and Letters, 271
Gracie Square (New York City), 221
Graham, Martha, 62
Grant, Frederic M., 37
Gray, Thomas, 40
Green, Harrison, 33
Green, Mildred Ormsby, 33, 34, 39, 48–49, 158
Greenwich Village (New York City), 209
Gruppe aus dem Tartarus (Schubert), 85
Gurdjieff philosophy, 33, 278n33
The Guardian (London), 203
Guild, Margaret (college friend), 44

Hale, Nancy, 181
Hallam, Mabel, 24
"Haller's Second Home" (WM), 89, 90–92, 111
Hanover Fire Insurance Company, 26, 30, 94, 102
Harcourt Brace, 181
Harlem Renaissance, The, 33
Harper and Brothers, 60, 63, 94; ends relationship with 187–88; and *The Folded Leaf,* 99, 100, 102, 129; and *Time Will Darken It,* 169
Harper's Bazaar, 98, 181
Hart, Moss, 26
Harts, John (Lincoln friend), 265
Harvard University, 45–46, 61, 90; and John Updike, 183
Harvill Press, 201
Hay, Sara Henderson, 128
Hazzard, Shirley, 45, 271–72
Hemingway, Ernest, 78, 164
Henderson, Robert, 43, 48, 85
Heran, Lafcadio, 59
Hicks, Granville, 201
Hill, Mr. and Mrs. Dean (family friends in Lincoln), 21
historiographic metafiction, 251–52, 295n37
H.M.S. Pinafore (Gilbert and Sullivan), 37

Hokinson, Helen, 64
Holden, Raymond, 80
Holocaust, 164
"The Holy Terror" (WM), 262
homes (of WM): Baptist Church Road, Yorktown Heights, New York, 2, 4, 93, 96, 135, 163, 271; East Eight-Sixth Street apartment, Manhattan, 1–2, 272; Lexington Avenue rooming house, Manhattan, 63; Murray Hill, Manhattan, 182, 225; Ninth Street, Lincoln, Illinois, 22, 25–26, 27, 29, 217, 264, 268; Park Avenue, Manhattan, 103; Park Place, Lincoln, Illinois, 29, 232; Patchin Place, Manhattan, 79, 86, 93
House of Paris, The (Bowen), 185
Howells, William Dean, 115
Howells Medal, 82, 115, 115, 182, 255
Hutcheon, Linda, 246, 251–52, 295n37

Illinois: as setting for work, 191, 208, 220, 222. *See also* Bloomington; Chicago; Lincoln; Logan County; Peoria; Sangamon County; Springfield; University of Illinois; Urbana
"infant amnesia," 76
influenza epidemic of 1918, 7, 10, 19–22, 65–66, 72, 77–78, 264
Inness, George, 37
Innsbruck, Austria, 225
Ipswich, Massachusetts (home of John Updike), 3
Irvin, Rea, 64
Italian Riviera, 168
Italy: Florence, 163, 166; Rome, 167, 198; San Remo, 168; travel in, 163–68; Venice, 21

Jackson, Mississippi (Eudora Welty home), 181
Jacob's Pillow (Becket, Massachusetts), 62
James, Henry (Jamesian tradition), 115, 192
jazz, 29
jazz age, 114
Johnson, Samuel, 39
Jones, Ernest, 168–69
Jones, Judith (Knopf editor): and *Ancestors,* 208–9; and *The Chateau,* 190–91
Joyce, James, 75; as literary inspiration, 8, 9, 216; *Ulysses,* 161
Jude the Obscure (Hardy), 39
Jung, Carl, 96, 108

Kazin, Alfred, 184, 185, 187
Kern, Jerome, 26
Kilvert, Reverend Francis, 258
"The Kingdom Where Straightforward, Logical Thinking Was Admired over Every Other Kind" (WM), 205
King Lear (Shakespeare), 39
Knopf, Alfred A. Jr., 187–88
Knopf, Alfred A. Publishers, 187–91, 236; and *Ancestors*, 208–9; and *The Outermost Dream*, 257; and *So Long, See You Tomorrow*, 255; and Zona Gale, 35
Knopf, Alfred A. Sr., 188, 190–91, 201
Knopf, Blanche (wife of Alfred Sr.), 200–201

La Boheme, 43, 86
Laffont, Robert (French publisher), 202
La Grande Mademoiselle (Steegmuller), 259
Lake Geneva, Switzerland, 166
Landis, Paul (university professor), 38–39, 68
"The Land of Counterpane" (Stevenson), 125
Latimer, Margery (Wisconsin writer), 278n33
Laurel, Mississippi, 216
Lausanne, Switzerland, 166
Le Grande Meaulnes (Alain-Fournier), 164
Le Monde (Paris), 203
Leningrad, 225
Levin, James, 119
Lewis, Sinclair: *Main Street*, 14
Lhevinne, Josef, 33, 48, 59
Lied v. d. Erde (Mahler), 85–86
Lincoln, Abraham, 22–23, 28, 57
Lincoln, Illinois: as childhood home, 13, 22–31, 217; departure from, 31, 242; history of, 22–25; and influenza epidemic, 20–22; John Updike in, 4; Lincoln Chautauqua, 23–24; Lincoln College, 263; Lincoln Country Club, 26; Lincoln High School, 14, 29; Lincoln Public Library, 264; Lincoln Rotary, 26; Maxwell friends and family in, 25–29, 101; as setting in WM's work, 1, 7, 14, 16, 36, 66, 177, 261, 262–69; Union Cemetery, 22; WM visits in adulthood, 31
Lincoln Courier-Herald: Billie Dyer obituary, 266; coverage of influenza epidemic, 20–22; coverage of World War I, 46; in *So Long, See You Tomorrow*, 231–34, 240, 242, 250–51, 252, 253

Lincoln Evening Star: coverage of Maxwell/McGrath nuptials, 29
Lobrano, Gustav (*New Yorker* fiction editor), 98, 129, 188
Logan County, Illinois, 262, 267. *See also* Lincoln, Illinois
London Independent, 120
Lord, James, 259; *A Giacometti Portrait*, 259
Lost in the Funhouse (Barth), 237, 247
"The Lotos-Eaters" (Tennyson), 102, 134
"Love" (WM), 124, 126, 135, 261–62

MacDowell, Edward, 62
MacDowell, Mrs. Edward, 61–62
MacDowell Colony (Peterborough, New Hampshire), 13, 61–62, 112
Mackinac Island, Michigan, 146
Madame Bovary (Flaubert), 189
Mailer, Norman, 78, 253
Main Street (Lewis), 14
"The Man in the Moon" (WM), 28, 261
"The Man Who Had No Enemies" (WM), 205
Marseilles, France, 163, 193
Martinique: travels to 31, 59–60, 164; unfinished novel based on, 59
Masters, Edgar Lee, 14, 31; *Spoon River Anthology*, 14
Matisse, Henri, 235
Mauritania (ocean liner), 170
Maxfield, James F., 138
Maxwell, Blossom Blinn (mother): and Blinn family, 27; bond with WM, 25–26; contracts influenza, 21–22; death, funeral, and burial of, 22; effect of death on WM's fiction, 42, 66, 138, 220, 230; and family life, 26; as figure in WM's work, 158, 176–79; gentle world of, 29, 71–72; gives birth to Blinn, 21–22; marriage of, 23; and Ninth Street home, 25–26, 72; opinion of Chicago, 30; and pregnancy, 21; as Red Cross volunteer, 20
Maxwell, Edward C. ("Hap," older brother): birth of, 23; and carriage accident, 27, 146, 261; and family life, 26; and high school, 31; inspiration for "The Holy Terror," 261; as lawyer, 27; and mother's death, 29; and *They Came Like Swallows*, 73, 100
Maxwell, Emily Brooke ("Brookie," younger daughter), 2, 7, 208, 271, 272
Maxwell, Emily Gilman Noyes (wife), 2, 4,

44, 93, 236; and chemotherapy, 272; childhood of, 104; courtship of, 103–4; death of, 272; engagement to WM, 104; and Eudora Welty, 182; and family life, 223; gives birth to Katharine, 184; letters to WM's father and stepmother, 164; marriage of, 129; meets WM, 79, 97; memorial service, 273; and "Over by the River," 224, 293n7; as reader of WM's work, 135–36; and Smith College, 103, 184; and "The Thistles in Sweden," 228; and *Time Will Darken It*, 145–49; travel to France, 104, 163–70, 202

Maxwell, Grace McGrath (stepmother): correspondence from WM, 94; and *The Folded Leaf* 100–101; funeral of 31, 93, 232; and kindergarten 137, 232; marriage to WM's father, 29; move to Chicago 30

Maxwell, Grandmother (paternal grandmother, born Margaret Turley), 27, 211

Maxwell, Henry (ancestor), 210–11

Maxwell, Katharine ("Kate," older daughter), 184, 222, 271–72

Maxwell, Robert (ancestor, Henry's son), 212

Maxwell, Robert Blinn ("Blinn," younger brother): and Billie Dyer, 266; birth of, 21–22; raised in Lincoln, 30; service in World War II, 91, 93; speaks at WM's memorial service, 272

Maxwell, Robert Creighton (grandfather), 212

Maxwell, William K. Sr. (father): and Armistice, 21; contracts influenza, 21; courtship of and marriage to Blossom, 23; courtship of and marriage to Grace McGrath, 29; and farms, 232; and *The Folded Leaf*, 100–101; funeral of, 31; and genealogical study, 210; and Hanover Fire Insurance Company, 26, 94, 283n31; letters from WM, 93–96, 98, 163–70; and mourning, 29; move to Chicago, 30; as namesake, 209; and neighborhood orchestra, 25; relationship with WM, 26, 94, 217; as Republican, 101; and Ted Blinn (brother-in-law), 28

Maxwell, William K., Jr. (WM): affinity with black household help, 27; artistic development of, 11–13, 178–79, 204, 209, 217–18, 220, 229–30, 238–41, 245, 262, 266; bachelorhood, 79–80, 89; birth of, 23; childhood, 25–30; correspondence of, 2–4;

courtship of Emily Gilman Noyes, 103–4; death, 8, 273; early years in New York, 210; as editor, 3, 95, 146, 184; final months of life, 272–73; infancy of, 26; marriage of, 97, 129; memorial service, 273; physical description, 1, 95, 186; playing piano 59, 85–86; politics, 101; psychoanalysis with Theodor Reik, 16, 96–100, 106–9, 215; relationship with father, 217; relationship with younger brother, 30; Scottish heritage, 210, 215; suicide, attempt at, 44–45, 285–86n82; university years, 38–45. *See also* individual works

Maybel (paternal aunt), 216; and Blinn Maxwell, 30; and Blossom's death, 29; as Clara in *They Came Like Swallows*, 27, 277n18

McCarthy, Mary, 77, 180, 214, 270; *Memories of a Catholic Girlhood* 77, 214

McGrath brothers (Maxwell's step-uncles), 30–31

McGrath, Grace. *See* Maxwell, Grace McGrath

McHale, Brian, 246–49

McKelway, St. Clair, 80

Melville, Herman, 185

memory, 84, 108, 220, 234, 238, 261

Memphis Bound (musical by Sally Benson), 103

Menaker, Daniel, 260

Mendenhall Hotel Restaurant, Mendenhall, Mississippi, 3, 182, 289n17

Metropolitan Museum of Art, New York, 272

Midnight's Children (Rushdie), 251

Midwest, the: landscape of, 10, 13–14, 105, 109, 115, 127, 212, 222, 239; language of, 16, 208, 236, 244–45; literature of, 13–16, 36, 115; midwestern homecoming theme, 206–7; as setting/theme in WM's fiction, 8, 28, 66, 143–49, 180, 191, 225

Moby Dick (Melville), 185

Modernism, 8, 11–12, 75, 246–48

Mont St. Michel, France, 163, 164, 207–8

Moore, George, 37

Moore, Marianne, 88–89; "In Distrust of Merits," 88–89, 282n21

Morris, Wright, 15, 232

Moss, Howard, 235

Mount Hood (Oregon), 104

Mount Monadnock (New Hampshire), 62

Moynihan, Senator Patrick, 76
Murdoch, Iris, 202
Murray Hill (New York City), 182, 221
Museum of Modern Art (New York City), 241, 244
music, 85
"My Father's Friends" (WM), 21

NAACP, 54, 57
Nabokov, Vera, 182
Nabokov, Vladimir: *Ada*, 237, 252; correspondence with WM, 3, 271; *The Defense* (also *"Luzhin Defense"*), 182–83; *The Gift*, 182, 252; and *The New Yorker*, 180, 181, 182–83, 214, 238, 252; *Pale Fire*, 182, 237, 252; as postmodernist, 246; *Speak, Memory*, 214
Nathan, Robert, 46 (*One More Spring*)
Nation, The, 127, 168
National Book Award, 184; nomination 191, 204
National Book Critics Circle Award for Lifetime Achievement, 272
National Psychological Association for Psychoanalysis, 96
National Public Radio, 205, 262
Netherlands, The, 96
"Never to Hear Silence" (WM), 80
New Criterion, The, 54
New Mexico (WM travels to), 95, 105, 109, 110
New Republic, The, 63
New York, New York: Fort Tryon Park, 81; Gracie Square, 221; Greenwich Village, 209; moves from Illinois to, 47–48; Murray Hill, 182, 225; setting in WM's work, 89, 177, 219–228; Washington Heights, 81; WM on, 222
The New Yorker, 37, 39; art meetings, 64; business practices 94, 164; censorship, 4; correspondence to father about, 93; and Emily Maxwell, 103; and Eudora Welty, 181–82; foreign correspondents, 163–64; geographic restrictions of, 89; history of, 5; leaves of absence from 82, 94–95; and Mary McCarthy, 77, 214; publication of WM's stories, reviews, and fables in 79, 80, 89, 125, 180, 205, 231, 258, 267; retirement from, 219; reviews of WM's work in, 104, 127–28, 168, 192, 213; and Robert Henderson, 43; and *So Long, See You*

Tomorrow, 235–38, 255; success of, 191; and Vladimir Nabokov 182–83, 214, 237; WM as fiction editor, 2, 64–65, 96, 98, 103, 146, 179–84, 201, 209, 213–14, 237, 239, 253, 256; WM hired 63–65; WM on 75th anniversary issue, 272; writers of, 151
New York Herald Tribune, 39, 78
New York Times, The: bestseller list, 191; obituary in, 8, 169; review of *The Outermost Dream*, 260
New York Times Book Review, 158
New York University, 256
New York World: and Zona Gale, 34
Nice, France, 163
Nicholas Senn High School (Chicago, Illinois): *Forum* (student literary magazine and yearbook), 32, 37–38; high school years, 31–32, 36–38; senior year, 36–38; student athletic association 37–38
Northampton, Massachusetts. *See* Smith College
Noyes, Emily Gilman. *See* Maxwell, Emily
Noyes, Katherine (Emily's mother), 129
The Nation, 81
Nyland, Mrs. Willem (Ilonka Karasz), 102

O'Connor, Frank (Michael O'Donovan), 77, 188–89, 259; *An Only Child*, 188
Oconomowoc, Wisconsin, 37
O'Hara, John, 3
The Old Man at the Railroad Crossing (WM), 205–6, 271
"Once More to the Lake" (White), 111
One More Spring (Nathan), 47
Oswego, New York, 103–4
The Outermost Dream: Essays and Reviews (WM), 1, 258–61; as example of late writing, 52
"Over by the River" (WM), 1, 92, 220–25, 226; and dog's point of view, 294n18; and Emily Maxwell, 224, 293n7
Over by the River and Other Stories (WM), 219, 271
Oxford University, 183
Oxnard, California, 30

Pacheco, Francisco, 145–59, 198, 243, 248, 249
"Palace at 4 A.M." (Giacometti), 179, 199, 235, 241, 243–44, 251
Pale Horse, Pale Rider (Porter), 77
Paramount Pictures, 63

Paris, France: affinity for 43, 86; in *The Chateau* 193, 202; Colette's home in, 1; expatriate writers in, 43, 163–64; Louvre, 197; Luxembourg gardens, 168; Palais Royal, 1, 197; St. Sulpice, 168; travels to, 165, 168, 202

The Paris Review 51, 270

Partisan Review, 227

Patchin Place (New York City), 79, 86, 93

"The Patterns of Love" (WM), 65, 92–93, 226

Peekskill, New York, 95

PEN/Malamud Award, 4–5, 271

Peoria, Illinois, 26

Perry, Dr. Robert, 4

Perry, Thomas (Tom), 93, 232–33, 242, 267

Perspectives U.S.A., 180

Peterborough, New Hampshire. *See* Mac-Dowell Colony

Philadelphia Art Museum, 255

Phinney, A. W., 204, 205

"The Pilgrimage" (WM), 172, 174–75, 207

play (WM, unfinished), 176–79

Plimpton, George, 9, 51, 68, 69, 87, 270

poetry (WM, written at University of Illinois), 39–42, 51

Pontorson, France, 165

Porter, Cole, 26

Porter, Katherine Ann, 77; *Pale Horse, Pale Rider,* 77

Portland, Oregon, 79, 104, 120

Postmodernism, 8, 246–53

Presbyterian Church, 210–11

Pritchett, V. S., 69–70, 259–60

Prohibition, 29

Proust, Marcel, 9, 88, 108

psychoanalysis, 16, 96–100, 106–9, 215; and *Ancestors,* 215, 217–18; and *The Chateau,* 194–96; and "The French Scarecrow," 175–76; and *So Long, See You Tomorrow,* 215, 217–18; and *Time Will Darken It,* 137–39; and unfinished play, 176–79

Public Burning, The (Coover), 251

Pulitzer Prize, 184; nomination 191

Purchase, New York (home of Alfred Knopf, Sr.), 188

Pynchon, Thomas, 246

Queen Elizabeth (ocean liner), 163

race (as subject in WM's work), 27, 49–51, 53–57, 140, 161–63, 262–69

Ragtime (Doctorow), 237, 251

Random House, 7

Rank, Otto, 96

Raskin, Judith, 85

Rasselas, Prince of Abyssinia (Johnson), 39

Reagan, President Ronald, 23

Realism, American Literary, 104–5, 113–16, 127–28, 237

Reik, Theodor (psychoanalyst), 96–100; birth of, 96; as character in WM's work, 175–79; flees Nazis, 96; as Freud protégé, 96; influence on *Ancestors,* 215, 217–18; influence on *The Chateau,* 194; influence on *The Folded Leaf,* 85, 96–100, 106–9, 121, 126–27, 129–30, 175, 273; and "The French Scarecrow," 175–76; influence on *Time Will Darken It,* 137–39; and law of psychic potentiality, 96, 97; as personal influence, 79, 85, 121; and unfinished play, 176–79; view of WM's career, 184

Remnick, David, 220

Remnitz, Tiana, 85

Rennes, France, 165

Reynolds, Joshua, 39

Rinaker, Clarissa (University professor), 39

Robinson, Edward Arlington, 43

Rodgers, Richard, 26

Roethke, Theodore, 80–81

Rome, Italy, 167, 198

Romeo and Juliet (Shakespeare), 102

Roosevelt, President Theodore, 22, 101, 193

Ross, Harold, 5, 64, 168; and geographic restrictions of *The New Yorker,* 89, 180; grants WM leaves to write *The Folded Leaf,* 82, 92, 94, 95; and Eudora Welty, 181–82

Rushdie, Salmon, 251; *Midnight's Children,* 251

Sachs, Hans, 96

Salinger, J. D., 2, 79, 146, 180–81; "Slight Rebellion Off Madison," 79

Salzburg, Austria, 166

Salzburg Music Festival, 163

San Francisco Chronicle, 169

Sangamon County, Illinois, 211. *See also* Springfield, Illinois

San Remo, Italy, 168

Santa Fe Railroad, 265

Sargent, John Singer, 37

Saturday Evening Post, 114, 116

Saturday Review of Literature, 128
Saxton, Eugene, 63
Schnitzler, Arthur, 97
science fiction, 176–79
Scotland, 210
"Scotland's Burning" (WM), 63
Scottsboro trial, 54, 57
Scribner's, 81
Scully, Jack (high school and college friend), 32, 37–38, 44
Seymour, Miranda, 201–4, 292n65
Shattuck, Charles, 10, 32, 44, 255
Shattuck, Susan Deuel, 3, 32, 44–45, 128
Shaw, George Bernard, 37
Shawn, William, 16, 180, 183, 236–38, 244, 253
"The Shepherd's Wife" (WM), 206
Sherman, The Honorable L. Y., 24
Slaughterhouse-Five (Vonnegut), 237, 247, 252
Smith College: and Edith Blinn Young (Maxwell's aunt), 28; and Emily Maxwell, 103, 184; panel discussion at, 187, 290n26, 290n29; *Sophian,* 187; speech given by WM, 184–87, 192, 197, 206, 213, 240, 249
So Long, See You Tomorrow: art of fiction as subject in, 197, 248–49; autobiographical basis of, 9; comparison to *Bright Center of Heaven,* 49, 50; comparison to *The Chateau,* 191, 197, 204; comparison to *The House of Paris* (Bowen), 185; as example of late writing, 52–53; and history, 250–51; honors for, 255–57; influence of Reik/ analysis in, 97, 243, 244; manuscripts of, 240; as masterwork, 8, 105; memory in, 108, 234, 238; as midwestern novel, 14–16, 236, 239–40, 244; and mother's death, 73, 78, 230, 243; murder in, 230–35, 241–42, 294n9; narrative technique/style in, 3, 12–13, 124, 235–56, 238–41, 244–53, 266, 292n65; narrator in, 1, 5, 9, 12–13, 186, 241, 244–46, 258; and *The New Yorker,* 235–38; and "The Palace at 4 A.M.," 179, 199, 235, 241, 243–44, 252, 253–54; plot of, 230; postmodernist qualities of, 246–53; publication of, 236, 255; as realistic novel, 237; receives William Dean Howells medal, 82, 115, 182, 255; reviews of, 230; structure of, 185, 235–36, 240–41; title of, 235; and Tom Perry, 93, 242, 263; women in, 158; writing of, 231–38, 240
"the sound of waves" (WM), 271

Spain (travels to), 164
Spanish influenza epidemic of 1918, 7, 10, 19–22, 65–66, 72, 77–78, 264
Spoon River Anthology (Masters), 114
Springfield, Illinois, 1, 45; Illinois State Historical Library, 231; and influenza epidemic, 21; race riot of 1908, 24–25, 57, 264; underground railroad, 264
Stafford, Jean, 179–80, 219
Steegmuller, Francis, 189–90, 196, 260, 271
Stevenson, Adlai, 101, 203
Stevenson, Robert Louis: "Land of Counterpane," 125; *Treasure Island,* 30; WM review of correspondence, 258
Stewart, Natasha, 181, 188
Stokes, Geoffrey, 145, 146, 270
Stone, Barton (pioneer minister), 211
Stories (with Cheever, Stafford, Fuchs), 179–80, 219
Strauss, Harold, 190–91
suicide, attempt at, 44–45
Sullivan, Walter, 230
Sunday, Billy, 24

Tchaikovsky, Pytor (B flat minor piano concerto), 49
Tennyson, Lord Alfred: childhood in, 16, 70–73, 76–77, 84, 125, 133, 138, 173, 194, 238; domestic life in 58, 71–72; 74–75, 110, 225; and *The Folded Leaf,* 9, 81, 100–101, 105, 106, 110; honors for, 78; influence of Virginia Woolf on, 61, 66–70, 74–76; and influenza epidemic, 72, 74, 77–78; and Knopf, 187; "The Lotos-Eaters," 102, 134; as midwestern novel, 14, 66–67, 180, 225; as modernist novel, 247–48; mother character in, 151, 213; narrative technique/style in, 11, 66–76, 111, 112, 140, 216, 247–48; plot of, 65–66; publication of, 65; reference in *To the Lighthouse,* 67; reviews of, 69, 78; and *So Long, See You Tomorrow,* 9, 262; structure of, 69; and Theodor Reik, 97; *They Came Like Swallows,* 61–78, 79; writing of, 61, 62–63, 68–69; 105, 113, 135
"The Thistles in Sweden" (WM), 67, 159, 220, 225–28
Thurber, James, 64
Tilden, David, 78
Time magazine, 201
Time Will Darken It, 24, 238; adult life in, 139–40; African Americans in, 56, 140,

161–63; autobiographical material and, 137–39; children in, 156, 159, 173–74, 223; comparison to *The Folded Leaf*, 140, 169; as domestic novel, 151, 223; and dream, 137–39; ending of, 160–61; and "The Front and the Back Parts of the House," 267–68; and gender, 149–61; and history, 141–45; influence of Theodor Reik/psychoanalysis on, 137–39, 160; and Knopf, 187; as midwestern novel, 143–49, 152, 180; and mother's death, 78; narrative technique/style in, 11, 140–41, 147–49, 154, 221, 229; narrator in, 217, 259, 274; and National Book Award, 184; plot of, 136; publication of, 163; and Pulitzer Prize, 184; reviews of, 168–70; sales of, 172; storytelling as theme in, 145–49, 192; title of, 145–49; and "The Trojan Women," 172–74; women in, 28, 140, 149–61, 227; writing of, 135–39

Tolstoy, Leo: *Anna Karenina*, 93; *Master and Man*, 74; WM as reader of, 2

Tom Jones (Fielding), 39, 113

Toomer, Jean, 33, 278n33; *Cane*, 33

Tours, France, 165

travel, 111–12. *See also* individual country and city names

Treasure Island (Stevenson), 30

Trilling, Diana, 107, 112, 127, 128, 129

"The Triple Murder" (WM), 231

"The Trojan Women" (WM), 90, 172–74, 180, 227

Turgenev, Ivan, 189

Twain, Mark, 167

Ullman, Natasha Stewart, 181, 188

United States, The (ocean liner), 182

University of Illinois (at Urbana-Champaign): college years, 8, 32, 38–45, 258; donates papers to, 2–4; graduate school, 46–47; graduation from, 45; introduced to *To the Lighthouse*, 67; poetry society, 39–40, 43; resigns from, 47; as setting in *The Folded Leaf*, 81; Sigma Pi fraternity, 46

University of Wisconsin at Madison, 34

unpublished works (WM): "Bloody Murder," 231; "The Triple Murder," 231; unfinished novel about Martinique, 59; unfinished play, 176–79

Updike, John, 2, 202; "The Beloved," 183–84; comment on "Over by the River," 224; comment on *Time Will Darken It*, 137; correspondence with WM, 3, 184, 271–72; "Friends from Philadelphia," 290n21; in Lincoln, Illinois, 4; and *The New Yorker*, 180, 183–84, 237; and Oxford, 183; relationship with WM, 2–4, 183–84, 271–72; "Wait," 183; "Who Made Yellow Roses Yellow?" 183

Urbana, Illinois, 85, 86; Garreta Busey home, 62, 74, 112, 113; as setting in The Folded Leaf, 88, 114–16. *See also* University of Illinois

"The Value of Money" (WM), 12

Van Vechten, Carl, 190

Vassiltchikov, Prince Marie, 258 (*Berlin Diaries*)

Venice, Italy, 217

Versailles, France, 169

Vienna, Austria, 96, 166

Vintage (Press), 188

Vogue magazine, 270

Vonnegut, Kurt, 78, 237, 246–47, 252, 253; Slaughterhouse-Five, 237, 247, 252

Waldorf-Astoria Hotel (New York), 177

War and Peace (Tolstoy), 273

Warner, Sylvia Townsend, 158

Washington, D.C., 4–5

Washington Heights (New York City), 81

Weirick, Bruce (university professor), 38–39

Wells, H. G., 37

Welty, Eudora, 181–82; "The Bride at Innisfallen," 181; correspondence with WM, 3, 181–82; "Kin," 181; memoir, 259; and *The New Yorker*, 180–81; "No Place for You, My Love," 181; *The Ponder Heart*, 3, 181–82; presents Howells medal to WM, 255–56; receives Howells medal, 182

Wertheimer, Linda, 261

Wescott, Glenway, 163

Wharton, Edith, 34, 150

"What Every Boy Should Know" (WM), 180, 222

Whilomville Stories (Crane), 114

White, E. B. (Ellwyn Brooks), 5, 64, 111, 215

White, Katharine, 63–65; 80, 98; and John Updike, 183; and Vladimir Nabokov, 182

Whitman, Walt (technique of), 221

Wilde, Oscar, 39
Wilkie, Wendell, 101
Wilkinson, Alec, 94, 103, 184, 271–72; *My Mentor: A Young Man's Friendship with William Maxwell,* 271–72
Wilson, Edmund, 76, 78, 104, 114–15, 127, 128
Wilson, President Woodrow, 193
Wisconsin: Oconomowoc, 37; Portage, 32–36, 112, 142; as setting in fiction 49, 54; University of Wisconsin at Madison, 34. *See also* Bonnie Oaks
Witham, W. Tasker, 119–20; *The Adolescent and the American Novel,* 119
"The Woman Who Had No Eye for Small Details" (WM), 206
"The Woman Who Never Drew Breath Except to Complain" (WM), 205
women: affinity for women's world, 71–72, 177; affinity for women writers, 150, 158; as subject/characters in work, 73–74, 149–61, 227–28; underappreciation of WM's female portraits, 158–59. *See also* Bogan, Louise; Busey, Garreta; Cather, Willa; Colette; Dineson, Isak; Gale, Zona; Green, Mildred; Maxwell, Blossom; Maxwell, Emily; Warner, Sylvia Townsend; Woolf, Virginia; Wylie, Elinor
Woolf, Virginia: comparison with WM, 9, 216; influence on *Bright Center of Heaven,* 51, 53, 58–59; influence on *They Came Like Swallows,* 66–70, 74–76; as literary inspiration, 8, 9, 48, 51, 158, 246, 258; "Modern Fiction," 74–75; *Orlando,* 186; *A Room of One's Own,* 93; *To the Lighthouse,* 39, 53, 66–70, 74

Wordsworth, William, 121, 129
World's Columbian Exposition (Chicago), 211
World War I, 10, 15, 19–20, 46, 69, 72, 77, 144, 152; the Armistice, 20, 65, 75; and Billie Dyer, 264, 266
World War II: and *The Chateau,* 11, 192–93, 198, 199, 207; Dresden, 252; election of 1944, 101; and Germans, 164, 193; in "Haller's Second Home," 90–92; Holocaust, 164; and Jews, 164, 192–93; New York City during, 220; WM and the draft, 93–94; WM's reflections on, 93–94, 96, 103–4
"The Writer as Illusionist" (WM, speech at Smith College), 184–87, 192, 197, 206, 213, 240, 249
Wylie, Elinor: "Castilian," 40; correspondence with Zona Gale, 34; "The Devil in Seven Shires," 40; "The Eagle and the Mole," 40; as literary influence, 39–40, 42, 48, 51–52, 158, 246; "Madman's Song," 40

Yale Review, 33
Yeats, William Butler, 2, 39, 48, 51
Yezierska, Anzia, 34, 150
Yorktown Heights, New York, 93, 94, 95
Young, Edith Blinn. *See* Blinn, Edith
Young, William (uncle), 29
"Young Francis Whitehead" (WM), 89–90
Youtsey, Annette. See Blinn, Annette (Nettie) Youtsey

Zabel, Morton, 85–86

BARBARA BURKHARDT is an associate professor of English at the University of Illinois at Springfield. She received her Ph.D. from the University of Illinois at Urbana-Champaign.

The University of Illinois Press
is a founding member of the
Association of American University Presses.

———————————————————

Composed in 10.5/13 Adobe Minion
by Barbara Evans
at the University of Illinois Press
Designed by Dennis Roberts
Manufactured by Thomson-Shore, Inc.

University of Illinois Press
1325 South Oak Street
Champaign, IL 61820-6903
www.press.uillinois.edu